The Entrepreneurial Parent®

The
Entrepreneurial

Paul and Sarah Edwards
and Lisa M. Roberts

JEREMY P. TARCHER/PUTNAM
a member of Penguin Putnam Inc.
New York

Parent®

How to Earn Your
Income at Home and Still
Enjoy Your Family,
Your Work, and Your Life

While the author has made every effort to provide accurate telephone numbers and Internet addresses at the time of publication, neither the publisher nor the author assumes any responsibility for errors, or for changes that occur after publication.

Most Tarcher/Putnam books are available at special quantity discounts for bulk purchase for sales promotions, premiums, fund-raising, and educational needs. Special books or book excerpts also can be created to fit specific needs. For details, write Putnam Special Markets, 375 Hudson Street, New York, NY 10014.

Jeremy P. Tarcher/Putnam
A member of
Penguin Putnam Inc.
375 Hudson Street
New York, NY 10014
www.penguinputnam.com

Library of Congress Cataloging-in-Publication Data

Edwards, Paul.
    The entrepreneurial parent : how to earn your income at home and still enjoy your family, your work, and your life / Paul and Sarah Edwards, and Lisa M. Roberts.
        p.   cm.
    ISBN 1-58542-163-4
        1. Home-based businesses—Management.
    2. New business enterprises—Management.   3. Work and family.
    I. Edwards, Sarah (Sarah A.)   II. Roberts, Lisa M., date   III. Title.
    HD62.38 .E386   2002   2001058589
    658'.041—dc21

Printed in the United States of America
10 9 8 7 6 5 4 3 2 1

Book design by Lee Fukui

Acknowledgments

From Paul and Sarah: First, we wish to acknowledge our co-author, Lisa Roberts, who is a brilliant collaborator, researcher, and writer. Equal to each of these is her role as a model of an entrepreneurial parent!

Second, we thank the more than seven hundred entrepreneurial parents whose wisdom, woes, testimonies, and inspiration appear on the pages of this book. Finally, we thank the good people at Aquent.com, Monster Talent Market, Ants.com, MBA Free Agents, and Oxygen Media who helped us identify the participants in the national survey that makes this book as reflective as any we've written of the real world of working at home.

Third, we wish to express gratitude to Joel Fotinos, Mitch Horowitz, Allison Sobel, Kelly Groves, and the others at Tarcher/Putnam who have helped to make this book, our twelfth published by Tarcher. We also acknowledge the helpfulness of our agents, Bob Diforio, Marilyn Allen, and Colleen O'Shea.

From Lisa: Becoming an entrepreneurial parent and then making it somewhat of a "mission" in life has been a long, strange journey peopled with some remarkable characters. I would first like to acknowledge and thank my sister-in-law, Beverly Hunter, who probably doesn't remember the conversation we had shortly after Jessica was born, when she suggested I look into working at home, and that the technology existed for me to do so. This led me to the library, where I discovered the wonderful early works of Paul and Sarah Edwards, whose voice in such books as *Working from Home* and particularly *Getting Business to Come to You* gave me hope that entrepreneurs didn't need an aggressive personality type to make a go of it. It has been truly an honor to work with Paul and Sarah on this project, and I thank them for the unparalleled opportunity and their boundless support.

I would also like to share my gratitude and respect for my favorite EP in the world, Deborah Sechrist, who co-founded en-parent.com with me, an online community full of hard-working parents who are a continual source of inspiration when it comes to making the tough choices between work and family. To me, among them, Deb will always be the "Wisest Woman of the Web." And many thanks go to Janet Gardella, a neighbor and friend, whose creation and analysis of the database surveys reflects equally on her competency and intelligence as it does on her generosity of spirit.

Above all, I'd like to thank my family: my husband, Ron, for insisting I stay the course, and my children: Jessica, for your wonderfully accurate keyboarding of the survey data; Jimmy and Thomas, for so many well-timed antics and commentary that lightened my load with a smile; and William, for your honest opinion after I asked you to read the book proposal: "Well, Mommy, I am sure for entrepreneurial parents this will be the most exciting book in the world, but for a ten-year-old, well, you know, it's kinda boring. . . ." This book is my future gift to the four of you. Someday you'll come of an age when you'll look back on your childhood and ask "Why?" and look forward and ask "What now?" I know I have not always met my EP goals with grace, but I do hope someday this book will have some answers for you, and, well, you know, maybe you'll find it kinda interesting . . . ?

Contents

PART II
ENJOYING YOUR FAMILY, YOUR WORK, *AND* YOUR LIFE

PART I

EARNING YOUR INCOME — at — HOME

The EP Opportunity

For most of us, driving with the flow of traffic seems like the right thing to do. Step on the gas pedal to pull ahead on the Interstate and you feel like too much of a risk-taker, tagged for a ticket. Lighten the pressure on the gas pedal to slow down and you feel like you're holding everybody up behind you, then inadequate as other cars pass yours by. Keeping up, keeping pace, is an easier ride. To go with the flow is natural.

But what happens when that flow breaks the recommended speed limit, or when traffic jams and you feel restless and stuck in a line of slow progression? With this new awareness, is keeping pace still the intuitive move to make? At what point do you decide to slow down, speed up, or exit the highway altogether and find a better-suited traffic flow for you on an alternate route?

The flow of workplace traffic for families today is dual-income households, constituting 63.6 percent of married-couple families with children under eighteen years of age, according to a population survey by the Bureau of Labor Statistics in 2000. After years of drifting with the prevalent current, many parents feel stuck in a routine rut that pushes children and parents alike into stifling schedules and a sense of entrapment. Others have grown startlingly aware that the frenetic pace of a full-time, year-round, double-income lifestyle may be putting their families at risk of a major emotional "collision." While they certainly hope that won't happen, as the rush of time whips through their daily schedules like a strong and persistent wind, they feel more and more vulnerable, more and more worn down.

Perhaps you, our reader, would like to slow down, speed up, or exit I-9-5 (Interstate "nine to five") altogether, or perhaps you already have. Even if you feel confident and secure in the road frequently traveled, it's important to have an alternate plan if for some reason you hit a road-block or otherwise need to take a detour. For those before you who have felt this strongly off course—or were thrown off course by a company layoff or other life-altering event—a new back road has been gaining ground, one that is surprisingly close by and is getting better paved and better serviced all the time. We call the travelers on this road "entrepreneurial parents" (EPs).

Entrepreneurial parents are working parents too, only they earn their living at home where they could put the brake on their work time whenever they need to without disrupting anyone else's flow or move full speed ahead when opportunity arises. Above all, they have a resolute need to be in the driver's seat around the clock when it comes to parenting their children. The entrepreneurial parent, as defined by Rich Minitir, author of the article "Entrepreneurial Parents Profit from More Time with the Kids; Family Values Driving New Work-at-Home Boom" (*Reader's Digest*, April 1999), are home-office workers who believe that family values are crucial to their long-term *business* strategy. They are designing businesses that will grow no bigger than the walls of their homes can contain, taking control of their careers so their time can stretch and flex around the everyday needs of their families.

> *"To me, an entrepreneurial parent is a parent who is proactively seeking a new and better lifestyle—one that successfully combines the excitement and realities of making a living with the excitement and realities of raising a family. So it's not about 'how to make money' or 'how to be successful' per se. It's about already knowing that a successful life starts with a successful family."*
>
> —PETER W. SILER, M.A., FATHERS FIRST

Entrepreneurial Parents:
An Emerging Work-Life Force

By opening up this book, you have opened yourself up to the world—and the strong work-life force—of entrepreneurial parents. Beyond the voices within these pages are those in your neighborhood and across the country. According to the annual household survey conducted by International Data Corporation (IDC), a research firm that tracks the small office/home office trend, an estimated 12.6 million American households in 2001 contained at least one parent of dependent children who was generating income at home. In 2001, Cyber Dialogue, Inc., found that out of an estimated 84.9 million adults who were on-line, 8.5 million were parents with children under eighteen years of age who described themselves as working at home *and* self-employed (21.7 million Internet users worked at home in total, including teleworkers). Between these two estimates, we project the number of EPs in the current workforce to hover around 10 million.

In addition, Cyber Dialogue found that of the self-employed work-at-home parents who were on-line, 57 percent were dads and 43 percent were moms. IDC also puts the male population of at-home workers slightly over female (55 percent to 45 percent). These findings indicate that while work-at-home moms (WAHMs) may have gotten all the press in recent years—*and* may be the gender more inclined to publicize their homebased work status through press releases and the like—work-at-home dads are indeed pulling slightly ahead, at least in sheer number. This is an important finding because the attention at-home working moms receive obscures the reality that this is a gender-blind work option. Despite our own study that yielded a database of 80 percent females, dads are embracing flexible technologies right alongside the moms so they can be more involved in their children's lives, they're just less inclined than their female counterparts to publicize the fact. So don't be fooled—an increasing number of those "soccer dads" and Little League coaches that populate the playing fields on a weekday afternoon are *breaking from* work—not *home from* work.

Yet while so many families have joined these ranks, the story of entrepreneurial parents is not yet fully told, and they are far from living happily ever after. Even though work and family are back under one roof, EPs still find themselves constantly torn between the two, with their career ambitions and parenting instincts locking horns almost daily. They also face isolation, burnout, and marital issues that are vastly different from their work-at-home counterparts who do not have to also care for a family. Finally, for those EPs with very young children, child-care responsibilities can hold back and/or put a cap on income potential so much so that frugal living often becomes a necessity.

This book was written to address these issues and more. In addition, like the dot-com panacea, there's been a lot of hype and myth enshrouding the "Work at Home!" option. Whether posted in a flyer on a telephone pole down the street or incessantly appearing in your e-mail inbox, bold proclamations of being able to work at home earning thousands per month (or week!) within a part-time framework abound. So to help you navigate your homeward journey, we bypassed the deluge of opportunity-seekers both on-line and off and went straight to registered members of selected freelance marketplace job sites: Aquent, Ants.com, Talent Market (of Monster Talent), and MBA Free Agents. Through them, as well as Oxygen Media's business and finance site (ka-ching.com) and the entrepreneurial parent on-line community itself (en-parent.com), we conducted "The National Survey of Entrepreneurial Parents," an on-line survey that ran from September 2000 to January 2001 (see Appendix for more details). This survey was developed to probe the work-life trend the authors of this book have been well aware of for a long time now, and it resulted in 606 respondents to our demographic survey as well as more than 700 pages of appended stories, upon which this book has been based.

Contrary to the hype, we learned that these parents for the most part are earning everyday livings by leading everyday lives: 58 percent indeed opting for a part-time workweek *but thereby part-time income* so they can be as available to their children as their personal needs dictate. In Chapter 2, you'll find 101 business/career profiles of entrepreneurial parents—freelancers, home business owners, and a handful of employed teleworkers—who tell in their own words how they made the transition to home employment, what their top revenue streams and marketing strategies are, and what their advice is for parents looking to break into their line of home-based work. Behind this business front you'll find a collective home front—rich with insight, inspiration, information, and ideas—in Chapters 3 through 7. You'll be encouraged to design your own solution, start or tie up loose ends of your business, manage your time, involve your family in your work, and pass the entre- preneurial parenthood work option on to the next generation.

Before we take a close look in their direction, however, it may be helpful to offer an aerial view of the workplace landscape, as it looks from a distance, at this time of writing. While we are certain this land- scape will alter by the time this book is in your hands, the seismatic shift in the economy caused by new technologies that have resulted in a 51 percent personal computer and 41.5 percent Internet penetration in American homes has already occurred (according to the August 2000 Internet and Computer Use Supplement, Bureau of the Census for the Bureau of Labor Statistics). Work life has irrevocably penetrated home life for the employed (after hours) and self-employed (all hours!) alike. The virtual genie, as they say, is out of the bottle.

How can this wired spirit knock down the physical boundaries that have been separating parents from their children in ten- to twelve-hour blocks of time throughout the workweek? Let's very briefly "rewind" the work scene a hundred years ago and then "fast forward" back to today. We'll see how modern technology threw American family life off course and how it is now directing us back home—for any parent ready to make the journey.

The Way We Were

A hundred years ago, the Industrial Revolution put Americans in a tailspin, breaking the natural order of everyday family life by send- ing the great majority of parents outside the home to work for the first time. Up until then, an agricultural economy was mainstream and oth- ers literally lived on top of their livelihoods—a flight of stairs up from the mom-and-pop shop below. For the past one hundred years, however, millions of families have struggled with the unnatural state of fathers working a good distance from home or, more recently, both parents tak- ing jobs miles and hours away from their children. While the financial, professional, and personal growth for a great many parents have flour- ished as a result, their children have been inadvertently left out of the loop (save the token "take your child to work day"), and they were told that doing so was in everyone's best interest.

That stamp of approval for working parents today has been mani- fested through the obscure lens of the television screen since the 1950s.

Appeased by watching popular childhood sitcoms, too many of us bought into the idealism that work and family had clean, clear lines of separation. Remember those black-and-white amiable programs such as *Father Knows Best* that gave Dad (the sole breadwinner) all the authority and Mom (the focused parent) all the heart of the family? Some of us even grew up in such homes, with Dad home in time for family supper at 5:30 and Mom (without fanfare) taking on part-time work only when her youngest child went to school full-time. More equitable parenting models in shows such as *Family Ties, Full House,* and *The Cosby Show* always presented a well-educated but unharried parent in the kitchen or living room, with their work life neatly tucked away in between commercials. Finally, ensemble casts like those in *The Mary Tyler Moore Show* and *Murphy Brown* turned co-workers into family members, completely skewing our expectations of what the workplace was all about. Here the work/family line blurred, merged, so much so that an all-career, no-family expectancy took hold. Where did children fit into this picture? Toward the very end of one's career, if ever. A tough model to follow when the median age of first-time moms is twenty-four years, according to the National Center for Health Statistics!

Of course, in the end, entertainment is just that, and we are each accountable for the decisions we make individually, but understanding how popular culture can affect our sense of self is important. Few loyal fans of Oprah Winfrey, for instance, don't know that *The Mary Tyler Moore Show* was an enormous source of inspiration for Oprah as she grew up and began her own highly successful career in broadcasting. For those of us who are married with children, however, there's a pull to be—or be married to—Laura Petrie, happy homemaker with a good-humored spouse, and Mary Richards, happy independent professional surrounded by co-workers (all men) who love and adore her. Both these polar life paths looked so appealing; turn off the tube and grow up, of course, and the battle with disgruntled co-workers, spouses, children, *and self* begins . . .

Fast forward to today. With cell phones, laptops, and instantaneous communication with anyone in the world, the net of alternative work options is growing wider and wider. Turn off the tube and go wireless, and working while sailing the seven seas seems possible, especially for the tech-savvy, ambitious, and well-connected. But parents aren't looking to go off on adventures—they're looking to simplify, to settle down, to go with their own personalized family flow. To meet this need, low-cost computer and communications technology are extending the welcoming hand of home-based work once again, and parents from every industry, stage, and experience are taking it—and with no apologies. These parents are part of a growing movement across the country and around the world aimed at using advances in technology and the proliferation of the Internet to bring work back home, where they could put another log on the fire and take an afternoon break to build a snowman with the kids. They are being fueled not only by technology-driven careers, but by the innate desire of parents to spend more time with their children and to pursue their vocation in a *true* family-friendly workplace. The Mary Tyler Moore myth exploded; the workplace is where, at last, children are not only back in the picture, but back "in the loop."

In summary, the road today's entrepreneurial parents are taking is actually an old path repaved. It is our hope, through the 700+ EPs who contributed directly to our research and the more than 1,000 who have registered as members of the en-parent.com online community, that you too can find a work-life flow that keeps pace with your priorities in the world we live in today.

EP Work Options

With modern technology nudging those of us who want to return to the homestead to do so—*without* sacrificing our education, career, income, or self-sufficiency—what exactly are our options? Must one be an envelope stuffer or a highly skilled computer whiz to join the home-working ranks? Where's the middle ground? We found many in our survey responses. Chapter 4 will highlight ten selected businesses through show-and-tell profiles—you'll see the public image of the business on the front of the page and the EP behind that business on the back. In Chapter 2 you will hear from 101 EPs who have developed home-based careers that fall into one of three broad categories:

- *"Tech-Lite" Home Careers*—which need minimal tech proficiency, if any.

- *"Tech-Heavy" Home Careers*—which need a higher level of tech proficiency because advanced software programs and other high-tech prerequisites are wholly integrated into the business operation.

- *"Internet-Based" Home Careers*—which are wholly reliant on the Internet and wouldn't exist without it.

It's important to note here that the selected career profiles are reflective of our survey respondents and do not come close to covering the entire spectrum of home career possibilities available to EPs. In *Finding Your Perfect Work,* the Edwardses identified 1,600 home-based businesses, with 612 of those being particularly family-friendly, and their book *The Best Home Businesses for the 21st Century* highlights comprehensive profiles of more than 100 of the most promising. In *The Entrepreneurial Parent,* we drew on the insights and experiences of parents in the at-home workforce to develop our profiles, asking questions that matter most to *them*. We asked:

- *What transferable skills can be exchanged between the traditional workforce and self-employment?* Because knowing that one can switch to and from traditional and alternative employment gives EPs peace of mind.

- *What's a "day in the life" of an EP like?* Because time management tops the stress factors for all working parents, including EPs.

- *How do they price and market their products and services?* Because sales and marketing is one of the top psychological barriers of entry for EPs who, for the most part, come from corporate rather than entrepreneurial career paths.

This latter point is an important finding in our study. Prior to becoming an EP, a full 74 percent of our survey respondents worked in the traditional workforce, with 53 percent already a parent working outside the home and 21 percent making the jump from outside of the home employment to home employment at the onset of parenthood (see Appendix, Figure 11). Only 15 percent of the EPs made the transition into home employment as a stay-at-home parent, and a mere 5 percent came from an entrepreneurial background. This finding begs the question, how did these parents discover the EP back road from the mainstream highway? Let's take a look at the most common routes.

The Telework Buzz: Is It Just a Murmur?

Far and away the most common question we receive from aspiring EPs is: "I want to work at home . . . I have a Pentium computer . . . do you know anyone who is hiring?"

The chasm between being gainfully employed and becoming apprehensively self-employed is gargantuan to most. Small wonder that when the concept of telecommuting—working as a full-time employee either part-time or full-time from home—first emerged as a work option more than twenty years ago, it created quite a stir. Employers took note of such bottom-line benefits as increased productivity and real estate savings, while employees worn out by the nine-to-five grind jumped at the opportunity to skip the commute a few times a week while retaining a full paycheck. With telecommuting, parents gain all of the flexibility of working at home with none of the risk. It's a sweet deal.

While fraught with new work-related challenges such as the perception that teleworkers are not serious professionals because they put their lifestyles first (false), co-worker resentment (true), getting squeezed out of the communications loop (true and false), and getting passed over for raises and promotions (false), the telework option overall has built a solid reputation of being a win-win arrangement for those who venture to give it a whirl. Employers who implement a formal teleworking program under the advice and direction of specialized telework consultants find the investment in proper protocol worth the extra effort. Employees lucky enough to be offered the opportunity often wouldn't trade their position in their company for any other. Bit by bit, companies from just about every industry sector and every size are beginning to flirt with the telework promise, albeit the great majority still on an informal, case-by-case basis.

What is discouraging for parents eager to work at home, however, is that teleworking more often than not brings only a little bit of breathing room into their overextended schedules. According to the 1999 Telework America National Telework Survey, conducted and reported by Joanne H. Pratt Associates for The International Telework Association and Council, today's 19.6 million teleworkers typically work only 5.5 days per month at home. When parents are feeling stretched and pulled by competing schedule conflicts, those 5.5 days a month are really just a drop in the stress-management bucket. For some families, they're actually just a tease.

So while telework may be on the rise, even when given the opportunity, many parents find the corporate tether is often too constricting. In Chapter 2, you'll hear directly from a few successful teleworkers, but you'll notice that most EPs we came across have taken—by choice or by necessity—the self-employed route. Not surprisingly, a good many have turned their former employer into their first client, providing the springboard to an independent career.

To learn more about teleworking, visit:

- Work Options, Inc. (for "FlexSuccess," a downloadable blueprint employees can customize for their own telework proposal) www.workoptions.com

- Gil Gordon Associates (a resource for telecommuters and managers, run by a renowned telework consultant) www.gilgordon.com

- International Teleworker Association and Council www.telecommute.org

- Canadian Telework Association (links to news, articles, studies) www.ivc.ca

The MLM/Biz Opp Scene: Is It All a Scam?

Right behind the question of whether we know of anyone who's hiring, often comes the question: "I want to work at home, but I'm afraid I'll lose money to a scam. Do you know of any legitimate business opportunities?"

Again, the prospect of being completely on one's own professionally—having to scramble to put together a home career from scratch with no support system in place—is overwhelming to those without any history of self-employment. Small wonder here, too, that those "Work at Home!" posters and "Unlimited Income Potential" e-mails can turn the heads of many frustrated parents looking for a more reasonable work-family balance but would appreciate the guidance of a parent company. Unfortunately, as too many have learned, when desperation and opportunism meet, unsavory business deals are too often made.

However, multi-level marketing (MLM) and home-based franchises can also be as wholesome as apple pie and the Tupperware you use for that one leftover slice. Indeed, there are many scam-free home-based business opportunities out there, enough in fact for Paul and Sarah Edwards to have written the book *Home Businesses You Can Buy: The Definitive Guide to Exploring Franchises, Multi-Level Marketing, and Business Opportunities* with co-author Walter Zooi. For those interested in exploring this type of work-at-home option—especially if you come from a strong sales background and/or are particularly enamored by a certain product line that you discovered at a neighborhood "party"—we highly recommend you turn to *Home Businesses You Can Buy* for guidance. However, because the National Survey of Entrepreneurial Parents yielded only a 2 percent survey response from network marketing/MLM consultants, and the Edwardses wrote an entire book on this subject, we will not be addressing this particular avenue here.

Before we move on, however, there's one important discovery we'd like to point out. Over the years we have heard from many EPs who have gotten their entrepreneurial start from the multi-level marketing or business opportunity industry, and either they have used the experience as a launching pad to their own independent home business, or they work in a dual capacity, both as a direct sales consultant and as an independent professional or entrepreneur. In other words, they have found that their investment of time and money in a turnkey operation or direct-sales opportunity gave them a hands-on "education" in entrepreneurship, and/or they saw it as an "entry-level" self-employed position of sorts. Explains Howard Dingman, an independent systems integrator in Maine, New York:

> Oddly enough, the best thing I did for our business was to become involved in a multi-level marketing organization. Not because we had any success in this MLM; in fact we "lost" quite a large amount of money. But the way we "lost" the money was by attending seminars and buying training materials. We received an education in business unlike any available in schools. We learned about business ethics, work ethic, and how to treat a business like a business rather than a hobby. We learned about attitudes, and how our own attitude would influence the growth of our business. We learned about success materials from au-

thors like Zig Ziglar, Og Mandino, and many others. We learned to associate with others who shared our goals and ideals, and to disassociate ourselves from those who would try to drag us down to share their quagmire existence. We learned that as we began to succeed, that others would call us "lucky," even though we worked hard to get there. And we learned that our hardships were our own, to be kept to ourselves, but our successes should be shared with everyone we could.

Besides the Edwards/Zooi book, these sites may help guide parents through the maze of business opportunities:

- www.WAHM.com

- www.Bizymoms.com

- Home-Based Working Moms, www.hbwm.com

Transferable Skills: Are They Enough?

Although former employers and MLM opportunities are common stepping stones to wholly independent home careers, many aspiring EPs bypass both and go straight to this question: "I want to work at home, and I have a dozen years experience in my industry, so how do I get started?"

Again, unlike innate entrepreneurs, the majority of entrepreneurial parents (74 percent in our study) come from a corporate upbringing and maintain a corporate mindset for quite a while. This places them on a distinctly different launching ground than their home-based entrepreneurial counterparts who are *not* parents, since it's not entrepreneurial blood running through their veins as much as their parenting instinct. Propelled by the desire for a true family-friendly workplace, these determined and career-savvy EPs took the years of experience in their industry and either put a spin on it or plucked certain skills from their salaried positions and wrapped a whole new career path around those strengths. Such transferable skills, they are finding, are not only surprisingly adaptable, but they help them bridge their employment opportunities between the traditional and alternative workforce as needed.

An excellent example of the ability to envision a home-based career that stemmed from a previous employment experience can be found in Janet Gardella, an aspiring EP to two children, ages four and two. In fact, Janet's use of transferable skills is reflected in the Appendix of this book, as she is the one who calculated, prepared, and reported the data results of our quantitative questionnaire.

Before becoming a parent, Janet worked in the consumer-product industry as a scientist for eleven years for such companies as Procter & Gamble and Johnson & Johnson. In addition to product development (her primary work), she managed scientific and consumer research areas that involved generating, analyzing, interpreting, and reporting data. Although most of her former career involved developing new consumer products such as name-brand facial moisturizer and cleanser, Janet plans to use her secondary but sharp market research skills to jumpstart her EP career. She hopes to assist journalists, researchers, and research firms in organizing, analyzing, interpreting, and presenting quantitative and qualitative data—a service easily operated out of a home office, during after hours (after-parenting hours, that is!)

> **Fun Fact:** Janet lives around the corner from Lisa, whose older children acted as couriers, transporting stacks of extended surveys into Janet's mailbox for quantitative analysis. After reading through all 700 pages herself, Janet commented: "I guess what I have learned the most is that you can make your EP experience be whatever you *want* it to be, and that you can make an EP experience out of whatever background you're *coming from*. For me, it is really the only career type that fits completely into my parenting goals."

Self-Employment: A Diversified Income Strategy

To be sure, the transition from turning to a single employer for one's livelihood to multiple businesses, clients, or customers is a good bit unsettling for most. EPs who choose self-employment to spend more time with their children often leave behind not only a steady paycheck but their comfort zone as well. Therefore, using marketing and sales to snatch that first client or account can be a monumental psychological hurdle.

Erin Staeck, owner of Catering to Computers, represents the sentiments of many EPs who have been cut off from their former sense of self:

> I think it is a shame that Corporate America has yet to realize that all their great talent has left the cubicle and are sitting at

home filling the role of Entrepreneurial Parents! They have yet to realize that very cost-effective contracts with people like us would allow them to not only gain the hardest working employees they ever had, but also help in securing the world's future by allowing us to participate in the upbringing of our children, make a decent living, and be productive members of society.

Indeed, convincing those first few clients that you've got the best talent, skills, and wherewithal to complete the project—on time and within budget, and better than anyone they already have on staff—is the stuff successful EPs are made of. The good news is that once you do develop working relationships with those first few clients, then losing any one of them is a much softer blow than losing a salaried position.

In fact, a comparison can be made as follows: self-employment is to a salaried position as mutual funds is to an individual stock. *In essence, self-employment is a diversified income strategy.* Interestingly enough, during the writing of this book the stock market oscillated from an extraordinarily high to a frighteningly low market value, the economy from an unprecedented tight labor market in the booming "new economy" to a widening sweep of layoff announcements in the wake of a national recession. With their versatility and diversity, independent home office workers are in a strong position to ride out such dramatic fluctuations—during this round and the one after.

Regardless of where the economy swings next, it's clear that the increasing use of the home office as a primary workplace is here to stay, as are parents compelled to spend more time with their children. While history is on the side of parents and children living and working in close vicinity, as a nation we've simply forgotten how this natural state of affairs works. How can we revitalize our instincts to stick together as families who work and learn side by side? By observing the modern-day EP, and traveling with them on the back road that leads to the street where you live. . . .

CHAPTER 2

101 EP Profiles

We have found that readers who are exploring an entrepreneurial career path not only want information and prescriptive advice, they also want to learn from the experience of others like themselves who have chosen a business similar to the one they are in or wish to pursue. The following profiles of 101 entrepreneurial parents are "in their own words" for this reason. While we have edited these profiles for grammar and flow, we have preserved the words and personalities of the people who shared them. Although we cannot personally endorse any of the following products and services, we carefully selected these profiles based on the breadth of home career options and hope you will enjoy their diversity and candor as much as we have.

To learn more about these businesses and a thousand others, take a look at the EP Business Directory at www.en-parent.com/directory, where you are invited to list your own when you're ready!

Tech-Lite Home Careers

ACCOUNTANT

DATAMASTER, LLC | www.DaycareRecordkeeping.com
Brigitte A. Thompson, 32 | Williston, Vermont | Ages of Children:
7 weeks, 4, 8

> *"I continue to receive full-time job offers from businesses outside my home, which include a generous salary as well as benefits I can only dream of while being self-employed. There is so much more to life than money, though. And while I do miss the increased financial compensation, I don't miss anything else and feel I am much more productive without the office politics."*

Office Oasis
A finished portion of our basement, about 300 square feet with two small windows, providing room for me to meet with clients, store supplies, and do my work.

Job Description
Accounting, bookkeeping, and payroll services. I also am the author of one printed book, *The Home Daycare Complete Recordkeeping System,* and one e-book, *Home Daycare Recordkeeping,* with another printed book in the works geared toward general business recordkeeping and tax issues.

Previous Career
I worked at an investment counseling firm for six years, providing a variety of services in the publishing department and bookkeeping services for the management team.

Transferable Skills
Transferable skills include computer work, customer service, order fulfillment, bookkeeping, bank deposits, credit card processing, transcrip-

tion, advertising, marketing, accounts receivable and payable management including collections, research, and purchasing. A bit of everything that I quickly learned could all be done from home or in an outside office!

Knowledge, Skills, Experience, and/or Education Needed

A clear understanding of federal tax laws acquired through classes and reading the publications of the Internal Revenue Service would be essential for your success. It is a good idea to keep up-to-date in this field since tax laws change frequently. An accountant should be someone who is willing to take the time to be sure client accounts are in balance and, when they are not, be patient enough to find the source of the discrepancy and fix it. Since working with numbers is the basis of this profession, one should be mathematically inclined. An ability to organize is also helpful.

Industry Insight

As long as entrepreneurs have to pay taxes based on their income, there will be a need for bookkeeping and accounting services. To get started in this field, I recommend networking with tax preparers and other accountants. They come in contact with your target market daily and will at some point have to turn away clients when their businesses have grown to capacity. If they are familiar with you and your business, they have someone to recommend.

On Marketing

My business has grown to the point where I can no longer accept new accounting clients, but while I was getting started I tried several marketing techniques. Networking worked the best. Tell everyone you know what your business is offering and that you are welcoming new clients. Mention it to friends, neighbors, relatives, and anyone who asks about your profession. You just never know where a new client will come from. I found the least effective method to be direct mailings advertising my services.

Top Revenue Streams

My largest source of revenue is monthly bookkeeping services. I provide a variety of services customized to the needs of each client. Some clients need help on a daily basis with cash deposits and expenditures, others need help once a week with billing services, but all of my clients require monthly reconciliation of bank statements and preparation of financial statements. These reports provide a wealth of information to my clients, which helps them operate their businesses and make decisions for the future.

The second largest source of revenue for me is payroll services. There are employee paychecks to calculate each period and payroll taxes that are due each month, quarter, and year. Payroll can keep you very busy!

Reconstruction is another top source of revenue. When businesses lose sight of their recordkeeping and can't file an accurate tax return, they call on a bookkeeper or accountant for help. This is a time-consuming project but very rewarding in the sense that what was once a pile of messy receipts and check stubs is now an organized financial statement.

Pricing Structure

I charge $25 an hour for bookkeeping services, $50 for accounting software set-up and training, and $50 to $75 per hour for accounting services based upon what is required. *The Home Daycare Complete Recordkeeping System* is available for $22.50 (available through Amazon. com, BarnesandNoble.com and my web site www.angelfire.com/biz/datamaster), and *Home Daycare Recordkeeping* (available through www. parentsmarket.com) sells for $15.95.

Additional Cost Items

A software program for accounting and taxes would be helpful. The programs I have seen start at approximately $100 and can get quite expensive based on your clients' needs and the size of your business.

ADVERTISING SPECIALIST/PROMOTIONAL ITEMS

JESA PROMOTIONS | jesapro@hotmail.com
Saba Kennedy Washington, 32 | Charlotte, North Carolina | Ages of Children:
9 months, 5 years

Office Oasis

A large corner of my bedroom; my closet is full of promotional samples.

Home Business

Jesa Promotions is a full-service advertising specialty, marketing, and promotions company, specializing in the embroidery and screen-printing of corporate logos onto promotional wear. We also offer promotional writing services for press releases, catalogs, product releases, and articles.

Personal Mission

I would like to see my business grow to support my children financially, emotionally, and spiritually. I look at my business as something intricately tied into the quality of life I foresee for my family.

Top Clients

- Reebok
- *Black Enterprise*
- *The New York Carib News*
- *PC Magazine*

Primary Market

Mid-to-large corporations, small businesses, any organization with need for my services.

EP Motivating Force

I want to have more control of my life and time. I want to be able to design my own financial destiny and professionally challenge myself. Most of all, I want to be the one to decide when I want to be with my own family. Working at home allows my children to see me as a self-sufficient and strong woman. I want them to grow up secure in themselves and their own potential. I do not want them to be dependent on anyone or any one source. I believe that seeing me work will provide them this blueprint for living. It is also important that they understand that "whatever one dreams, one can achieve."

EP Advice

Stay focused and believe in your vision. Associate daily with positive people who share your dream of living on your own terms. Also, remain persistent, frugal, and consistent, and hold on to your faith.

EP Vow

Never again will I allow anyone to put me in the position where I have to choose between my work and my family.

Recommended Resources

BOOKS

- *The Seven Spiritual Laws of Success* by Deepak Chopra
- All the financial freedom books by Suze Orman
- *To Build the Life You Want, Create the Work You Love: The Spiritual Dimension of Entreprenuering* by Marsha Sinetar

WEB SITES

- www.en-parent.com
- www.womencentral.com
- www.cindykick.com
- www.wsj.com

AMERICAN INDIAN ART DEALER

COYOTES CORNER | www.coyotescorner.com
Janis M. Calouro, 52 | East Providence, Rhode Island | Ages of Children: 7, 26, 28

Home Biz and Mission Statement

Coyotes Corner was developed to help bring awareness and recognition to American Indian art and artists. The American Indian pieces that we sell are authentic and come from "cottage industries." We hope to be able to expand and export our products globally. Our target market is the world! Everybody can use another blanket!

Most Popular Services and Pricing Fees

Our most popular products are our T-shirts and our dream catchers. The prices of the dream catchers vary according to size and whether or not they are made with grapevine or a metal hoop. The T-shirt prices also vary. It depends on what I paid for them. Frankly, on some of our pieces, I don't know that I have found the right price! Usually, I consider what I paid for it and what my competition is selling it for (if it's the same quality). Then I try and price it so that I'm appealing to that part of our brain that says, "Wow . . . that's a great price!" Personally, I'd rather make buckets of dimes than a handful of one dollar bills.

Favorite Products and/or Services

My favorite products are the coyote face mandellas. Each year thousands of coyotes are slaughtered, simply for fun. Some folks go and collect as many of the carcasses as possible. The carcasses are cleaned, and then honored. The mandella is a very powerful piece. It has a copyright. Coyote taught humans many things. Coyote teaches us how to raise our young. Coyote is teacher and trickster. Coyote is adaptable and loyal. To be able to honor the coyote is a great thing.

Marketing Strategy

First of all, everybody gets a card. I put business cards in with my checks when paying bills. I carry cards when we go out walking. We also use flyers. We work powwows, street fairs, and festivals, so we hand out flyers with a list of upcoming sales. (For example, in November, all of our candles will be on sale.) I also write daily tips and suggestions on living less toxically. I am developing "The Frugal Environmentalist," but right now the tips link with Coyotes Corner. That helps because most folks want to live with fewer toxins and save money. Finally, I'm working on developing a "class" to help welfare recipients get free, used computers and bring them on-line. I think that many of these people will end up being customers, either as retail or wholesale clients. I offer discounts—veteran discounts, senior citizen discounts, powwow-dancer discounts, etc. Sometimes, I'll give a "many children" discount. For instance, if we have flutes that sell for $3.00 each and a parent with four children is interested in them, we can drop to four flutes for $10.00. I try and make it so each client feels special and feels as though he or she received a great deal!

Recommendations

I see many vendors who are married to their stocks and their prices. The object is to turn the product or service into cash. Why limit yourself? Why box yourself into a price . . . then you'll end up carrying that item back home, rather than cash. I don't lose money on my items, but I don't have to squeeze each one for every penny! Let me tell you, those folks who know that I gave them a break—they always come back, and they talk about us to others!

ARTIST/PAINTED FURNITURE AND HOME ACCESSORIES

WHIMSICAL NOTES | www.whimsicalnotes.com
Jane Kavanagh Morton, 49 | Newark, Delaware | Ages of Children: 14, 16

Office Oasis
Spare room is my studio, and office is on first floor.

Job Description
Creator of designs to fit personalities.

Previous Career
Accountant.

Transferable Skills
Organization, marketing, networking, web site design, time management can be of help no matter which direction you are headed.

Knowledge, Skills, Experience, and/or Education Needed
I am self-taught as far as my art work, but my business experience comes from being in the nine-to-five work life.

Industry Insight
My field is slow right now because the economy is not good, but branching out and offering to do murals and smaller pieces seems to be a good way to go.

On Marketing
I've been using eBay to have cash flow and get my name out. Having other people market me is just too expensive and not very productive.

Top Revenue Streams
Murals and painted furniture are my most successful lines. Price depends on detail and size.

Additional Cost Items

Buying furniture wholesale is a bit of an investment up front but will pay off over buying retail.

Recommended Resources

I learn what I can from everybody I meet. Can't say that one person or source has been outstanding. I learn a little bit from a lot of sources and it adds up.

ATTORNEY/BANKRUPTCY

MARJORIE J. HOLSTEN, ATTORNEY-AT-LAW | marjholsten@yahoo.com
Marjorie J. Holsten, 37 | Maple Grove, Minnesota | Ages of Children: 6, 8

"I have never been criticized for being unprofessional—only thanked profusely."

Office Oasis

We built our home with the idea that I would work out of it. My office is a separate room (though it has no doors on it) right near the front door, so that when clients come over I don't have to clean more than the entryway. (My office is always clean, because children and husbands are not allowed to play there.)

Job Description

Attorney, practicing in the areas of real estate, bankruptcy, and estate planning. I do a lot of closings for people selling their homes, and I draft many wills.

Previous Career

Associate attorney with a law firm.

Transferable Skills

If an attorney (aka "esquire," or "Esq.") can type and operate a computer and word processor, virtually all aspects of a law practice can be done from the home. If a secretary or legal assistant is needed, a home-based practice would be more difficult. "Self-sufficient" attorneys are the most valuable, both at home and in the workforce. Should I ever go back to a law firm, I will not need a secretary (which increases my "cost" to the firm by $40,000 or whatever).

EPs in the area of law have the world at their fingertips today. Clients shop on-line for attorneys, so an EP Esq. who wants to attract clients needs only to set up a web site. Legal research resources abound on the web for free. Voice-mail on a separate office line allows a professional presence, and since nine-to-five jobs utilize e-mail and voice-mail, clients are used to it.

If an EP Esq. is looking to reenter the workforce and hopes to get into private practice, an established client base is their ticket into almost any firm they want.

A law practice from home can take as many hours as you want to give it. A friend of mine does two wills a month (a husband and a wife). This is enough to pay for her license fees and a few other things, plus it also allows her to truthfully put on her résumé that she is in solo practice. Gaps in employment make it difficult to reenter the legal workforce. Another friend of mine took five years off totally to raise her children. She spent two years after that trying to get a job with a law firm, with no success. She was perceived as being "rusty," had no client base, and now works in a flower shop. The mommy track is a very real and scary thing in law. Mommies are not taken as seriously by the male-dominated powerful majority.

Knowledge, Skills, Experience, and/or Education Needed

This is a tough one for the average person. To be a lawyer, you have to graduate from law school and pass the bar exam to get a license to practice law. If a parent thinks, "I'd like to be an attorney to work from home," my advice is "*Run*—in the opposite direction." To get into law school, you need a college degree and to do well on the LSAT. Law school is three miserable years—that were difficult for me even before husband and children. I personally cannot imagine trying to juggle parenthood along with law school.

Industry Insight

Once someone is a lawyer, many avenues are open. There is a high degree of job dissatisfaction among lawyers, due to powerful greedy senior partners who demand associates work bazillion hours a week and dangle a "partnership carrot" for incentive. Most (women in particular) do not realize how easy it actually is to hang out their own shingle. Simply put, it takes confidence and a computer.

On Marketing

There is *so much* work out there. Once you do a good job for someone, they will tell all their friends, and soon your practice will be booming. I have not spent a penny on advertising in the past nine years. In the early days of my solo practice, I did a lot of speaking (to advertise myself— quite a bit of it for free), teaching about "your rights," etc. Nowadays, I do less speaking, but I get paid a whole lot more.

My most effective marketing method has been speaking in churches about wills. I throw in pertinent Bible verses and some off-the-wall humor. Each such speaking engagement brings in twenty or more wills (which I have promised and am able to do at a significant discount because I have explained the process to twenty people at once, rather than each individually). *Every parent* needs a will, and so few can afford to spend hundreds of dollars on them. Thus, speaking in churches has been a win-win situation for many. Wills are also relatively simple to get "up to speed" on, and they can be done easily with a computer and the right forms.

My second most effective marketing is teaching classes. I have knowledge of mortgage foreclosure, real estate, and bankruptcy laws, and I teach classes to social workers, county welfare administrators, realtors, and other professionals on what to do with someone when they are in foreclosure. Often, the last and only possible resort is filing for bankruptcy, which can only be done by a licensed attorney. Thus, many of my students refer clients to me. These are great clients, also, as they have been well screened by the well trained professional and have a basic understanding of the process. I am trying to get away from bankruptcy for a while now though. It is very draining, there are constant emergencies, and many times I do not get paid.

My least effective marketing method was advertising in the Yellow Pages, which a "mentor" told me to do when I first started my practice. It was expensive and only wasted my time. Many people would call, but they were almost always fishing for free legal advice and shopping around for attorneys. (That's fine, but each phone call was fifteen to twenty minutes, several times a week, which added up to hours and hours of time.) Some of the phone contacts may have resulted in business coming in, but overall I probably broke even or lost a bit on the advertising expenses. The best is word of mouth. When a friend gives a recommendation, someone is not interested in shopping around—they want me specifically.

Top Revenue Streams

Drafting wills, speaking, and teaching.

Pricing Structure

My hourly rate and pricing structure varies a bit depending on what I am doing. Overall I hate keeping track of my time because there are constant interruptions (mostly kids, though telephone, laundry, etc., come into it), so I charge whatever I can on a flat-fee basis. If a couple attends my class, I will do their wills for $150 (total—husband and wife each get a will). Actually, most often they pay $200 to attend the class, and the church keeps $50. I do real estate closings for $250, and bankruptcies are about $800. My hourly rate is $125. (It often takes eight hours to make five "billable hours" however.)

Additional Cost Items

A copy machine; mine cost $250 used.

Recommended Resources

Find a mentor. The best would be another EP Esq. We support each other. As a one-person shop, it is impossible to be more than one place at once. I have many friends I call on to cover court hearings for me, and frequently call them to get their insights. It works both ways. Also, my EP Esq. colleagues who call me for advice often provide me a much-needed break during which I can speak to another adult (who isn't a client in crisis). Home officing can be lonely.

In Minnesota, I am on a panel of home-based office attorneys. I encourage many to go for it! I am always flattered when another attorney calls to see how I do it. Many meetings with aspiring EP Esq.'s have been in my home, and they bring their children to play with mine. We have a cup of coffee and a wonderful visit. I benefit from having adult conversation and a new potential resource for when I may need help.

ATTORNEY/ESTATE PLANNING

LAW OFFICE OF PAULA AIELLO
Paula Aiello, 46 | San Ramon, California | Ages of Children: 5, 15, 17, 19

Office Oasis
Laundry room.

Job Description
I serve clients of all ages with estate planning needs (wills and trusts, mostly) and legal issues related to aging and death.

Previous Career
Attorney since 1986; previously a high school teacher.

Transferable Skills
Most important, develop initiative and self-reliance. Even if you work "for" others, treat yourself as a professional working mostly for yourself. You are your own boss no matter who pays the salary!

Knowledge, Skills, Experience, and/or Education Needed
- Knowledge of people—how to listen to them and learn about what they need and want
- Law school degree and a license to practice
- Desire to serve others, not just make money

Industry Insight
If you are an attorney and have experience in this area, there will never be an end to this need.

On Marketing
I do not really have to market anymore. All of my clients come by word of mouth from other clients and by connections made during my other activities (it's like meeting "the right person" to marry—do what you love and you'll find one!).

Pricing Structure
$150/hour.

Additional Cost Items
Professional materials and books are helpful, but access to a good library will do!

Recommended Resources
Strength of my desire to be my own boss and have low overhead so that I would be freer to do the work I want to do rather than work I *have* to do just to pay the big overhead bills.

Initially, I relied heavily on connections through the local senior center (i.e., connect with your target clientele).

AUTHOR/BUSINESS REFERRAL CONSULTANT

BNI-WISCONSIN, INC. | www.bniwis.com
Craig Campana, 40 | Menomonee Falls, Wisconsin | Ages of Children: 6, 9

Office Oasis
Living room armoire with laptop, and quiet location downstairs for presenting my tele-seminars.

Education and Awards
- B.S. degree in film and television production, certification as a networking trainer, certified teleclass leader
- U.S. director of the year for Business Network International (BNI) (11/11/00)
- BNI Founder's Circle 1997–2001
- Contributing author to *Masters of Networking; Confessions of Shameless Self-Promoters,* and *Masters of Success*
- Author of *Turning Career Adversity Into Power for Success*

Previous Career
Worked in television broadcasting as a commercial producer, writer, and editor for television commercials at a small market station in Kalispell, Montana. I also directed the nightly news (which proved to me what sheer stress was). Worked in the corporate setting as director of video services for a book publisher in Milwaukee, Wisconsin, before being downsized in 1994. Then we opened our first small business producing video programs, and in order to grow our business we founded the first

BNI chapter in Wisconsin in 1995. Now six years later, BNI is our business. We own the BNI franchise in the state of Wisconsin and have more than 1,000 members.

Home Biz

BNI is a business and professional networking organization whose sole purpose is to generate referral business for our members. See www.bniwis.com. We only allow one person per profession. Being a member of a chapter is like having a sales force of 25 people out promoting your business to the contacts they have.

Primary Market

Small business owners

Top Revenue Streams

- Membership development
- Tele-seminars

EP Motivating Force

We started working at home out of necessity. The very day I was downsized we took in a foster baby (we were a licensed foster home for Milwaukee County at the time.) We ended up adopting that baby (our son Timothy, who is challenged with cerebral palsy). Due to the care he needed, it was important that our business was out of the home, so we could respond quickly to his needs and those of his brother Corey.

Home Career Advice

Employ a call center to take your calls. I didn't for the first three years, and it was difficult to get anything appreciably done in a day. I was constantly interrupted by phone calls routing me in a different direction from where I wanted to go. Two years ago we routed all calls through a call center named American Business Solutions, and then we could focus on what we needed to get done. We received our messages via e-mail three times each day so we could plan our callback times.

Recommended Resources

- www.ceoexpress.com
- www.toolkit.cch.com

- www.parentingideas.com
- www.sba.com

AUTHOR/COLUMNIST

ANCHORED DREAMS | www.azriela.com
Azriela Jaffe, 42 | Yardley, Pennsylvania | Ages of Children: 3, 6, 7

Office Oasis
Converted living room.

Previous Career
Fifteen years as a human resource director for large New England companies.

Degree
Master's in business administration; bachelor's in social work.

Home Biz
I am a published author of ten non-fiction business and self-help/inspirational/religious books, a novelist, and a syndicated newspaper business advice columnist. I also write columns for a variety of web sites that are interested in work/family and entrepreneurial couples and family issues. Occasionally I will coach individuals, couples, and partners by telephone and e-mail on issues of work/family concerns. I also speak professionally at conferences around the country, primarily as a keynoter and workshop leader for small business conferences and synagogues. I split my time between serving business audiences, because of my first several books, and synagogues and other spiritual communities because of my last two books, *Create Your Own Luck* (which is basically about partnering with God), and *Two Jews Can Still Be a Mixed Marriage*. I also publish two free e-zines for subscribers, the *Entrepreneurial Couples' Success Letter,* for entrepreneurial couples and families, and *Create Your Own Luck,* an e-zine to help people partner with God and create more blessings in their life.

Mission Statement

I assist individuals, couples, and business partners to find solutions to creating the quality of work, family, and spiritual life that they strive to create for themselves.

EP Musings

Recently I screwed up on coordinating with my husband. I was scheduled for an early morning radio interview, live, while he was out of town, and I had three young and active children in the house. The radio show was at 7:00 A.M., so I couldn't very well hire a baby-sitter, and even worse, I had misplaced the contact info so I couldn't call the radio show to reschedule. Oh well, time to punt! I got up extra early that morning, made sure that the kids knew I was going to be on the radio and then took out the old weapon—bribery. If all three would watch TV in my bedroom (far away from my downstairs office) and would stay completely quiet for the whole time I was on the radio, they could have anything they wanted for breakfast, and I mean, anything. Well, they thought this was way cool, it worked, they stayed completely out of the room, and I don't even want to tell you what they had for breakfast before going off to school!

EP Advice

Be realistic about what you can accomplish in your business and still be available for your children, or you will end up feeling like an ineffective parent and an unproductive business owner. Unless you are going to work early in the morning, or late in the evening, don't expect of yourself a full-time work schedule. Only people who have never tried it believe that you can park your children in front of Barney or a coloring book for hours at a time!

Also, be patient, persistent, and prepared for a long, adventurous ride with lots of ups and downs, but a fun ride nonetheless!

Recommended Resources

- *Transitions* by William Bridges
- *Small Miracles* by Yitta Halberstam
- *Men Are from Mars, Women Are from Venus* by John Gray
- *Divorce Busting* by Michele Wiener-Davis

AUTHOR/ORGANIZATIONAL EDUCATOR

LET'S GET IT TOGETHER | www.OrganizingU.com
Debbie Williams, 40 | Houston, Texas | Age of Child: 5

Office Oasis

Family room, where I use my laptop computer and small file crate. I do still have a dedicated office with a door but have cut back on my business hours so that I can work more comfortably downstairs on the sofa.

Home Biz

Let's Get It Together, a professional organizing and time management service for busy parents.

Mission

To help parents balance work and family by offering organizing tips and teaching time-management skills.

Top Products

- My book, *Home Management 101* (Champion Press, May 2001)
- Teleclasses for the public and other professional organizers through OrganizedU
- Organizing newsletter (*The Organized Exchange*)
- Syndicated articles
- E-mail consulting
- Telephone consulting
- Keynote presentations

Primary Market

Mothers with children living at home

Home Career Defining Moment

When I received writing assignments and requests for interviews on-line after being in business only one month! What a great networking opportunity that was.

EP Rewards

When you stay at home to raise your kids, you don't seem to need lunch money, working wardrobe, or day care fees. If you are creative, you find bartering systems for baby-sitters, are able to go to work in play clothes, and learn to like peanut butter and jelly every day of your life. It's so rewarding to watch your kids at work or play and secretly catch them being good!

EP Advice

Work around your children's schedule. Provide special toys/activities for your children that are only to be used while you are working, such as a basket of toys or a desk beside your computer. This keeps them mildly distracted while you do a small bit of work. Use naptime to make phone calls, and Mom's day out is a great time for running errands. If you work around your kids, rather than expect them to work around you, things run much smoother. Also, don't be afraid to take a risk—if you keep your costs to a minimum, you don't have much to lose except your efforts. And you will never know if it could be unless you try!

Recommended Resources

BOOKS

- *How to Get Business to Come to You* by Paul and Sarah Edwards
- *How to Raise a Family and a Career Under One Roof* by Lisa Roberts
- *Organizing Your Home Office for Success* by Lisa Kanarek
- *Teaming Up* by Paul and Sarah Edwards
- *Getting Publicity* by Tana Fletcher

WEB SITES

- *Entrepreneur Magazine,* www.entrepreneur.com
- SCORE, www.score.org
- Let's Get It Together, www.organizedtimes.com
- Home Office Life, www.homeofficelife.com
- Guerrilla Marketing Online, www.gmarketing.com
- Press Access (a free service for press release distribution), www.pressaccess.com

AUTHOR/PARENTING EDUCATOR

PARENT TO PARENT | www.parenttoparent.com
Jodie Lynn, 44 | St. Louis, Missouri | Ages of Children: four children
between 10 and 22

Office Oasis

My office is located upstairs overlooking our backyard. The computer is
strategically placed so I can look out of the window and watch my children playing outside.

Current Employment

- Parenting columnist, five years
- Parent educator, sixteen years
- Author, five years

Previous Employment

- Taught preschool through high school
- Account executive for various firms

Degree

The only education I like to talk about is the fact that I am a mommy,
i.e. a counselor, jury, judge, police officer, cook, cleaner, bottle washer,
nurse, doctor, playmate, coach, and friend!

Mission

Through my parenting column, "Parent to Parent," my books, like
Mommy—CEO (Constantly Evaluating Others): 5 *Golden Rules*, speaking engagements, and other writings, I am trying to make a difference in
today's society for children and their parents: If you care—you will share!

Top Products/Services

- Parenting/family speaker
- Freelance writing: Parenting/family columns, articles, and stories
- Radio and TV spokesperson for parenting today's children

Recent Clients

- National Association for the Education of Young Children (NAEYC)
- The Knight-Ridder/Tribune News Service (more than 350 newspapers throughout the United States)

- The Midwest Women's Show
- The Professional Business Women's Association
- Toastmasters
- Senator Tom Wyss

EP Advice

Don't try to work while the kids are determined to get your attention. Put things aside and spend a little time with them. Put yourself in their place. Computers are hot competition. They will probably leave you alone for a longer period if you'll spend time with them now. (Besides, you can enjoy the break as well!)

Don't get so uptight and involved in your work that you forget what your real job is: PARENTING! Pace yourself and take mini-breaks. Try to eat right and exercise! If you have a major project to get out and fast food is the only answer, always eat a piece of fruit before or after to break down and help absorb the fat. Drink plenty of water. Keep music handy and change it after a couple of hours. Get your body out of your chair and do a little dancing! Don't become too serious too fast.

Recommended Resources

BOOKS

- *Mommy—CEO*
- *The Road Less Traveled*
- *Sibling Rivalry*
- *How to Raise a Family and a Career Under One Roof*
- *The Family Manager*
- *The Psychology of Winning*

WEB SITES

- www.parenthoodweb.com
- www.oxygen.com
- www.fathersworld.com
- www.amazingmoms.com
- www.KRTDIRECT.com
- www.babyuniversity.com
- www.mommytips.com
- www.bluesuitmom.com

- www.singleparent.com
- www.amomslove.com

ORGANIZATIONS

- The Professional Business Women's Association
- Toastmasters
- National Association for the Education of Young Children (NAEYC)
- YWCA
- YMCA

BED-AND-BREAKFAST INNKEEPER

WINDOW ON THE WINDS B&B | www.windowonthewinds.com
Leanne McClain Rellstab, 40 | Pinedale, Wyoming | Ages of Children:
4 months, 2, 6, 10

"I wanted to be a stay-at-home mom with an income so I created a lifestyle for myself that would combine both jobs. As an innkeeper, I can make cookies for my guests and my family—all in the same batch!"

Office Oasis
Family room—hardly an oasis!

Job Description
As a bed-and-breakfast (B&B) innkeeper, I am a hostess, concierge, chef, maid, marketer, and bookkeeper. I enjoy cooking and making people feel good the most.

Previous Career
Archaeological consultant (a business I also ran from my home).

Transferable Skills
As an innkeeper, you will have to do every job that a larger company may hire several people to do, from the position of CEO to the maid. In addition to basic business management skills like computer, accounting, and marketing, you'll especially need:

- **Phone Skills:** Good phone skills are one of the most important aspects of the job. The phone is often your first contact and first impression with a potential guest.
- **Personnel Management:** Most innkeepers hire out some of their work, such as house cleaners, chefs, inn managers, and hostesses. Most will at least have a repair person, a lawn care service, interior decorator, and other similar types of help. Hiring and firing people is an important relevant skill.
- **Parenting Skills:** Running a B&B is very similar to being a good parent. You have to have a genuine concern for your guests. Are they well fed? Warm enough? Do they have sunscreen? Are they having fun? What can you do to make their stay (i.e., their lives) the best that it can be? Then after you have taken care of their every need, you have to clean up after them!
- **Cleaning Skills:** Keeping yourself well-groomed and your house and guest rooms clean are of the utmost importance. You have to be well organized, and be able to clean up quickly and immaculately.

To get started as an innkeeper, stay in as many B&Bs as you can to learn how someone else does it. Join a local or state organization to meet fellow innkeepers, and learn the nuances of innkeeping in your area. For instance, regulations vary from state to state and county to county. You have to know the rules. Also join a national organization like PAII. Read trade publications and follow your instincts.

I am unsure of career options for reentering the traditional work force, though a number of jobs in the tourism industry or as a consultant to others in hospitality professions come to mind. If cooking is your specialty, you could also be a chef.

Knowledge, Skills, Experience, and/or Education Needed

Good people skills and a willingness for your job to be an intimate part of your life are crucial. A lot of our business is common sense. My friends tease me that I am the ultimate housewife. I started the B&B without any previous hotel or restaurant experience. I have learned to be a good B&B owner through trial and error and eleven years of experience. I read as much as I can in trade publications, attend conferences, and network with other B&B owners. I do have a B.A. in history/anthropology . . . perhaps studying people in the past has given me some insight into people today?

Industry Insight

This is not a get-rich-quick kind of business. Innkeepers can make a rather nice salary as they grow, however. The B&B industry is being taken more seriously now. Innkeepers are seen as professionals, not just old folks with an extra room in their house. Our industry is growing.

I started our B&B in order to stay at home and to travel less. I do make enough money now to contribute to our household income, pay the utility bills, buy some of our food, and provide a nice house for my family to live in. I get to send my kids off to school every day, and I'm here when they get home. My children have also met a variety of wonderful people (our guests), and have learned some manners and people skills. It has allowed me to live in a beautiful area that I choose to raise my family in. I don't have to commute, and, for the most part, I can work my job schedule into my family's schedule.

On Marketing

The Internet is the most effective marketing tool I have. It really levels the playing field with larger hotels. My web site costs the same to produce as a large hotel chain's would. I cannot afford full-page ads like they can, so I try to use the latest Internet tools available, like on-line reservations. There are hundreds of B&B sites that list B&Bs (like a guidebook online). I have offers every day to join these so you really have to stay on top of them. They range in price from being free to costing hundreds of dollars.

Direct mail is usually effective. It is important to stay in touch with previous guests. Recommendations, word of mouth, and repeat guests produce a large percentage of my income. Therefore, doing a good job in the first place is very important.

"Traditional" marketing methods such as print ads, signs, or radio ads just don't work. While it's always tempting to put an ad in a magazine because you feel that you have to get your name out there, such advertising really doesn't produce guests (income) and is exorbitantly costly.

Top Revenue Streams

- Overnight stays, $45 to $125 per night. I have tried packages (overnight stays and activities) without any success.
- I also sell **Window on the Winds** B&B coffee cups and T-shirts, at $12 to $20. I make a little money this way, but not really enough worth mentioning. Mostly it's more of a branding technique.

Hourly Rate

I base my prices by the season and number of guests. $45 is the rate for a single person in the winter on a corporate rate; $125 would be for four people in the summer.

Additional Cost Items

I had to buy the property to run the B&B, which cost $110,000. Then I had to buy furniture, linens, dishes, decorations, amenities (soap, lotion, etc.), and so forth. I also added bathrooms and did some other smaller remodeling. So my total start-up costs were high, at around $50,000. As for office equipment, the only additional items needed were a reservation software program ($500), and my credit card terminal ($400).

Recommended Resources

- The Professional Association of Innkeepers—getting started, handling new situations that arise, and keeping you up to date with the latest information.
- The Internet—the single most important tool in marketing, as well as operating a B&B.

BUSINESS LETTER WRITER

EXECUTIVE REWRITES | www.exec-rewrites.com
Janet Tilden, 43 | Fremont, Nebraska | Ages of Children: 2, 13

Office Oasis

First-floor room with a window and a door that closes (yesss!!!) right next to the kitchen.

Job Description
Write and edit letters for business clients.

Previous Career
Project editor for Scott, Foresman.

Transferable Skills
Attention to details, written communications skills, self-discipline, task orientation, familiarity with the business world, marketing experience, interest in people

Knowledge, Skills, Experience, and/or Education Needed
Undergraduate degree in English, at least five years as an editor, *meticulous* attention to details.

Industry Insight
My ongoing challenge has been converting web site visitors to paying clients. In my opinion, there's a great need for my services, but people are wary of hiring a service provider over the Internet.

On Marketing
I'm still trying to figure this out. A background in marketing would have been very helpful to me. Right now, I'm using a low-energy approach—web site, contact with past clients, follow-up with visitors who fill out a form on my web site.

Top Revenue Streams and Pricing Structure
- Part-time telecommuting job for a former employer (twenty hours per week)—employer would prefer that I not state my income
- Freelance editing of college text (ten hours a week at $24/hour for an established client who pays within two weeks and keeps sending large projects my way)
- Writing and rewriting business letters ($40/hour)—small jobs for ongoing and new clients
- Participation in an affiliate program run by a related web site ($25 per sale made from my site)

Pricing Structure
$40/hour.

Additional Cost Items
None.

Recommended Resources
Keep reading and learning everything you can!

BUSINESS START-UP ADVISER

STRATEGIC MANAGEMENT RESOURCES, LLC | debsmr@snet.net
Deborah Polydys, 44 | Southington, Connecticut | Age of Child: 2

"Originally I went into business to have control over my time and my life, but like most entrepreneurs I spent most of my time working on the business versus pursuing my original goal. Now that my son has arrived, he has brought me face-to-face with my original goal."

Office Oasis
Spare bedroom.

Job Description
Business adviser to start-ups and established businesses. I work with business owners to help their businesses and reach their potential. If they're in trouble, I work with them to turn them around.

Previous Career
I've been doing this for fifteen years, long before I became a new mom.

Transferable Skills
My three major transferable skills were: (1) the ability to sell, (2) the ability to focus, and (3) the ability to discipline myself in a home-office environment. Although I had worked for a company, I worked by myself in running the Connecticut operation so I always had to motivate myself to work. When I went on my own, I found all three of these skills invaluable. In talking and working with other entrepreneurs, many found

it very difficult to stay focused and motivated working out of their homes as they were too easily distracted. And many found it extremely difficult when they realized they had to "sell" in order to be in business and make money. As for being a parent, you quickly learn how to organize, multi-task, negotiate, and focus quickly. These skills transfer well in the work world and should not be undervalued.

Knowledge, Skills, Experience, and/or Education Needed

It is important that you are fluent with word processing, can use e-mail, and can easily move around the Internet, as these tools can help you work more effectively. My ability to communicate and work on-line as well as off-line has been very effective in increasing my outreach to clients, while also increasing my ability to balance my work and personal life. I had a well-rounded business background that encompassed business development, sales, personnel management, recruiting, budgeting and projections, as well as networking, all of which greatly assisted me in my line of work. But most important was my ability to communicate what I knew, explain how my experience related to a prospective client's project, and state why I was the best person for the job. Most people have no idea that I have a B.A. or an M.A.; they are more interested in my ability to communicate and relate to them.

Industry Insight

There is a great deal of confusion in the marketplace as to whether prospective clients need a coach or a consultant. You need to be able to identify your strengths and focus on that market, as that's where there will be opportunity for growth. My strength has been my experience in running a small business in addition to being a small business owner for fifteen years. I stay focused on business-to-business ventures and in-tangibles, as both represent my strengths. Another consultant may be an expert in the retail market. People need advisers to help them make their businesses grow.

On Marketing

I consistently speak and conduct workshops throughout the year to groups that represent my marketplace. That is my greatest source of new business in addition to client referrals. My work is so relationship-based that I find being able to get in front of business owners is more effective for me than direct mail or advertising.

Top Revenue Streams
- Business planning
- Management of other businesses
- Sales management for clients

Pricing Structure
$165/hour.

Additional Cost Items
None.

Recommended Resources
I consistently read magazines like *Inc.* and *Entrepreneur* to get ideas as to what others are doing.

CAREER COUNSELOR/MOMS

COLLAMER CAREER COUNSELING | www.jobsandmoms.com
Nancy J. Collamer, 43 | Old Greenwich, Connecticut | Ages of Children: 10, 13

Previous Career
In my first life, before children, I spent ten years in corporate human resources and three years as the co-owner of an employment agency.

Degrees
- M.S. in career development
- B.A. in Psychology
- Certified Meyer-Briggs administrator

Home Biz
I provide career guidance and telephone consulting to women in search of new career directions, strategies for finding flexible employment, and assistance with creating meaningful home-based business options.

Mission

To empower women with the knowledge, resources, and guidance needed to make optimal decisions regarding their career direction and work-life balance.

Top Products/Services

- Telephone consulting
- E-books
- Freelance writer/career issues

Primary Market

Women.

Home Career Defining Moment

I am so fortunate to be in a line of work where getting thank-yous is a frequent occurrence. I love it when my clients land a new job or start a new business. One of my favorite moments this past week was hearing from a client who successfully negotiated a wonderful part-time tele-commute arrangement and even got a raise in the process!

EP Motivating Force

My motivations were two-fold. First, I wanted to start my own business so that I could have the flexibility I need to enjoy a fulfilling personal life and a career simultaneously. Second, I felt (and five years later, still feel) that there were not enough quality services available to help women make these critical decisions for their lives. Jobsandmoms.com helps to meet this need.

EP Musings

One of the great features of being an entrepreneurial parent is there is no typical working day! I adjust my schedule as needed to accommodate my personal needs. Sure, there are times when I have to work evenings or weekends. But, the trade-offs are most definitely worth it!

EP Advice

Be patient! It takes a while before business starts to roll in, and that can be very frustrating. Working on your own takes discipline, energy, and patience, so finding work you love is key to success.

COMMUNICATIONS SPECIALIST/CORPORATE

SIMPLY WRITING | www.simplywriting.com
Sandra Linville-Thomas, 49 | Shawnee, Kansas | Age of Child: 14

Office Oasis
Upper floor dedicated office with windows overlooking the adjacent woods.

Job Description
Write copy for various marketing and corporate communications projects such as publications, newsletters, print ads, web sites, direct marketing campaigns, retail advertising campaigns, scripts for PC-based presentations, and more.

Previous Career
Managing editorial services/publications for Fortune 100 corporation and West Coast private university.

Transferable Skills
Organizational skills used in any company are important in your own business. As a freelance corporate communications writer, you basically do what a nine-to-five corporate communications staff person does—but for many clients as opposed to one company.

Knowledge, Skills, Experience, and/or Education Needed
It helps to have a bachelor's degree in journalism, communications, public relations, marketing, or similar field, however as long as a freelance writer has excellent writing and editing skills, it doesn't matter what the field. Many times, it helps to have a specialty, such as science, technology, or health so you can take your degree in another field. However, you must combine that with very strong writing ability. A freelance writer needs strong marketing skills, also.

Industry Insight
If you are in a large enough metropolitan area, the prospects are good. However, in most cases you need to make peace with the "feast or famine" aspect of freelancing. You also have to remember to market

yourself at all times. In my opinion, this can be very difficult for writers. If you enjoy writing copy for many different projects for many different clients, it is ideal. The variety of opportunities is very interesting. Learning about a multitude of companies and their products is challenging as well as rewarding. I don't think there is one best way to break into the field. In my case, I had a lot of experience as a staff member of corporate communications departments at several organizations. This helped considerably. However, others have started right from college or moved from other careers.

On Marketing

I make cold calls, send postcards to both current and prospective clients, send e-mails to prospective clients, maintain consistent and ongoing communications with my past and current clients, ask current clients for referrals, send packets of writing samples to prospective clients, and maintain a web site. My most effective marketing in the first days of my business was to send e-mails to potential clients. I am now very careful about that since the volume of e-mail has increased. Marketing is the most difficult part of this business for me. I love the work so much it is easy to bury myself in a writing project and forget (or ignore) the need to continue to market so I have projects in the pipeline for later. Consistent marketing helps alleviate the dreaded (for me anyway) feast or famine.

Pricing Structure
$50/hour.

Additional Cost Items
An appropriate reference book library is helpful, but that's about it.

Recommended Resources
A very good resource with a wonderful section on marketing for corporate communications writers is *The Well-Fed Writer* by Peter Bowerman.

COMMUNICATIONS SPECIALIST/EDITORIAL MANAGEMENT

INKSPINNERS | www.inkspinners.com
Tonya Poole, 30 | Reno, Nevada | Ages of Children: 6, 9

"Being an entrepreneurial parent means juggling all the joys and challenges that come with having the best of both possible worlds. I'm at once the financial provider, creative director, emotional supporter, adviser, homework helper, family backbone, mentor, role model, friend, and partner-in-crime. I get a great amount of satisfaction from being able to accomplish my family and professional goals simultaneously."

Office Oasis

We found a great house with a large loft area on one floor. It's wide open, very sunny, and roomy enough to spread out and not feel confined to a single working space. We've split it up into two separate work stations, a small library and a casual sitting area. This allows me to move from one "mood" to another easily, which is essential in a creative work environment. It also allows me to invite the kids in our office with me when necessary without worrying about being crowded or distracting each other.

Job Description

I'm teetering on the edge between operating as an independent freelancer and operating as a small business. I provide a variety of communications, content, and editorial management services for other small and home offices, and I have also moved our services into the nonprofit and civic agency markets.

Previous Career

When I began working from home, we were a military family and the frequent transfers resulted in constant job-hopping. I've been an administrative assistant, event planner, records manager, newsletter administrator, copywriter/editor, and research assistant.

Transferable Skills

The most valuable skill that transferred from such a wide range of experience was the short-term, project-oriented, flexible work style, which has been instrumental in managing freelance projects. Transferring from job to job, I was forced to learn fast, organize well, and manage a variety of skills within very short time periods. This has been crucial in being able to think fast on my feet and switch seamlessly from project to project. In addition, I don't care how talented, creative, or flexible you are— if you're unable to manage time and projects effectively, keeping afloat as an EP can be nearly impossible. Plus if you can develop these skills on an entrepreneurial level, they can be a powerful ally in rejoining a traditional career.

Knowledge, Skills, Experience, and/or Education Needed

To provide creative communications of any kind, an independent professional really needs to have a solid understanding of how people interact with each other and with the organizations and public around them. Add to that a strong command of the language, the flexibility to switch hats and styles to accommodate different clients, and the creativity and innovative nature that allow you to come up with fresh, original ideas for each project. A degree in communications, English, marketing, or journalism is helpful. And yes, technology is often very important—as much of the work you'll do is created and delivered electronically.

A Day in the Life

My work schedule changes with the needs of my kids, as well as my clients. I work on a project basis, so no two weeks are ever the same. Some days I'll have a break in my work load and will catch up on administrative or marketing functions (or, if the kids are home, take them to the lake instead!).

Other days I'll have more project-oriented material than I can possibly accomplish in a day's time, and I'll have to map out very specific hours that sometimes extend from 7:00 A.M. to 10:00 P.M., with the necessary breaks in between to tend to personal and family activities.

The hours can be long, and immersive projects can sometimes extend for days (or weeks) at a time. It's at once exhausting and invigorating—but provides both the revenue and the satisfaction necessary to keep the business alive. It's a constant trade-off.

Industry Insight

This field is growing steadily but is very competitive. The market is relatively saturated with thousands of creative professionals, and to compete you must position yourself very strongly in a way that makes you stand out from that crowd. If you're talented and driven, build a strong portfolio of your work and get out there and meet some people in the market you're interested in serving. Remember that while confidence is important, arrogance is a turn-off. A lot of newcomers make the mistake of believing their talents will win them contracts, when in fact it's most often your professional demeanor and reputation that creates such successes for you.

On Marketing

I work a lot with e-mail in my marketing campaigns and rely heavily on my web site as a marketing tool. My URL is printed on all my materials, and I keep a portfolio of work there for potential clients to browse. In the nonprofit markets, I search out very specific companies I'd like to work with and contact them directly. When they know I'm truly interested in learning about the organization and how we can work together, that goes a long way in establishing a mutually respected relationship.

Top Revenue Streams
- Copywriting and editing (both for web and print)
- Publications management
- Marketing and editorial materials

Pricing Structure

I rate by the project, depending on the level of time and intensity it requires and the materials I need to do the job. My average hourly rates run between $40 and $65 per hour—with significant discounts given to nonprofits as well as long-term projects based on volume.

Additional Cost Items

Design and publishing software, both for print and web media, is essential, such as Adobe Pagemaker, Microsoft Publisher, Quark Xpress, FrontPage. Adobe programs can be pricey, $600+ each, but the quality is outstanding. Microsoft programs are a solid, inexpensive alternative at around $200. For my work, a commercial quality color printer was necessary and has been a great convenience to clients who wished to have their design and printing done by one provider.

Recommended Resources
During non-peak periods, on-line project marketplaces such as eLance. com, FreeAgent.com, and Guru.com have been a terrific way to stimulate some additional income in between regular projects. Most of these also offer a great variety of general resources as well, applicable to many of the issues that face freelancers and entrepreneurs.

COMMUNICATIONS SPECIALIST/MARKETING

DH COMMUNICATIONS, INC. | www.dhcommunications.com
Dianna Huff, 38 | Amesbury, Massachusetts | Age of Child: 3

> *"I put my son in day care at six weeks, which killed me. When I started working from home, I cut those hours back to twenty a week. I don't mind day care; it's necessary especially if you have a demanding business. But I just can't stand being away from my son more than twenty hours a week."*

Office Oasis
A second-floor third bedroom.

Job Description
I specialize in marketing communications and PR for high-tech and industrial companies.

Previous Career
Marketing communications specialist at a Fortune 500 in Silicon Valley.

Transferable Skills
Prior to my last full-time job, I was the office manager for a small manufacturing firm in the Silicon Valley for seven years. I hated that job. I felt it was so beneath my capabilities. Now, I thank my lucky stars that I was

fortunate enough to have that experience, because I did payroll, A/R, and A/P, marketing, shipping and receiving, and much more. Naturally I was able to do all those chores for my own business with little mishap. My accountant was pleasantly surprised at how clean my files were. I'm organized. I know how to market myself. I understand cash flow—at my traditional job, I was the one responsible for making sure we had the cash to meet payroll. I am not afraid to call clients and ask for money owed me since I did this for seven years. To sum up, I've had little difficulty in *managing* my business.

Knowledge, Skills, Experience, and/or Education Needed

I read industry trades constantly, plus pubs such as *Industry Standard* and *Fast Company*. As for my own education, I'm not really fluent in software, although I do use Quickbooks, MS Word, and Excel regularly, as well as Quark occasionally. As for education, I have an M.A. in English (tee-hee), but I also have a strong background in science as my original major was nursing. Plus, I've always been interested in how things work, which means I get excited when I get to write about a new subject. I have no formal training in marketing communications. Everything I know, I either learned on the job or taught myself.

A Day in the Life	
Up at 6:00 A.M.	Shower, dress, breakfast
7:30 A.M.	Drive son to preschool (if my spouse is traveling; otherwise, he does it)
8:00–9:00 A.M.	Run
9:00–11:30 A.M.	Monday, Wednesday, Friday—work; Tues only—until 2:30; Thursdays my son is home with me
12:30–1:30 P.M.	Lunch, prepare for nap
1:30–3:30 P.M.	Work while son naps
3:30–5:00 P.M.	Errands, chores, play dates, etc.
6:00–8:00 P.M.	Dinner, bath, bedtime
8:00–11:00 P.M.	Work if necessary or time with partner
10:00–11:00 P.M.	Bedtime

Industry Insight

For the last five years, this market has been healthy. Back when I was in school, there weren't any formal education programs, but now many universities offer marcom (marketing communications) and PR degrees, so that's one route. Most companies will ask to see your portfolio, so make sure you have one. I spent ten years building mine before going out on my own.

On Marketing

Most effective: direct mail, networking, and the web. Least effective: advertising and cold calling

Top Revenue Streams

- Freelance writing
- Marketing communications consulting
- Teaching (I teach one quarter per year at Northeastern)

Pricing Structure

$ 80–$100/hour.

Additional Cost Items

None.

Recommended Resources

BOOKS

(and I recommend these to *everyone* who asks me how to get started in this line of work):

- *How to Raise a Family and a Career Under One Roof* by Lisa Roberts
- *Solo Success: 100 Tips for Becoming a $100,000 a Year Freelancer* by David Perlstein
- *Secrets of a Freelance Writer: How to Make $85K a Year* by Robert Bly

WEB SITE

- Robert Middleton's Action Plan Marketing, www.actionplan.com

CORPORATE PERFORMANCE CONSULTANT

EFFECTIVE LEARNING SYSTEMS | Lorcandela@aol.com
Lori Candela, 38 | Monroe, Connecticut | Ages of Children: 2, 4

> *"I love doing what I do and having the flexibility that enables me to take time for my family and myself."*

Office Oasis

At home, my office is located in what would have been the dining room. I also currently have an office that I lease outside of my home, which is a part of a group of offices in a large suite. We have an office manager and administrative support that we share. It has been wonderful, primarily because it is a space all my own.

Job Description

I founded Effective Learning Systems in 1990. I am a performance consultant, working with corporations to link business goals with employee performance expectations and in turn creating appropriate interventions for learning and development. I have been in this field for seventeen years and have been focusing primarily on large corporations experiencing organizational change and transition.

Previous Career

Prior to founding Effective Learning Systems, I was the director of training and employee development for Penn Savings Bank, in Wyomissing, Pennsylvania.

Transferable Skills

As a performance consultant, I follow the basic human performance technology model (from the International Society of Performance Improvement), which focuses on performance analysis, cause analysis, and intervention selection. The skills required are many; however, the ability to facilitate and analyze data with regard to business objectives and human performance is key.

Knowledge, Skills, Experience, and/or Education Needed

It's helpful to have experience in one or more of the following disciplines: organizational development, training and development, organizational psychology, or instructional design. It also requires a desire to help people and the ability to tie together the human and business aspects of an organization. I have found that my M.Ed. in training design and development has been extremely beneficial. There are also several programs and workshops that are good and that I would encourage others to consider.

Industry Insight

The market is great given the constant change taking place in corporate America that requires a change in performance.

On Marketing

In the eleven years that I have been in business, the way that I have been able to maintain a relatively steady stream of income has been through networking. In my field, advertising doesn't seem to work. If someone in a corporation is looking for someone who does what I do, they typically tap into their own network to find out who has had success with the consultants that they have used. So my most effective marketing method has been networking; least effective, advertising—particularly in the Yellow Pages.

Top Revenue Streams

- Custom designed solutions
- Linking performance goals to business needs
- Evaluating results

Pricing Structure

My per diem rate is currently $1,500 to $2,000 (depending upon the type of work and the skills required).

Additional Cost Items

None.

Resources

IN GETTING STARTED

- Paul and Sarah Edwards' *Finding Your Perfect Work*
- The Bridgeport Regional Business Council
- Service Corps of Retired Executives (SCORE)
- The Entrepreneurial Women's Network

IN OPERATING

- Various mentors, professional organizations, and peer networks.

COURT REPORTER

Bonnie Elliott, 36 | England | Ages of Children: 7, 14, 23

Office Oasis

My office is situated outside our house with a lovely view over the garden and fields beyond. It was originally two rooms: a coal shed and a storage room. We knocked through the wall between them, plastered over the pitch-black walls, and converted it into the comfortable office it is now.

Job Description

I transcribe court proceedings from audio tape.

Previous Career

Secretary.

Transferable Skills

Audio transcribers with experience of court transcription are a rarity in England. The work is ideal for EPs because tapes are recorded in court and sent to them for transcription at home.

Knowledge, Skills, Experience, and/or Education Needed

Must have excellent grammar skills, outstanding typing speed and accuracy, and legal experience. People who are able to travel are very much in demand.

Industry Insight

At the moment, in my experience, there is a shortage of audio transcribers in England.

On Marketing

Most transcription companies in England are listed on the transcription panel with the courts. I wrote a standard letter of introduction to them when I first arrived in England and, later, a second letter advising of a change of address. Neither elicited much response. A marketing consultant friend then said that every sentence should be saying to the client "what you will get" as opposed to "what I do." I revised my letter accordingly in October last year. I've been totally swamped by work ever since!

Top Sources of Revenue Streams

- Courts
- Army courts martial
- Police interviews
- Medical tribunals
- Conferences

Pricing Structure

Prices vary from one company to the next and are based on a folio rate of seventy-two words.

Additional Cost Items

A specialized playback machine with four channels is required, at a cost of about £800 (approximately $1,152 U.S.). It is also useful to have your own recording equipment, which is between £500 (cheapest, $720 U.S.) and £1,400 (the Rolls-Royce, $2,016 U.S.).

Recommended Resources

- I subscribe to Philip Humbert's weekly newsletter. He is a personal coach and his advice on goal setting and positive thinking have been invaluable: www.philiphumbert.com
- And naturally, EPnews, EPnews-subscribe@yahoogroups.com

EDUCATIONAL PRODUCT INVENTOR

NERDKARDS | www.nerdkards.com
Nick Giorgis, 65 | Huntington, Connecticut | Ages of Grandchildren: 12, 26, 31

Former Home Biz

My first attempt to start a business from my home was in 1986 when I invented a gadget to measure acceleration in a high school physics class. With the help of a former student, I took an HP ink jet cartridge, modified the electronics so that a drop of ink would eject every 100th of a second, and attached it to a toy car so that the cartridge would leave a trail of ink drops on scrap paper on the floor. Each drop of ink was "exactly" .01 second apart. The students could measure that trail of ink drops and calculate the acceleration of the toy car. It could also measure the acceleration due to gravity of freely falling objects on a ticker tape moving at right angles to the accelerating object. For that I was awarded Patent # 4,761,658 and I called it IJIT, an acronym for Ink Jet Impactless Timer, and that was the start of my company, IJIT.

I quickly discovered that the cost of the patent was about $3,000 and the start-up costs brought it to a sum of $20,000. I advertised in *Physics* magazine, went to conventions, rented tables to "show my device," etc. All in all it took me five years to get my investment back. This device gave way to the computer, so if anyone wants to buy my patent rights, they are welcome to make an offer!

Current Home Biz

I taught physics for thirty-four years at Staples High School in Westport, Connecticut, and retired in 1992 to become an educational consultant for Wesleyan University in Middletown. As part of my duties, I visited more than twelve high schools all over the state and observed students trading cards, not only sports cards but serial killer cards as well! I decided that there had to be an *educational* card featuring scientists and mathematicians with valid biographical information so that students could learn.

I spent the next three years developing a set of "Science and Math Cards" (sold by the IJIT company since I already had a Connecticut state ID number on file).

Marketing Strategy

I went to San Francisco to a science teachers' convention, set up a booth, spent $3,000, and sold about $250 worth. Went to a similar convention in Reno the following month and spent $1,800 and sold $150 worth! I was quickly going down the "black hole" of the entrepreneurial self-marketing abyss.

I did my own marketing research by "hanging out" at local fast food restaurants and discovered that grandparents liked the cards. So I bought an ad with *Modern Maturity* magazine, 20 million circulation for a one-time insertion ad the size of a credit card (2" × 3"), for a price of $10,000 cash six months in advance. I plunged and took a bath! (I received four orders—so much for paid advertising.)

Then one day a reporter and photographer from *New Haven Register* ran a story on their front page. Nerdkards was coined, and the story hit the AP wire services and the resulting publicity spread across the USA via radio, TV, and print. I am on my second printing and re-cooped my $45,000 investment!!

Recommendations

If you want to produce a product, you are on your own. I tried to get sixty Fortune 500 companies to buy my Kards and use them as a promotion. FORGET IT! They will not take you on unless you are already successful. You have to manufacture it yourself and multiply your cost by four in order to compete. K-Mart wants a UPC code on my Kards and a $2.5 million liability policy, paid for by ME! (UPC code will cost $1,300.)

The media by way of feature stories is the way to go. If you can get a feature writer to tell your story, you can get a lot of mileage.

ERRAND SERVICE/OFFICE SUPPORT ADMINISTRATOR

www.wedoiterrandservice.com
Robin Boland, 33 | El Cajon, California | Ages of Children: 6, 8

Office Oasis

My office is in what would be the formal dining room. Right smack dab in the middle of the house.

Job Description

We take the mundane tasks that busy people don't have the time or the desire to do *and get them done*. We spend our hours lightening the loads of everyone from the busy professional to the overworked mom!

Previous Career

Administrative support for an insurance agency.

Transferable Skills

Basic office skills, typing, customer service skills, computer skills. Telephone skills!!! Oral and written communication skills. Organizational skills, prioritizing skills.

Industry Insight

Fabulous for this line of work. People do not show any signs of slowing down. In this "give me it all" society, the need for errand services/personal and office support services will continue to grow! Breaking into the field would be as simple as setting up your business.

- Know what you will offer
- Know what you will charge
- Be confident and excel in the service that you offer

THEN . . . network, network, and network. When you have done that, network some more.

As for target market, beyond the small business is now what is known as the "microbusiness." I am a microbusiness. A microbusiness is one that is run by a single person (or a few). These individuals are the chief cook and bottle washer of their businesses. They often generate enough income to support themselves but not a staff. Therefore many times they are overworked and can really use some relief. The great thing about these business owners is that they are usually very flexible when it comes to the hours that you work for them. And another great thing is that there are so many of them that you could be busy forever.

On Marketing

Did I mention network? That's been my most effective. Least effective (surprisingly so) has been direct mail. Basically, providing excellent service to one busy person leads to more busy people (they're also busy talking!). As a business owner, I have grown, and each day I am amazed that all this has been built by my believing in myself, by trying to do a good job at everything I do, that by building others' businesses I have built my own. I give back to my group of clients and associates and fellow women in business, and it shows every day in referrals and kudos and a growing business.

Top Revenue Streams and Pricing Structure
- Providing office support services (filing, organizing, researching, and even simple billing), $20/hour
- Running errands (drug store, shopping, cleaners), $15/hour
- Word processing/desktop publishing, $20–$25/hour

Additional Cost Items
Cellular phone is a must!

Recommended Resources
I found the Internet as a great resource, giving me the opportunity to see what others across the country offer. I attend small business symposiums and meet with other women in business. I learn from helping others. I learn from experience. I am not afraid to make a mistake. I have made plenty, and I am better for each one.

FASHION DESIGNER

SÜZKNITS | www.suzknits.com
Suzanne Gentes, 41 | Amherst, Massachusetts | Ages of Children: 12, 14

> *"My home is so overtaken with bolts of fleece, clothing racks, yarn, marketing materials, and more that my kids are worried that they'll soon have to sleep in the yard!"*

Office Oasis
My studio is based in a large, sunny room above our two-car garage, but I store stock and fabric all over our house—all of the guest bedroom and parts of the dining room, living room, finished basement, and of course, the garage.

Job Description
Since 1991, self-employed designer, producer, and marketer of a line of limited-edition women's garments and accessories, artfully combining fleece with hand-loomed knit accents.

Previous Career
Worked for a Simon & Schuster subsidiary, producing an elementary school reading textbook series. Prior to that, I worked for Lotus Development Corp. in marketing communications.

Transferable Skills
Having grown up as one of six sisters, I've used my lifelong sewing and knitting experience to design and produce my own line of garments and accessories. My corporate jobs often entailed being the manager of the details and schedules—invaluable in keeping multiple projects moving forward while continuing to produce my line.

Knowledge, Skills, Experience, and/or Education Needed
I've found that being an efficient and organized administrator has allowed me to take advantage of key marketing opportunities and stay on top of important buying trends. In addition to daily e-mail, I use several Microsoft programs: Access (to track my customers' buying histories and to prepare multiple mailings each year), and Excel (to track my finances), plus I've learned some simple HTML to update my web site.

Industry Insight
As long as there are wealthy women who like to adorn themselves, there will be a market for "wearable art." The key is finding where they shop and creating work that continues to appeal to their sense of style and individuality. By targeting this high-end market, I've been successful in selling a seasonal line virtually year-round.

On Marketing
My products are marketed at high-end, juried retail craft shows throughout the Northeast, through nationwide craft galleries, boutiques, museum shows and "wearable art" fashion shows and exhibitions, and via my web site. My customer mailing list (1,800+) is by far my most precious marketing tool. I do multiple postcard mailings to them throughout

the year. I also plan to start an e-mail list to update customers on new colors, patterns, etc., as they become available. Local newspaper ads have been ineffective for me; instead, I've learned to mail press releases announcing upcoming shows with photos of my work. This saves me money and carries much more authority with their readers.

Pricing Structure

I retail my product line from $14 to $50 for accessories and $89 to $359 for the garments.

Additional Cost Items

I've invested quite heavily in my studio. I operate two industrial serger sewing machines, a straight seam machine, two electronic knitting machines, a professional-grade steam iron, a $144 \times 78"$ industrial cutting table, and improved lighting and ventilation. To replace it all would easily cost over $15,000. I have also significantly upgraded my display with sleek clothing racks, shelves, a full-length mirror, track lighting, comfortable flooring, and more.

Recommended Resources

I urge any craft artist to subscribe to *The Crafts Report*, considered the bible of the crafts business. Also, networking with other exhibitors while doing shows is not only helpful, it's essential to avoid the solitude of working alone at one's craft.

FINE ARTIST

T ROBESON STUDIO | www.trobeson.com
Teresa Robeson, 37 | Bloomington, Indiana | Ages of Children: 3, 5

"Trust your instincts—in parenting and in business—and aim high!"

Office Oasis

We built our house about three years ago and had designed it so that I can use a spare bedroom downstairs as my studio. As the kids get older and move downstairs, I will convert their current bedroom into my studio. The important thing was to have the studio (whichever room it is) close to running water and a bathtub (for watercolor paintings).

Job Description

I create original fine art, specializing in portraits, but I also do landscapes, pets/animals, and still lifes. My media of preference are: pastels, watercolors, charcoal, colored pencils, and conté crayons.

Previous Career

Research associate for a psychology professor.

Transferable Skills

Graphics editing and DOS programming (any type of computer programming is a good skill to have).

Knowledge, Skills, Experience, and/or Education Needed

While many professional fine artists have B.F.A. (or higher) degrees, a large number are self-taught. What's important is that you are continually refining your skills and pushing your creative limits.

Industry Insight

The consensus is that in healthy economic times, more people will buy fine art. However, the market can be promising any time if you know how to sell yourself and network well. My advice is for people to network with local artists, read many books on the topic of art as a career, and learn about running a business in general.

On Marketing

Recently, I have been doing mainly on-line marketing, joining home-based business organizations (such as www.hbwm.com and www.parentpreneurclub.com), and placing ads in e-zines. This has netted good exposure for my web site but has yet to yield any commissions. I plan to do more local networking and raise my profile around the community by having shows in various places that display local artists' works. Since word of mouth is probably the best advertising in this field, one good way to market is to get my artwork into homes of friends who will recommend me to their friends. Another thing to do for exposure is to create greeting cards, which is an affordable way to get the public to start recognizing my name and work.

Pricing Structure

I charge an hourly rate plus costs for materials (paints, papers, etc.). The hourly rate may vary depending on the medium the client has chosen. I use the same basic formula for pricing non-commissioned works.

Additional Cost Items

The sort of materials and equipment you need depends on the medium you work in. I needed a big work table (bought used) and easels (which were new purchases, ranging from $75 to $150). Those who were hobby or amateur artists before going professional have probably accumulated enough equipment over the years and do not need much more to begin a business.

Recommended Resources

I find joining support organizations to be extremely helpful in terms of commiserating, networking, and sometimes funding. Some of the organizations I belong to are Society of Children's Book Writers and Illustrators, American Society of Portrait Artists, and Indiana Wildlife Artists.

HEALTHCARE RECRUITER

WIEDERHOLD AND ASSOCIATES, INC. | www.wiederholdassoc.com
Jim Wiederhold, 47 | Marietta, Georgia | Ages of Children: 14, 18

Home Biz

Wiederhold and Associates, Inc., is a contractual search firm in the healthcare industry for physicians and non-physicians, offering coaching programs, a one-day seminar, résumé writing, and more.

Top Services
- Job search
- Coaching
- Seminars

- Résumé preparation
- Networking
- Newsletter

Home Career Defining Moment
My greatest home-career-related achievement was pulling the whole thing off. I started with one contract, which was not even enough to pay the bills, and I never looked back. It forced me to believe in myself, and sometimes we are at our best when our backs are against the wall.

Home Career Advice
Make sure that you can meet and exceed the parameters you have set with the company you have built. I have been on both sides of this where people take on more than they can handle to the detriment of all. Also, believe in yourself, and do not keep putting off your dreams because there will never be the perfect time. If you are waiting for that, it will never happen.

EP Motivating Force
My goal is to grow this business not so much to increase revenue but to give back more—we give 5 percent to children's charities. I also work in the summer with Camp Sunshine and do some work with children in Hospice. I want it to be an ethical organization where everyone walks away from a completed project feeling good. I would also like to reduce my hours of work and achieve greater balance.

INDEXER

MARY COE INDEXING SERVICES | coeme@aol.com
Mary E. Coe, 35 | Rockville, Maryland | Ages of Children: 3, 5

"My husband and I enjoy our home careers but are not totally absorbed by them."

Office Oasis
Private office in the top floor of home.

Job Description
I create back-of-the-book indexes, database indexes, and finding aids for the publishing industry.

Previous Career
Part-time in-house editor.

Transferable Skills
Wholly—can work in the same capacity as staff or freelancer.

Knowledge, Skills, Experience, and/or Education Needed
Anyone can learn how to use indexing software, how to format indexes and the business side of it all, but what is truly important is whether or not you have the indexing "knack." In other words, it's a true vocation. You can either do it (i.e., read the text and know what's important) or you can't. That said, other aspects can certainly help.

Professionalism is important, especially since meeting deadlines is a VERY important part of the job; if you don't get the index to the publisher on time, they won't call you again!

People skills are minimal, but it does help to be able to establish a good rapport with your clients. Negotiating an indexing contract or marketing can be difficult for the shy.

Industry Insight
The market is very strong. Most indexers (established, not newbies) are turning down work or at least are at a comfortable level, due largely to the expanded opportunities the Internet provides, i.e., on-line indexing such as web sites or embedded indexing. That said, aspiring indexers must be prepared to spend time building their business and client base. Cold calls will bring minimal results at first but can be a way to get started, and then word-of-mouth and repeat business takes a strong hold. My best advice would be to network, network, network with other indexers, editors, publishers—anyone likely to need an indexer or indexing assistance.

On Marketing
A few years ago I sent out "cold call" marketing packets to a carefully chosen target list and enjoyed a good response. My most effective form of mar-

keting is networking; the least effective is cold calling by phone. Lately, marketing involves repeat or word-of-mouth referrals almost entirely.

A Day in the Life

Because my husband is also self-employed, we're able to enjoy a "tag team" schedule that works well for our family. Dad works mornings from 8 A.M. to 1 P.M.; Mom works afternoons from 1 P.M. to 6 P.M. On Thursdays, Mom works all day, and on Saturdays Dad works all day. Sunday everyone's off! Sometimes there's also evening work after the children are in bed and Sundays occasionally, but we really try to avoid that.

Top Revenue Streams

Primarily database indexing, with a few back-of-the-book (BOB) indexes thrown in for interest. This type of work fits in better with my lifestyle as the deadlines are more relaxed than BOB indexing, and the work is steady.

Pricing Structure

Usually charge by the item or by the indexable page. Rates vary greatly, though the average hourly wage for indexing is $30.

Additional Cost Items

Indexing software ($500) and indexing-related references. Professional development such as indexing courses or conferences should be budgeted in, especially for a newbie who needs to network. My other expenses have included items such as a microfilm reader, but that's project specific.

Recommended Resources

- American Society of Indexers
- Index-L (listserv for indexers)
- Local newspaper (classified section)

INTERIM EXECUTIVE

ROLCO | rolco@mindspring.com
Richard Lewis, 52 | Salisbury, North Carolina | Ages of Children: 8, 26

Office Oasis
Basement.

Job Description
An interim management company serving executive management teams. I have worked with high-tech companies, medicine, manufacturing, transportation, finance, business services, and telecommunications. Interim executive means I contract my services to other companies. Some of my opportunities include developing new distribution channels; establishing a brand; marketing management; crisis management; strategic planning; general management; financial modeling; negotiating; divisional turnaround; structuring data warehousing for strategic database marketing; competitive analysis; market research; media planning; competitive intelligence; using the Internet; e-commerce and integrating people, processes, and technology into organizations; developing and building an international reseller organization; researching and writing business/ marketing plans; finding investors; finding new manufacturing locations; and developing and executing a direct marketing campaigns.

Previous Career
Fortune 200 companies in sales and marketing.

Transferable Skills
The skills you have learned while working for someone else can be transferred directly to being an EP. One major thing to keep in mind is how you perceive your role as an independent consultant in your client's (the organization's) culture and environment. You can't go in as a gun fighter if you've been hired to herd sheep. Later, if you decide to go for a salaried position, you can place on your résumé the activities you have performed as a contract employee.

Knowledge, Skills, Experience, and/or Education Needed
Depends on what you want to do. My education and experiences allow
me to interact at an executive level. My education is:
- Duke University, Durham, North Carolina: Executive MBA, 1998
- Woodrow Wilson College of Law, Atlanta, Georgia: J.D. of Law, 1980
- Georgia Institute of Technology, Atlanta, Georgia: B.S. Industrial
  Management, 1972

For what I'm involved in, experience and knowledge of business are critical.

Industry Insight
The market outlook is excellent. I only work with two or three clients at
a time. Some of the assignments I have had for more than a year. On the
average most last between six and nine months. There are many companies outsourcing now. If someone has a particular skill, some company
is willing to contract for it.

On Marketing
I am constantly talking to others about business problems and offering
solutions. My most effective strategy to attract new consulting gigs is to
voluntarily sit in on a problem/brainstorming session and offer ideas, at
no cost to the company. If it doesn't cost anything, companies are willing
to have you there. Usually what comes out of such meetings is an idea
that no one on staff has the time or knowledge to implement. That's
when my name usually pops up. You get to meet a lot of people and your
name gets associated with problem solving and implementation.

    My least effective—and the one I absolutely deplore—is what I
call a "tombstone ad." The Yellow Pages are full of them. It's the
"here's my name, here's my company, here's the business we are in, etc."
These types of ads offer no compelling reason for anyone to do business
with you.

Pricing Structure
Project-by-project basis: could be a fee to complete, sometimes a daily
rate, it depends on the assignment.

Additional Cost Items
Use a headphone; it frees up your hands. Get an old typewriter; not
everything can be done on a computer.

Recommended Resources
Writings by Dan Kennedy, Ben Suarez, Jay Abraham, Michael Gerber, David Ogilvy, John Caples. I have pulled many of my ideas over the years from these people.

INTERIM MINISTER

PEOPLE POWER TRAINING | www.peoplepowertraining.com
Dennis J. Hester, 49 | Shelby, North Carolina | Ages of Children: 11, 13

> *"I am a thinker and a dreamer but also a procrastinator. I have so many ideas that I find myself being slow on the doing. My son Nathan helped me realize how this was holding me back professionally when he said, 'Dad, why are you always coming up with great book titles but never writing any books?' Eighteen months later, my first book came off the press."*

Office Oasis
Over-the-garage study behind our home.

Job Description
Ordained Southern Baptist minister who specializes in helping churches through transitions. Also a church consultant who conducts workshops for churches, nonprofit organizations, and small businesses, focusing on conflict management, transitions, and communication. Author of the book *Pastor, We Need to Talk! How Congregations and Pastors Can Solve Their Problems Before It's Too Late.*

Previous Career
Newspaper reporter, auctioneer, and most recently a full-time minister/ pastor.

Transferable Skills
I've always been a storyteller and salesman at heart. I grew up on a farm in North Carolina with two brothers (country people love to tell stories about childhood and everyday adventures), and along the way I learned to play the guitar and sing. I began writing poetry in the first grade and eventually wrote songs as a teenager. I often entertained family and

friends. My writing skills developed in college where I began writing inspirational newspaper columns and worked a few months as a newspaper reporter. I went on to write magazine articles and compiled three books on a famous Southern evangelist, Dr. Vance Havner.

My writing skills, music, entertaining, and storytelling all were very beneficial to me as a minister. My professional auctioneering skills along with my ability to entertain a crowd has helped me to be a leader and to sell myself to individuals in networking and to groups as a trainer. Everything I've ever failed at or been successful at has been "grist for the mill," meaning, every experience, talent, and skill I've picked up along the way has gone into my "toolbox," and has contributed to the effectiveness of my work today as a professional, speaker, trainer, and writer.

If I stopped what I was doing today I could seek employment as a salesman, supervisor, customer-relationship person, human resources administrator, or counselor. The skills I've learned in helping churches to make transitions from losing one minister to calling on another minister would be helpful in training employees in making sense of change and transitions, conflict management, communication skills, creating a mission statement for your organization, and how to build teams, make decisions, and rediscover lost dreams and goals.

Knowledge, Skills, Experience, and/or Education Needed

The desire to analyze oneself and be willing to be counseled before helping others in this area is important. Formal education such as college is always helpful, but training and counseling others can be learned by almost anyone who has had some psychology, people skills training, and counseling skills. You should also have a desire to change, a love for people, and enough compassion to want to help them change, in addition to strong communication, listening, and conflict management skills. This type of work is "low-tech and high-touch." You, your experiences, your understanding of human behavior, and your ability to help lead others to a deeper understanding of self that would help them make decisions to enhance their lives is what you are selling. You, essentially, are the product.

Industry Insight

There'll always be a need for people who are counselors, helpers, and trainers to guide other people to a higher level of living and productivity, whether it be spiritually or professionally. There'll always be a need for written material such as self-help and how-to books, as well as inspirational lectures from teachers, trainers, and motivational speakers. To be a Christian minister, one must have a spiritual calling from God. To be a writer, start writing and send out your articles. To be a trainer/workshop leader, start volunteering to work and lead other people as you receive training in helping others. The more you do, the more you learn and the more others will seek out your advice and skills if you are compassionate and passionate about what you do for others.

On Marketing

Writing newspaper and magazine articles helps bring in extra income and helps to market me to a larger audience. Writing a book opened up doors to speaking and sold me as an expert in my field of church consulting and conflict management. Doing volunteer work at churches and nonprofit organizations gets my name out in the public. Speaking at clubs and organizations helps to market my abilities and skills. I do a lot of free speaking and consulting that leads to paid jobs. I try to see how much I can give away of my service and myself, and I hope to eventually reap the rewards of sharing myself with others in many ways besides money.

Top Revenue Streams

Writing, speaking, and consulting.

Pricing Structure

Approximately $50/hour.

Additional Cost Items

Minimal.

Recommended Resources

Every friend and foe, teacher, preacher, adviser, and every person I've built a relationship with has contributed to who I am and what I am doing today.

INVENTOR/ALLERGY AWARENESS PRODUCTS

CONRAD CONCEPTS, INC. | www.allergywatch99.com
Stephanie Conrad, 42 | Bartlett, Illinois | Ages of Children: 8, 11

Office Oasis

My husband and I converted our living room into an office. I have my desk on one side of the room; he has his on the other. We have a little den attached to the living room, which we call our hobby room. This room is where I store all my inventory and make all my products.

Previous Career

Sales service supervisor for fifteen years for a commercial printing company. Our company printed retail advertising circulars for national retail stores, comics, and TV guides. I was also a freelance commercial artist for a few years.

Degree

B.S. in graphic communications, commercial art diploma from Art Institute of Pittsburgh.

Home Biz

Conrad Concepts, Inc., develops allergy awareness products for children. Our Allergy Watch products can be worn by children, to alert others that they are severely allergic to certain foods or substances. All our products can be personalized with any allergy.

Mission Statement

To raise the awareness level in our communities of the severe allergies and chronic illnesses our children are faced with every single day of their lives. They are becoming more prevalent with each passing day, and we need to help our children to stay safe. Watchful eyes can save lives.

Top Products

- Allergy Watch stickers
- T-shirts
- Buttons
- Key chains

- Magnets
- Many more products to come!

Top Clients
- Children with severe allergies
- Allergists
- Schools
- Pediatricians
- Family doctors
- Day-cares
- Churches
- Camps

Home Career Advice

Start out slowly and really think about what you want to accomplish. Set small goals, and as you accomplish them, set new and greater ones. Writing a business plan is very important, but if your business is small and you really don't know how to set up a business plan, taking one small step at a time is the best advice I can give.

Recommended Resources
- Food Allergy Network, www.foodallergy.org
- www.allergymatters.com
- Asthma and Allergy Foundation of America, www.aafa.org
- www.allergywatch99.com

JUVENILE PRODUCT INVENTOR

SEW BEAUTIFUL | www.cozyrosie.com
Jeanette Benway, 41 | Mt. Kisco, New York | Ages of Children: 6, 10, 13

"Recently I briefly considered getting a 'real' job. When I mentioned this to my kids they were horrified."

Office Oasis

The family room—which is used for computer work, sewing projects, playing games, school projects, and my desk and filing cabinet. There are large sliding glass doors to the deck and a beautiful view of the back-yard. It is a wonderful place to spend the day.

Job Description
I manufacture, market, and distribute Cozy Rosie, a patented fleece blanket that stays on your stroller to keep baby warm without falling off or dragging on the ground.

Previous Career
The three years before starting the business, I had been a full-time, stay-at-home mom. Before that I was a computer trainer for a large company that manufactured computerized blood chemistry analyzers for the medical laboratory.

Transferable Skills
The transferable skills include sales and marketing and public relations. Also, familiarity with purchasing and contracting with manufacturing companies.

Knowledge, Skills, Experience, and/or Education Needed
Experience in PR and sales and marketing is a plus although you can learn this by trial and error. Easy use of a computer is helpful for accounting, communicating via e-mail, and developing marketing materials that streamline your business and give it a professional image.

Industry Insight
The baby business is changing. Although 4 million babies are born each year, the number of specialty juvenile stores is dwindling, so it becomes more important to break into the larger stores and catalogs. Then, if you do manage to break into a large store, they end up controlling your business. So it really is tough to bring a juvenile product to market as a lucrative home-based business. It helps to have an absolute belief in and love for the product.

On Marketing
The most effective marketing method for me has been sending press releases to baby magazines and newspapers. The editorial press coverage is free, gives your business credibility, and attracts customers. After edi-

torial coverage has brought in business, monthly advertising in those targeted parenting magazines has also been effective. Another effective marketing method has been demonstrating Cozy Rosie directly to consumers at baby shows. The least effective method for me has been attending trade shows because of the competition for the buyers' time from the large number of vendors and the small number of buyers.

Top Revenue Streams
My revenues are from wholesale and retail sales of Cozy Rosie.

Pricing Structure
Currently, Cozy Rosie retails for $50 (solid colors) and $56 (prints).

Additional Cost Items
The largest expense of starting my business has been manufacturing the blankets, which involves purchasing the materials and labor.

Recommended Resources
- *How to Market Your Product for Under $500*, by Jeffrey Dobkin
- www.publicityhound.com by Joan Stewart
- My association with other women promoting home-based businesses has also led to PR opportunities, including en-parent.com, The Mompreneurs, and Little Did I Know.com

---

KEYNOTE SPEAKER

MEMORY MAKERS | silvanac@msn.com
Silvana Clark, 48 | Bellingham, Washington | Ages of Children: 12, 28

"Sondra, my twelve-year-old, helps me carry supplies when I speak at conferences, sells her books at the back of the room, and knows how to shake hands, make eye contact, and more. She's comfortable speaking in front of large groups. Recently she spoke to 4,000 people and raised $10,000 in one weekend for a relief organization. Those are skills she'll use throughout her life."

Office Oasis

I have a small and cozy office to which my husband added a bay window and French doors, so it's bright and airy even though it's small. Three deer "hang out" in the backyard and actually position themselves so they can see me at my desk while they lie and chew their cud.

Job Description

I'm a professional speaker, presenting keynotes and workshops across the United States, Canada, and overseas. The three most requested topics are: "Marketing with a Big Imagination and a Small Budget," "Motivating Employees," and "Balancing Work and Family." I've also written seven books and 150 magazine articles, and I speak to businesses, parent groups, and associations ranging from the Canadian Llama Association to the Roller Skating Association. Frequently my eleven-year-old daughter comes with me and presents also. She's written two books, distributed by Simon and Schuster, and has appeared on the *Donny and Marie Show, 700 Club,* and others. We often appear on television shows together, and since my husband often travels with us, it's truly a family event. She's been asked to be a "spokeschild" for Childcare International, a relief organization for children in Third World countries. In October 2000, we all went to Africa for two weeks so she could film a documentary. Since we returned, our family has decided to promote Childcare by taking a year and traveling around the U.S. in an RV. I can still continue my speaking from the road, plus we'll have more family time together. Chevy has even given us a new truck to use for an entire year as we travel!

Previous Career

I was the recreation supervisor for Bellingham Parks and Recreation for ten years. I supervised staff, did major budgets, ran classes, concerts, and special events for thousands of people.

Transferable Skills

Self-discipline, problem-solving skills, creativity. You really have to be dedicated to working for yourself. I'm at my desk by 7:00 A.M. just to get started on the day.

A Day in the Life

6:00–6:20 A.M. My husband and I have a "candlelight" breakfast. He eats and I talk! It starts our day off right.

6:20–6:45 A.M. We do maintenance at our community clubhouse. I clean bathrooms, he checks the pool and vacuums. We took the job to help Sondra see that there is nothing wrong with physical labor. She rides in limousines and has lunch with Donny Osmond, so we want her grounded. In the afternoons and the summer she is in charge of emptying wastebaskets, arranging pool furniture, etc. We are saving money for 2002, when we plan to make a nine-month trip around the world.

9:00–3:30 After Sondra goes to school, I make calls, write articles, and prepare for speeches. No interruptions, no lunch with friends. Allan comes home for lunch three times a week and we take a brisk forty-minute walk through the park.

3:30 P.M. Sondra comes home. My "workday" ends. Allan is home by 4:30, so we play. We watch very little TV. It's straight family time until bedtime.

Knowledge, Skills, Experience, and/or Education Needed

As a professional speaker, you definitely need "platform" skills. People often say, "I love to talk so I'd be a great speaker," but it also takes research on your topic, a flair for drama, and people skills to make an effective presentation. You may only speak for sixty minutes, but there are hours involved with preparation, travel, writing proposals, preparing handouts, and searching for new material.

Industry Insight

The market is tight. More and more people want to get on the "speakers' circuit." Begin by giving a free speech to Rotary or Lions clubs to get feedback. When you see a professional speaker, they make it seem so easy. Many speakers rehearse down to each pause and hand gesture. The National Speakers Association has great resources also.

On Marketing

As I've mentioned in my book *Taming the Marketing Jungle*, a key aspect of marketing is standing out from the competition. In my case, I frequently tie in a "jungle" theme with my keynotes. I wear a complete safari outfit, even a pith helmet. Audiences love it. Even though they forget my name, they will call and say, "Are you that jungle lady?" Sometimes people pick me up at the airport and the first thing they say is, "Why aren't you wearing a safari outfit?" The costume really stands out in their minds. I use the jungle picture on my business cards and web site.

I'm also known for using lots of props in my presentations. Instead of just saying, "Studies show that a piece of chocolate reduces stress . . ." I toss out chocolate to the audience. When telling stories about silly gifts we've received, I bring up an audience member and have them put on a poncho made from an old umbrella (spokes removed!). People remember the visual aspects of my presentations.

Top Revenue Streams

Professional speaking and writing books are my best revenue producers.

Pricing Structure

When beginning as a speaker, you'll be thrilled to get $25 for an hour-long speech. As your skills improve, you can raise your fees. Many speakers' bureaus seldom even represent a speaker who gets you less than $2,000 for a speech. The size of the group doesn't matter. I just received over $3,000 for speaking to thirty-eight people. Look up "speakers' bureaus" on the Internet and you can find many bureaus who list their speakers' fees. It's not uncommon to get $6,000 to $7,000 for a one-hour speech (although I haven't reached that level yet).

Additional Cost Items

No special equipment is needed, though you do need several "professional" outfits to wear while speaking. (Sweatpants don't go over too well in front of a group of corporate executives!) You'll need professional looking one-sheets, brochures, and business cards also.

Recommended Resources

- National Speakers Association

MANUFACTURER/AUTO LIGHTS

AUTOGEM | www.auto-gem.com
Tom and Ann Hinderholtz, 45 and 42 | Caledonia, Wisconsin | Ages of
Children: 7, 8

> *"It's important to set limits to protect family time. We really use the early
> morning to do "catch-up" work and spend most of the weekend with our
> kids and family members. Ann serves on volunteer boards and requests
> that meetings are during daytime versus evening."*

Office Oasis

Our home office is located primarily in the kitchen, with two computers, multiple file cabinets and many, many piles of paper. The manufacturing business also has an office and work area in an outbuilding.

Job Description

AutoGem sells marker lights to the automotive industry, specifically the motorcycle industry, worldwide. Our products are distributed through after-market motorcycle parts distributors, motorcycle dealers, and direct to consumers via catalogs (JandP Cycles), and at swap meetings, trade shows, and direct mail. AutoGem began production in 1997 with one product in four colors; today there are five products in a variety of colors with many more ideas in the works. As co-owner of AutoGem with husband, Tom, my responsibilities for the company encompass all of the administrative, office management, AR and AP, accounting, and marketing for the business. Tom handles all of the manufacturing, sourcing, research and development of new products, travel to swap meets, and more. In addition, in a separate home business, I am the owner of Offsite Solutions, which offers office management solutions from training office staff in customer service or hard skills to strategic planning, marketing consulting, and purchasing of office equipment based on needs.

Previous Career

Have worked for large call centers including Pleasant Company (Middleton, Wisconsin), and Gander Mountain (Wilmot, Wisconsin).

Transferable Skills

From the traditional workforce it's important to borrow the "routine"—specifically the ability to start at 8 A.M. and work until 5 P.M., and if at all possible avoid working the sixteen-hour days because the office is right in your home. The skill that can be brought back into the workforce is the ability to take on all tasks, including those you've never had experience doing before. There's no such thing as "that's not my job." There's also a sense of commitment and dedication you learn while in your own business that the traditional nine-to-five would welcome. Even though I had no experience in the automotive industry, and even less in the motorcycle industry, I learned to quickly assimilate common sense practices to marketing techniques.

Knowledge, Skills, Experience, and/or Education Needed

It's most critical to be organized and focused. It is also critical to be resourceful and creative and know where to find the information—or who to ask when you don't know the answer. I do not have a degree, but work experience and the can-do attitude have taken me far.

Industry Insight

Tom identified this product and market out of a love for the industry. He is an avid motorcycle enthusiast with a love for the quality of products produced in the 1950s and 1960s, which brought him to his original product, the AutoGem Marker Lights. These are 1" round glass chisel-cut lenses in a stainless steel pan that are lit up with an incandescent 12-volt light bulb, equipped with a hollow stud. These lights hold your license plate on the motorcycle. You hook the light to the electrical system, and you have a nice marker light giving you extra visibility and a nostalgic look. Since the "cruiser" market often looks for the classic nostalgic look, our product is a perfect fit and has a fair price. Tom did extensive work sourcing the best materials while using local vendors whenever possible. He spent hours in the library going through the Thomas Register and countless hours on the Internet and telephone. He consulted with friends in the industry for feedback and developed a prototype. From there we hired a lawyer to trademark the name "AutoGem" and located an artist to design packaging. As with anything, there is a system of steps that need to be taken.

On Marketing

The fact that Tom developed something for an industry that he is enthusiastic about and already has the network to work within helped. He understands his market and the kind of product that appeals to that market. He spends much time out and about talking to consumers to find out what they like and what they want. This helps drive the research and development of future products.

Top Revenue Streams and Pricing

- AutoGem Marker light pairs available in red, green, amber, and blue, retail $19.95
- ShotGun lights (pair) designed for Harley-Davidson Road Kings available in red, retail $49.95
- Deringer lights (pair) designed for Harley-Davidson Soft Tails available in red, retail $49.95
- Baby Bullet lights (pair), which work on all types of bikes, available in red, amber, and blue, retail $69.99
- Replacement bulbs (pair), retail $5.99
- Replacement lenses (pair) (for Baby Bullet Lights) available in red, amber, and blue, retail $14.99
- Handlebar kits (pair), retail $5.99

We expect our top seller this year to be the new Baby Bullet light, the smallest bullet light available at a very good cost, and universal in use. This light can be bolted on the bike wherever there is a suitable hole.

Pricing Structure

Products are priced based on actual cost with approximately a 40 percent to 75 percent markup depending on the customer (distributor versus dealer versus consumer).

Additional Cost Items

Dies for manufacturing purposes—costs are in the area of $20,000 additional. The nice thing is that once you have a good die, it will last for years with good maintenance. The cost of goods sold is figured into the markup of the product. The cost of the individual parts that make up a product will go down based on the quantity of parts purchased. We use high-quality parts with our product and all are made in the United

States; therefore our parts expense is high. Other additional costs include artwork, packaging, and the usual office expenses.

Recommended Resources

The very first thing I did when I started my business in 1995 was to join an entrepreneurial organization: Wisconsin Women Entrepreneurs. The networking and friendships I have made have been invaluable. I have also served on the board since joining in 1995 and will continue in that capacity. It has given me the opportunity to hold multiple board positions, providing me with additional skills I did not have before. Tom has also created relationships with key people in the industry, and we work collaboratively with them to advance all businesses.

MANUFACTURER/CHILDREN'S PHOTO ID CARDS

KIDDIE ID | www.kiddieid.com
Holly Jo West, 42 | San Marcos, Texas | Ages of Children: 2, 5, 8

"My husband and I feel like we are great role models for our children. They will never be afraid to go out and try their own ideas. They'll have learned it's not an easy road, but a satisfying one."

Office Oasis

Converted carport.

Job Description

I sell children's photo ID cards to schools and day-care centers.

Previous Career

Education agency data modeler information systems analyst (currently employed full-time and moonlighting as an EP).

Transferable Skills

Interpersonal skills come in handy with direct sales to day care directors. PC knowledge helped me in choosing software packages to use and designing templates for cards and advertising. Other skills developed in my line of work are:

- Experience in many computer software programs
- Working with digital camera equipment or Polaroid camera
- Scheduling: ability to be a project manager
- Problem-solving techniques (So what if I accidentally hit the wrong button and all the kids' faces are blue in my digital shots? My attitude is *everything* is fixable!)

Knowledge, Skills, Experience, and/or Education Needed

I would say you could be a success if you have common sense and an ability to communicate and relate with other people. So many women underrate themselves and don't give themselves enough credit where credit is due. Techno-savvy comes in handy, but can also get in the way.

Industry Insight

Unfortunately I think the market looks good for a need to identify children quickly and easily. With population growth and cities getting larger, there is always a growing concern for disappearing children. I would advise aspiring EPs to research their competition and know the facts.

On Marketing

My most effective marketing method to date was to network with fellow women in the business world—it's how my product was seen on the Oprah Winfrey show. My least effective? Taking no action at all, expecting things to just fall into my lap. Currently I am trying to breathe new life into my Internet endeavors and broaden my scope of customers. I'm currently collecting e-mail addresses for a newsletter and look forward to sharing information and ideas with past, present, and future customers. Shop, shop, shop around when it comes to marketing. I am *the* frugal marketing shopper. I don't like to spend money unless I have to.

Top Revenue Streams

Basic ID card.

Pricing Structure

$5/card; $19 for special packages.

A Day in the Life

5:00 A.M.	Wake up
6:00 A.M.	Kiss the boys and dad good-bye for the day
7:00 A.M.	Arrive at work
9:00 A.M.	Check e-mail messages on break
12 noon	Check e-mail and voice-mail for business messages
3:00 P.M.	Break; call West Coast consultants to check on work load pipeline for Kiddie ID
4:00 P.M.	Leave work
5:30 P.M.	Pick up Katie from day care on the way home
6:00 P.M.	Arrive home, kiss husband good-bye as he goes to some meeting
7:00 P.M.	Help with homework while whipping up something for dinner
7:30 P.M.	Bathe children
8:00 P.M.	Brush teeth, read stories, and get settled into bed
9:00 P.M.	Try to talk Katie into going to bed . . .
9:15 P.M.	Clean kitchen
9:30 P.M.	Rest for five minutes
10:00 P.M.	Start small business work load
11:00 P.M.	Load laundry (which is conveniently located near office)
12 midnight	Finish up current project
12:30-1:30 A.M.	Go to bed!

This is a typical day for me during the week. Some weekends are spent at fairs and festivals, working long hours away from family, but on the average I try to keep those down to a minimum.

Additional Cost Items
Digital camera and laminator; prices vary but are becoming more affordable.

Recommended Resources
- Little Did I Know, www.littledidiknow.com
- Vista Print (free full-color business cards), www.vistaprint.com

MANUFACTURER/NATURAL CARE PRODUCTS

MOSSBERRY HOLLOW NATURAL CARE PRODUCTS | www.mossberry.com
Paula Polman, 36 | Edmonton, Alberta, Canada | Age of Child: 22 months

"What better coffee break can a worker have than to sit down with your child and snuggle in front of a favorite video while he drifts off to sleep? And where else can you wear slippers and sweats all day long and nuke the same cup of coffee three times before you finally get to finish it (ice cold, of course!)?"

Office Oasis

Basement (storage of everything), spare bedroom (office), and kitchen (production, shipping).

Job Description

I develop, manufacture, and market natural care products in the personal care industry.

Previous Career

My career path has been quite varied—my immediate prior employment was as a corporate account sales manager in the computer/IT industry; before that I worked in the tourism/meeting planning industry, did computer consulting for a SOHO business, and was an office manager for a nonprofit, volunteer organization.

Transferable Skills

While each position was quite a drastic change from the other, many skills were expanded and layered in a way that I could not have learned from a school or a single job. People management, sales, administration, small business development, marketing, customer service, and more. I am able to apply all these skills to my home business.

In addition to the general business, financial, and time management skills anyone running a business picks up, some of the major skills specifically from this business would include: research/reference development of products and ingredients, government regulations management (tracking, interpretation, paperwork, revisions), product marketing research and development, self-directed studies and skills development.

Knowledge, Skills, Experience, and/or Education Needed

Within this industry many people are simply knowledgeable hobbyists. Some take their business seriously and do a lot of learning and research on their own; some are less dedicated to understanding their products and ingredients. However, having some education in holistic health (aromatherapy, herbal therapy), chemistry, or biological sciences is a definite asset in understanding the production of the items being created.

Industry Insight

If someone wanted to break into the industry, I would recommend first making a lot of product, then refining your recipes so you can try them out in low-cost farmers' markets and craft fairs to test your products and packaging. Once you have a feel for what you like to make and what people want to buy, then decide where you want to take it. Retail,

A Day in the Life

It's hard to give a typical day's schedule, but I'll give you today's. This survey is estimated to take about twenty minutes to complete, but I've already been working on it for over four hours. In between, I made changes to my web site, answered some e-mail, rescued my boy twice from being stuck in a drawer he was climbing into, changed a poopy diaper, did two and a half loads of laundry, started on the breakfast dishes while handling a phone call, fed my son his lunch, and had a snack myself. Then I was off to a meeting with a banker, then with our real estate agent. Rescued my boy again, dried some tears, changed another diaper, and managed a couple more phone calls while giving our ferrets some food and water. My son is now having his supper after my having read him a couple of books.

And the day isn't over yet. I still need to finish the changes I was making to my web site, sit on the phone for some tech support, finish laundry, make supper for the adults, package a couple of orders to be shipped, take my kids and the dog out for a walk, then bath time and bed for the kids around 9:30. After that I'll catch up with the rest of the day's e-mail over a cup of tea and go to bed typically around 11:30. It is irrelevant if it's a weekday or weekend. This is an average day, every day . . . doing fifteen things concurrently and hoping that I'll actually complete 30 to 40 percent of them.

wholesale, home parties, markets, and crafts shows are the primary ways to sell your products.

On Marketing

While my business in the startup phase was concentrating on retail sales through markets and fairs, I am shifting now to a wholesale marketing effort. A presence at some major industry trade shows is planned for this year. Effective marketing still tends to be word of mouth, writing articles for e-zines and local pulp publications, and booths at popular seasonal gift shows and markets. Least effective has been Internet banner and shopping mall links. Marketing decisions will vary widely depending on your product focus and target audience. In your business plan, you need to clearly outline that so you get what you are trying to accomplish straight in your head. Otherwise your marketing efforts will result in a haphazard effort that yields minimal results.

Top Revenue Streams

- Wholesale
- Retail—markets
- Consignment
- Retail—Internet

Pricing Structure

Product prices are based on a formula that includes the cost of the raw materials, labor, packaging, and overhead. From that I can determine my wholesale and retail prices, quantity break points, etc.

Additional Cost Items

This is a business that can be started with basic kitchen equipment. A complete set of mixing and measuring utensils, pots and pans, and mixing bowls is recommended, separate from the ones used for personal food preparation. A good scale is the single most important and expensive item that you'll need to initially purchase; you can get decent ones for $100 to $500. For anyone with small children and a home-based business, a roaming headset for your phone is an invaluable tool. You can do a lot more if you can wander through your home and yard while talking on the phone hands free.

MATHEMATICS ENRICHMENT INSTRUCTOR

MERC: THE MATH ENRICHMENT RESOURCE CENTER
SAI: THE SUMMER ALGEBRA INSTITUTE FOR KIDS
bhazen@mbusa.net
Bob and Sarah Hazen, 50/48 | St. Paul, Minnesota | Ages of Children: 13, 17

Office Oasis
Ground floor.

Job Description
Teaching, consulting, writing, training, and speaking about broadening, connecting, and elevating mathematics for elementary students, including sales of booklets on math games and math ideas, and of videos on math games.

Current Career
Bob works as a full-time mathematics teacher and moonlights as an EP on the side. Sarah worked previously in office administration.

Transferable Skills
Chutzpah, creativity, initiative, persistence, love for math and kids.

Knowledge, Skills, Experience, and/or Education Needed
Mathematics, algebra, and a love of teaching and of kids.

Industry Insight
The market for our business looks good. We teach challenging, substantive algebra to students in grades three through six. We have built a successful business in the Minneapolis/St. Paul area and are well known regionally. There is a national market for what we are doing, and we are looking to expand via satellite locations and/or franchise opportunities.

On Marketing
Effective marketing methods have been ads in parent/family periodicals in the Twin Cities area, along with word-of-mouth advertising (since we have a good reputation) and our Internet web page.

Pricing Structure
Varies, on the order of $20–$40/hour.

Additional Cost Items
Math manipulatives, from $100 up.

OFFICE SUPPORT SERVICE

HAPPY FINGERS WORD PROCESSING AND RÉSUMÉ SERVICE
www.HappyFingers.com
Barbie Dallmann, 47 | Charleston, West Virginia | Age of Child: 15

> *"I didn't really start making serious money until I joined a national asso-*
> *ciation and began attending conventions. That's where I really learned*
> *about pricing and smart work habits. My success in business and in life is*
> *so much greater, I believe, because I am constantly taking risks and step-*
> *ping outside my comfort zone to try new things."*

Office Oasis
Ours is a three-story house built into the hillside. The bottom floor is the garage and storage area, the second floor is my office, and the third floor is our living area (three bedrooms, kitchen, living room, dining room, etc.). When we bought this house the second floor had a family room, a bedroom, and a smaller kitchen. Now the bedroom is my son's, the family room is my office, and the kitchen is for storage of office supplies.

Job Description
In addition to writing résumés and other self-marketing documents, I also offer a wide array of office support services, including word processing, desktop publishing, bookkeeping, payroll, editing, writing, and business consulting.

Previous Career
Secretary.

Transferable Skills

The skills I use regularly in my work include my secretarial skills (word processing, organization) as well as writing and editing. As a result of owning my own business, I developed the additional skills of business management, bookkeeping, and marketing. Not only do I use these skills to enhance my own success, I have managed to work them into profit centers that generate a much higher hourly rate than the traditional secretarial skills of typing and word processing. If I were to reenter the nine-to-five workforce at this point, I could easily market myself as an office manager, rather than just a secretary.

Knowledge, Skills, Experience, and/or Education Needed

For résumé writing, it's important to know current hiring trends as well as marketing. One must have an excellent command of the English language and be an excellent writer as well. Continuing education is necessary to keep up with trends and to sharpen one's skills. As for office support services, the basic secretarial skills were enough to get me started. A keyboarding speed in excess of 100 wpm didn't hurt either! It is necessary to keep up with software changes and also to know basic office procedures. I have had some college, but most of the skills I relied on for starting the business were learned in high school.

Industry Insight

My client base continues to grow, and there seems to be an increasing need for people with excellent office support skills, particularly for small business start-ups. Résumé writing, too, is a growing field, becoming more complicated and more difficult with the advent of Internet job search strategies. It takes special knowledge and continuing education to do an outstanding job.

On Marketing

Since the beginning, I have relied heavily on Yellow Pages advertising to bring a steady stream of new customers. Over the last several years, however, the stream has steadily declined, and I find my most reliable source of new clients now to be referrals from friends, clients, and business associates. I found direct mail to be my least effective approach. I think my constant self-marketing has also reaped wonderful benefits (I give out lots and lots of business cards).

I also do a lot of follow up with first-time clients. I always send a customer satisfaction survey to a first-time client. Then I follow up with postcards once a month for six months. The postcards highlight various services offered by my company. I believe in offering excellent customer service, and I think that's an important aspect of marketing.

Top Revenue Streams
- Bookkeeping
- Résumé writing
- Word processing

Pricing Structure
- Bookkeeping, $40–$50/hour
- Résumé writing, $100/hour
- Word processing, $35–$45/hour

Additional Cost Items
In addition to a transcriber and headphones, photocopying equipment is also a must for a secretarial service. The last two copiers I purchased were "used" machines with prices around $3,000, and each had an expected life of around five to six years. Each has paid for itself through copies I make for my clients. Don't be fooled by a copier with a very low purchase price—the operation costs may drive your per-copy cost up to more than 15 cents a copy! Look at all the costs involved in making copies (machine, toner, service) and then figure a per-copy cost in comparing prices.

Recommended Resources
I strongly recommend affiliation with an industry-specific organization. The information I learned through membership in such organizations was vital to my company's growth and success, and the friendships I gained through them have been among the best in my entire life. Going to national conventions and talking to people who had become successful in the industry was like discovering pure gold! The three I recommend are:
- The Association of Business Support Services International
- The National Résumé Writers Association
- The Professional Association of Résumé Writers

PROFESSIONAL ORGANIZER

ORGANIZE YOUR LIFE! | www.momtime.net
Cheryl R. Carter, 39 | Uniondale, New York | Ages of Children: 5, 8, 11

"I have self-published five time-management books, and by far my biggest tip is to keep my biz, home-schooling, and personal goals ever before me so I don't become an at-home workaholic. When you're doing what you love, it can be very easy to become driven."

Office Oasis
My home office is located right in my schoolroom, which is my former master bedroom.

Job Description
I teach people how to set goals, manage their time, and organize their space (home and office) through seminar teaching, writing, and practical workshops. My specialty is time management and organizing for parents and children, which entails home management, time management, and study skills for teens. I have been a professional organizer (PO) for ten years, but with each new baby and school grade, it gets more difficult to get out to clients. As my family needs increased, I gradually phased out the individual-consultant end of the business and am concentrating on the seminar speaking and writing (although I still work with schools and community groups.) Since the fees I got for speaking exceeded the fees I got for consulting, it was a natural transition for me. I have also written five books: *Organize Your Life, Organize Your Home, Organize Your Home Office, How to Get Started as a Professional Organizer* (an e-book), and *400 Ways to Organize Your Child,* which my kids co-wrote with me. It started as a joke to see if we could list ways kids could be organized. I added a few questions and parenting principles, and before we knew it we had written a book together. I try to include my kids in my business as much as possible. As a home educator, I find it best to go with the tide than to work against it. Kids cooperate more when they are included.

Previous Career
A very unorganized schoolteacher. (I learned to be organized after I became a mom.)

Transferable Skills

Interestingly, most professional organizers are people who have transitioned from other careers, and they come from various backgrounds, including secretaries, construction workers, and corporate managers. This profession is growing as people are busier than ever and need help putting their lives in order. Aspiring professional organizers would do well to look at their own organizing skills and how they relate to their current job experience. For instance, my teaching experience has given me credibility to enter the schooling market, and my parenting experience gives me credibility with parenting groups. Some of my colleagues work in the corporate field or management as their experience opens doors for them. Secretarial experience is excellent for organizers. This is a relatively new field. A lot of people still do not know what professional organizers are or what they do, yet the field is expanding.

Knowledge, Skills, Experience, and/or Education Needed

To be a professional organizer, you really need a basic knowledge of technology so you can recommend software to your clients. Some professional organizers specialize in teaching people how to use and maximize the effectiveness of technology. This niche field is quite lucrative but requires a thorough knowledge of computers and software. There are no education requirements for POs, but remember you cannot enter a field where your experience is not respected (i.e., I could not advise a corporation if I never worked in management and could not understand corporate needs). If you like to organize and can pair your experience with a specialty, this can be a great biz for EPs.

Industry Insight

The market for POs is great. *U.S. News & World Report* listed it as one of the fastest-growing home businesses. Presently women make up the majority of POs but this too is changing. I would suggest reading as many organizing books as possible and visiting the web sites of prominent POs.

On Marketing

My freelance writing tends to bring in a great deal of inquiries. Word of mouth continues to bring in the most inquiries and business. My web site also helps to bring in business. A great business card I have and T-shirt I like to wear to the park says, "Let me help you Organize Your

Life!" The name of my business always sparks inquiries especially among the moms, my target market. Always keep business cards and brochures handy wherever you go.

Top Revenue Streams
- Seminars/Speaking
- Writing
- Consultations

Pricing Structure

When I consult with schools, working with teachers and individual students, my rate is generally $50 an hour. (When I found out that county substitute teachers earn this rate, I knew my work would be easily approved if the rate was right.) I also earn income through the sales of my books and reports. Other professional organizers fare better and make from $35 to $150 an hour or more, depending on their specialty. Business POs make much more, and specialized POs, such as for home offices, can also earn more than a home-management consultant.

Additional Cost Items

None—just a telephone, a smile, and a desire to help people be more productive.

Recommended Resources
- The National Association of Professional Organizers, www.napo.net
- The Entrepreneurial Parent, www.en-parent.com
- Home Office Life, www.HomeOfficeLife.com

PROJECT DEVELOPMENT MANAGER

ANN BETZ CONSULTING | annbetz@peoplepc.com
Ann Betz, 37 | St. Louis Park, Minnesota | Age of Child: 5

"Working at home has meant that everything goes a lot smoother. Our family pace is easier, and I'm able to stop work and start dinner so that everything isn't in such a rush every night."

Office Oasis

Spare bedroom on the second floor of home.

Job Description

Independent consultant, offering organizational development and project management for nonprofits, primarily in the areas of education, youth development, and community development.

Previous Career

I was employed full-time for a nonprofit research and education organization. When my position was eliminated due to funding cuts and reorganization, I looked for full-time work and took on projects as a consultant. For a brief while I took on a part-time salaried job, but it wasn't a good fit, so when one of my independent clients asked me if I would manage a project half-time as a consultant, I agreed and became self-employed full-time.

Transferable Skills

The primary skills I draw on are project-management skills—keeping everything organized and juggling the demands of multiple projects at once so that *nothing* falls through the cracks. It is actually a lot like parenting and running a household. Sometimes I have to be careful that one demanding project isn't taking all my attention while a quieter one languishes.

Knowledge, Skills, Experience, and/or Education Needed

E-mail is an absolute *must*. I often do chunks of work in the evening when my son has gone to bed, and e-mail makes it possible to communicate with my project team at my convenience. I even network by keeping my name in front of people with casual e-mails. I know a few software programs but mostly just need really good familiarity with Word and some facility with Microsoft Publisher. My work doesn't require me to have a high level of tech savvy, but it has been useful that I have a network of skilled people I can call on for those areas (like web-site design and print materials design) that *I* am not skilled in.

I have found that my ability to draw on a number of skills not only makes me a more valuable resource, but it keeps me more engaged. I have projects where I do a great deal of writing, others where my main work is designing and facilitating training, and others that have me doing city-wide organizing. It can be a little schizophrenic, but an ability to deal with all that is a valuable asset in my work.

Industry Insight

Since I work exclusively with nonprofits, I watch the funding situation as closely as I can, which is somewhat tied to the general economy. In terms of breaking in, my field is all about relationships and networking and, frankly, having very strong skills. There are indeed a lot of organizations out there that seem to need discrete projects developed and run—this may have to do with the general move toward outsourcing that we've seen in other areas of the economy. My recommendation is to find one steady client who will guarantee a certain number of hours per week for an extended period of time, and then find a handful of other clients who can fill in your workload with smaller projects.

A Day in the Life

A typical week would have me home about 30 to 40 percent of the time, off in meetings the rest of the time. When I'm home, I'm generally e-mailing, writing, or setting up appointments. I usually stop work about 4:00 or 4:30 and go for a walk with my neighbor or a run with my dog, or I get dinner going. I pick up my son from day care around 5:15, and then we have dinner as a family. I often go back to work after he goes to bed at 7:30 or 8:00, and work until 10:00.

On Marketing

For me, it's all about networking. My most effective marketing method is to be as helpful as I can to everyone—making connections for them, introducing people I think may be able to help each other, positioning myself as a resource, and keeping my name in front of people as much through friendship as possible. I don't need any new business right now, but I still try to have a networking event each week. If I did need business, I'd be having breakfast and lunch out every day possible!

Top Revenue Streams
- Training development and facilitation
- Project development and management

- Writing
- Coaching

Pricing Structure

I started at $50 an hour two years ago. This was for a client that guaranteed me thirty hours per week, so I used a lower rate than I would have otherwise. I now charge between $60 and $75 per hour, depending on the client and scope of work.

Additional Cost Items

- Office equipment and supplies
- Car maintenance
- Professional development/network

Recommended Resources

I started a support group for job seekers and consultants, and that's been wonderfully supportive. I could have benefited from a nuts-and-bolts, starting-your-small-business class instead of having to figure most things out myself.

RÉSUMÉ WRITER

CAREER CHANGE RÉSUMÉS | www.careerchangerésumés.com
Rita Fisher, 29 | Columbus, Indiana | Ages of Children: newborn, 2

Office Oasis

Spare bedroom at back of house.

Job Description

I'm the chief visionary, the writer, marketer, public-relations professional. The only thing I don't do in my business is my taxes.

Previous Career

Proofreader, bookkeeper, and administrative assistant.

Transferable Skills

Organization, writing, marketing, PR, interviewing, rapport building.

Knowledge, Skills, Experience, and/or Education Needed
I'm a certified professional résumé writer. Certification is awarded upon completion of rigorous studies set forth by the Professional Association of Résumé Writers (www.parw.com).

Industry Insight
People will always need résumés, and it's not hard to break into. The key is knowing how to position yourself within your chosen niche and excellent writing/customer-service skills.

On Marketing
My most effective is to offer free advice as a résumé expert on Internet discussion boards. My least effective was a magnetic sign on my car.

Top Revenue Streams and Pricing
I have only two prices for résumés: $179.00 for everybody except for senior level executives, $300.00 for senior level executives. This price includes only the development of a professional résumé.

Pricing Structure
$55/hour.

Additional Cost Items
None.

Recommended Resources
- Professional Association of Résumé Writers, www.parw.com

RETAILER/CANES

THE CANE GUY | www.thecaneguy.com
Charlie Burns, 46 | Milford, New Hampshire | Ages of Children: 14, 16

Office Oasis
Basement.

Education
B.S. in administration, University of New Hampshire.

Previous Career

I came out of the electronics manufacturing industry. My background is primarily sales, having been a direct salesman, an independent manufacturer's rep, as well as a sales manager on both the national and international level.

Home Biz

The Cane Guy: A cane should be a fashion accessory, not a clumsy appendage. If you have to walk with a cane, it should enhance your image, not make you look and feel like you just fell out of an institution. My canes make great gifts for parents or grandparents who walk with a cane.

Primary Market

Baby boomers with aging parents.

Top Products

- Flashlight Cane—a walking cane that incorporates a flashlight into the handle as well as a rear-blinking safety light for walking at night, with a "secret" storage compartment in the handle for medication.
- Other stylish and affordable canes.

EP Motivating Force

I was in a severe accident in 1992. While playing with my kids at the beach, I was hit by a wave and broke my neck and back. I have recovered from quadriplegia to walking with a cane. Starting a home business was my way of getting back into life again.

EP Highlight

My greatest achievement has been to be working at all. When something happens to you like what has happened to me, you have a choice. You can quit, feel sorry for yourself, and let life happen to you, or you can make life happen.

EP Advice

Besides making sure there's really a market for your produce or service, I'd say involve your kids in your business. Make them feel a part of it. The lessons they get here will be with them for their entire life.

Favorite Quote

There are three kinds of people in this world: those who learn by experience, those who learn by the experiences of others, and those who never learn at all. Which one do you want to be? (My dad used to say this all the time when we were kids!)

Recommended Resources

I use Ask Jeeves, www.askjeeves.com, for everything!

RETAILER/POTPOURRI AND SCENTED CRAFTS

Maggie Smith, 45 | Washington Grove, Maryland | Ages of Children: 16, 19

Office Oasis

Spare bedroom.

Job Description

Make and sell potpourri, sachets, and fragrant crafts through boutique craft shows, a web site, and wholesale orders. I grow and dry many of the flowers and herbs that I use, so I'm busy in the garden.

Previous Career

Waitress for more than twenty years.

Transferable Skills

How to deal effectively with people, plus some bookkeeping and a little computer experience. The day-to-day running of a business I learned from working at a small, family-run restaurant.

Knowledge, Skills, Experience, and/or Education Needed

Definitely a love of gardening as so much time is spent outdoors. Knowledge is gained through experience and experimenting with different scents/blends of flowers and essential oils. If making sachets, an ability to sew well. Good imagination for creative designs.

Industry Insight

The sales of potpourri and sachets stays steady since consumers enjoy having flowers, fragrances, and scented items in their homes. Learn/read about potpourri, aromatherapy, essential oils, and experiment with fragrances, colors, and flowers. Study the area where you want to market your products—what are the consumers buying? Cater to their tastes, as potpourri can be made in many styles and scents (a few examples are primitive, country, victorian, and woodsy).

A Day in the Life

My workday begins at 4:00 P.M. I start with the garden—weeding, gathering flowers, herbs, planting, watering. Then, a quick shower and onto the computer to check e-mail and devote two hours to marketing. If I have potpourri to blend, it's one to four hours of mixing flowers, spices, herbs. Then adding oils and a few hours of sewing sachets. Back to the computer to check e-mail, more research on marketing, get additional links for site. My business day stops at 4 A.M. If I have a craft show to get ready for, it's a longer day, with bagging, ribbons, boxing, and waiting for UPS to show up. The only drawback is as I work nights to stay on my family's schedule and spend time with them, it's sometimes hard to communicate by telephone with wholesale accounts and suppliers. Their day stops when mine begins, and they don't like to communicate through e-mail nor do they comprehend that there are people who work a night shift, even at home!

On Marketing

My most effective marketing method to date was a free ad in *Freebies* magazine (snail mail) for a sample of potpourri ($2 charge). I then saved all the addresses and sent offers of special deals on sachets to the subscribers who ordered potpourri samples, working on a special "new" potpourri offer to same. My least effective was advertising on a "freebie" web site. On that site, people expect a totally free product, no shipping charges at all. My other marketing efforts have been signing my web address on all e-mail, sending business cards with all outgoing snail mail (be it bills or whatever), and whenever asked what I do, wherever I am, handing out a business card. Remember you need to devote a few hours every day/ evening to marketing. If you have a web site, this could mean getting listed in every search engine, trading links with other craft/art/business sites, and offering specials on your site. Also try to promote your business through a local newspaper article, tying it in with special occasions for that month. And look for opportunities where you can donate an item for a charity or other community event to get your business noticed.

Top Revenue Streams
- Advertising and selling to the wholesale market via web site
- Sending regular updates on new products/specials to existing mailing list of previous buyers
- Boutique craft shows during spring and fall months
- Web site retail sales
- Home craft shows

Pricing Structure
Cost of materials/supplies $\times$ 3 = wholesale price. Retail is double the cost of wholesale. I then check out the competition's price; if my prices are much lower or higher, I try different flowers/materials to stay within that price range. If I'm shipping potpourri to a show, the cost of shipping is added; for wholesale orders, the buyer pays the shipping costs.

Additional Cost Items
- Dried flowers and materials, about $100 investment
- Essential oils (best quality you can find), about $50–$100
- Packaging supplies, $50

Recommended Resources
- *The Crafts Report*
- Barbara Brabec's books on crafting as a business
- *Herbal Treasures and the Pleasure of Herbs* by Phyllis Shadys
- Other professional and calendar crafts on-line forum posts and archives to network with fellow craftspeople and learn of upcoming craft shows

---

SALESPERSON/HORSE SUPPLIES/RIDING APPAREL

THE PACIFIC EQUESTRIAN TACK SHOP | pacificequestrian@msn.com
Claire Sutherland, 35 | Wildomar, California | Age of Child: 3

"During the week, I miss having someone to talk to who is more than three feet tall. But all my customers adore my son and come in to buy things to help support us. He's a good little salesman too."

Job Description

I own a business that sells riding apparel and horse supplies at horse shows and through mail order. My son and I travel from Arizona to Washington state. We spend approximately six months on the road each year.

Previous Career

I worked in the film industry.

Transferable Skills

As a film person, I transferred tenacity, long work hours, and sales and accounting skills to my new business. If ever I went back to work for someone else, I would bring in the ability to work long hours, computer and sales skills, future customer contacts, ability to drive a big truck, and the ability to survive.

Knowledge, Skills, Experience, and/or Education Needed

- Basic business education
- Commercial drivers license
- Good sales skills
- Own and ride horses

Industry Insight

The industry is good but limited because of finances and number of customers in my specialty, which is dressage. My advice would be to buy an existing business.

A Day in the Life	
7:00 A.M.	Feed horses
8:30 A.M.	Take Colin to preschool
9:00–noon	Ride horses
Noon–3:00 P.M.	Mail order
3:00 P.M.	Pick up Colin from school
3:30 P.M.	Return to work at home with Colin
6:00–7:30 P.M.	Feed and care for horses

On Marketing

We do monthly mini-catalogs (in color), which is our most effective method to date. Least effective was horse show sponsorship.

Top Revenue Streams

The top revenue streams for my business are horse supplies and riding apparel, but other similar fields might be:

- Horse laundry and blanket repair
- Consignment tack store
- Horse sitting/daily stall cleaning service

Pricing Structure

Regular retail markup.

Additional Cost Items

- Truck and trailer, $38,000
- Inventory, $35,000

Recommended Resources

The best small retail book I've come across is *Retail in Detail,* by Ronald L. Bond, Oasis Press.

SALESPERSON/STORK SIGN RENTALS

STORKS AND FRIENDS | www.StorkandFriends.com
Judith K. Diamond, 37 | Rancho Palos Verdes, California | Ages of Children: 4, 6

> *"[A corporate job] sure was easier work in the sense that it wasn't some-thing I thought about (almost) every waking moment. I wake up think-ing about my business and go to sleep thinking about my business. When I had a corporate job, I could take a vacation and not think about the job. Now when I'm on 'vacation' it gives me even more time to think about my business!"*

Office Oasis

A dedicated room in our home.

Job Description

I rent six-foot colorful painted wooden stork signs for display on front lawns that announce the birth of a baby, and also sell personalized chocolate bars. The wrappers have personalized messages and are purchased by individuals and businesses who are looking for a unique promotional item.

Previous Career

Project manager in the aerospace industry for thirteen years, dealing with airline modifications. During a layoff period at my company, I was able to negotiate a modest severance package and used it to make the jump to entrepreneurial life. It was one of the best decisions I've ever made for myself and my family.

A Day in the Life

6:00–7:30 A.M.	Prepare breakfast for children and get everyone ready for preschool/school
7:30–8:30 A.M.	Drop children off at school
8:30–11:00 A.M.	Work on business (typically from my second office—my car. This includes follow up calls, place and deliver orders) or run errands (business and personal)
11:15 A.M.	Pick up my preschooler
11:15–1:00 P.M.	Lunch, play with children, get ready for naptime
1:00–2:30 P.M.	Daughter naps while I work from home
2:30–6:00 P.M.	Pick up kindergartner. Do homework, play with children, make dinner.
6:00–8:00 P.M.	Dinner, clean up, bath time, bedtime for children
8:00–9:00 P.M.	Housework
9:00 P.M.–1:00 A.M.	Work at home

Typically weekends are spent with my family. Also, during this time, orders are processed and I on occasion will participate in local trade shows/fairs.

Transferable Skills

In my corporate life, I was responsible for managing projects. I am responsible for managing several projects at one time. This includes marketing, sales, community relations, and finance.

For those EPs returning to the nine-to-five work life, having the responsibility for all facets of one's business may be to their advantage. Most likely they would stand out as a job candidate because of their proven dedication and commitment to day-to-day work.

Knowledge, Skills, Experience, and/or Education Needed

In my particular line of work, I needed to have the basic knowledge of how to run a successful home-based business. This included setting goals, schedules, and having self-discipline to follow through. Although I may not have initially had all the education I needed to be a successful EP, I learned to research, research, research. Knowledge of basic accounting software, database management, and marketing continue to be an important part of my business.

Industry Insight

Luckily for my stork business, hundreds of babies are being born every month in our area so the market is strong. With regards to the promotional chocolate bars: The trend for personalization is overwhelming! Let's face it, lots of people love chocolate and seeing their name in print. I would advise EPs to track similar trends in their local market.

On Marketing

Networking provides a great source of business for me. Finding (or even creating) groups that can be a forum to promote your business can be of great help. The most effective marketing methods that I have used to date involve the creation of strategic alliances with similar businesses. Being a very active member in our local chamber of commerce has been a considerable asset in promoting my business. I've been able to meet several people that I would not have necessarily made acquaintances with had we not had that common tie to the local business community. Personally, I find marketing to be one of the most exciting parts of any business.

Top Revenue Streams

Renting the stork signs have been my top revenue-generating product. The addition of the personalized chocolate bars was a great complement to my existing business. The particular line that I carry has more than one hundred designs. The designs range from birthday and holiday items to promotional items for businesses. Offering the latter has created another market for my business.

The storks rent anywhere from $30 to $70 . . . depending upon the rental period and whether or not a balloon bouquet is included. Since the signs are rented and not sold, the overhead is low.

Additional Cost Items

A portable phone headset, $40 approximate cost, has been one of the best investments I've made. As an EP, I can be involved with a business-related phone conversation and do light housework (laundry, dusting, making beds, etc.) at the same time—a great time saver (and does wonders for your posture!).

Recommended Resources

For educational resources, I recommend the local SBDC (small business development center) and classes through local community colleges and adult education programs aimed at small businesses and one's local chamber of commerce. I also strongly recommend working with other businesses that share your concerns. I have learned a lot from others who are in the same industry, are home-based, and are EPs like myself.

STRESS MANAGEMENT COACH

STRESS MANAGEMENT AND RELAXATION TECHNOLOGY
www.SMARTaichi.com
Bill Douglas, 44 | Overland Park, Kansas | Ages of Children: 17, 19

> *"The direction of the economy seems to be moving for more and more people to become independent contractors, or employees enabled via the Internet to work at home. This will solve many problems by simply bringing parents back into children's lives. Most crime is committed by kids between 3:00 and 7:00 P.M. when parents are working or fighting traffic to get home."*

Office Oasis

My wife and I both have our own offices, which can double as guest rooms when needed.

Job Description

My wife and I teach classes on stress management, tai chi, and qigong, both on-line and off; produce video and audio instructional programs on stress management (which we ship from our home); and write columns for magazines and e-zines on the subject. I also wrote a best-selling book on tai chi/stress management called *The Complete Idiot's Guide to Chi and Qigong* (Macmillan Reference, 1999). I am the tai chi expert on America Online's Alternative Medicine site, and I appear in monthly chats the first Tuesday of each month (AOL Keyword: alt med).

Previous Career

Administrator in human resources for a Fortune 500 company, and my wife was products traffic manager for an international corporation.

Transferable Skills

I got my computer skills from corporate training and also learned marketing from my previous careers, which has enabled me to get the most advertising bang for the least amount of bucks. My people skills were honed as well as my bookkeeping skills from previous corporate careers.

Knowledge, Skills, Experience, and/or Education Needed

My computer experience enabled me to create my own marketing brochures and correspondence as well as to set up a mailing list database for marketing postcards. However, what helped me the most was learning how to deal with "stress" on the job during my corporate years. This enabled me to learn how to create effective stress-management training programs for others to benefit from, which is the essence of my business—stress-management training.

Industry Insight

I encourage all people to try to find the most healthy and fulfilling way to live their lives, and then that trailblazing way of life will create templates or formulas they can offer to others struggling with the same demands of job and family. There will always be a market for healthier ways to live. Just look at the self-help shelves at the book store—they're packed.

On Marketing

We advertise in local wellness magazines and place public service announcements in newspapers, on the radio, and on TV. We offer free workshops to introduce people to our services, through libraries, community colleges, business groups, and community associations, and we write articles for related publications. We also send out postcards, because they are only 20 cents each to post. Each of these brings in more business, and it all adds up.

A Day in the Life

I get up at 8:00 A.M., after my daughter has already left for high school. I jog a mile, do tai chi, lift weights, meditate, and then have breakfast.

Then I go to my computer and begin contacting, marketing, e-mailing, writing, telephoning, faxing, and generally creating, while my wife does her exercises and then gets Internet orders off AOL and begins filling video and audio orders.

When our daughter gets home from tennis practice at 4:00 P.M. we begin preparing dinner and relax, talk, sometimes wrap up work a bit as our daughter does her homework. Then we watch a little TV and go to bed. The next day, the adventure begins again!

Top Revenue Streams

Stress Management Training is our biggest seller. Videos on stress management techniques is second, and audios are third.

Pricing Structure

We charge a percentage of the income from public classes, ranging from 50 percent to 70 percent of the tuition. In this way, we benefit from a successful class, rather than making a static wage. It stimulates us to be the *very best* we can be.

Recommended Resources

- *The Tao of Sales* by E. Thomas Behr, Ph.D.
- *How to Get on Radio Talk Shows All Across America Without Leaving Your Home or Office* by Joe Sabah

TECHNICAL WRITER

ENGINEERING INK | www.engineeringink.com
www.absolutekidsbooks.com
Pamela J. Waterman, 45 | Mesa, Arizona | Ages of Children: 7, 10, 12

"I use a small digital timer in my office every day, or I'd never remember to do the school pick-up."

Office Oasis

With our four moves I've been fortunate enough to always have a private office (a spare bedroom). In my current house this bedroom (office) is away from the other bedrooms, so it's nice and quiet.

Job Description

My primary business for the past ten years has been freelance technical writing, from a marketing point of view. I write articles, brochures, technical reports, business plans, and proposals, both for corporate clients and for magazines, mostly about engineering design software and hardware. I get regular assignments from one magazine, and occasionally I am commissioned by companies to write articles for other magazines. I also sometimes write my own pieces and find a market for them.

In a totally different writing application, in March 1999, Sourcebooks published a book I wrote on children's theme-based activities, *The Absolute Best Play Days*. Since then, I have become immersed in an unexpected second part-time job of book promotion, as I discovered the hard way that unless you're Tom Clancy even big publishing companies do almost nothing for you. I have written a marketing plan and now spend at least five hours a week calling and writing to magazines or web sites trying to get my book reviewed, doing demos at a booth I set up at local bookstores, festivals, and moms' play groups (selling copies I have purchased myself), doing a story/craft time at local bookstores, and writing articles on parenting that I sell or give to magazines or web sites, in order to get my name and the book's name "out there." I also do radio interviews at crazy hours, as set up by the publisher. This could be a full-time job if I let it happen, and I have to consider how much time to put into it, as well as whether to continue writing such books.

Previous Career

I was an electrical engineer for seven years, then an editor/technical writer in two jobs for four years.

Transferable Skills

Project planning skills as an employee have helped me in prioritizing monthly/weekly/daily activities as an EP. The people skills I developed are now applied to networking towards new clients and managing current ones. And keeping a "paper trail" so I always knew where I stood on each project now helps me to constantly update my résumé and portfolio, which I use to gain new clients or secure a bank loan if I wanted. Current EPs looking to reenter the nine-to-five world will definitely need to document their project-management skills to show how well they worked both independently and alongside clients. In addition, the multi-tasking that EPs do shows skill in both time management and financial planning, and the marketing skills picked up as an entrepreneur can be valuable on a résumé as well. Other transferable skills came from my volunteer experience. My project-management experience for various activities within the local section of Society of Women Engineers (SWE) helped me organize my business tasks. My public speaking experience on Air Force projects and for SWE outreach (school) programs gave me the confidence to make presentations to potential clients.

Knowledge, Skills, Experience, and/or Education Needed

A strong knowledge of basic engineering skills has enabled me to land projects even in areas outside of my particular engineering experience, so my B.S. and M.S. seem to open doors. Clients believe that I will not be "afraid" to delve deeply into technical lingo. I think that my seven years in design/manufacturing goes a long way to establishing credibility. Equally strong writing skills are also essential; the less editing a magazine has to do on your pieces, the more receptive they are to giving you assignments. Other skills include asking the right questions to get to the point, admitting you need something clarified, staying on schedule, and being able to do extensive web research.

Industry Insight

The market is great, as many companies have downsized their internal marketing departments and are looking to outsource. Technical magazines are also always looking for solid writing on hot topics. New EPs could find a magazine that interests them and propose a topic that would fit in with their readership (called pitching a story, or sending a query). You may have to write the entire piece and send it in "on speculation," but that will show your style and thoroughness. Keep copies of every report, white paper, business plan, newsletter, brochure, or article you've already written or edited (even if for free) to build a portfolio.

On Marketing

Most effective for magazines: sending a query and clippings of similar articles. Most effective for corporate clients: word of mouth. Least effective: short business write-ups in newsletters or in web directories.

Top Revenue Streams

- Technical articles on assignment by corporate clients
- Technical brochures on assignment by corporate clients
- Technical articles on assignment by magazines

Pricing Structure

$75/hour, or I bid a fixed price plus 10 percent overage for large projects.

Additional Cost Items

None.

Recommended Resources

Attending a SCORE seminar was the best $20 I ever spent! It answered my basic licensing and tax liability questions, so I felt I was legally covered to get started. Beyond that, I subscribe to several magazines and newsletters, both for engineers and for freelance writers. I have another set of contacts, web sites, and magazines I read for my parenting writing. In general, I get information and support from local meetings of the Society of Women Engineers and the Arizona Entrepreneurial Mothers' Association. I also belong to the Arizona Book Publishers Association and the Society of Manufacturing Engineers, and I subscribe to several web newsletters, especially HBWM (Home-Base Working Moms).

WOODWORKER/CABINET MAKER

LACREWS, INC. | www.lacrews.com
d.b.a. Mark Crews, "The Cabinetmaker"
Mark and Andrea Crews | Culpeper, Virginia | Ages of Children: 5, 8

Office Oasis
- *Year 1:* LaCrews was a sole proprietorship in our town home, using part of the basement and our bedroom for the shop and office.
- *Years 2–4:* We purchased a bigger home while both working full-time elsewhere, moonlighting with our cabinetry business. LaCrews was a S-Corporation and rented about 900 square feet from our home for storage, shop, and office. We intermittently used a woodworking co-op and self-storage shed.
- *Years 5–6:* LaCrews rented about 1,300 square feet of our home for storage, shop, and office as well as a self-storage unit and woodworking co-op space.
- *January 2001:* Relocated and physically moved LaCrews to an outside office. LaCrews, Inc., now rents a 2,000 square foot shop/office space in Culpeper, Virginia.

Home Biz and Mission Statement
We offer custom cabinetry to contractors, builders, and residential clients, including matching finishes, designing and building cabinetry and built-in furniture, and the sale of Merillat Cabinetry.

Most Popular Services and Pricing Fees
Most projects are designing and building residential custom kitchen cabinetry. Our rate is $65/hour plus mark-up of materials based on fair market value.

Favorite Products and/or Services
Mark really enjoys creating custom furniture as it provides a creative outlet.

Marketing Strategy
Personal networking has worked the absolute best for us. Our marketing/advertising includes: web site, lead share groups, membership in

chambers of commerce and trade associations, Yellow Pages, trade shows, ads in local church bulletins, and a directory of services listing in a local paper. Andrea gets leads on-line, by referral, and by phone. After qualifying these leads on the phone or e-mail, Andrea closes the sales face to face or on the phone.

Recommendations
- 50 percent of your time is marketing/sales
- Maintaining good personal credit
- Using a CPA
- Having long- and-short term goals

Recommended Resources
- Local chamber of commerce
- Local trade associations
- Woodworking/artisan co-op

WRITER-SPEAKER

LIVING HOPE, INC. | www.writerspeaker.com
Carmen Leal, 46 | Lake Mary, Florida | Ages of Children: 17, 19

"I like the fact that my kids do not think anyone owes them anything. When parents work outside the home, it's as if the money is there by magic. But my kids know where the money comes from, so they don't think anyone owes them anything."

Office Oasis
Third bedroom.

Job Description
I am currently a freelance writer and speaker. I write and speak in the area of Huntington's Disease and a variety of Christian topics. I also write books (such as WriterSpeaker.com) and articles for writers and speakers on using the Internet more effectively. In addition, I teach workshops and seminars in that area. The mission of Living Hope, Inc., is to help the hurting world accept finite disappointment while accept-

ing the infinite hope of eternal salvation through Jesus Christ. This is accomplished by the publication of books and articles, the production and performance of music, and relevant public speaking and training.

Previous Career

Before writing full-time, I owned my own marketing firm in Hawaii for ten years. I specialized in working with small businesses, churches, and nonprofit organizations. I did event-planning, copywriting, wrote commercials, wrote "junk mail," created marketing strategies, etc. Prior to that I was the telemarketing and marketing manager for Honolulu Cellular doing much of the same thing I did for clients once I opened my business. I also sold radio advertising space and had a number of other sales jobs.

Transferable Skills

- Phone skills
- Sales (closing!)
- Accounts payable and receivable
- Collections
- Writing concise reports

Knowledge, Skills, Experience, and/or Education Needed

There will always be a market for writers and speakers. However, I suggest those interested in eventually writing full-time learn to write advertising copy and to do technical writing. Yes, it might not be the great American novel, but it will put food on the table and pay some bills. Be prepared to follow the rules of publishing. Also, start with articles and move up to books. Write nonfiction based on a platform, and then create speeches that complement the book so the research goes both for the speech and the book. Learn to network. Understand that this business is a "who you know" business, so writers' conferences, professional organizations, and the like are essential. Eventually you will build the credits needed to write what you want and actually get it published and make money, or you can charge big bucks for your speaking.

On Marketing

Most effective is without a doubt the Internet. Learning how to effectively network on-line, create and market my web page, interact in chat rooms, and use forums and e-mail lists has accelerated my career. In the four years I've been writing and speaking, every project I've done is as a result of the Internet. My fourth book comes out this June, and I've spoken all over the United States. In fact, I have a speaking tour lined up this fall in Great Britain, thanks 100 percent to the Internet. Word of mouth is a close second. Worst? Advertising of any sort, including direct snail mail.

Top Revenue Streams
- Writing
- Speaking
- HTML and web page development

Additional Cost Items
None.

Recommended Resources
The Internet!

Tech-Heavy Home Careers

ADVERTISING/MARKETING SPECIALIST

DOBBEN INK | kdobbenink@aol.com
Kelly Dobben-Annis, 34 | Portsmouth, New Hampshire | Ages of Children: 4, 5

> *"One time my son and I were walking down the street and a FedEx truck drove by. He yelled, 'There goes the Dobben Ink truck!' I thought that was cute but a little sad . . ."*

Office Oasis
Spare bedroom, plus living room as a meeting area for clients.

Job Description
I act as an external marketing department for larger companies that have an in-house marketing department but have an overflow of projects. For smaller companies that don't have a department or the budgets to hire larger advertising firms, I *am* their marketing department. The majority of my work is designing catalogs, brochures, direct marketing material, and CD packaging. I also do some consulting for smaller companies. I help them with marketing strategies and planning for the upcoming year. I try to help companies get the most out of a small budget.

Previous Career
Marketing communications specialist, graphic designer, waitress, aerobics instructor—that about covers it.

Knowledge, Skills, Experience, and/or Education Needed
As far as skills and education go, in my field I must know the programs inside and out and stay educated on new products and new ideas/styles. I involve myself in lots of things just to see other people's perspectives and ideas. As far as knowledge and experience go, it's really important that you enjoy working with many different types of people. If you're one that thinks working for yourself makes you the instant boss then

you're way off. With each client comes one or two new bosses. And, nine to five means nothing when you work for yourself; you'd be safe to set your watch on FedEx time.

Industry Insight

The market for a graphic designer seems to be nice and steady. There is an endless amount of work out there; you just need to figure out what your goal is (or your market) and start chipping away at it.

On Marketing

Fortunately, for me I've had to do little to market my company. I've been lucky to make great contacts along the way in positions I've held with other companies. Almost all my work comes by word of mouth. Things I highly recommend doing are joining clubs, advertising and graphic clubs as well as the chamber of commerce in your area. And, do some free work to get your name out there. Each year I try to donate my services to three organizations that benefit children, the environment, or cancer. I may design a logo, lay out a road race application, or do a brochure for an event. Also, getting your own web site is helpful but may not be a necessity. If you're just starting out, your money may be better spent on marketing yourself in other ways.

Top Revenue Streams
- Catalog and brochure design
- Direct marketing pieces
- Logo design
- CD packaging design for musicians (my favorite)

Pricing Structure

I charge $45 to $75 per hour, depending on the project, and usually charge a flat fee based on projected hours/project.

Additional Cost Items

It's good to have other people you can call to help you with projects. I have a copywriter I work with, two illustrators that have completely different styles than myself, two graphic designers whom I can call when the work load gets too out of hand. For me, I work at home so I can be flexible and spend more time with my kids, but I also have to remember my clients are counting on me to get their project done perfectly and in the time I agreed upon. That means I need knowledgeable backup at times, which I gladly pay for.

Recommended Resources
- *Communication Arts Magazine*

BUSINESS SUPPORT SERVICES

DUNCAN BUSINESS SERVICES | VDuncanCO@aol.com
Vicki L. Duncan, 43 | Loveland, Colorado | Age of Child: 3

> *"I feel working at home helps our daughter understand the value of time management and also illustrates to her that we value our family time. She's at an age now where she doesn't need constant supervision or interaction with me, but I like feeling that I'm available if she needs me."*

Office Oasis
Major portion of walkout basement.

Job Description
We provide a broad range of services to our clients from bookkeeping to transcription and word processing. Two new, and growing, aspects of our business are database design/management and bulk mail services.

Previous Career
Secretary/administrative assistant for more than twenty-three years. Insurance claims adjuster for more than five years.

Transferable Skills
My many years of experience as a secretary/administrative assistant helped me build strong communication and organizational skills, not to mention the requisite typing, writing, and resourcefulness necessary for the jobs I held in the corporate world. While I couldn't profitably do this type of work without above-average technical skills (typing, writing, editing, computer skills), I think the communication skills, organizational

skills, and the ability to be very resourceful have played an important role in turning my "hard" skills into a profitable business.

Knowledge, Skills, Experience, and/or Education Needed

In any business requiring the use of computer technology, you must stay informed about new products, software, and trends and strive to stay on the leading edge of technological advances. By doing so, you can recognize changes in your industry and develop ways to use them to your advantage to help you (1) work smarter instead of harder, and (2) recognize and develop new profit centers. As for skills, in my business it is absolutely necessary to have above-average typing speed and formatting skills, knowledge of grammar and punctuation, and the ability to listen to and communicate well with your clients. I believe my corporate experience has helped me a great deal in attracting corporate clients in that I understand the processes involved in decision making in a large corporation and the time pressures often involved in large projects.

Industry Insight

The business support services industry is very adaptable to a changing economy. In "boom" periods when there aren't enough qualified employees to fill the jobs available, outsourcing to a business support service is a way to handle the volume of work when a qualified employee isn't available. During economic downturns, many times companies have to lay workers off even though the volume of work remains unchanged—again making outsourcing to a business support service a smart way to handle the volume. My experience thus far has shown that high-caliber, professional business support services are in demand by small business, corporate clients, *and* individuals. Most people these days are too busy to get everything done—especially if they too are entrepreneurs trying to build/run their own business. Finding a qualified professional to assist them frees them to do what they do best—and they can leave the details to us!

On Marketing

There's nothing better than word-of-mouth advertising, and it's free! I have invested time in getting to know the folks at one of our local print shops. I have the pleasure of referring my clients to them for fast, affordable printing; and they reciprocate whenever one of their customers need business support services. This mutually beneficial relationship has turned into one of the most effective forms of marketing for me since our recent relocation to another city. Yellow Pages advertising has consistently paid for itself. Now, having touted Yellow Pages advertising, I have to say that all the advertising in the world won't do you any good if you don't answer your phone. I can't tell you how many times, when asked why they chose our services, clients have said, "No one else answered their phone!"

Top Revenue Streams
- Database design/database management/data entry
- Bookkeeping services
- Bulk mail services
- Word processing/typing/transcription
- General administrative services

Pricing Structure
$25 to $40/hour.

Additional Cost Items
We recently invested in bulk mail equipment when we decided to offer that as a new profit center. I researched my equipment purchase and decided to purchase good, used equipment to start out, and I found someone who was selling their business. This enabled me to purchase about $30,000 of equipment for less than $15,000.

Recommended Resources
I had the extreme good fortune to be associated with a local network of professional business support service owners when I first started my business. These local and international associations have been a tremendous source of information, support, assistance, and referrals for me. I highly recommend:
- The Association of Business Support Services International, Inc. (ABSSI), www.abssi.org

COMPUTER SERVICES TECHNICIAN

ADVENTURE TECH | www.medicinebow.org/adventure/
Laura Wheeler, 36 | Medicine Bow, Wyoming | Ages of Children:
4, 6, 7, 9, 12, 13, 14

"My transition from being a SAHM to an EP was seamless . . . I simply started replacing pastimes that did not pay for ones that did."

Office Oasis

Small rented office down the road, but I homeschool seven children so moved both business equipment and school items to the new space. This keeps the entire *home* the "oasis"!

Job Description

I began by offering a wide variety of computer services. Slow but consistent growth and some new product lines (bulk foods, nutritional herbs, and cosmetics) have required that I streamline my business and eliminate many of the smaller services so I could focus on computer sales and repair, and the new product lines.

Previous Career

Stay-at-home mom, all self-taught.

Transferable Skills

- Attention to detail was gained from homemaking.
- Typing was learned in the course of computer use.
- Budgeting for the family trained me for balancing business books.
- Time management was learned in the home.
- Teaching my children prepared me to teach clients and assistants about our products.

Knowledge, Skills, Experience, and/or Education Needed

I learned what I do by doing it and by reading about it and asking a lot of questions. I simply worked with my talents and increased them to the point where they could compete in the marketplace. Then I kept it all up when I got discouraged.

Industry Insight

When I began doing computer work, I just did odd jobs for people who had no computer (like typing résumés and printing Christmas newsletters). I think three things helped me succeed. First, I was willing to develop my business slowly. Second, I kept learning new things. And third, I was willing to be flexible. If I advertised that I could scan photos, sure as anything, someone would want me to fax something for them. People thought of me for things I never advertised to do, and if possible, I did the job they asked me and did not complain. When you are starting out, sometimes the thing you prefer to do is not the thing that you end up needing to do. I would not say that you should not pursue a dream but be willing to let that dream take you someplace new too. I always thought I would hate having a boring store. Now I focus mostly on sales and manufacturing, and I find I enjoy what I never thought I would, because that is what people want me to do here. You really have to recognize the unique possibilities of your area and tailor your solutions to those needs and limitations.

On Marketing

I market on-line and locally. We live in a small town with no news service, so things work a little differently here. My most effective marketing method is to check in on help lines to offer tech solutions. I also offer some free services locally (Internet access to students for homework and free computer classes to seniors), which helps me become a trusted expert to those I help. Least effective has been classified ads—no one seems to read them or pay attention to them. That said, the best way to grow a business like mine is to back up what you say. A business that is run well, by an honorable owner, will grow based on its reputation and eventually will pick up momentum even without high advertising dollars. If you take on too much too fast—get twenty new customers, say—but lose them all because of poor quality work or not backing up your product or service, or by being impolite to your clients or customers, then you are back at square one, always paying high dollars to get new clients, and your business never does gain momentum. I spend almost nothing on advertising and have very slow growth as a result, but I have repeat customers who refer other customers to me. I have customers who tell me that they don't care if they can get it for less elsewhere, they can rely on what I sell and my reputation is worth paying a little more for.

Top Revenue Streams

Computer manufacture, used computer sales, web design, and bulk food sales. All are highly competitive or have a highly specific target market. I am successful in each in a very small way, reflective of the town in which I live. Talking to my clients in person makes more of a difference than what I sell seems to.

Pricing Structure

I don't charge by the hour because open-ended hourly fees seem to scare the little folk. I price by the job and base it on the average for the area for that service. Once quoted, I do not change the cost. I used to have to lower it a lot for some people to afford it, and I did it to get my business underway, but I no longer have to take underpaid jobs.

Additional Cost Items

I started with just the basics. Over time, I found that some older computers (low cost ones . . . many of them just our own castoffs) helped for testing used parts. A demo computer—one you build yourself—is of course a must if you want to build computers. An extra computer with an Internet connection comes in handy if you want to offer tutoring or other services where the client uses your computer. It's almost essential when starting in computer sales that you *do not* have an inventory. Prices decline too fast and you can lose too much money. I set up suppliers who can get me what I need quickly, and order on demand. You do need an Internet connection, and it is best if the computer system you have is a newer one (more impressive to prospective clients). Otherwise, equipment costs are very low or optional.

Recommended Resources

The QUE computer books have been some of the most helpful for learning the computer skills I needed. Quickbooks or Peachtree Accounting make the process simpler for tracking inventory, calculating profit and loss, paying sales tax, and more.

DESKTOP PUBLISHER

DESIGN/TYPE | dsigntype@aol.com
Heather Lee, 37 | Centerville, Minnesota | Age of Child: 9

"The life of the work-at-home parent often feels like a constant and very delicate balancing act. Every day we're charged with meeting the needs of our clients, our children, our spouse, and ourselves, and successfully dealing with these seemingly irreconcilable forces is, at times, tremendously challenging . . . but also tremendously rewarding."

Office Oasis

In 1999, I was in the midst of reorganizing my business and planning to close the executive suite I had operated for the past six years. I was also in the market for a new home, which put me in the unique position of shopping for a house with my home office needs and desires clearly in mind. Now my home office is located on the lowest of four levels. It's close enough to the family room that I'm able to keep tabs on my son when he's home, yet far enough away from the main living areas that I'm not distracted by household tasks during the workday. In addition, there's a patio with a lake view just outside my office door, providing a convenient getaway when I need a quick break during a particularly stressful day.

Job Description

My company provides desktop publishing and design, research, writing, and editorial services and, to a lesser extent, word processing and transcription services. My niche market is independent consultants (marketing, financial, etc.), for whom I create presentation graphics and adjunct training and handout materials. I also work with various corporate clients on the development of identity systems, collateral materials, and other communication pieces.

Previous Career

I was a patient coordinator in the neuropsychology department of a pediatric hospital. My business began as primarily a medical transcription company, so the contacts I made in this setting were very helpful during my company's start-up phase.

Transferable Skills

Transferable skills would include keyboarding, proficiency with a variety of software programs, creativity and design skills, mastery of core secretarial/administrative skills, management experience (personnel, facilities, operations), communication abilities, and relationship skills.

I would urge anyone interested in getting into this business to be sure that his/her skills are absolutely solid. Be honest in your assessment; if there are areas in which you need improvement, get some additional training before you start looking for clients. Pay attention to the "business" side of the business, and understand the basics of marketing, financial management, and strategic planning.

As to post-entrepreneurial career options, a number of possibilities come to mind. A corporate desktop publishing position is the most obvious. Other possibilities, depending on your relative strengths, might include graphic design, copyediting and proofreading, senior-level executive assistance, office management, or sales and marketing.

Knowledge, Skills, Experience, and/or Education Needed

Proficiency with a variety of software programs is key. Equally important, however, are a creative mind, a keen eye for design, top-notch language skills, the ability to handle multiple and unrelated projects simultaneously, and the ability to communicate effectively with a diverse group of people. In my experience, it's also extremely worthwhile to seek out some education in marketing, business operations, and financial and human resources management for the business end of it all.

On Marketing

Now that I'm fourteen years into the business, I actually do very little in the way of marketing, aside from Yellow Pages advertising and occasional participation in trade shows/business expos. Most of my new business now comes from referrals (from clients and colleagues), and I am very selective about the clients I take on. Word of mouth is certainly my favorite marketing tactic, but I'd have to say that Yellow Pages advertising has been a consistently effective producer.

Hourly Rate

I bill on an hourly basis, using a tiered-rate structure—$35 to $100 per hour—depending upon the type of work I'm doing. I do have some "per project" prices, typically for very straightforward DTP projects, that start at about $300 for a two-page piece and go up from there.

Additional Cost Items

Specialized software, such as Adobe PageMaker (approximately $500), Adobe InDesign (approximately $700), Adobe Illustrator (approximately $400), and Adobe Photoshop (approximately $600). These programs, along with my basic word processing/presentation/spreadsheet suites (i.e., Microsoft Office, Corel Office) are upgraded every two years or so, at a cost of roughly $150 per program.

Recommended Resources
- Association of Business Support Services International, Inc.
- MN-ABSS, a local business support services association that I founded in 1995

ENTERTAINMENT WIRE SERVICE PROVIDER

THE STAR WIRE | www.thestarwire.com
Tonya Parker Morrison, 30 | Lake Charles, Louisiana | Ages of Children: 5, 6

"I clean up after the kids only after they're in bed. If I clean up after them all day, that would mean I'd clean up after them ALLLLL DAY!"

Office Oasis
Living room.

Job Description
I own an entertainment wire service that provides reviews, interviews, and other info to newspapers, magazines, and e-zines all over the world. We are like the Associated Press, but with only entertainment-related stories.

Previous Career
I worked mostly as a secretary or personal assistant. Watching my bosses multi-task helped me learn about prioritizing my day and also helped my

organizational skills. Maintaining successful relationships with clients also helped me transfer that skill to my own business. I am a diplomat, boss, employee, teacher, student, and parent all rolled into one.

Transferable Skills

Multi-tasking! I used to curse bosses who wanted me to answer the phone, plan an awards banquet, type an urgent letter, and take dictation all at the same time. Now, I use that experience juggling a hundred balls in the air every single day.

Knowledge, Skills, Experience, and/or Education Needed

Communication skills are the biggest asset in my industry. You have to be able to convince publishers or editors to spend extra money to use you when they already have a full staff; convince a PR firm that its clients *need* you to interview them to help their career; convince celebrities that you can give them proper exposure; and convince yourself that you can do all that and more with your hands tied behind your back. I use my journalism background—including marketing, accounting, debating, acting, and creative writing—on a daily basis. If you're not using your right and left brain simultaneously, you're dead in this business. Having a writer's creativity won't help you much when it's time to meet deadlines and pay the bills.

Industry Insight

Unfortunately, the market isn't great in this line of work. The Associated Press has been around a *long* time and many editors are terrified at the prospect of making enemies of AP by using another source. Sometimes, I have to be just another freelancer or I wouldn't get my foot in the door.

On Marketing

Marketing is everything! I am constantly querying editors from magazines and newspapers around the globe, as well as attending every entertainment activity I can physically get to. Networking is the most effective tool in my business, as well as reliability. If you can't sell yourself, then you certainly can't sell your product.

A Day in the Life

Monday through Friday

6:00 A.M.	Get kids ready for school
7:00 A.M.	Walk kids to bus
8:00–11:00 A.M.	Return phone calls, check status on upcoming stories and interview requests, open e-mail and snail mail
11:00 A.M.–?	Various multimedia interviews scheduled. Conduct interviews via phone, label tapes for later dictation
11:30 A.M.	Husband returns home; run various errands (grocery shop, pay bills, get supplies, etc.)
Noon	Breakfast/lunch at desk while surfing Pollstar for upcoming concerts to ensure I have offered interviews to everyone within an artists' upcoming tour itinerary
1:00 P.M.	E-mail potential and existing clients offering copy
2:00 P.M.	Work out at the gym for one hour
3:00–4:00 P.M.	Get kids off the bus, get afternoon snack together, catch up on what they did that day in school, free play time
4:00 P.M.	Start preparing dinner and continue interviewing
5:00 P.M.	Enter day's interviews from cassette into computer
6:00 P.M.	Dinner with the family
7:00 P.M.	Go review movie
9:00 or 9:30 P.M.	Come home, put kids to bed; read manuscripts, cookbooks, novels, whatever is necessary; watch screeners or films on people to be interviewed the next day
10:00 P.M.	Continue typing in that day's interviews, as well as any reviews necessary; begin washing uniforms for next day if necessary, as well as rest of laundry; clean up
12:00 A.M.	Make sure all research for next day's interviews is completed, as well as list of questions; e-mail for status on story queries; get organized for interviews with new tapes, batteries, etc.; get kids' stuff together for school: pack lunches, refrigerate; lay out clothes (find shoes and socks!); make sure I've read all notes necessary and send any supplies and/or money needed
2:00 A.M.	Finish up work, fold and put away laundry, get to bed

Top Revenue Streams and Pricing Structure
- Features: $100–$200, depending on difficulty of interview. Assigned interviews cost the same as those I already have on hand.
- Entertainment news reporting (infrequent, usually on-line): $100 per subject
- Movie/CD/Book/Other reviews: $50–$75

Hourly Rate
Varies with the hours of research, interviewing, and story creation involved. Also, sometimes it takes me weeks of trading phone calls, e-mails, and faxes to land a particularly difficult interview, so I could never charge by the hour!

Additional Cost Items
My best friend is my tape recorder—a Sony handheld model—with a microphone jack. Without that, I couldn't tape my interviews with any sort of sound quality. You have to have those taped conversations—all of them—in case anyone ever regrets a quote and claims it never happened.

Recommended Resources
I've owned, at one time or another, every thesaurus, encyclopedia (especially Encarta), dictionary, and writing manual out there. The AP Handbook helps with technical aspects of writing, but devouring magazines like *Writer's Digest* also help. Financial literature (even if it makes you yawn) is invaluable when you cannot yet afford to hire an accountant.

GRAPHIC DESIGN/HIGH END PRESENTATION

SUSAN THESING GRAPHIC DESIGN | susan@onol.com
Susan Thesing | Decatur, Georgia | Ages of Children: 5, 6

> *"My husband and I are foster parents and so we have children who have unusually high needs. My schedule fluctuates wildly; work flows around my childcare commitments but I'm fortunate to have a husband who takes up the childcare slack if I am slammed with work."*

Office Oasis

A spare bedroom that I share with my husband (who works in a traditional office but sometimes works at home in the evening).

Job Description

I'm a freelance graphic designer who has carved out a niche in high-end presentation design. I create custom illustrations, graphics, or business models for my clients.

Previous Career

As a research architect for the VA Hospital, my responsibilities included various graphic design duties such as creating research presentations and editing a newsletter. I cut back to part time, which is easy to do with the federal government, and started picking up graphic design jobs from local agencies. When I felt I had the hang of the off/on schedule of a freelancer, I left my government job completely. It was a direct transfer of skills, but the change in scheduling was challenging.

Transferable Skills

This is a pretty straightforward transition out of and back into the work force. I would reenter the work force as a senior graphic designer, and with my experience, would hopefully be qualified for a position as an art director soon after returning to an office.

If I were moving into self-employment now, I would send a creative, eye-catching résumé and leave behind book (or stand out means of conveying design skills) to all of the creative firms in the area and other businesses that outsource creative work. People with a limited creative background in larger cities can look for placement agencies that might be able to place them in lower level jobs while allowing them to train on software at the agency.

Knowledge, Skills, Experience, and/or Education Needed

Typically, this career requires an art/design/creative background. Most designers have a two- or four-year degree in graphic design or art, but I have a B.S. with a major in architecture and an M.S. in environmental design research. The art and design skills transfer pretty easily from my architecture degree.

This profession also requires strong knowledge of graphic design software, depending on the specialty. Traditional print designers use Photoshop, Illustrator or Freehand, and Quark XPress. I also use Powerpoint as the interface for my end user. Web designers have their own software, including Flash. I taught myself to use the software that I need and pre-press skills (how to prep documents to send to an outside print vendor) while at my job as a research architect. One agency I work with also allowed me to come in and train on their software, which was a huge help. I am currently teaching myself Flash because it interests me, will broaden my marketability, and has a higher pay scale than the work I currently do.

People skills and organizational/time-management skills are also very important in this profession. Clients are often on a very tight schedule and meeting deadlines, managing client expectations, and maintaining calm with demanding clients is essential for repeat business and referrals.

In my specialty of business presentations, art, and statistical models, my research background serves me very well. I am able to help clients organize a logical argument and sort through complex data to help determine what needs to be presented and how, depending on the intended audience.

Industry Insight

This industry is very susceptible to the ups and downs of the economy. I lost a significant portion of my clients in the fall of 2000 when many dot-coms and tech companies went under (75 percent of my business was in this sector). I gradually rebuilt but had another setback after 9/11 since so much of my business is presentations/corporate events. When business people don't fly, they don't need presentations. Several prospective projects disappeared. I know other freelance graphic designers who have also had a difficult time the last eighteen months.

On Marketing

Until eighteen months ago, work just came to me. I had more than I wanted, and I didn't do any marketing at all. Much of this work came through a graphic design placement agency. Since my business slowed down, I have contacted two other placement agencies (both of which have since gone out of business) and sent leave-behind books (mini-portfolios that are a design piece on their own) to several key clients. Neither of these produced much work.

Things have been so slow lately that I have begun to pull together a design for a web page that I hope to put up soon, am pulling together a sample CD to send to production companies, and am learning a new skill (Flash) that I can market through the graphic design placement agency that has sent work to me for the last seven years. I have a good relationship with them and I am confident they will make an effort to find work for me once I have created a few samples which will provide the experience I need to keep learning.

Word of mouth has been good to me. Many past contacts who were laid off from dot-coms have contacted me after finding new jobs, and I also get referrals from people who I have worked with in the past. This hasn't produced the steady stream of work I had prior to fall 2000, though, in part because many of my old contacts are not allowed to outsource.

Marketing myself is the hardest part of this job. I am not good at it, and I don't like it. Things have gotten so very slow though that I find I have to get over it and get moving!

Top Revenue Streams

My greatest income over the last year is from Aquent—a placement agency that sends work my way when they get leads on work that can be done from a home office. It is very difficult to quantify top revenue streams because the last two years have been so tumultuous. Two other agencies that I have worked with have gone out of business. Many clients have also gone out of business or experienced severe cutbacks. I also find that when a contact is laid off or leaves for a new job, I often lose that client. My contacts often remain in touch with me, but I have found these contacts often get new jobs at firms with in-house design departments and, in such tight times, can't get approval to outsource work.

Hourly Rates

- Work from agencies, $25/hour (taxes taken out/participation in 401k with some matching)
- Freelance presentation, $50/hour
- Freelance design (logos, art), $60 hour
- When I start accepting Flash work through agencies, I will earn $30 to $35/hour. Once I am confident enough to seek freelance work in this area on my own, I will charge $70 to $75 per hour.

Additional Cost Items

- Graphic design software depending on specialty (these prices are from the product web sites; it's possible to find them cheaper at other e-stores, and some can be bundled for greater savings).
  - Quark, $870
  - Photoshop, $550
  - Illustrator/Freehand, $400 each (only need one, though having both is good)
- Other useful software includes Adobe Acrobat (writer and distiller), Powerpoint, and Adobe Streamline.
- Fonts and clipart/stock photos are important too. Free stuff can be found on the web with some work.

Recommended Resources

- Aquent, www.aquent.com, 877-227-8368

GRAPHIC DESIGN/NEWSLETTERS

CREATIVE COMMUNIQUE, INC. | www.creativecommunique.com
Sharon-Kaye Hector, 35 | Silver Spring, Maryland | Ages of Children:
15 months, 3 years

"Being an EP allows me to be the parent that I am and still have something that is mine."

Job Description

I design newsletters, logos, brochures, mailers, and web pages—both static and dynamic web pages, including flash designs.

Previous Career

Programmer/system administrator for Unix and web servers.

Transferable Skills

From project specifications to code development to implementation while documenting it along the way, my programming skills are the most transferable hard skill. The most transferable soft skill is time management, and if you have spent any time at home attempting to do work for clients as a contractor, independent professional, or freelancer, knowing how to multi-task is a must. The ability to do several things at once, prioritize your projects, be a self-starter and motivate yourself are an absolute must. Personally I view everything as mini-projects, including my children. This way I am able to handle whatever is thrown at me. I am also a quick study. I learn things quickly, and I use this to my advantage.

Knowledge, Skills, Experience, and/or Education Needed

My educational background is in technology; I have a B.S. in computer systems engineering and a M.S. in computer science. My skill set is database and programming for system applications, and my prior work experience includes designing databases and installing servers. While acting in this role, I also started up and designed an employee newsletter, just to keep everyone abreast of what was happening at the workplace. Around the same time, in my private life, I designed and assisted in editing (and still do) a local church newsletter. All this sparked my interest in design. I then branched out and sought information on the whole process of design—the "artsy" stuff—this just fascinates me. My first "real" design job came when I was asked to redesign a logo for a client who wanted her logo to be more professional. She loved it, and so did I. Since then I have designed newsletters, brochures, catalogs, web sites, and business cards.

Industry Insight

This industry is constantly changing—the nature of the beast requires that you appeal to human nature, so how people perceive things drives the changes that are seen. I have found that if something is well liked, though it may be revamped, the basic concept remains the same. For anyone interested in this arena, my route may not be the best, since it's so important to have a portfolio so people can see past work. Taking a class or two on the topic where you get an opportunity to design something is a definite plus. If you wish to go for the degree, by all means do; there is something to be said about understanding the reasoning and the history of the industry and the concepts of design. If this is not an option, then do things like design invitations, newsletters, flyers, logos, and such for friends and family. The nice thing is that if they really like what they see, you will get paid. Do whatever it takes to gather the experience and develop that portfolio. Nothing speaks volumes more than a good portfolio, even if it contains only five good things.

On Marketing

Primarily word of mouth. Whenever I can speak about what I do, I take that opportunity. You would be surprised by the number of people who say, "You do that? Great! Do you have a card?" I have found marketing to be a necessary pain to endure. You need to get comfortable with talking about yourself and always have a stack of business cards on hand.

Top Revenue Streams

- Newsletter design
- Brochure design
- Web site design

Pricing Structure

- Newsletters/layout, $25 per hour
- Graphic design, $50 per hour
- Web design, $75 per page (sometimes I just charge a flat fee depending on the size of the project)
- Programming (JavaScript, CGI, PHP, etc.), $50 per hour
- Business cards, $200 flat fee

Additional Cost Items

Flash, Dreamweaver, Fireworks, Adobe, Freehand, and more, for a total cost of about $1,500.

Recommended Resources

GETTING STARTED

- www.hbwm.com
- www.creativebusiness.com
- www.bizymoms.com
- www.inc.com
- www.en-parent.com

BOOKS

- *Mompreneurs*
- *Marketing Online for Dummies*

HELP AUTHOR/DEVELOPER

JTF ASSOCIATES, INC. | www.helpstuff.com
Char James-Tanny, 44 | Lynn, Massachusetts | Age of Child: 3

> *"I met my husband Jim after I was an E but before I was a P. I was finishing a Help file the day before I delivered, but then I didn't do any training or traveling for three months after my son was born. I know it's not politically correct to place a child in day care, but our son is there only until 3:30, and it's important for both him and us. He gets to socialize, and he loves to read, sing, play music, march, build castles, and play house and with trucks, while I get a guaranteed six hours of work five days a week, around the entire calendar year (not including sick and vacation days, of course!)."*

Office Oasis

My office was probably intended as a nursery or child's playroom. It's an extra room at the side of the house, accessible through a doorway in the dining room. My husband ran wires into the room so that I can listen to the radio while I work. It's not very big—8x10, maybe—and it holds two desks, six computers, three printers, and bookshelves.

Job Description

As a Help author (or developer), I teach folks how to create on-line Help files and I develop on-line Help files for clients as well. I have written two books on Help authoring and speak frequently at on-line technical communication conferences.

Previous Career

I started in 1981 as a software technical writer. After going back to school to get my bachelor's, I started consulting but hated the commute. In 1991, I chose to only work from home.

Transferable Skills

Skills borrowed from the traditional work force would be any tools, as it gets easier to learn new tools if you already know at least one. As for returning, I would point to:

- Discipline—you'll get much more work out of EPs returning to the work force, as they are used to focusing and getting the job done.
- Research—we have to buy our own hardware and software and get answers to questions.
- Work ethic—OK, this is a generalization, but in spite of the fact that most people think that I sit around all day eating bon-bons and watching TV, I actually work for the better part of fourteen hours a day. And so do the other home-based folks I know.

Knowledge, Skills, Experience, and/or Education Needed

I had been creating user documentation for ten years when I made the move to on-line documentation and Help. I still create hard copy but on a limited basis. Mostly I create on-line Help files for all platforms (Windows, Mac, and UNIX). I have a journalism degree, although it is possible to get a technical communication degree or certificate. Writing, editing, and usability standards are necessary. Programming isn't a requirement, although it doesn't hurt to have.

Industry Insight

Right now, this line of work continues to prosper. Companies realize the benefits that technical writers bring to their product. We write user documentation, specs, read-me files, and anything else that needs a wordsmith. Most folks are aware that all products come with instructions (from toasters to word-processing software to the space shuttle). You'll find tech writers at software companies (like Macromedia and Microsoft), hardware companies (Toshiba), and also at companies like Gallo (the winery) and Ben & Jerry's (ice cream).

If you want to break into this field, make sure you have good writing and editing skills; are self-motivated; can meet deadlines; can learn software quickly (especially the tools we use for development, such as RoboHelp Office, ForeHelp, Doc-To-Help, or AuthorIT). It helps if you know Microsoft Word, but that depends on the tool that you'll be using.

On Marketing

I only started actively marketing two years ago. Before then, I handed out business cards and answered questions in on-line forums. In early 1998, I started my web site, and later that year I started exhibiting at conferences. Word of mouth is actually my most effective marketing method. Of course, it's also the least reliable. One year, I made candy bar wrappers and handed them out at a conference . . . and never got one response, which qualifies it as the least effective. Now, I rely on the web site, exhibitions, and my conference sessions to let folks know who I am and what I do.

Top Revenue Streams

Writing, editing, Help development, document conversion (hard copy to online), and speaking at conferences.

Pricing Structure

According to the WinWriters Salary Survey, consultants in the top 10 percent make between $60 and $160 an hour. I'm somewhere in this percentile. I use an hourly rate for projects that can't be nailed down (for example, software in development). I use a flat rate for projects where I can comfortably scope the requirements.

Additional Cost Items

My PC is a 900MHz with 512M Ram. Some of the tools listed below use a lot of processing power! Also, we have DSL (through iNYC), which expedites delivery of Help files and web sites. I also have a Toshiba laptop and a Macintosh iMac (for testing purposes). The prices below are for new licenses and, if possible, for electronic delivery. Upgrades are less. Many products listed here have trial versions available.

- A laptop for traveling and presenting ($1900).
- Microsoft Office
- Adobe Acrobat to create PDF files ($299)
- Help development tools (RoboHelp Office, $899; FAR, $38; AuthorIT, $199)
- HTML tools (HomeSite, $89; Dreamweaver, $299)
- Graphics (Adobe Illustrator, $399; Paint Shop Pro, $99)
- Other tools (HTML Tidy, Xenu Link Sleuth, and so on, FREE)
- Subscription to *ArtToday* (clipart and graphics)

Recommended Resources

- Training: Provided through Solutions. I took classes on editing, indexing, design—pretty much anything they offered.

- Books: *Designing Windows 95 Help, Developing Online Help for Windows,* skills books for HTML, Dynamic HTML, JavaScript, and graphics
- On-line: Web sites, such as WinWriters, WebReference, and STC. Mailing lists, such as HATT and ForeHelp on Yahoo (these can be customized so that I can read off the web site, get individual e-mails, or get one e-mail that includes everything).
- Subscriptions to newsletters: *WebReference, HTML Goodies, Gibson Research*
- Conferences: WinWriters, Help Technology Conference, STC
- Tool specific: RoboHelp Office, ForeHelp, AuthorIT, Doc-To-Help, FAR, and more

---

HIGH-TECH CRIME INVESTIGATOR

Dana Brown | Florence, South Carolina | Ages of Children: 6, 12

"When I have a family emergency it always comes first, although this has been difficult at times. If I receive a page about a missing child who was taken as a result of a computer pedophile, I know that if I don't start my computer investigation soon the child may not be recovered. But my own children need me too. This is tough."

Job Description
I own a high-tech crime investigations firm with sixty-four employees. We catch computer hackers and pedophiles, and we work for large companies and banks.

Previous Career
Technical writer.

Transferable Skills
General computer skills and an analytical mind.

Knowledge, Skills, Experience, and/or Education Needed
Obtaining MCSE (Microsoft Certified System Engineer) is very helpful. Our work is done using Unix so familiarity with Unix is a must. Certification as a high-tech crime investigator is required and can be obtained

from the HTCN (high-tech crime network). Knowledge of Omniquad Desktop Surveillance and Digital Detective is also a must.

A Day in the Life

I wake up to a page or when I feel like getting up. I put on a robe, juice a drink, and then step into my office oasis with its fountain bubbling and plants all around. After a few minutes of enjoyable peacefulness, I start perusing through my current client list and the day just takes off from there. Since my company is a twenty-four-hour operation, we encounter the same stresses as a surgeon and others on-call 24/7.

Industry Insight

This field is very new and will continue to grow over the next several years. To break into this field, obtain a degree in computer science.

On Marketing

I do not market or advertise my company.

Pricing Structure

$200/hour.

Additional Cost Items

A server is necessary and ranges from a few hundred to several thousand dollars. You will also need to obtain a device that will allow you to quickly and accurately make several copies of a computer's hard drive.

Recommended Resources

- The High-Tech Crime Network
- HTCIA (High-Tech Crime Investigation Association)

ILLUSTRATOR (TRADITIONAL)

PAMELA STUART STUDIOS | wstuart2@san.rr.com
Pamela Stuart, 43 | San Diego, California | Ages of Children: 14, 19

"When my husband and I are on our walks, especially at the beach, we're really having a business conference! Talking out what we'll work on that day or who we'll call or brainstorming and thinking creatively. We aren't workaholics—we make sure we have time for fun."

Office Oasis
A 20' × 20' family room on the front of our house, which has its own entrance from the street (great for client visits!).

Job Description
I produce illustrations and product designs for the gift, craft, and educational markets.

Previous Career
Worked full-time for a greeting card company.

Transferable Skills
At the greeting card company, I learned about marketing and designing for specific markets. I also taught myself how to analyze sales reports and determine what would sell well.

Knowledge, Skills, Experience, and/or Education Needed
If you're an artist, you should learn to use computer programs such as Quark, Photoshop, and Illustrator. You can take classes at a local junior college (they are intensive programs but needed to work in this competitive industry). Don't be afraid to try them. They may seem intimidating when you first start, but once you start learning you won't want to go back to traditional illustration. Photoshop has a tool that you can actually airbrush with—better than a traditional one—you won't believe how cool it is!!!

Industry Insight
I have worked in many companies, and every time I always left because of people being mismanaged. I always worked hard but never made the

money I thought I deserved. I know lots of people feel that way. I don't feel like artists are treated fairly. Artists don't unite to be a strong force, so they get used and used up. I plan to join an illustrators guild and start an illustrator's critique forum in the near future. I enjoy sharing my talents with the community, and I feel that more people should try to give at least four hours a month back to their community. Think what a different world it would be if that happened!

A Day in the Life

Our days fluctuate depending on the projects we're working on . . . especially when we do murals on site. We then work from 9:00 A.M. to 5:00-ish and are not home when our fourteen-year-old gets home. She lets herself in, and our college-age daughter can usually be home for her. If not, she is comfortable to stay alone for a couple hours. Many times we also work on the weekend too. It is not a drudge and the days sometimes meld into each other. We have to work on jobs we get, because we never know when the next project will come in. We are looking forward to the day when we can work on artwork anywhere in the world, via computers, fax, and e-mail.

On Marketing

I create files on the computer and e-mail them to possible employers, which saves money on mailing and printing. I also attend trade shows as a designer and approach companies who might be able to use my work. It's been slow in coming.

Top Revenue Streams

Murals in homes and businesses are very hot in our area, but you do need an art background and talent for this.

Pricing Structure

For murals, we now can charge $500 a day; other industry work such as freelance illustration depends on the job.

Additional Cost Items

Software programs such as Photoshop and Quark are very expensive ($500–$800), but worth the investment.

Recommended Resources

Artists and Graphic Designers Market—essential in learning the free-lance market. It lists companies who work with freelancers and give guidelines on what to charge and how to submit artwork. It's the best!!

IT BUSINESS/MARKETING PLAN DEVELOPER

Q COMMUNICATIONS | ssegars@mindspring.com
Susan Segars, 39 | Roswell, Georgia | Age of Child: 7

> *"I am a much more relaxed person these days. I smile more. I don't miss endless meetings and political struggles at all. I can really be a parent and keep up with my personal life (bills, finances, cleaning) for once in my life."*

Office Oasis
A loft overlooking the family room.

Job Description
I create business and marketing plans for new IT businesses who are seeking venture capital or angel money. I also create brochures and web pages (copywriting and graphic design work).

Previous Career
Vice president of marketing, with ten years in the ad agency business, then another seven in corporate marketing. All of the corporations that I worked for were relatively new IT-related companies.

Transferable Skills
A top skill to borrow from the traditional work force is the ability to maintain a schedule with goals/benchmarks for progress. A top skill developed as an EP that can transfer to the nine-to-five world is improved judgment based on the knowledge that a paycheck isn't just going to appear every two weeks. Someone who has been on their own has more empathy for company management's need to generate revenue/profits and for overall accountability for actions. Working in this entrepreneurial environment has made me particularly qualified for what I do. I fi-

nally made the leap about five years after I decided to eventually go out on my own. My key to success has been that I never burned bridges with past employers, who are now my primary source of clients.

Knowledge, Skills, Experience, and/or Education Needed
Primary skill needed: you must be a renaissance person. I have to be very proficient on several software applications. My clients are almost all Internet-related, so on top of that I also have to be abreast of historical, current, and future IT trends, as well as financial market trends (mostly venture capital). Because creating high-quality documents is part of my job description, I have to be fluent in desktop publishing packages and graphic programs (PageMaker, InDesign, Photoshop, etc.). I also have to create financial models with Excel, which requires an understanding of the principles of finance/revenue and cost projections. I do rely on my journalism degree for my writing skills, but beyond that my skills come from years in marketing and management and being exposed to strategic planning.

Industry Insight
I depend on start-up companies for my business. With the economy slowing and venture capital investments dropping off, it would seem to be a concern although that hasn't been the case as of this writing. I represent a less expensive alternative for my clients (vs. incubators and ad agencies), so I seem to be benefiting from the current economic climate. I would advise anyone wishing to get into this line of work to get experience in strategic planning, business writing, and presentation. The best place to get that quickly would be to work as an associate for a company that does business/strategic plans, or to work in a top-notch ad agency.

On Marketing
The most effective has been maintaining and fostering relationships with past business associates, while looking for opportunities to contact people who refer business whenever I see an excuse, such as an article that they might be interested in. This often leads to a call with some referred business within thirty days. Since it takes a minimum of thirty days to close new business, I have to keep the pipeline active. Least effective? None, so far. Other comments: I could (haven't yet) enhance

my efforts with the addition of a web page for potential clients to get access to my portfolio. I also plan to extend my networking to local organizations related to the venture capital industry.

A Day in the Life	
7:30 A.M.	Walk son to school
8:00–8:30 A.M.	Run or read the paper, eat breakfast
8:30 A.M.–2:00 P.M.	Work
2:00 P.M.	Walk to school to pick my son up
2:30–7:30 P.M.	Various activities with my son
8:00–11:00 P.M.	Work, surf the net, read, or watch TV

Top Revenue Streams

Top revenue generator: business plan creation. Second: marketing services. As an aside, my strategic planning/overall experience allows me to become a trusted adviser who can charge more than twice what I could if I only had good writing/design skills ($100+/hour vs. $40/hour).

Pricing Structure

Business Plans: $90–$110 per hour. Some flat fees, depending on the project. A complete business plan is usually about $7,000 to $10,000, and it takes one to two months to complete.

Marketing Services: $85 per hour for copywriting and web content, design/layout, logo work, etc.

Additional Cost Items

Beyond the basics, I have to spend more on a computer, since I need a really fast Macintosh (vs. PC) for graphic work (about $2,700), plus graphic software, which is about $5,000 to start with, plus upgrades.

Recommended Resources

I've gotten business from Guru.com, a great web site that matches companies with providers. Their support services (medical insurance providers, tax advice, etc.) have been helpful. Also, I have a friend who has been indispensable in managing my technical setup (I call him my system administrator). Not worrying about computer problems has helped a lot!

MARKETING COMMUNICATIONS/MULTIMEDIA SPECIALIST

DIGITAL XESTO | www.digitalxesto.com
Eileen Tuttle, 36 | Plain City, Ohio | Ages of Children: 2½ years and 6 months

"My goal is that my children will never spend more conscious hours in a day care than with me."

Office Oasis
Spare bedroom.

Job Description
I'm employed full-time in the electric utility industry as a marketing/communications specialist. I'm also two years into owning my own home-based multimedia production/marketing company, with marketing/communications as the core service and multimedia productions as our niche. It was clear to me, going into business ownership, that we needed to distinguish ourselves from the competition. My husband's interest in digital video editing fit so nicely with my experience with computers and marketing.

Previous Career
My work experience has almost always involved both sales and marketing as well as computers. I began working from home part-time during my first maternity leave from a real estate and construction company, where I was office manager and marketing coordinator. When my employer reorganized the office during my leave, my job was eliminated. That's when we officially launched our company. However, we've really struggled with putting our personal resources into its success or failure. Launching a business such as ours requires smart financial planning and resources, and we jumped into it not by plan but by default. As a result, the first eight months were very rocky. When my primary contract fell through (my ex-employer) and my primary subcontract relationship didn't result in enough business, we didn't have the resources to go it on our own. Since we already had incurred substantial debt, my husband and I decided the best way to manage it was to put growth plans for our business on hold while we shored up our financial situation. I took a full-time job.

Transferable Skills

I couldn't be an EP without my experience with business decision-making and politics in the traditional work force. It allows me the insight to better position my small business and sell my skills. It also helps me keep the rejections in perspective, as politics and business timelines control so many decisions. As an EP, it's critical to develop time-management and self-discipline skills. These have really paid off for me in the nine-to-five world. Since I've launched my business, I am more focused on the job, accomplishing more in less time, which means I work an eight-hour day in the office, not nine or ten.

Knowledge, Skills, Experience, and/or Education Needed

Multimedia production is a very technical field. Computer experience with a variety of graphics programs is essential. Artistic talent is important too. Experience developing messages for a wide variety of audiences gets me "in the door." And salesmanship is necessary, so you can get the job!

Industry Insight

The personal computer has brought not only an influx of readily available technology to the home but has created interest in those who have no time to deal with it. Electronic media has achieved a great deal of recognition, but not everyone is savvy enough to create it or plan for it. Those people who can navigate the electronic world for others stand to gain in the future marketplace. I truly believe that those who can bring professionalism and talent to the world of multimedia communications will succeed.

On Marketing

Absolutely the best form of marketing for us has been word of mouth. Who do we know? Who do they know? My husband and I joke that we should have saved receipts for the local coffee shop over the past two years because we've derived more business leads from hanging around talking with people there than almost any other source!

Top Revenue Streams
- Sports teams—highlight film editing

A Day in the Life

Working full-time *and* running a business is hectic. Our sons leave for day care (grandma's house) with Dad before 7:00. This gives me just enough time to finish up odds and ends for our business before I head to the office for my full-time day. Lunch hour is never lunch: it's generally spent on Digital Xesto issues.

Evenings working on projects are usually traded between my husband and me, depending on what deadlines we face. While one of us concentrates, the other corrals the boys and does the chores, sometimes with all of us in the office together.

The real test is the weekends, when the bulk of our sports video business is done. We rarely work together on a project, so that one of us is available for the kids. And virtually every weekend includes at least two blocks of time when one of us is involved in a project.

- Small businesses—web, commercials, presentations, printed materials
- Personal video/photo collections—editing, copying

Pricing Structure
Editing or other technical time is $65 to $75 per hour. We frequently discount our rates to about $50 per hour for large projects and repeat clients. The goodwill it buys has helped a lot in our word-of-mouth promotion.

Additional Cost Items
We invested carefully in a non-linear video editing computer suite and a first-rate pro-sumer video camera with lights and mics to the tune of about $15,000. I wouldn't recommend doing it any other way.

Recommended Resources
The variety of small business web sites has not only helped with resources but given me insight on how I can sell my services to other small business owners.

RECORDING ENGINEER

MIRABOO GROUP | www.miraboo.com
Mark Nathan, 29 | Woodland Hills, California | Ages of Children: 3.5, 9 months

> *"My home studio is a palace for Mira to play and gain interest in piano, music, and creativity. She loves singing into a microphone that I have just assigned to her only, even with it unplugged. She thinks she's Annie. When she's performing, I also think she's Annie."*

Office Oasis

My office is in the back of the house, and I control who comes in and out by placing a baby gate in the doorway. This allows me to keep a part of what's going on at the same time keeping a distance so I can continue working. Mira loves to walk up to the gate for the occasional chat. It's a fun getaway from some of the potential work chaos.

Job Description

Audio recording, mixing, and editing for radio, TV, and film (the real talent behind the scenes of music making!). My work also includes video and motion graphics for DVD and film.

Previous Career

Have always been an entrepreneur.

A Day in the Life

I work seven days a week. My nights start around 7:30 P.M., after my kids go to bed. I can continue up until 2:00–3:00 A.M., which is when I usually take a baby shift and feed Matthew, which gives my wife some time to sleep. I then sleep, and I am up by 9:00 A.M., usually with the help of Mira (my girl). My wife gives me a little more time to sleep. I get up, hang for a few moments with my family, and then head straight to the office to check the day's e-mail. I then start the phone calls and prepare for a labor-intensive workday. This schedule is pretty standard Monday through Sunday, although I do spend less time working during the days Saturday and Sunday (while still working through the nights).

Transferable Skills

My profession doesn't lend itself to traditional work. I have worked for myself 85 percent of my life and opted to stay an EP *because* of my dislike of a traditional work force. I've been spoiled and can never be happy in the herd of sheep that do the daily nine-to-five grind. My ability to function comes from my gut instinct, people skills, and ability to reason logically. My decisions are always that, mine! That said, if I did ever choose to follow the route with a traditional nine-to-five job, skills as a business owner would definitely assist me in staying strong and honest as an employee.

Knowledge, Skills, Experience, and/or Education Needed

The technical side of the music industry is a trade skill—similar to becoming an electrician, contractor, or plumber. Schools are available but will not prepare a young individual to the *harsh* reality of poverty while attempting to create a name for yourself. Luckily, I found a mentor who opened his heart to me. I also come from a family of musicians—I'm a piano player with a good ear for pitch. This helps me navigate through my peers who just can't find the beat. If you have an ear for music, *then* the next step is knowing the technology, including hardware and software.

Industry Insight

The music/recording industry is evolving dramatically. In the last five to eight years, recording and technology school programs have popped up all over the country. Probably 99 percent of them produce lousy candidates for what I do, while the 1 percent with any real talent all "jock for position." Record labels are paying less and late (so be prepared). You *must* wrap your talents up as a package in order to sell. If you can provide an entire solution and maintain solid relationships with the producers of the music, you can have a very prosperous run of luck and work. Be prepared to have others try knocking you off your pedestal, but no matter how mad you get *don't burn bridges*. Everyone in LA/NYC/Nashville talks, and one episode can—and will—affect your ability to continue working.

On Marketing

Word of mouth and my name have been good enough for some time to keep work flowing. Trade shows are semi-important for exposure. Selling myself as a self-contained package with recording gear and equipment helps to validate my rates. I keep my options open to opportunities when they appear. My most effective marketing is how I treat my active client base. Loyalty is hard to come by here in Los Angeles!! Oh yeah — and remember, if you do 'spec' work, don't 'spec' to get paid!

Top Revenue Streams
- Protools editing and recording
- Mixing
- Video art and motion graphics
- Technical consulting for audio and recording
- IT specialty in the downtime

Pricing Structure
- Hourly rates start at $85
- Day rates for engineering, $750 (always a twelve-hour block)
- Day rates for mixing, $1500 (always a twelve-hour block)
- Day rates for protools in home, $750
- Materials charge (CDs, DATs, tape backups, DVD-R, Mini DV)
- Do not charge for travel (if any)
- Do not charge for time on technical support phone calls by clients

Additional Cost Items
My space is loaded with three different computers with three others hidden in the background. Costs to have a basic setup will start at $15,000. Be prepared for the price tag to go up as you invest in your future. Commercial recording studios have millions in gear alone. Most that are interested in this industry will quickly learn on their own what they need to compete.

Recommended Resources
Trade magazines helped my awareness. Technical books have helped me *privately* find answers to questions I didn't know.

RÉSUMÉ WRITER/JOB SEARCH COACH

ABSOLUTE ADVANTAGE | www.janmelnik.com
Jan Melnik, 44 | Durham, Connecticut | Ages of Children: 13, 13, 11

> *"I think the key to being a successful and happy EP is ensuring that you love, really love, and excel at the work you select to do. I know that's why I have such a high degree of job satisfaction . . . which translates into life satisfaction!"*

Office Oasis
A dedicated office with separate entrance adjacent to our home, which has immediate access to the kitchen.

Job Description
As a career management expert, I write résumés and coach my clients during their job search.

Previous Career
I worked for several Fortune 500 corporations, moving from administrative to line management.

Transferable Skills
A significant amount of human resources and direct hiring experience, which directly parlayed into current work.

Knowledge, Skills, Experience, and/or Education Needed
Proficiency in MS Word and Excel, Adobe PageMaker, and Quicken/QuickBooks helps, plus a strong user-friendly relationship to the Internet, with the ability to quickly (hence, profitably!) post résumés on-line, convert files to ASCII text, download and upload client files, and more.

Industry Insight
As the economy has begun to tighten up a bit with the continuing "bottoming-out" of the stock market and creeping interest rates, employment opportunities are not quite as prevalent as they had been for the past three to four years during a boom economy. Therefore candidates need every advantage in effectively marketing themselves—something a

career-management professional can greatly assist with. For aspiring EPs to break into this field successfully, they need a strong editorial background, good HR/interviewing skills, excellent listening skills, and an ability to understand/draw parallels between skills and employment requirements.

On Marketing

Yellow Page ads consistently have been the top source of first-time clients; thereafter, it's heavily referral/repeat clientele. The second largest source of first-time clients is a nationally syndicated radio program, MoneyWatch, for which I am the career and work-at-home expert.

Top Revenue Streams

- Résumé writing
- Job search coaching
- Business plan writing
- Marketing

Pricing Structure

Ranges from $52/hour for office support/word processing to $140/hour for all editorial, career counseling, consultations, and résumé-writing services.

Additional Cost Items

Memberships in professional associations in my industry have been important, particularly with the career search coaching/résumé-writing services (this includes membership in Career Masters Institute, the Professional Association of Résumé Writers, and the National Résumé Writers Association); complementing this is attendance at annual conventions. Totaled, the cost for memberships/conference attendance/professional certification testing exceeds $3,000 per year.

Recommended Resources

- Books by Paul and Sarah Edwards
- Jay Conrad Levinson's Guerrilla Marketing series
- Subscriptions to *Entrepreneur* and *Inc*.

SELF-PUBLISHER/CALENDARS

CALENDAR SYSTEMS, U.S.A | www.thefamilyorganizer.com
Amy Knapp, 36 | Kalamazoo, MI | Ages of Children: 6, 8

Home Biz and Mission Statement

Calendar Systems, U.S.A., is a small publisher that specializes in functional calendars. The Family Organizer is a unique calendar that sets time management strategies used in business into a format design for the home. Being a publisher entails much more that just printing a book.

Bidding out the project and selecting a printer was the easy part. I also had to establish distribution channels in both the book and gift markets as well as develop a marketing plan to sell the calendars once they are on the store shelves.

Most Popular Services and Pricing Fees

The Family Organizer is a spiral-bound desk calendar. Each week includes appointment scheduling, to-do list, perforated grocery list, menu planning, and personal journaling/goal-tracking. In the back of the calendar are two pages of color-coded stickers to help identify birthdays, school events, car maintenance, and bill payments. I developed this layout when I became a stay-at-home mom. I needed a calendar to coordinate my new responsibilities.

Favorite Products and/or Services

The calendar will retail for $15.95. This price was set after determining the cost to produce the calendar at various quantities. Once this base cost was set, I had to determine the industry's standard markup. These two elements combined with market research to determine competitors pricing produced the final price.

Marketing Strategy

My past experience in advertising and promotion has really paid off. For me learning the distribution channels was the most difficult. Before the Family Organizer even hits the shelf of a single book or gift store, more than 500 review copies will be sent to parenting and child-related magazines. Our web site will provide access to an ordering link as well as an interactive format where families can share time-/home-management tips. Press releases will be distributed to newspapers in major metropolitan areas. Having an aggressive marketing plan has really helped me get into bookstores and thus increase my sales. I have found that it is not the stores' responsibility to sell the book (calendar) to the public; this task lies with the publisher. They are hesitant to purchase books with no marketing support for fear that they will occupy valuable space and not produce the revenues. This first year, I expect that the majority of the sales will come either directly or indirectly from the Internet. My goal for this year is to sell enough calendars to break even on the project; anything more will be frosting on the cake.

Recommendations

I think that having a realistic goal is very important. Don't be greedy when setting your goal. Greed tends to lead to unwise business decisions.

SELF-PUBLISHER/FICTION

CHISTELL PUBLISHING | www.chistell.com
Denise Turney, 38 | Bensalem, Pennsylvania | Age of Child: 11

Home Biz and Mission Statement

My business is books! We write, print, publish, and distribute books. Readers are our treasures! Without them, we would not exist.

Most Popular Product and Pricing Fees

My new book, *Love Has Many Faces,* a multicultural suspense, is selling fast! *Portia,* the story of how a woman deals with breast cancer, continues to sell very well. Shipping and handling for both *Love Has Many Faces* and *Portia* is free. Studying the market is how we found the right price for both books—that and listening to our readers. A product that is priced too low is seen as being "cheap" by consumers. On the other hand, if you overprice, consumers think your only concern is money and not quality or their best interest. It's crucial to price each product right; otherwise you could lose sales or gain a reputation for being either cheap or too expensive.

Marketing Strategy

We market via phone (leave a message about our business on voice-mail), e-mail discussion lists, "targeted" newsgroups, a top-notch news-letter that features incredibly successful writers/publishers around the world giving out solid, valuable advice, press releases (everyone in business should send press releases each month), business cards, T-shirts and our web site.

Recommendations

Treat your customers right, and they will treat you right. Make people feel like you are more concerned about providing them a service or product that will enrich their lives than you are about making money. Do business with integrity and always remember that the greatest value is human value. Provide excellent customer service! "Connect" with your customers.

SENIOR TECHNICAL WRITER

WING GROUP, LLC | www.wing-group.com
Wendy Wing, 29 | Temple, New Hampshire | Ages of Children: 2, 4

> *"I'm transitioning from being a remote-staff employee to an entrepreneur. Although I'm just starting out I already have a two-month contract worth as much as four months at my salaried position. My husband is quitting his full-time job to stay home and help out with the kids (otherwise they would be in full-time day care)."*

Office Oasis

Spare bedroom on the first floor, near living room and kitchen.

Job Description

I am a senior technical writing consultant. I write user documentation (owner manuals) and on-line Help for high-tech companies who sell computer hardware and software, telecommunications, and electrical products. I work either at the client's site or at my home office depending on my client's needs.

Transferable Skills

I am transferring my knowledge of various software programs, technical-writing skills, and project-management skills from my previous employer.

Knowledge, Skills, Experience, and/or Education Needed

Two of the most important skills I need for my home business are marketing and time-management skills. For marketing/sales, I recently joined a writing organization that has a special-interest group for writers who have started their own business, which has a wealth of information about marketing and selling one's business. Because I need to be constantly marketing myself and, at the same time, working on client projects, time management is very critical.

Industry Insight

The technical documentation industry (writers, editors, and illustrators) is booming. There is a great need in the technology industry for good writing communicators. A well-written manual can save a company money by reducing customer support calls and field technician visits. Anyone who wants to break into the technical-writing field should first have a college degree, preferably in technical writing or technical communications, or some college-level courses in technical writing. They should also know how to use current documentation programs such as Adobe FrameMaker, Adobe Acrobat, and Microsoft Word; current on-line Help programs such as e-Help RoboHelp; and current illustrating programs such as CorelDraw and Adobe Illustrator. Before venturing out on your own, an aspiring EP should work for an agency that specializes in technical-writing assignments. An agency sends you out on long-term or short-term contract assignments to a variety of companies. They can usually find entry-level assignments for beginners. These assignments can give you the experience and portfolio to start your own business down the road.

Top Revenue Streams

- Technical writing
- Technical illustrating
- Technical editing
- Web site designing
- Marketing writing

A Day in the Life

My workday starts at 8:00 A.M. I start working on a daily prioritized "things to do" list that I created from the previous evening. All my projects have a schedule of deliverables that I keep posted on a corkboard mounted on the wall behind my computer screen, so I always know when something is due. I read my e-mails first thing in the morning, then work on my list, periodically checking e-mail throughout the day. If an e-mail request comes up for something not listed or scheduled, I generally try to resolve it right away so that it doesn't linger or I don't forget to do it later. At 9:00 A.M. I take a short break to drive my daughter to preschool.

When I return, I work several more hours until I need to pick my daughter up from preschool. Then I am usually done working until my girls go to bed. I don't work a straight eight-hour day but rather four to five hours during business hours and another four to five hours at night and sometimes weekends. However, I am always available to my clients via my cell phone during business hours.

Pricing Structure

My hourly rate is $50–$75. Which rate I use is based on whether I received the assignment through an agency or on my own, as well as where the client is located (besides my own state, I will travel to three surrounding states for on-site work). I also quote a project fee if my client prefers. If my quote is close to the actual time I spent working on a project I can make close to $100/hour.

Additional Cost Items

None.

Recommended Resources

Society for Technical Communication, www.stc.org

SOFTWARE DEVELOPER/ENTREPRENEUR

BUNGALOW SOFTWARE, INC. | www.StrokeSoftware.com
Clay D. Nichols, Jr., 34 | Hillsboro, Oregon | Ages of Children: 8-month-old twins

"It's easy to get caught up in the passion and focus of business-building and working toward goals. But few tasks are more urgent than the momentary needs of a child. Easy to forget. Important to remember."

Office Oasis
Upstairs in the second master bedroom, 20 by 10, with storage space in the attic.

Job Description
My wife, Terri, is a speech and language pathologist. I started creating software for her patients as a way to practice my software-engineering skills in preparation for a new job. After much tweaking and tuning, the programs became very popular and now we create, market, and sell speech therapy software that stroke and brain injury survivors use to help regain their speech, language, and cognitive (reasoning) skills. As the local TV station described it, it's "Stroke Software" since it's primarily for those who have had a stroke.

Previous Career
Telecommunications Engineering Consultant (four years) then software engineer for a video conferencing company (three years).

Knowledge, Skills, Experience, and/or Education Needed
Software engineering experience, plus a strong willingness to spend a lot of time learning about marketing, sales, production, publishing catalogs, and more of the business operation end.

Transferable Skills
- Software engineering (programming)
- Knowledge of customer is absolutely vital. Luckily, my wife is a speech therapist, so she understood the customers: other speech therapists and their patients.
- Ability to explain technical issues in an easy-to-understand way to

a non-technical audience. We sell a high-tech product that addresses a complex problem (brain damage). The customer has to understand it before they can use (or buy) it.

- Cost-analysis. I've always been inclined to cost-analysis—calculating what something will cost. It started in college when I calculated what each bowl of chili or spaghetti would cost and what percentage of the total cost each ingredient was. ("Hmmm . . . we can double the amount of meat in this for only a 24% increase in the cost per bowl.") As a telecommunications engineer, I was responsible for estimating whether a projected service would make money, and how much and when it would break even. That involved cost-estimation and analysis of pricing structures. This may be boring to the average person, but sadly, it's fascinating to me!

Industry Insight

There is always room for another competitor. We really worried early on about other companies (competitors) and whether there was room in the "market" for another speech therapy software company. One of our competitors has been around for twenty years. However, we found that there's plenty of room in the market. We've thrived, and I don't think it's been at the expense of other companies (i.e., we're not stealing shares from other slices of the pie; there's just a lot of pie for everyone).

Be yourself; focus on the customer. Don't worry about your competitor other than to get possible ideas. Don't worry about keeping up with the competition; instead focus on keeping up with your customers. If they are doing something new/clever, decide if it will work for your customers. If not, don't do it. I've seen our competitors do things that I'd like to imitate until I think, "How does this help our customer?"

On Marketing

Our web site has been the most cost-effective marketing strategy. We do our own web site maintenance and it's something I enjoy, so our out-of-pocket expense is embarrassingly low ($16 monthly) for the return we get on it. We are also active on relevant Internet groups/list servs, which are a good place to be helpful and "plug" your service at the same time while helping to cultivate a reputation as a subject matter expert. In addition, we use print advertising and a newsletter.

Our least effective marketing technique has been direct marketing.

We sent out 2,000 pieces but only made a couple of sales. Probably the failure was largely that we were expecting the mailing to do too much. We should have kept it short and simple, like an advertisement—just enough info to get them to call for more info.

Top Products

- AphasiaTutor 1: Words $99.50
- AphasiaTutor 2: Sentences $99.50
- Sights'n Sounds: $129.50

Pricing Structure

- Programs vary in price from $69.50 to $199.50 (for professional-grade therapy programs for speech therapists).
- Typically, charges for custom work start at $60 per hour. We do some custom programming and individual speech therapy.

Additional Cost Items

- Contact Manager; we use ACE, www.goace.com, $40, but the program hasn't been updated in a while and may not be supported in the future. The "gotta-have" feature of a contact manager is the ability to track old e-mail addresses by who they were sent *by* or *to* so you have a history. We track over 10,000 prospect records. We tried handling sales/support calls for four days without the computer, but I was a nervous wreck because it's impossible for me to keep track of all that without a nice organized system. The other gotta-have feature is the ability to automatically import e-mailed forms (with name/address, etc.) into the database. Goldmine seems to have all of these features, but has a steep learning curve and costs more ($200). If you're just starting and you want something fairly good and cheap, I recommend www.goace.com. Seems to be much more stable on our new 1.5 Ghz PC.
- A web site. Gotta have this. Cost is $16.00 per month (at www. Interland.com)
- Digital Camera (1 mega pixel), $200

Recommended Resources

- Free fax to e-mail service, www.efax.com. This saves us a phone line and fax machine since we get our faxes as e-mail attachments.

It also includes HotSend, which allows you to print from any program to a self-reading file that you can send to anyone on a PC (and now, apparently Mac too) where it can be read. This is great for sending complex documents; for example, if we need to e-mail an invoice to a customer in Romania (as I did this morning), I just send it as a self-viewing HotSend file.

- Service Core of Retired Executives (www.SCORE.org). We showed our counselor our catalog and got great feedback and suggestions on pricing. I'd guess that his advice alone increased net revenue by 20 percent.
- www.experts-exchange.com
- IhelpDesk, http://www.adventive.com/lists/ihelpdesk. This newsletter is hosted by Eva Rosenberg, known as the "Tax Momma." Great source of peers to whom you can pose questions ask for help.

SOFTWARE DEVELOPER/TELEWORKER

AIRLINE INDUSTRY TELEWORKER
Mark DuRussel, 32 | Madison, Wisconsin | Ages of Children:
2½ years old, 5 months old

"Ultimately, I'm very glad I decided to telecommute because it has met all our goals financially and personally. It has even enhanced my career, as I've spent much of the last year learning about web-based technologies, which I might not have been given the opportunity to do if things had taken a different twist."

Office Oasis
Spare (fourth) bedroom upstairs; not fancy at all.

Job Description
Software developer in the airline industry, developing an internal web-based application.

Previous Career
Software developer for the healthcare industry.

Transferable Skills

Whenever I visit the company's office, I'm reminded that there are other valuable ways to interact with people besides e-mail or the phone. On the other hand, working at home has made me more of an independent thinker. Now when I have questions about my work, I don't necessarily feel the need to call someone within the company for help—especially with the advent of the World Wide Web as a research tool.

Knowledge, Skills, Experience, and/or Education Needed

My current role requires a certain combination of experience in the air-line industry plus a software development background—regardless of whether I work at home or not.

A Day in the Life

My schedule is very fluid. I try to do most of my work Monday through Friday, but my customers are in Australia and New Zealand, so sometimes I find myself working on Sunday when they've already started working their Monday.

I don't usually get started until mid to late morning, with 10:00 or 10:30 A.M. being an average start time. I usually like to take a forty-five- to sixty-minute lunch, so if I am to work 8 hours, I have to go until 7:00 or 7:30 P.M.. However, my family sometimes is ready to eat dinner together around 5:30 or 6:00 P.M., which causes me to take a break sooner than I expected, which in turn requires me to make up the time later that evening or some other day.

Usually one or two nights a week, I stay up late working (after everyone else has gone to bed) to make sure I stay on top of things. Normally this just ensures that I'll attain my goal of a forty-hour workweek, but occasionally I need to work more than forty hours, especially before an important deadline.

Industry Insight

An aspiring EP needs to differentiate him/herself just like anyone else, by promising to deliver a product or service of exceptional quality and/or with some unique attributes.

Additional Cost Items

A network hub so that I can split my high-speed Internet access for use at two different computers—one for work and one for home use. This raises a good point, which is that it's generally a smart move to use separate computers for work and personal activities.

Recommended Resources

I used cnet.com for helpful recommendations when trying to decide what hardware/software to purchase. I'm very pleased with the space-efficient HP Office Jet multi-purpose unit—a combination printer/copier/scanner/fax machine (all in color or BandW) that fits neatly on top of a file cabinet. I found it after several hours of combing through other users' reviews of similar hardware at cnet.com's product review section.

SYSTEMS INTEGRATOR

HOLOCOM COMPUTER SPECIALISTS, LLC | www.holocom.com
Howard Dingman, 44 | Maine, New York | Ages of Children: 4, 7

> *"Don't think that your life is going to be stress-free. You'll have stress as an EP too—it's just a different kind of stress. In the meantime, remember why you got married, and why you had the kids. Love each person for who they are, and be thankful we live in a country that allows us to be an EP if we want to."*

Office Oasis
Basement.

Job Description
Systems integrator, computer consultant, and custom programmer working in the warehouse and distribution vertical market.

Previous Career
In my last corporate job, the company decided to close our department, planning to drop all their customers and just walk away. We decided to start our own business to pick up the slack.

Transferable Skills
Most important are a positive attitude and a strong work ethic. Results count. Excuses don't. Zig Ziglar said that employers tell him "Give me

an employee with a positive attitude, a good work ethic, and a willingness to learn, and I'll TEACH them to run the gizmo that makes the widgets." It's a rare consultant who can bring the job in on time and on budget. Customers appreciate results.

Knowledge, Skills, Experience, and/or Education Needed

Networking and interpersonal skills are an *absolute must*. (This was an extremely difficult thing for me originally, and I still have to work at it.) Every line of business has its own buzzwords. You don't need to know them all, but you should become familiar with the vocabulary of your target market. You're the consultant, and you're expected to have all of the answers. None of their people have all the answers, but that doesn't matter. You should. It's not as hard as it sounds, though. For instance, have a general understanding of business *and* finance because you will be thrust into meetings with many people, and sometimes that includes finance people who want to know costs and "ROI." Perhaps there will be manufacturing people who want to know about inventory levels and "MRP." Or maybe there will be computer people who want to know how your implementation will affect their "IS infrastructure." Maybe it's "IT" instead of "IS." Maybe it will be a top-level manager or VP or CEO. They will mostly listen, and maybe ask one or two pointed questions, but they will evaluate you *immediately* based on your answers to those questions. If you make an impression as one who is recommending something because it benefits *their* company, in terms of the ROI for them, and you are informed and aware of the way *their* business runs, the evaluation of you as a vendor will be much more favorable than if it looks like you haven't "done your homework." And, of course, if you don't know what business terms like "approved vendor list" and "PO" and "net 60 days" mean, you're in for some rude awakenings.

Industry Insight

Technology is only beginning to spread into this market. The price of the equipment has dropped radically, making it much more affordable. It's not an area where most computer professionals choose to go—out into the warehouse with all of the dirt, grime, and heavy work. There are significant savings opportunities for most companies. These may be in terms of accuracy or inventory reduction, or may be just in terms of order turnaround time. I start from a question like, "If I could do one thing to improve the process here, what would it be? If I did it, what would it cost the customer, and what benefit would it give them? Would it make financial sense for the company to do it, in light of the costs and benefits? How long would it take for the customer to pay back the investment with savings?"

On Marketing

Two of the first purchases we made for the business proved to be critical in the revenue stream, and they're not what most people would think about: a two-part spiral-bound telephone message book and a small Rolodex. The book is where *all* of the business messages go, and two-part so they stay there. Years later, I still have occasion to look up a contact name from old phone records. Perhaps a book isn't the most efficient tool, but we still have all of the messages back to our beginning. The Rolodex makes it easy to be a little more organized than just chronological order. People appreciate being remembered, and it adds a personal touch to your company's service that helps to differentiate you from your competition.

Top Revenue Streams
- Telephone support for software.
- Software installation, integration, start-up, and training (I "take it out of the box, put it together, and make it all work.")

Pricing Structure
$125/hour, $1,000/day, plus expenses if on the road. Not always hourly, many jobs are large enough to be bid on a by-the-job basis rather than by-the-hour. $75/half-hour for telephone support.

Additional Cost Items
Cell phone.

Recommended Resources
- Books, tapes, and materials from Ziglar Training Systems; attend a live seminar with Zig if you can—it's worth every penny.
- Bob Burg's seminars, books, and tapes; "Endless Referrals" and others
- Books by Og Mandino

A Day in the Life

6:00 A.M.	Rise and shine.
6:30 A.M.	Walk dog, go to corner restaurant for breakfast. Catch up on town news.
7:30 A.M.	Home to office, start up systems, and pick up e-mail. Start replies and SPAM cleanout.
8:30 A.M.	Walk to bus stop with first-grade son. Wait for bus.
8:45 A.M.	Back to office, plan schedule for day. Take care of urgent calls/e-mails. Second cup of coffee. "Commute" to work: "Honey, I'll be down in the office."
9:00 A.M.	Project work and phone calls.
11:45 A.M.	Figure out what time lunch will be. Phone rings, customer crisis.
Noon	Lunchtime, working customer call while having sandwich.
1:00 P.M.	Back to the grind for a while. Maybe work on a quote or two.
3:30 P.M.	Walk to bus stop with three-year-old. Meet first-grader when bus comes home.
3:45 P.M.	If weather is good, take kids out for sleigh riding, kite flying, or bicycle riding. If bad weather, play game or read. Play for an hour or so.
5:00 P.M.	Dinner time. Normal chaos of scouts, ball games, etc. for a while.
8:00 P.M.	Kids go to bed. Peace and tranquility return. Back to work. Usually, this phase is done in the living room in the recliner with the laptop. It plugs into the network, and can access all of the systems and the Internet. Look at current projects, milestones, deadlines. Rough out a plan of action for tomorrow.
11:00 P.M.	Shutdown, bedtime.

Also, avoid one caveat when starting out: good lawyers and good accountants cost good money. "Respectable" firms have earned that respect by doing quality work for their clients. Hiring a "cheap" lawyer or accountant may be the most expensive decision you make and may cost you your business.

TRANSLATOR/INTERPRETER

TANAKA TALKS TRANSLATION/INTERPRETING
gailtanaka@earthlink.net
Gail Tanaka, 47 | Eagan, Minnesota | Ages of Children: 17, 19, 24

> *"I find that having an office in my own home has eliminated over 60 percent of my stress and is allowing me to be there more for my teenagers. Working at home has definitely given me an edge on parenting. Before I was so stressed out that when I came home from work I wasn't much good for anything. I have become a more low-key mother and a lot better listener."*

Office Oasis
One-half of the upstairs master bedroom.

Job Description
Japanese to English translator for written language and interpreter for spoken language, specializing in the legal field doing document review, translation, and consulting for intellectual property cases.

Previous Career
International customer service rep, bilingual executive assistant, and international staff liaison.

Transferable Skills
The industry skills I learned in the corporate world have enabled me to gain insight into how companies work, which helps me in negotiating with prospective clients. Because of my former employment, I can now write a killer résumé, have great interviewing skills, and am more business savvy.

Knowledge, Skills, Experience, and/or Education Needed
A degree in linguistics, language, or a technical field is important, as is certification from American Translators Association (ATA) or some other industry-related field. Above-average WP skills as well as some type of graphic arts software, plus the ability to compress and decompress various types of files as the majority of work is delivered and received electronically.

Industry Insight
The market looks very good right now because of continued global expansion. If you're fluent in a second language or multiple languages and have strong writing skills, my advice going forward is to identify a niche.

On Marketing
Networking is very important in the beginning. My most effective marketing methods have been direct mailings as well as being a member of ATA. Other ways I marketed myself were:

- Studying related Internet sites to see what kinds of skills were being sold
- Purchasing and reading books on working as a freelance translator
- Joining translation/interpreting associations to get my name listed and to participate in industry-related events
- Creating an effective marketing letter
- Purchasing client lists and conducting direct mailings
- Listing myself on several translator job listing sites

Top Revenue Streams
My niche of patent translations, followed by medical and financial. To bring in specific jobs I use:

- Proz.com (job-posting web site)
- E-Groups.com (an e-mail membership that notifies me of available translation jobs)
- Established customer base that I promote my services to

Additional Cost Items
Some translators use CAT tools ($700–$1,000+), which create a glossary database on your system for automatic recall of phrases and terms. Glossaries and dictionaries are important tools (I use both hard copy and electronic versions). Also essential is an adequate storage and filing system, both electronic and hard copy.

Recommended Resources
Translatortips.com

VIDEO PRODUCER

ALIQUIDREALITY.COM
Ryan O'Connell, 23 | Phoenix, Arizona | Age of Child: 2

> *"My daughter is only 2 years old so she can't help much with my work, but she's cute as an angel. I take her with me when meeting clients. It makes me look like a wholesome person, and everyone loves her."*

Office Oasis
The third bedroom of my house, which currently houses four computers, such as my Athlon 700 with 9×12 graphic pad for animation work, a dual processor Mac G4 for video editing, and a Titanium PowerBook for on-location work.

Job Description
As a freelancer in the graphic design industry, I handle any jobs from complex video production and 3D animation to simple flyers, web design, and CD and package design.

Previous Career
Worked in a Phoenix pre-press shop.

Transferable Skills
At the pre-press shop I learned the intricate details of printing, such as creep, bleed, and trapping. What I didn't learn was how to both be a manager and work in production at the same time. As an EP, you take on both roles, so learning time management is essential.

Knowledge, Skills, Experience, and/or Education Needed
You can never know too much. The only crime is thinking you know enough. Software is always changing, so it's not as important to know one particular software as it is to know how software programs work. With that knowledge, you can adapt to any new program, software update, or any other curveball you're thrown. In addition to whatever you're skilled at, you need to be proficient at economics, law, and accounting. If you're too right-brained for that, you may need to enlist a friend or spouse to tackle that important area of business or you won't make it.

Industry Insight
The only way to break into the design field is through viability. Never turn down a job when you're first getting started because the work you do will help you get other jobs. There's a lot of competition and who you know makes all the difference. So get out there, and GET KNOWN!

On Marketing
Word of mouth is definitely the best advertising. If you can get other people talking about you, you're doing something right. I've found the worst way to advertise is handing out flyers, because nobody wants an extra piece of paper (no matter how cool it looks!). Fliers are better stacked somewhere so if prospects are interested, they can take it for themselves.

Top Revenue Streams
- Web sites—everybody wants one
- Corporate identity—making business cards, letterhead, and envelopes. The best thing is every time they move or an area code changes, you get more work redesigning.
- Flyers—club and dance flyers are great because the places are always having new events.

Additional Cost Items
In my field of work, Adobe is the greatest. I use their suite of software from Photoshop to After Effects, though they're pricey (even when buying as a bundle, you're still looking at about $2,000). Then there are 3D programs ranging in price from $100 to $10,000. More expensive programs give better renderings and have more features. Finally, if you are going to do web work, you *need* Flash. It lets you make your site as cool as you want, like aLiquidReality.com. My favorite piece of hardware is my Wacom 9×12 drawing board. It's under $500 and it lets you draw with a pressure-sensitive pen instead of a mouse.

Recommended Resources
An unrelenting desire to succeed and the love of your children are your greatest resources!

Internet-Based Home Careers

AFFILIATE MANAGER

CLUBMOM, INC. (remote staffer) | BabyLounge.com (own biz)
Shawn Collins, 31 | Millburn, New Jersey | Ages of Children: newborn, 2

> *"It was never really much of a question for my wife and me about whether we would be entrepreneurial parents. Both of us grew up in homes where there was always a parent around, and we wanted the same for our children. We faced the common problem of one salary not covering the family, so we decide to start a company of our own."*

Office Oasis

We converted our unfinished basement into a finished office with all of the amenities, including a crib and TV/VCR for those times when we have to be an entrepreneur and baby-sitter at the same time.

Job Description

Full-time affiliate manager at ClubMom, where I manage 9,000 affiliates in promoting ClubMom. Outside of this position, I run the BabyLounge.com site, write freelance, and consult in web design and marketing.

Previous Career

Before the Internet, I was working in magazine publishing. Soon after getting married, I made the random jump into Internet marketing at a start-up company.

Transferable Skills

EPs should definitely apply traditional work force skills, such as time management and budgeting—two essential skills for an EP. As a publisher of my site, BabyLounge.com, I've accumulated some skills that are very valued in the workplace, such as HTML knowledge and Internet marketing through affiliate programs and search engines.

Knowledge, Skills, Experience, and/or Education Needed

In order to succeed with your own web site, one of the most important skills is a willingness to learn—free tutorials and software such as Front-Page and DreamWeaver enable even the most technically challenged to be publishers on the Internet. It's also essential to learn the ropes for marketing a web site—no prior knowledge or education needed—everything you need to know is available for free on-line (though any sort of background in sales or marketing is helpful).

Industry Insight

My site is based around affiliate programs, where I earn money based on my performance (commissions for getting people to fill out forms and buy things on-line). The affiliate marketing business model is the darling of the Internet now—all industry experts are pointing toward performance-based marketing as the future.

First, create a web site based around a topic that is interesting to you. Then, go to the affiliate program directories, such as Refer-it.com, CashPile.com, and AssociatePrograms.com to find affiliate programs that focus on the same topic as your site (example: if your site is about soccer, join the Sports Authority affiliate program to sell soccer balls and cleats, and join the Amazon program to sell books and videos about soccer).

On Marketing

I have an opt-in newsletter on my site where I gather e-mail addresses. (I e-mail this list once a month or more with content and targeted offers through my affiliate links). Also, there are strategically placed affiliate links throughout my site (for example, my wife, Vicky, writes book reviews for our site, and then I add links to buy the books she reviews). We also have our own affiliate program, where we sell Mom Software (similar to Net Nanny) and our affiliates get paid when they refer sales to us.

The most effective method has been to exchange links with similar sites, so we share very targeted traffic with each other. The least effective method has been to send out direct mail to an off-line mailing list. I highly endorse GoTo.com, where you pay for placement in their search engine. This enables you to drive reasonably priced traffic to a web site right away (it takes weeks or months to get into the search engines).

Top Revenue Streams

- Affiliate programs
- Web consulting, marketing, and updates to sites for clients
- Reseller of Mom Software
- Freelance writer

Pricing Structure

This varies depending on the revenue stream. Affiliate programs pay a flat fee or percentage of a sale; consulting, marketing, and updates to sites ranges from $40 to $70 per hour; we sell Mom Software for $20 (delivered via the Web) and pay a percentage for each copy as a license fee; freelance writing varies depending on the place—generally $0.50 to $1.00 per word.

Additional Cost Items

- Domains ($15/year)
- Web site hosting ($15.95/month)
- Search engine marketing ($200/month)
- Assorted promotional items such as shirts, postcards, etc.

Recommended Resources

Weekly reading of *Industry Standard, Business 2.0, Internet World,* and *iMarketing news.* Also:

- www.clickz.com
- www.searchenginewatch.com
- www.refer-it.com
- www.associateprograms.com
- www.cashpile.com
- www.revenews.com
- www.associate-it.com

BRAND CONSULTANT

BLUE SAGE GROUP | www.bluesagegroup.com
Genece Hamby, 50 | Morrisville, North Carolina | Age of Child: 5

"Since I started working from home, my spirit has been more nurtured; home and work have integrated into a soulful journey."

Office Oasis
Spare bedroom.

Job Description
I work closely with clients in helping identify and build their brand architecture from the ground up, including concept development, market research for validation, brand strategy and positioning, clarifying core messages, brand identity, package design, and more. For the solo entrepreneur, the branding process affects all forms of communications—how they present themselves to the public—it is the intentional declaration of who they are, what they believe in, and why their customers should put their faith in them. It distinguishes them from their competition. And most important, branding is a promise—a promise that they must keep to their customers. A strong brand identity builds mindshare—the strongest marketing and communication tool imaginable.

Previous Career
I have been working with entrepreneurs for twenty years. Primarily, I worked with small to mid-size companies and agencies as an independent brand and packaging consultant. I've worked from home most of these twenty years, with a few years where I had an outside office (though I didn't enjoy it).

Transferable Skills
Entering the market as a brand consultant usually requires strong marketing skills and an understanding of brand methodologies and brand architecture. The best way to transition into this career is to start with what you know most about branding and niche yourself to a specific market. Skills that can be successfully transferred over are strong communications skills, a knowledge of market research and marketing communications, and creativity or ability to design. If you decide to reenter the traditional workforce, there are a lot of options for the brand consultant. You can move into a corporate environment as a product brand manager or senior brand manager. You can also easily transfer into other marketing roles such as a marketing communications director or a public relations agent. Other options are advertising or creative brand agencies.

Knowledge, Skills, Experience, and/or Education Needed

A brand consultant needs to be a highly creative, strategic thinker. One must thoroughly understand that branding is a marketing communications process—one that is planned, strategically focused, and fully integrated. It conveys the essence, culture, character, and purpose of a company or product. It's the heart and soul of the brand from which all outward expressions emanate. A bachelor's degree in marketing or communications, or having six to eight years equivalent experience in marketing, branding, advertising, or public relations, would help make you a more effective brand consultant. Additional experience in a creative ad agency or corporate environment in consumer brands are a plus.

Industry Insight

Being a brand consultant is a fairly new field, and there is room for consultants that find a specific niche of expertise in branding. For example, specializing in branding consumer products.

On Marketing

As Blue Sage Group, I have focused my brand consulting career on a specific niche—branding *the solo entrepreneur*. To market my skills and build brand awareness, I provide a weekly newsletter to 1,000 current subscribers nationwide (a circulation that continues to grow), write articles and professionally speak on "branding the solo entrepreneur," while authoring a book and interviewing successful solo entrepreneurs, attending networking events, and pursuing on-line marketing efforts to increase site traffic.

The most effective marketing method to date has been the weekly newsletter, networking events, and word-of-mouth referrals. My approach to marketing is highly strategic and very focused. Each one of the methods I'm currently using to market myself are working. One of the greatest successes I'm having is due to the way I build relationships with everyone I encounter. Clients know my strong work ethic and experience such great results from the work we do together that they become my greatest cheerleaders, spreading the word.

Top Revenue Streams

- **The Blue Sage Journey,** a unique brand process designed exclusively for the solo entrepreneur that is a one-on-one consultation.

An average brand session is eight to twelve hours and costs between \$1,200 and \$1,800.

- **Brand In A Box™**, a line of pre-packaged tools exclusive to the solo entrepreneur for do-it-yourself branding. Each Brand In A Box™ includes an instructional step-by-step audio cassette along with other tools to help the solo entrepreneur identify and define their core message and communication strategies for a consistent brand. Cost is \$99 per Brand In A Box™.

- **Brand Clinics,** learning clinics provided over the telephone via a conference call as an opportunity to experience the power of the creative branding process, tips and strategies for effective branding, and techniques to benefit the solo entrepreneur's business. Cost is \$60 per person, per hour.

- **Brand Packaging,** converting a solo entrepreneur's specialized knowledge and quality information into commodities that can be packaged and sold to others as books, eBooks, eZines, workshops/ seminars, audiotapes, videos, and CDs to name a few. Packaging costs are quoted based on the project.

Additional Cost Items
None.

Recommended Resources
Over the years, I've taken classes and have been an instructor through small business development centers located throughout the U.S. This has been one of the best resources for learning "how-to" complete a business plan, designing effective marketing strategies, financing the business, and more. Another great resource has been hiring other consultants that have an expertise that I don't possess to help me in my business. For example, hiring an accountant, freelance graphic artist, or marketing strategist. I also find using the Internet one of the most valuable resources for forming strategic partnerships, building name recognition, new client development, and more.

CAREER SITE PRODUCER

Womans-Work.com
Kirsten E. Ross, 35 | Warren, Michigan | Ages of Children: 2½ years, 6 months

> *"Working in an Internet business makes you feel kind of anonymous. I think that the perception of site visitors is that we are a big organization—they don't realize that I'm responding to their requests from my little home office and that hearing some feedback from them would make my day."*

Office Oasis

My office is in a large room in our basement, but we live in a quad so I am not so far below ground (just a few steps below our family room).

Job Description

I have an Internet site that is dedicated to helping women find professional alternative work arrangements. I have a job-search application that women use to search by the alternative arrangement they are looking for (part-time, telecommute, flex time, etc.), and I provide resources to organizations who want to implement alternative work arrangements.

Previous Career

I worked in human resources for a large organization. After having my first son, I went back to work part-time in a professional-level position and loved the balance I was able to achieve. I felt that with my background in human resources (certified senior professional in human resources and master's degree in labor and industrial relations), I could help women looking for alternative work arrangements find organizations who were progressive enough to use these arrangements as a powerful recruitment tool. After starting the web site and doing both for a number of months, I decided to give up the part-time job to work exclusively from home on the web site.

Transferable Skills

In my case, most of my skills were transferable to my business because the topic is related to my former profession. I am a human resource professional and now provide human resource expertise to organizations that are interested in implementing family-friendly benefits or alternative work arrangements. I also used my past experience to design my site. I know what it's like to post a lot of open positions, so I developed a site that is user-friendly to recruiters who need to post opportunities. As for EP skills transferable to the nine-to-five world, I would say all of them! Particularly in the beginning, you do it all—you're an accountant, biller, web designer, human resource professional, marketer, writer, business planner, secretary. Any new skill that you learn while performing these functions should go on a résumé. In addition, the initiative and creativity that it takes to be an entrepreneur are skills that an employer knows they cannot teach someone. They are, thus, highly desirable.

Knowledge, Skills, Experience, and/or Education Needed

The field of human resources does not have a certification or education requirement. However, to be a successful career site producer, you should have a strong working knowledge of human resource recruiting. The site should be user-friendly to individuals who are posting jobs, and you should be able to help your corporate members conduct a targeted search. If you are offering career advice or human resource consulting, you really should have a strong background through a combination of education and experience. There are many laws and practices that you need to be aware of. There is also a widely recognized certification program through the Society of Human Resource Management that can add a lot of credibility, which includes a professional human resource (PHR) designation and a senior professional human resource (SPHR) designation. Each certification requires successful completion of a very comprehensive test, and there are continuing ed/practice requirements to maintain the certification. I would strongly recommend getting certified.

Industry Insight

The topic of flexible work is very hot right now. Almost every organization is, at a minimum, talking about it. Job candidates and current employees want additional life balance. There are thousands of people looking for alternative work arrangements. However, there is still a lot of education involved. It is not necessarily an area that organizations are ready to jump right into. They are familiar with the concept but are not fully aware of the advantages and cost effectiveness of offering these kinds of arrangements. And it often requires a culture change to implement. So the field is exciting and evolving but definitely still a challenge as far as building a client base.

On Marketing

I have operated with a very low-budget marketing strategy. My most effective method has been use of the media. I have been lucky to have been interviewed on the topic of alternative work arrangements, with articles that have been picked up all over the United States. I even ended up on *NBC Nightly News* with Tom Brokaw as a result of one of the articles. The media is a great free place to get exposure! I also take every opportunity to be included in publications like the EP book and have applied for and won awards like the Mompreneur of the Month on iVillage. It takes time to fill out questionnaires or be interviewed, but the exposure can be wonderful.

Reciprocal links and networking are very important also. It takes time, but you need to find as many sites as you can that are relevant to your topic and request reciprocal links. And in some instances, I have made phone contact with individuals who have particularly interesting sites or services. One of the great things about the Internet is that there really is a small community feel when it comes to helping each other out. People with web sites relating to alternative work are often crusaders, and we keep each other in mind when there are opportunities for free publicity.

Top Revenue Streams and Pricing Structure

- Job postings on the web site—$70/job, also some annual packages
- Home business ads—$40/ad
- Freelance posts—This is a referral program. I receive $1 each time an individual posts a profile and $15 each time an organization purchases work through my site.

Additional Cost Items

Web development has been my biggest expense. I did a lot of the site myself but needed some help with the more technical aspects. I also have my monthly hosting charges and an annual digital Secure Socket Layer web server certificate.

Recommended Resources

- www.selfpromotion.com—An absolutely wonderful search engine submission site. I wish that I would have found it sooner!

- www.womensforum.com—A network of women- and girl-oriented sites
- www.sba.gov/—Small Business Administration
- www.workingwoman.com/wwn/home.jsp—*Working Woman* magazine and network

---

CONTENT WRITER

OneWriter4Hire.com
Theresa Grothe, 40 | Rolling Meadows, Illinois | Ages of Children: 10, 13, 17

Office Oasis
Dining room area.

Job Description
Writing articles for on-line magazines, creating columns for on-line web sites, Webmistress, advertising, writer, researcher. I do it all.

Previous Career
"Stay-at-Home Mom (SAHM)"

Transferable Skills
"People" skills, getting along with others.

Knowledge, Skills, Experience, and/or Education Needed
Creativity, patience, privacy, and time to do what needs to be done.

Industry Insight
There are always new things popping up on the Internet, so the field is wide open for writers. Start small and keep a positive attitude!

On Marketing
My web site has been a very effective marketing springboard.

Top Revenue Streams and Pricing Structure
- Ghostwriting (price varies)

- Web site revamping for individuals and businesses (prices vary from $30 to $60 per day)
- Writing reviews of different web sites on the Internet (approximately $10 each)

Additional Cost Items

None.

Resources

- Bigstep.com (www.bigstep.com) launched my first web site and helped a great deal to build my confidence and convince me that I *can* actually run a business.

E-BOOK PUBLISHER

WorkOptions.com
Pat Katepoo, 43 | Kaneohe, Hawaii | Age of Child: 19

"'Stay focused' is one of my favorite time-savers. An otherwise-worthy business goal, which clouds the vision that originally inspired me to start my business, is often a wasteful distraction. Staying focused on who I'm serving and why sparks creative business direction and keen decision-making."

Office Oasis

A room off the kitchen is dedicated to my home office.

Job Description

Through my web site, WorkOptions.com, and my e-workbook, *Flex Success: A Proposal Blueprint and Planning Guide for Getting a Family-Friendly Work Schedule,* I help working mothers and others negotiate a flexible work arrangement at their current job so they can have more time with their families.

Previous Career

Director of nutrition services for a forty-physician outpatient medical clinic (my formal training was as a registered dietitian); also, marketing director for a business law firm (second career).

Transferable Skills

A public relations and marketing background provides a useful foundation for writing and marketing a web site and e-book. An ability to gather information and analyze material helps in overall e-book development. Writing effective sales copy for the web and experience in on-line marketing strategies have marketability in the nine-to-five world.

Knowledge, Skills, Experience, and/or Education Needed

Research and writing skills are necessary to build an e-book of substance that also fills a well-defined and marketable need; Internet marketing skills and all that entails is an ongoing necessity; media-relations savvy helps; keeping up with the trends of e-publishing is a must.

Industry Insight

Flex Success started selling on-line in mid-1997, catching the wave of rapid Internet growth (which has since slowed considerably in the United States), yet not drowning in a sea of e-books that now glut the market. During most of the late 1990s, time and technique were enough to get high rankings in the search engines for free. It's a different and greatly saturated Internet world now; I think it's more difficult and more expensive for an e-book by an "unknown" author to get attention. That said, publishing an e-book remains fairly inexpensive and I'd advise those aspiring to do so to consider it if they have the knowledge of, and passion for, their subject. Speaking only from my personal experience, I think it helps to find a narrow niche and fill a need within that niche that originates from something you know and love. Also, don't publish an e-book in response to hype that labels it a "sure-fire, on-line, money-making opportunity." Wrong motives yield wrong results. Be committed to the reader/user and to the ongoing marketing process required to reach those who can value from whatever you have to offer.

On Marketing

In the early days, time devoted to search engine optimization strategies paid off handsomely in visitor traffic, regular print and on-line media attention, and sales growth. Good search engine rankings that allow individuals to find WorkOptions.com and purchase *Flex Success* remain fruitful, yet paid placement is now a necessary part of the mix. I believe the testimonials on the web site are critical to converting interested visitors to buyers.

My experiments with off-line print advertising proved to be least effective. Marketing must be ongoing for steady sales. It helps if you find the marketing process fun (which I do), especially when it comes to learning and trying new things. Expect to spend some money. While there remain many effective marketing strategies that cost mostly one's time, the nature of the Internet now requires reaching your market through some paid means in order to see new sales growth over long periods of time.

Top Revenue Streams
- Daily sales of *Flex Success* provide the main revenue stream.
- Consulting with individuals by telephone is supplementary.

Pricing Structure
Since 1999, the selling price for *Flex Success* has been $39, having first started at $19.95 two years prior. Experimenting with pricing in response to demand, regularly upgrading the product content, and switching from manually processing orders to an electronic distributor to handle the growing number of transactions were the mix of factors that pushed the product price up. In getting the *Flex Success* proposal blueprint, people are paying for speed and format, as well as proven content, so it's a fair price for the value received while providing comfortable profit margins. In 2001, I sensed I could meet a consumer need with a new proposal blueprint e-book, *Telecommuting Proposal Express*. Because of the minimal incremental costs in adding another product, and because it's less-detailed and shorter than *Flex Success*, it made sense to offer it at a lower price point.

Additional Cost Items
None.

Recommended Resources

ON-LINE RESOURCES

- Since first firing up my modem in January 1995, I've learned from thousands of individuals by way of hundreds of hours of on-line reading. Besides the treasured cyber colleagues with whom I continue to exchange ideas, information, and support, these are the on-line sources that proved especially useful.

- MarketPosition Monthly, http://marketposition.com—In the early days of building my site, this newsletter was very valuable for learning how to build web pages that ranked well with the search engines.
- Ralph Wilson's Web Marketing Today, http://wilsonweb.com—This newsletter and site is a current and constant source of instructive and practical Internet business advice.
- Search Engine Watch by Danny Sullivan, http://searchenginewatch.com/
- I-Sales and I-Search Discussion Lists from Adventive: The Internet Knowledge Exchange, http://adventive.com/
- SelfPromotion.com, http://selfpromotion.com/
- Useit.com, http://useit.com/

OFF-LINE SOURCES

- A wonderful book that returned its $30 price many times over as an ongoing private tutor: *The Non-Designer's Web Book* by Robin Williams and John Tollett

E-COMMERCE MARKETING DIRECTOR

Trophies2Go.com (Remote Staff Position)
Jodie Pettit, 34 | Lakewood, Washington | Ages of Children: 2, 8

"Before, when I was working full-time, my daughter didn't know how to make her bed or clean her room, because she didn't have to (and I didn't have the time or energy to enforce it). Now we no longer have a cleaning service; I am modeling appropriate housecleaning habits and have both the time and energy to teach her basic skills."

Office Oasis

I chose to locate my "office" in the heart of the home, rather than tuck myself into a back bedroom. I rearranged my living room to include a small desk and work area.

Job Description

I handle customer-service issues, marketing, and general business operations for Trophies2Go.com, a major awards and recognition corporation.

Previous Career

Vanpool operations supervisor for our local transportation authority.

Transferable Skills

It is important for a work-at-home parent to be very organized and able to multi-task well. I am constantly interrupted, so it is important to know how to get back on task without losing the integrity of the project.

Knowledge, Skills, Experience, and/or Education Needed

Whether working at home or in the traditional workplace, it is imperative to be fluent in several basic software programs (the Microsoft Office Suite) and special computer languages, depending on your trade. My skills, knowledge, and experience are *vital* to the position I hold.

Industry Insight

With all the uncertainty that surrounds dot-coms, e-commerce and the on-line business world need to focus on those who prefer to work at home. An employer has a lot to gain by offering work-at-home options. Most people own a computer at home, so the employer has less "equipment costs"—less overhead due to less office space and the resources needed to maintain the space (electricity, phone support, administrative expenses, capital expenses, etc.).

FREE CONTEST SITE PRODUCER/WEB DESIGNER

ContestHound.com | FlooringGuide.com
Bob Gunther, 36 | London, Ontario, Canada | Age of Child: 2

> *"It was shortly after the birth of our daughter, Neva, that I became a stay-at-home father. I soon realized the value of actively participating in the rearing of a child. For the first time in my life, I really knew what it meant to be a parent. Not just a father or caregiver but something much deeper, much more intuitive . . . developing a bond that continues to transcend the everydayness of living."*

Office Oasis

A second bedroom and a corner of the dining room.

Job Description

In short—everything. I design and manage web sites for myself and for others. This includes all aspects of design, content, advertising, marketing, promotion, complaints, correspondence, and anything else related to the day-to-day operation of a web site.

Previous Career

Professional wholesale sales and specification of flooring products to retailers, architectural, and design professionals.

Transferable Skills

Problem-solving skills that I have gained from the work force have been a fantastic benefit. Regardless of previous occupation, we all have confronted frustrating moments when things are not going as planned. Having seen my way through such moments makes the task of parenting and working at home much more manageable. It may be cliché, but "Been there, done that" is invaluable in maneuvering through those times when I need to be a parent and entrepreneur all at the same time. It is those problem-solving skills that help me manage the self-imposed deadlines I have with the web sites while not losing my patience with Neva. I can take appropriate actions first to deal with Neva and then still manage to meet deadlines.

If I were to go back into the workforce, I think the most valuable skill I have developed is the ability to work on multiple tasks at the same time without suffering major anxiety attacks. It is difficult to switch gears in midstream and back again, but with my experience of parenting and running a couple of web sites, I had little choice but to master this.

Knowledge, Skills, Experience, and/or Education Needed

I am primarily self-taught and as such am continually learning. I think the key is to accept that things change rapidly, and to resist this change can be damaging to the business. I read most everything that I can, time permitting, and I think about the issues and how I can incorporate them. I am never afraid to learn something new, even if it means that I need to totally scrap my original direction.

Industry Insight

Although many people have become rich overnight on the Internet, it is unrealistic to think that is normal. To make a living, you need to work hard in promoting your web sites and constantly reevaluate your approach. Focus on a niche, create content strictly related to that niche, and promote, promote, promote! Use your web address and a tag line on your e-mail signatures, participate in newsgroups related to your content, participate in on-line forums—asking and answering questions and signing them with your e-mail signature. Find related sites and trade newsletter links, banner advertising, or even content. Make sure you have a newsletter and that you correspond with your subscribers regularly; this is invaluable to promotion and earning money.

On Marketing

For me, web site traffic is the most important element in terms of generating income. I do this by marketing my web sites through my e-mail newsletters, link exchanges, and pay-per-click search engines. The most effective to date has been the search engines, using specific terms that are related to certain areas of the web site that generates income. Also very effective is the e-mail newsletter. The least effective was when I was unprepared to accept the traffic that a search engine generated. I hadn't yet completed the content before the search engine started sending visitors. On the Internet, I feel that banner advertising has seen better days, and so I avoid most types of banner exchanges.

Top Revenue Streams

- Web design
- Affiliate programs
- Advertising revenues

Pricing Structure

All my web design is done a project quote basis. I have built web sites for as little as $500 and as much as $12,000. It all depends on the complexity of the site.

Additional Cost Items

The only additional computer costs I incurred were upgrading to a high-end computer and monitor. I also purchased a digital video camera and related hardware and software to be able to offer video on web sites.

Recommended Resources

- www.Dreamweaver.com—for building web sites; it allows me to do both hand-coding and visual layout.
- Justweb Inc., who hosts my sites, has a php-based server so I am learning how to write php code and build a database from scratch.
- www.PHP.net—for help
- www.hotscripts.com—for all flavors of scripts
- Meta Medic—meta tag analysis, www.northernwebs.com/set/set simjr.html)
- Dr Watson—HTML checker, http://watson.addy.com/

HIGH SCHOOL REUNION PLANNER

Reunited.com
Jonathan Miller, 40 | Weston, Florida | Ages of Children: 3, 6, 10

Office Oasis
Fifth bedroom.

Job Description
Management of high school reunion events in South Florida. Management of reunited.com web site, a database of more than 300,000 high school alumni.

Previous Career
Corporate marketing and public relations at American Express, Citibank, and Racal Electronics.

Transferable Skills
Time-management skills are critical for the EP. Balancing the limited number of hours available to work in the office, spend time with your kids, take kids to their activities, exercise, sleep, and spend time with your spouse is a huge juggling act that has its own unique level of stress.

Knowledge, Skills, Experience, and/or Education Needed

The ability to understand and troubleshoot computer issues is huge. Knowing how to keep a network running and staying on top of technology can not only save money but lots of time as well.

Industry Insight

We are fortunate in that, like death and taxes, there will always be high school reunions. Our web site is also a vehicle for high school classmates to stay in touch with each other over the years, and that is also a phenomenon that has no expiration date.

On Marketing

I find that working on charitable events is an excellent way to garner exposure for my company and my skills. I select events that are pertinent to my industry (hospitality) and my market (long-time local residents). One of the most important things we did was convert our business from "Inc." to ".com." Most of the daily processes that we were performing manually are now being done in a decentralized method on the web. We also have created a steady stream of income by offering products on our web site that can be purchased year-round, rather than our traditional "reunion season," which is May to September.

Top Revenue Streams

- Reunion admissions
- Reunion merchandise
- Reunited.com site memberships

Pricing Structure

Income generated from per-person admission to reunion events and products sold on our web site.

Additional Cost Items

We have made a large investment in audio-visual equipment, decorations, and other event items that would normally need to be rented from hotels at each event. In the long run, this has saved us lots of money. Printing and postage is a big expense in our business as well. We have looked at professional mailing systems but have never been able to justify the investment.

Recommended Resources

The Internet has by far been my biggest resource. The ability to order products, get information, and communicate via the web has truly made our business possible.

INTERNET JOB SEARCH COACH

STRATEGIC POSITIONING FOR PEOPLE IN BUSINESS
www.inter-net-working.com
Nancy Halpern, 43 | New York, New York | Age of Child: 6

"Have brutally frank conversations with members of your family and try not to be defensive or judgmental. Get their financial and emotional support but be realistic—they're entitled to have fears and doubts, even if you don't like it!"

Office Oasis

My "office" is the living room. We have a New York City apartment, so "sharing" is tough.

Job Description

I'm an executive trainer and coach specializing in Internet-related job-search strategies, especially the development of virtual communities and on-line networking. I also help clients improve oral and written communications for improved business performance.

Previous Career

My previous employment has ranged from being an executive director of a ballet company to a divisional vice president of a billion-dollar-plus importing company. This is now my third career—and the first one run out of my home—and was created as a response to my dissatisfaction with corporate life and being downsized!

Transferable Skills

Career strategies that have been helpful? Learning that career management is not something you do between jobs—it is your main job! Improving my listening skills, learning that the best communicators are those who can answer their customer's questions, learning that we all have customers, and realizing that integrity is the single most important quality you can have—it will never give you sleepless nights and it will contribute to you loving what you do. Other transferable skills include:

- organizational abilities
- balancing conflicting priorities
- marketing of ideas and concepts to a number of constituencies
- time management

Knowledge, Skills, Experience, and/or Education Needed

You don't have to be incredibly literate, but a basic understanding of Windows, Word, and Excel is almost a requirement in all work. Also a real user's understanding of the Internet is helpful—mostly as an interactive tool and information resource.

Industry Insight

The market is good, but more important is to know your place in it. Who are your target customers? What do you bring to the table that no one else does? What problems keep your clients up at night? I would advise aspiring EPs to do lots of research—go to professional association meetings, subscribe to newsletters, look at some web sites, and talk to trusted friends and colleagues about your goals, objectives, ideas, and ideals.

On Marketing

Marketing is tough, almost a full-time job in itself. I now work for a small consulting firm three days a week as a contractor. This guarantees some definite income stream, allowing me more time for family and work/life balance, while still keeping a small private practice and continuing to define my niche. Writing is a great way to self-promote, as is finding one or two small clients who can grow with you.

Top Revenue Streams

Interview skills coaching, résumé writing, and presentation preparation.

Pricing Structure

A daily minimum for a corporate client is $500 a day, or $150/hour, though sometimes I charge double that. For individuals, it's $100/hour.

> ### *A Day in the Life*
>
> It's so varied. I can take a two-day trip to visit a client or fly up for one day and then back home that evening (that's probably only once a month). Or I can see a private client at Starbucks and then go somewhere quiet to write. Or I can go to a client's midtown office and spend the day there. It really depends on my bookings.

Additional Cost Items

Minimal—a cell phone, association dues, and reading material to keep current.

Recommended Resources

Hmmm—an understanding spouse, dedicated time, careful scheduling, professional colleagues to help you on your way, and realistic expectations, especially that first year. And, of course, you must write both a business plan and a marketing plan.

INTERNET PORTAL FOUNDER

Amazingmoms.com
Kit Bennett, 37 | Vancouver, Washington | Ages of Children: 8, 12, 20, 21

"We've been able to achieve the goal of 'being there' for school functions, class help, home after school, etc., but I often wonder if we'd get more focused time with the kids if my office wasn't always 'there'!"

Office Oasis

Up until our recent relocation, my office was in our laundry room. For now, my "office" (which consists of a computer desk and bookshelf) is camped out in our kitchen/dining area.

Job Description

I do all of the design, writing, marketing, images, and more as the founder of Amazingmoms.com, an information portal for moms.

Previous Career

I was an artist, teacher, and children's entertainer/event coordinator.

Transferable Skills

From my professional experience, I carried over the classroom skills of lesson planning and implementation, as well as my personal experience with children and family issues. If I were to reenter the traditional work force (though I can't imagine ever wanting to!), I am now a self-taught web designer and developer. I imagine that this hands-on experience with software would be very marketable.

Knowledge, Skills, Experience, and/or Education Needed

I knew nothing of this industry when I first started, but rather used my God-given talent of creativity and self-motivation, which no amount of formal education can provide. However, my learning curve was very steep and as a result it took a very long time to launch my business. I would therefore recommend basic HTML and graphic program courses to shorten the learning curve. A previous career in marketing, writing, graphics, and editing would all make a natural transition into being a founder of an Internet portal as well.

Industry Insight

We are all witnessing the changes occurring within the Internet industry—large sites are failing due to overspending and lack of insight; dotcom start-ups that dropped all traditional avenues are finding that their dreams of getting rich quick were just that—only dreams. When Amazingmoms was first conceived, my intentions were to generate revenue through advertising dollars, but since then the industry has changed dramatically, requiring me to make adaptations to my business plan.

On Marketing

I have spent the past two years "spreading the word" about Amazingmoms.com and marketing myself as a family fun expert. It's actaully a much smaller world than we assume. To date, Amazingmoms has yet to spend advertising dollars, though I have worked on developing relationships with other sites through shared content, and the site's visitors are growing monthly. The two most effective marketing methods for me have been prominent search engine placement and site branding.

Top Revenue Streams and Pricing Structure

- Web advertising inventory—banner ads cost between $4 and $8 per 1,000 impressions; newsletter ad space can vary per account.
- Membership subscriptions—Amazingmoms Family Weekly costs $12/annually.
- Affiliate program revenue—we receive 5 to 20 percent commissions.

Additional Cost Items

- Domain name registration cost $15 to $75.
- Server costs vary depending on visitors.
- Media kits cost $10 to $40 each (not necessary but recommended).
- Graphics software and HTML editing software (if doing your own site development); otherwise expect to pay a minimum of $5,000 to hire a web developer.

Recommended Resources

The Internet itself has become my most valuable resource. I constantly surf, read, and subscribe to Internet-related newsletters. The amazing people I've met along the way constantly provide insight and inspiration.

INTERNET RESEARCH CONSULTANT

MCKINNON INFORMATION SERVICES | www.Internetresearch.bigstep.com
Heather McKinnon, 34 | New Glasgow, Nova Scotia, Canada |
Ages of Children: 7 months, 6 years

Office Oasis

Spare bedroom.

Home Biz and Mission Statement

McKinnon Information Services provides professional and reliable information search and retrieval services for professionals. Our mission is to assist the client in making their jobs easier by doing their research for them. By doing so, we help the client save time and money. Target market includes business owners (large and small), lawyers, doctors, and the general public.

Most Popular Services and Pricing Fees

My services include Internet research and instructing Internet workshops. I usually charge $20/hour for research and retrieval (which includes information gathered and compiled into the preference of the client, usually a spreadsheet or Word format) and $35/ hour for teaching Internet workshops. I teach Internet workshops to small business owners at our local Business Service Center using a course that I created. My rates are negotiable as sometimes the client has more than one need and we work out a payment system that works for both of us. In addition, I am an IT field rep with Nova Scotia Information Technology Human Resource Sector Council (part-time).

Favorite Products and/or Services

I absolutely love teaching the Internet course. I enjoy helping others learn and feel that I have found my "niche" doing so. I can relate so well to my students as we are all small business owners, and they look to me as I am "there" right along with them building a business. I also thrive on my research skills—believe it or not, but I get a "buzz" finding exactly what my clients want and need.

Marketing Strategy

I started out going door-to-door to potential clients, passing out business cards and brochures to everyone I knew. I belong to a network of other small business owners in my local area at our business service center, and we meet once a month for brainstorming ideas. I started doing exclusive work for a local lawyer and built up a great relationship with him doing legal research. After two years, this process continues. However, I have found that my market stalled locally and I needed to expand. I then began a web page, learning as I went along. I listed myself on almost every available freelance directory. The one I found the most successful for me was eLance.com. I started doing research for some of the staff of eLance and I now have clients all over the world—Japan, Bulgaria, California, Texas, Florida, Massachusetts, British Columbia, and Ontario. All of my contact is either on-line or by phone. Work is delivered either on-line or fax.

Recommended Resources

I have found the free services of Bigstep.com a terrific way to build an on-line business. When I started developing my web page, I used Geocities and learned HTML skills as I went. I am self-taught in all of my computer skills. I then discovered Bigstep.com; they have been more than helpful and I have found that my business took off after starting with them. Everything is step by step. If you have a problem with anything, they respond to you within a day.

LIVE ON-LINE TECH SUPPORT

CRC CONSULTING | www.chrisricci.com
Chris Ricci, 34 | Ontario, Canada | Ages of Children: 11, 4

> "My children see that Daddy can work from home and make money doing something I enjoy, rather than Daddy always coming through the door miserable and grumpy (to put it in their words)."

Office Oasis

Living room/dining room.

Job Description

Computer technical support services, web site creation, Internet promotion, and marketing.

Previous Career

Started in technical support at IBM Canada and worked my way up to Help desk manager.

Transferable Skills

Meeting deadlines, gathering research from the Internet, problem-solving, accountability, dependability, customer contact skills, and customer service.

Knowledge, Skills, Experience, and/or Education Needed

Windows platforms, computer hardware, Internet technologies.

Industry Insight

There is much room and this is a much-needed service. Trust is a big factor in gaining loyal customers.

On Marketing

Word of mouth still beats all others. I encourage referrals by offering current clients discount prices on the invoices I have. Also, since local customers are key, local advertising in community is important. I tried a business web site several times only to find that it doesn't help me. Mainly because in this country, there are not that many "computer savvy" people. They resist new technology somewhat. "Truck magnet advertising" is effective—and a nice parking spot with plenty of access to the road for drivers to see.

Top Revenue Streams

Repairs and support, computer parts.

Pricing Structure

$55/hour, 15 percent markup on all parts.

Additional Cost Items

SPARE COMPUTER PARTS

- HD cables: $5
- Printer cable: $10
- CD-ROM audio cable: $2
- Video card: $50
- HD Card: $257
- Spare HD: $100
- Spare floppy drive $25
- Power supply: AT, $30; ATX, $35
- Spare Ram: 20 pin, $50; 72 pin, $50; SDRAM, $75

TOOLS

- Computer repair briefcase, $200
- Or regular briefcase, $50
- Computer repair toolkit, $50
- Special magnetic screw driver, $10

Recommended Resources

A good van with a nice clean surface to put your truck magnets for advertising.

ON-LINE RETAILER/CHILDREN'S BOUTIQUE

OneOfAKindKid.com
Kim Machaux, 40 | Roanoke, Virginia | Ages of Children: 3, 10, 12

> *"My goal has always been to raise decent human beings who are kind, moral, and hardworking. I think working at home has actually helped me to teach them these values."*

Office Oasis

We are using our den as an office and the living room as our family room. Our dining room is our shipping department. The office has built-in bookshelves and cabinets, a huge desk in the form of two filing cabinets with a door lying on top, and a row of tables for printers, extra computers, etc. There's also a long rack of clothing that I'm working on at any given time in the office, and a computer for the kids, and toys on the floor! (Not so sure it's an oasis . . .)

Job Description

I have three businesses: a twice-a-year children's consignment sale; OneOfAKindKid.com, which is an on-line children's clothing store; and Snips'nSnails.com, an on-line store just for boys.

Previous Career

I have a master's in accounting and worked *very* briefly before having children. I have always stayed home with my children, working odd jobs that fit around my husband's schedule, mainly retail in children's clothing shops. I started my first business seven years ago to earn extra spending money, and it's grown tremendously over the years (I now make way more than I ever did working for others). My e-commerce company, OneOfAKindkid.com is growing rapidly too.

Transferable Skills

I've learned loads of computer skills and basic web-site design. Learning what marketing and advertising works and what doesn't is transferable—I also go to market and buy inventory, trying to choose what will sell. Customer service is important—prior retail experience is too.

Knowledge, Skills, Experience, and/or Education Needed

I think you need good business sense, great customer service skills, a sense of what will sell, and retail experience to open an on-line store. Computer skills are helpful too. I don't necessarily think formal education is needed—just the ability to learn quickly, the desire to be successful, and the willingness to work hard. Probably being disciplined is helpful since there are so many distractions. But absolutely loving what you're doing helps with that!

Industry Insight

The nice thing about e-commerce is that you can work 24/7; i.e., you can work on-line anytime. The only drawback I see is lack of sleep! But it's one of the few entrepreneurial ventures you can pursue without giving up your day job. While it's definitely time consuming (there aren't any short cuts on the time commitment to be successful), there is unlimited growth opportunity. You're marketing to the world! I *love* working for myself! I work seventy-plus hours/week, but I never miss my children's plays or school events, and my kids have me here when they're sick. I can't imagine ever going back to a traditional job.

On Marketing

Marketing takes a lot of time, even if you have loads of money to spend. I spend hours each day promoting my site. I look for sites to exchange links or to pay to advertise. One of the most common mistakes e-businesses make is assuming just because they are selling a great product at a great price, customers will just magically find them. You're kind of just out in the wilderness on-line—you really need to let your market know you exist! Networking and advertising are a must on-line!

I definitely have a limited advertising budget, so I've worked very hard to get the most bang for my buck. I have concentrated on "mom sites" and had great luck with them. I sponsor contests on selected sites and I pay to be featured on some sites, both informational sites and malls. Link exchanges with companies that are trying to reach the same target market but with a noncompeting product are great! OneOfAKindKid. com has teamed up with a couple of other mom-owned companies like GeniusBabies.com and BabyUniversity.com to do joint marketing we couldn't afford individually.

OneOfAKindKid also has an affiliate program (seventy-five affiliates to date). I highly recommend this as a very cost-effective method of advertising. The least effective marketing method for us has been banner ads—just not worth the money. We get tons of calls from companies wanting to sell us advertising on their site. The one thing I've learned after a year in business is that the harder the sell, the worse the results! If it's truly a great site to advertise on, they don't need a hard sell, and in general, they don't need to be calling people to advertise.

A Day in the Life

6:00 A.M.	Check e-mail, make coffee, answer e-mail, check site stats.
7:00 A.M.	Get kids up and off to school. Three-year-old watches Barney until 8:30, then three days a week she goes to a church preschool until noon. The rest of the time, we work together for a few hours. When she is more restless, we go out to the store or the zoo—something to get out of the house for a while.
Noon	Lunch and nap for my preschooler. During her nap I work.
3:00 P.M.	Wake her up and carpool. Kids do homework and play outside until dinner. All play together and with neighborhood kids too. I can get lots done while they are playing.
6:00 P.M.	My husband comes home and cooks us dinner and gives baths while I work more (I do stop working so we can eat together).
8:00 P.M.	After kids are in bed we pack and ship orders.
Midnight	Go to bed.

Top Revenue Streams and Pricing Structure

Selling children's clothing on-line is my biggest revenue source. I also have a twice-yearly warehouse sale to clear out excess inventory. We buy off-price or receive goods on consignment, so we have a normal keystone markup.

Additional Cost Items

- A professional camera and tripod (more than $1,000), to create photos of inventory
- A fast Internet connection (in my city, which has no cable modem or DSL, this was expensive as I had to get an ISDN line—$250 to install, modem was $750 and monthly charges are $300)
- An 800 number (I get many phone orders from catalog shoppers who just aren't comfortable shopping on-line yet)

Recommended Resources

While I went into this e-biz knowing retail and children's clothing, I'm not a "computer geek" and had no idea how to design web pages or program. Choosing what software to use was overwhelming—there's so many details like what shopping cart to use, what security system, what merchant account, what worked with what. I spent a lot of time researching different options and chose Yahoo! Store. It is incredibly easy to use and gave me the exact layout I wanted. It's all integrated—plus we are included in Yahoo! Shopping, an added benefit. I can't stress how easy it was to set up a store. I did my entire store myself.

For my inventory, the best malls/sites I've found are BabyUniversity. com, MyBabyShops.com, BabyEShop, and ChildrensMall.com. All are very reasonable and send targeted traffic.

I also highly recommend GoTo, which is a pay per click directory, but you need to watch it carefully. Those $.25 clicks add up pretty quickly! I spent the time to buy a lot of very targeted key words that fit my store perfectly and cost less than $.05 each.

ON-LINE RETAILER/MAIL PACKETS

FUNMAIL4KIDS | www.funmail4kids.com
Michelle Wilson, 28 | La Vernia, Texas | Age of Child: 6

> *"I am in a much better mental state when my husband gets home. This has improved our marriage dramatically."*

Office Oasis
I have an office in my home that is right off the kitchen and living room.

Job Description
I create educational sheets for children, mail monthly packets complete with craft kits, and maintain and promote my web site.

Previous Career
Before starting FunMail4Kids, I worked outside the home in the computer field as an EDI coordinator and system support specialist.

Transferable Skills
I have found that there is a lot to learn about owning your own business. There are so many wonderful sites available that offer great information concerning the legal aspects of business. As for skills, I brought everything I knew with me to my new business. I think that the toughest job in the world is raising children. The skills required for that position, such as scheduling and responsibility, are the most valuable of all.

Knowledge, Skills, Experience, and/or Education Needed
I had to learn web design but luckily that came very easy for me. I found all the information and answers to my questions from the web. In my business, my knowledge of children and dedication as a parent were the most valuable. It gave me the understanding of what other parents want their children to receive.

Industry Insight
I believe that the web commerce industry is the way of the future. I would advise anyone who is interested in started their own web-based business to do a lot of research. Start by studying other on-line busi-

nesses that are closely related to yours and understand that it takes at least one year to actually see your work start paying off.

On Marketing

I have joined a wonderful group of other WAHMs (www.littledidiknow. com), which has given me support and guidance through the last year. We have made great strides by pulling together to create a unique cooperative of small home businesses. We are in the process of having a catalog published and we have a representative of the group who will be doing the introduction on *The Rosie O'Donnell Show* on April 12, where she will hand out catalogs and promote everyone in the group. This is the best group of ladies!

Top Revenue Streams

Our monthly mail packets are the heart of our business. We are not currently raking in the bucks, but we are starting to see an interest in our product. We only recently started promoting our site heavily and expect to see an increase in sales during the next six months.

Pricing Structure

We sell our packets for a yearly subscription price of $96. We also offer three- and six-month packages, as well as individuals.

Additional Cost Items

I have the expense of several software packages that I rely on for designing children's sheets. I use Microsoft Picture It Publishing (I believe the cost was around $60) and several less expensive graphic packages. Everything else is really just the basics.

Recommended Resources

The Little Did I Know group started by Darcy Miller, who is truly gifted, is the most unique and inspiring group I have come across. We are working together to change the world, one mom at a time!

ON-LINE MEDIA/PROMOTION SERVICE PROVIDERS

HARMONYNET MEDIA GROUP | www.harmonynetradio.com/
Patrick & Gina D'Arce, both 40something | Escondido, California |
Age of Child: 6

Office Oasis
Upstairs room off of a loft, with sunny view of neighborhood.

Job Description
Publishers of media/promotional programs on-line.

Previous Career
He: technology/marketing computer wizard; she: organizational development/psychology/MFT.

Transferable Skills
This one is easy. Business/legal/marketing are essentials for an EP. The scale is less; the stress is less; the payback is higher. One of the most important is time-valuation work (different from time management), where the nature of tasks is more vital than the time allotment. Since intellectual/emotional capital is at a premium for EPs, it's important to allocate them for work that is purposeful and profitable.

Knowledge, Skills, Experience, and/or Education Needed
A good sense of humor. Time-juggling expertise. The ability to say *no* often and nicely. A lifetime interest in learning is far superior to credentials, diplomas, or (heaven forbid) career experiences.

Industry Insight
The Internet has proven to be a largely niche area for sales at the retail level. The true arena for the Internet is in niche test marketing and product launches. With 100,000-plus niches on the market, there is much to do. Anyone with a background in market research, focus groups, PR, or advertising would be well-suited to explore the promotional values represented by the Internet.

On Marketing

Doing private labeled work is the most steady. My most effective marketing method has been pilot testing an idea and introducing that to the key players in the market. My least effective has been setting up a web site and playing the search engine game. Basically, knowing your customer first is rule number one. Rule number two? See rule number one.

Top Revenue Streams & Pricing Structure

- Private test marketing on-line, $150 to $500 per hour
- Twenty minutes of greatness promotional audio, $45 to $100 per hour
- Private labeled radio programs, $1,000 to 1,500 per show
- Marketing coaching, $150 per month

Additional Cost Items

- Typical installation is any PC/Mac that's multimedia compatible with around 1,500 upgrades for memory/sound cards/editing software.
- Marketing investment is around twenty to forty hours per project at your billable rates, to set up the pilots.

Recommended Resources

- *How to Win Friends and Influence People*
- Motivational seminars/tapes
- A spouse that forgives easily
- Sitting in the spa at sunset

RETAILER/ON-LINE CARE PACKAGES

TheSmileBox.com
Shannon Rubio, 31 | Spring, Texas | Ages of Children: 3, 5, 7

Office Oasis

We have a four-bedroom house—office is in fourth bedroom; inventory is everywhere else.

Job Description

The Smile Box is an on-line gift basket business. I am co-owner of this business with my mom, who is a self-employed attorney. My half of the business involves designing and maintaining our two web sites, coming up with all the product ideas and getting them photographed and up on the web, advertising and marketing, and overseeing our two employees that package the products. Basically, everything *but* the accounting and bills!

Previous Career

I have been a WAHM on some level since my first child was born in 1993. Immediately prior to this business, I had my own post-partum doula service which was *great*. The last out-of-home job I held was as a genetics social worker.

Transferable Skills

I taught myself to build a computer from the case up, so I can repair computers (and have to a lot around here!) and know how to design and maintain web sites. These skills can easily be transferred to a salaried position.

Knowledge, Skills, Experience, and/or Education Needed

My first dot-com was my best education, even though I still owe my dad $1,000 from that venture. It cost $1,500 to launch NetNuts.com, which sold mugs and other promo material, but it was well worth the education. I learned how to design a Yahoo store myself, taught myself HTML and graphic editing, learned about the printing industry and the true costs involved (printers never tell you about their setup fees!), and what works and what doesn't with on-line advertising. All this has helped us successfully launch TheSmileBox.com

Industry Insight

It seems like every time I look, there are new care-package companies, compared to only one or two when we first started. Regarding web sites in general, if you can find a niche, I think the market is there if you are able to get the word out about your site, find a market in the on-line world for it, and market it properly.

On Marketing

We spend no more than $100 per month on advertising, which is basically for the web hosting services of Yahoo. Our most effective marketing method is the careful selection of keywords and key phrases in the site description of our Yahoo storefront. For us, "Mother's Day," "gift basket," and "Get Well" keywords have worked wonders. Our least effective has been $3,500 for an ad at ShopNow.com. We're listed on the top, but we got maybe three sales from that.

Top Products & Pricing
- Get Well Gift SmileBox, $35
- Thanks a Million SmileBox, $40
- Happy Birthday SmileBox, $35
- College Care Package, $35

Additional Cost Items
- $1,500 spent on inventory (one case each of miscellaneous gift items)
- $1,500 on bright yellow gift boxes with logo
- $750 for logo design
- $300 for a digital camera ($350, Kodak DC215)
- $200 to hire a photographer to take initial pictures for the site
- $75 in domain name registration fees

Recommended Resources
- www.wilsonweb.com

SEARCH ENGINE PRODUCER

KinderStart.com
Sara Lewis, 48 | Pasadena, California | Ages of Children: 1, 5

Previous Career
More than fourteen years in the entertainment industry, including as vice president, Hallmark Entertainment; vice president, Republic/Spelling Entertainment; kindergarten teacher—Children's Hospital, Los Angeles; substitute teacher—Los Angeles Unified School District.

Home Biz and Mission Statement
KinderStart.com is the definitive, all-inclusive search engine for information about adoption, child development, health, community, parent-

ing, learning activities, pregnancy, birth, and the wide range of issues related to children seven years and under. Our mission is to be the information source for parents, would-be parents, or anybody interested in infants, toddlers, and young children.

Primary Market
Parents of young children and would-be parents.

EP Start
Wouldn't it be great to find a search engine that focused on child-related issues and nothing else? That's what was percolating in my mind when (a) I found out I was pregnant with my second child, and (b) I started thinking about what I could do careerwise that might combine my business, teaching, and parenting skills while keeping me at home. Incredibly, an old friend of mine, Victor Goodman, who had successfully developed another search engine, had been having similar thoughts. After sweating out a round or two of financing arrangements, our work began in earnest. I was given free reign to start designing a user-friendly, inclusive index/search engine about young children. The technology, which I had previously viewed with skepticism, has enabled me to work at home and with staff people from coast to coast. On a personal note, the first time my sister asked me for advice about her sick child and I could tell her to go look it up at KinderStart, I thought I might be on to something.

SITE PRODUCER

FathersFirst.org
Pete Siler, 45 | Herndon, VA | Ages of Children: 12, 14, 16

Office Oasis
Unfinished basement, a plethora of full-spectrum fluorescent lighting.

Job Description
I am the web-site producer of the FathersFirst.org web site. There are many responsibilities required in keeping an informational web site up and running. Most important is keeping the site's content up-to-date

and relevant. I also manage and write a periodic fathering e-mail news-letter to help keep site visitors abreast of any new information.

Previous Career

I have more than twenty years of experience in the computer field. I am a former assistant vice president and director of research and development for high-tech software firms. Most recently I returned to graduate school and earned a master's degree in psychological services.

Knowledge, Skills, Experience, and/or Education Needed

- Ability to provide outstanding content and community development to gain repeat audiences
- Innovative thinking about what makes compelling web resources and content
- Ability to prioritize, meet deadlines, apply creative problem-solving
- Strong sense of interface and content design, as well as in-depth understanding of the web
- Strong working knowledge of HTML code plus experience working with multimedia and interactivity tools *or* capital to hire a professional web designer/developer

Transferable Careers

Like desktop publishing, web publishing borrows heavily from two ever-green vocations—graphic design and writing—so EPs with a strong skill in either discipline are attracted to this field. In addition, community development/customer service skills are a must. Site producers looking to reenter the job market can look into the fields of writing, publishing, web design, and association management, in accordance with the skills they feel most fluent in.

The Market

The market is wide open, but choosing the right niche is critical. On the Internet, the tighter the niche the more valuable a resource your site can become. On the other hand, if it's too small the traffic won't support paid revenue streams. Once you select your niche, the best ways to reach your market is through on-line promotion such as domain name registration in search engines, cross-linking, electronic press releases, writing articles for like-minded sites, and joining discussion groups and including your URL in your signature. Off-line promotion includes printing your URL on all marketing material, writing op-eds for print publications, and sending out press releases to newspapers and other print publications. More than most types of businesses, this one takes off through word of mouth in the Internet community.

A Day in the Life

Early A.M.—Upload ready files for daily site update. Answer e-mail, which is used for responding to visitors; manage interactive features of the site (such as QandAs, polls, discussion groups, contests); create contacts; write letters to the editors of on-line and off-line magazines and newspapers; respond to the authors of on-line articles; connect to on-line communities; subscribe to e-zines of interest or competition; and more.

Late morning—Analyze visitor log stats to note trends and strategize site changes. The logs give important information, such as which pages visitors stay on the longest, where they come from, which keywords were used if they came from a search engine, which keywords they use for the site-search feature (indicating what type of content they are expecting to find), and more.

Early afternoon—Work on fresh content for either the e-zine or web site.

Late afternoon/early evening—Kid break!

Late evening—Maintain, research, and/or consider adding such interactive community tools as bulletin boards, opt-in e-mail lists, visitor surveys, contests, and awards. Prepare pages for next day's site update.

Industry Insight

The Internet has created a dynamic, diverse, and daunting new marketplace for professionals who have an editorial, graphic design, and/or membership development background. As people in the mainstream learn to take up recreational web surfing as easily as they click the TV remote, there are more and more opportunities for entrepreneurs with a penchant for publishing and a passion for a particular subject to "reach out and touch someone." A site producer develops content and resources that meet the needs of a specified target audience and is responsible for the creation, maintenance, and continual improvement of the site.

If you already have Internet access, see if your Internet service provider (ISP) offers free personal web page construction (most do). Tools are designed for the nonprogrammer and are generally very easy to use. With these tools, set up your own web page and test your selected market with a trial run. Get a feel for the ebb and flow of the daily tasks involved and get to know your target audience. Can you serve their needs well? Are they responsive to your content? Do you enjoy the work? If, after several months, you believe you've found your niche and you have the fundamental skills to succeed, obtain training on web design software to become proficient. Read books on the subject, take courses, join mailing lists, frequent on-line web design and publishing communities, and experiment.

Additional Costs Items
- High-speed access to the Internet, $360–$600/year + $100–$300 installation fee
- ISP, web hosting, and domain name fees, $500

Top Revenue Streams
- Advertising—banner ads and e-zine sponsorships
- Affiliate programs (but be very selective, keeping your target audience in mind at all times)
- Membership and/or subscriber fees
- Internet access and web hosting
- A product line and services specifically developed for your readership

Key Resource(s)
- Internet Professional Publishers Association, www.ippa.org

SITE PRODUCER/NICHE

PAM HUNTER ENTERPRISES / HUNTER'S PONY FARM |
www.huntersponyfarm.com
Pam Hunter, 46 | Amboy, Washington | Ages of Children: 9, 19;
five adult children

"I would rather lose money and time doing the right thing for a client or person than keep that money for myself knowing I have not done my duty as a valuable part of society."

Office Oasis
At the end of a long hallway in an alcove, approximately 12×10 feet.

Job Description
Artist and designer by nature, have developed a very popular equestrian web site for information and fun (www.huntersponyfarm.com with more than 40,000 hits per month). Duties include marketing and of course everything that goes with being an executive: financial decisions, accounting, personnel, taxes, juggling family and work, payrolls on occasion, and more.

Previous Career
Administrative assistant for the fur industry while also running my own house-cleaning business with fifteen employees.

Transferable Skills
EVERYTHING! The skills I learned working in an office and working closely with the executives in the fur business helped me develop the discipline and know-how to accomplish running my own business. Having been self-employed now for more than twenty years in some form or another, I find it unthinkable to have to reenter the work force. But, if circumstances dictated a need, I believe I would make an excellent manager. My skills are well rounded, well balanced, and extensive. From accounting to human resources, computers to skilled craftsman, there isn't a whole lot I wouldn't be qualified for.

Knowledge, Skills, Experience, and/or Education Needed

To be a successful EP, one needs to be disciplined. I have had three years of college (still trying to get that B.A. in between other obligations) with majors in business and psychology, minor in biology. The courses I have taken helped me immensely in keeping business records, having a basic understanding of people, having a basic understanding of the law, knowing how to do research, knowing where to find resources, and, again, being disciplined.

Industry Insight

As far as the web site–design aspect of my business is concerned, I am really not pursuing it now. There are thousands of designers and IT professionals out on the streets right now, and I have found it to be a very *slow* market. I subscribe to five industry-specific printed and several e-mail publications, and things aren't looking too good right now. However, my art and design business is going *well*. Paintings, home decor items, and so on are in high demand. People are "nesting," which I believe comes from uncertainty in the economy and increasing violence in society. People, families, are staying home more, looking to create that "perfect" home environment that is safe, secure, welcoming, and low stress. This is a boon for my art!

On Marketing

I use the Internet to market most of my art. This means I need hits! So I spend a lot of time signing guest books, sending out my own equestrian e-mail digest with links to my auctions and on-line store. I hand out business cards and e-mail my friends and family with updates and interesting developments in our sites or businesses, so they may tell someone else or forward my e-mail on.

The least effective marketing method? I *don't* use the Yellow Pages. I tried that once and it was very expensive and yielded no results, *but* I also think it depends on the kind of business you have. Most of my clients are on-line, so I market on-line. It wouldn't pay me to market on-line products and services to people who are not on-line!

The most effective marketing method I have used is *banner ads*! OK, I know the industry is saying they don't work, but they do *if* you target them to the audience you are trying to reach. I never just put my banner ads out there to show up on just any web site. I tried that at first, but it wasn't a success. Once I began targeting my ads on web sites that were somehow related to mine, I saw a 400 percent increase in hits. That translated into more business and more money!

I also contributed to a couple of articles on another very popular animal web site that is affiliated with AOL. This brought a lot of traffic to my horse site, which in turn brought traffic to my other sites. I wrote a book *Fighting the Gangs: One Kid at a Time* that I give away FREE online to any interested person. This book is used by law enforcement agencies across the country. It has brought more business my way. http://www.geocities.com/gangfyter

Top Revenue Streams
- Art and design—home decor—on-line marketing of my designs and products on my store site www.huntersgifts.com
- Marketing on the Internet and using search engine placement and banner ads to draw clients
- Using auctions to market my designs and other miscellaneous goods

Pricing Structure
I try to make products that pay me about $10 per hour, although some things bring more, some less. Web site design brings me about $30 per hour.

Additional Cost Items
All my software was free except Quicken. I purchase florals, paints, and other art supplies either on sale or wholesale. For my business, talent is the greatest asset other than knowledge of marketing.

Recommended Resources
- www.zdnet.com for software, free industry-specific printed and on-line publications
- www.linkshare.com for banner ads
- www.ehits.com for search engine placement
- www.netmechanic.com to keep my computer up and running
- www.antivirus.com to protect my computer

- www.ebay.com for selling products
- www.bigstep.com for my on-line store using the domain name www.huntersgifts.com
- Publications such as *eWeek*, *Internet Week*, and *Javapro*

VIRTUAL ASSISTANT/ASSOCIATION MANAGEMENT

THE ADMINISTRATIVE EDGE, LLC | TheAdmEdg@aol.com
Lizanne Fiorentino, 40 | Suffern, New York | Ages of Children: 6, 10

"When my five-year-old son answered the phone and said, 'Good Morning, Matthew speaking, Mommy's in the bathroom,' I wanted to crawl under a rock although now I view the incident as having been very symbolic. We always want everything to go smoothly and put our best foot forward professionally, but the fact is I am not just a businesswoman, I am a mother, wife, and businesswomen (the order of which changes minute by minute). Whatever success I may achieve in life and business is a result of how I manage that combination."

Office Oasis
My office is located in an extra bedroom downstairs next to the family room. Ugh. Loud, but convenient when I need to referee a dispute.

Job Description
I provide "virtual" business support (word processing, database management, communications, desktop publishing) to entrepreneurs and small- to medium-sized companies as well as association management services to nonprofit organizations.

Previous Career
Vice president with an international investment management firm responsible for administration/investor relations and regulatory compliance.

Transferable Skills
My organizational and technology skills were the most transferable. When managing multiple clients, each one must feel like your only client and main priority. Remembering names and dates are always ap-

preciated, as is being proactive in suggesting to a client how to make an event or assignment run smoother, sharper, or most cost effective the next time around. The ability to "make a sale" is a skill that works well in the corporate environment as well as in the EP world. Whether you are selling your product/service to a potential client or selling yourself and your abilities to a prospective employer or current manager, the ability to close the sale is vital.

Knowledge, Skills, Experience, and/or Education Needed

Working in a "virtual" world it is no longer a matter of location, location, location. It is, however, a world where success depends on communication, communication, communication. I find it essential to be proficient in several software applications, particularly word processing and spreadsheet programs. Proficiency in a multimedia application and page-layout programs are also beneficial if not essential. The greater your technical expertise the greater value you provide to your client. Moving information via e-mail, fax, and even PDF file is becoming a standard of business; proficiency in these applications is essential. You don't have to be able to rewire a PC or program a NASA launch, but you should be well versed in the bells and whistles of the software you use. Communication is vital in a business where very often long periods of time may pass between face-to-face meetings. Just because you don't see your clients everyday, you don't want them to ever forget about you or have them think you forgot about them.

Industry Insight

With more and more corporations downsizing their work forces, more people are making the decision to strike out on their own. Those people need support, thus making business support services a wide-open field. Additionally, as we become a more time-compressed society, the ability or willingness to volunteer for service or industry associations is on the wane while members' demands for better services is increasing. The role of association management fills that need.

On Marketing

I rely heavily on networking and lead generation groups for business. I find that in this business, particularly on the association management side, referrals are the best source of new business. I have obtained association clients as a result of virtual support clients, and the reverse has also been true. Association management clients tend to be retainer clients, which has been beneficial as cash-flow management has been one of the greatest challenges I have had to deal with. The least effective marketing tool is print advertising. It is cost prohibitive and in order to be meaningful must be a long-term investment.

Top Revenue Streams
- Association management retainers
- Word processing
- Data entry

Pricing Structure
Most functions are billed at an hourly rate; word processing and administrative functions are billed at one rate while multimedia and desktop publishing are billed at a higher rate. Data entry is billed on a "per record" basis as are mailing functions; i.e., collating, stuffing, sealing. Out-of-pocket expenses are billed accordingly. Fees range from $25 to $40 per hour.

Additional Cost Items
Not much to mention, except quality ergonomic equipment and a multi-line phone/answering machine.

Recommended Resources
I find networking with other professionals (both colleagues and people in other professions) to be helpful. The ability to talk about common issues and brainstorm solutions with others is always productive. Additionally, business related web sites and e-groups can be excellent resources. Their usefulness, however, may be offset by the time factor involved in sifting through the volumes of available information in order to find information of value.

VIRTUAL ASSISTANT/CERTIFIED

ROSANNE KUPIEC, CPVA | www.professionalva.com
Rosanne Kupiec, 51 | Utica, New York | Ages of Grandchildren: newborn,
14 months, 3 years

> *"I am convinced that it takes a village to raise children—not strangers who do not have a vested interest in their well-being. I became an EP grandparent because I don't believe day care providers have the same loving connection to my grandchildren as I could have. It took a lot to switch careers at fifty years old, and sometimes I wonder if I was crazy to do that. But when they are with me, I know that I'm perfectly right to try starting over. They're worth it."*

Office Oasis

Formerly my grandson's nursery before my daughter moved into their new home. Beautiful light, light-turquoise sponged walls, blushed oak armoire holding computer, scanner, etc. Big, bright window.

Job Description

I am a certified professional virtual assistant (VA), providing office management, consultation, and specific tasks/projects to overwhelmed entrepreneurs and small business owners.

Previous Career

Executive level administrative support of twenty years (fifteen years with a major airline).

Transferable Skills

Communication skills, organization, intuitive listening, creative brainstorming. For reentering the work force, all skills and knowledge learned via today's new technology in regard to software, research via the Internet, and resources of what/where/how to better support executives are all transferable.

Knowledge, Skills, Experience, and/or Education Needed

I trained on-line for five months to become a certified VA, while working full-time. It was a grad-level course—very difficult and intensive. I would say you must be very computer literate, Internet savvy, creative, have a great command of English language and excellent communication and voice skills, and have solid administrative background in support of those in decision-making positions. A personal quest for continuous knowledge, education, and improvement of one's own skills all help, plus a sincere desire to create value in another's business with a keen emphasis on trust and confidentiality. Last but not least, you must enjoy being in a *support* position.

Industry Insight

Per the U.S. Department of Labor, 8.5 million people in the United States now identify themselves as independent contractors, independent consultants, or freelance workers. People are starting home businesses at the rate of 2 million per year, and they could use a VA to help them grow! I would advise EPs to quantify their skills, ask themselves if they truly enjoy being in a support position, and if the answer is yes, seek certification and begin marketing (with cash reserves on-hand . . .).

On Marketing

My most effective marketing method has been to answer an ad for someone seeking virtual support (on-line). My least effective has been mailing letters. I recommend reading a variety of books, subscribing to on-line newsletters, and seeking professionals with information to guide and mentor you. Visibility and credibility are key. Join business groups, give presentations, and make your name and face known.

Top Revenue Streams

- Internet research
- Travel arrangements
- Personal and business calendar scheduling
- Niche development (doing all the research and leg work associated with a client's particular niche, such as getting lists, publications, memberships into associations, creating brochures and marketing letters, and more)
- Event coordination and planning

Pricing Structure

$35/hour for a minimum of eight hours retainer per month. Otherwise, hourly rate is $40/hr.

Additional Cost Items
None.

Recommended Resources
We did not have Business Network Int'l (BNI) in our area, so I spearheaded efforts and am now president of our chapter. Also, an article in a local newspaper on my business has led to contacts. Speaking engagements at local business groups, colleges, and high schools have helped. Also, Small Office Home Office (SOHO) trade shows and networking trade shows.

VIRTUAL ASSISTANT/GENERALIST

LISA IVALDI | lisa.ivaldi@home.com
Lisa Ivaldi, 39 | Brampton, Ontario, Canada | Age of Child: 3

Office Oasis
Converted spare bedroom on the second floor of house.

Job Description
I provide administrative services such as word processing, Internet research, newsletters preparation and distribution, and seminar and meeting planning. I also attend meetings to take minutes.

Previous Career
I worked for more than twenty years in administration from secretary to manager in several different sectors (real estate, waste management).

Transferable Skills
All.

Knowledge, Skills, Experience, and/or Education Needed
For my type of business, you must have good computer and keyboard skills as well as a pretty good knowledge of how to work on the Internet. I have a university education but I don't think that is necessary to be successful in this type of business. However, experience is essential. You must have some idea of what is expected of you and how to do it. Your clients are not paying you to learn as you go.

Industry Insight

I think off-site administrative work is growing. Companies find it cheaper to hire a contract worker to do what is needed rather than hire some-one full-time and pay their benefits, etc. Many small companies do not want to hire full-time or even part-time staff. They may not have the room to set them up with all the equipment needed. Off-site contract employees provide their own space and equipment. The best way to break into this field is to network. You have to let people know you are out there and what you are doing. Speak to everyone you know—friends, your doctor and dentist, former work associates—and let them know what you are doing and ask if they know anyone who might be able to use your services.

On Marketing

For me, face-to-face or on-the-phone networking has been my best mar-keting method. I have also sent marketing to human resource depart-ments of local government offices and big companies to offer them an alternative to temp agencies.

Pricing Structure

I charge between $15 and $25 CDN (roughly $9–$15 U.S.) per hour, depending on the client and the job. If a client requests it I will put a cap on the per hour rate to get a specific job done.

Additional Cost Items

None.

Recommended Resources

- Local board of trades or chambers of commerce and other local networking groups

---

VIRTUAL ASSISTANT/MEETINGS AND CONFERENCES

THE VIRTUAL SECRETARY | www.annabaron.com
Anna Baron, 31 | Allen, Texas | Ages of Children: 3, 13

> *"Don't get too involved with a client that is demanding and needs every-thing yesterday. This creates too much pressure on you and reflects on*

*your interaction with the family. My goal is to earn extra money—not
stress myself and my family out."*

Office Oasis
My office is merged with the living room where we watch TV so that I
am always available to my family. We have three computers in this area
so everyone can be on a computer—even the three-year-old! She has
several CD games (Sesame Street, Clifford, Richard Scarry games, Tele-
tubbies, etc.), and she is very efficient at turning the computer on and
using the mouse and understanding the games.

Job Description
Virtual assistant, offering desktop publishing, web design, and administrative support.

Previous Career
I worked for ten years as an executive level assistant or executive secretary. My boss(es) traveled frequently, and I was used to not only working unsupervised but working via phone/e-mail/fax, just as I do from
home now.

Transferable Skills
All.

Knowledge, Skills, Experience, and/or Education Needed
Virtual assistants don't necessarily have to have skills beyond a regular
office support service, but it is essential to have experience. A business
management degree wouldn't hurt but isn't necessary. I don't have
one; I just wish at times I did! I would suggest taking community
courses on business management and keeping your skills and software
up to date.

Industry Insight
I have obtained only one client on-line. It seems more difficult to find
them on-line. Although I am a "virtual" assistant, it seems clients still
want their assistant to live close whether they see them or not. I have
found this a problem several times. My solution was to hook up a video
cam to my computer so I can now perform teleconferences with clients.

On Marketing

Every year I choose a charity or foundation to donate time and services to. Last year it was a tournament for a battered women and children's shelter here in Dallas. Generally my company is listed several times in the brochure or program for that event because I do administrative work, desktop publishing (programs, flyers, brochures, menus, etc.), and web site design. I always donate all of my services and that results in the directors/managers of the event really talking me up to everyone they come in contact with. I also get included in all of their advertising and marketing for being a "major sponsor." Great way to help people, meet new people, and find new clients!

Top Revenue Streams and Pricing Structure

- Administrative, $20–$25/hour
- Meetings/conferences, $25–$30/hour
- Desktop publishing, $30–$35/hour
- Web sites, $40–$50/hour (each page=$100–$150)

Additional Cost Items

- I have done TONS of transcription; if you anticipate doing transcription, machines cost about $200.
- Zip drive is needed to store each client's files in case of theft/crash of computer. I perform a weekly backup of these files and each client has their own "disk" to back up.
- Cable or DSL connection; it's fast and speeds up your time researching info on the net, and it doesn't tie up your phone line. It's also nice to give info to clients on the phone at lightning speed instead of saying "It's still downloading, hold on . . . "
- Cordless phone
- Computer cam for teleconferences

Recommended Resources

- www.headhunter.com
- www.inc.com
- www.elance.com
- www.dallasnews.com (I find most of my clients through the local newspaper; I answer ads for part-time secretaries or anything part-time I think I can handle. I get 60 percent of my clients this way)

WEB AND GRAPHIC DESIGNER

ART BY CHRIS, INC. | www.artchris.com
Chris Agro, 40 | Fort Lauderdale, Florida | Ages of Children: 8 and 8 (twins)

Office Oasis
My office is located in the front Florida room.

Job Description
Consultant and designer for advertising and marketing materials, web site design, and e-commerce sites.

Previous Career
None.

Transferable Skills
There are more ways than ever to make a living today—Internet e-commerce, franchises, work-at-home opportunities, etc. No matter what track you choose, if you are going to make a go of it on your own, remember that those who succeed tend to focus more on the fundamentals of growing a successful business—business and marketing plans, client acquisition and retention, future plans, etc.—than where they do it from. If you are focused and self-motivated, most if not all your workforce skills will come in handy at one point or another.

Knowledge, Skills, Experience, and/or Education Needed
Talent. As a small business owner of a graphic design and web site design studio, I wear many hats. Entry-level positions would go to those who have a good working handle on the programs we use to create the projects. Working on the same computer platform is also a benefit. Most freelancers who work from their homes have Internet access with e-mail. Education is not a requirement in my view; talent and a good working knowledge of the programs would rank higher.

Industry Insight
As a graphic designer for the first eighteen years of my professional career, I saw no end or slowdown in sight. Now with the Internet, smart graphic designers have also entered this field. No matter how the mar-

ket swings, one thing is certain: the Internet is here to stay. How it all turns out is anyone's guess, but those who get involved and go with the flow of what the Internet brings to business will prosper greatly as time passes.

On Marketing

Most effective: I have had a business-card-sized Yellow Pages display ad in my local directory for some years. Many people doubted the power of this directory, but I have found it to be an asset. I recently landed an account with a five-star resort in the Bahamas. They found me while in town at a boat show by looking me up in the local Yellow Pages! Another form of marketing has been focused on promoting my web site through search engine placement, which I also learned at home on my computer! Least effective: local papers, membership directory ads in private organizations.

Top Revenue Streams
- Seminar programs
- Web site design
- Printing brokerage

Pricing Structure
- $95/hour for concepts and design
- $72/hour for post-design production

Additional Cost Items
- Web site design: Macromedia Dreamweaver/Fireworks 4 (approximately $500)
- Graphic design: Quark Xpress, Adobe Illustrator, Adobe Photoshop (approximately $500 to $700 each)

Recommended Resources
- *Home Office Know-How* by Jeffery D. Zbar
- www.recourses.com

WEB APPLICATION PROGRAMMER

LODESTONE SOFTWARE, INC. | www.lodestone-sw.com
Lara J. Fabans, 33 | Los Gatos, California | Age of Child: 3

Office Oasis
A study, though sometimes the laptop heads downstairs and outside, depending on what's going on.

Job Description
Plan, architect, design, code, test, and integrate web-based applications written in PHP, Perl, HTML, XML, Java, JavaScript, etc., to meet the customers' requirements. Document code, testing, etc. Fix other people's code.

Previous Career
Computer scientist, software testing, project management, technical phone support.

Transferable Skills
- Project management
- Communication skills (e-mail, e-mail management; knowing when to do the extra phone call to calm a nervous Nellie customer)
- Self-discipline
- Ability to plan and to estimate

Knowledge, Skills, Experience, and/or Education Needed
I have a B.S. in electronic engineering. A bachelor's or associate degree in computer science would suffice, or you can learn on your own by reading technical books, taking on-line training/tutorials, and practice, practice, practice. An important skill is persistence. I had to learn good business skills on the fly (taxes, payroll obligations, cash flow planning).

Industry Insight
The future is bright and getting better all the time. Once you learn the good programming skills of one language, they are transferable to all other languages. Customers hire me for my ability to problem-solve and to create their application. As long as I stay flexible and organized, I am

able to deliver. I am constantly turning down new work; I'd rather ensure a high quality of what I do commit to and produce.

On Marketing

I have a simple web site, and I post my résumé on technical job posting lists (www.prgjobs.com) and technical organizations (Software Contractors Guild). People find me. I got a lot of responses from putting my résumé on Monster Board, but it was mostly a waste of time. The recruiters did not read my résumé as to what I was looking for, and I spent hours calling back people telling them that I wasn't interested since I felt it was good customer service to return all phone calls. The best marketing is having a proven track record of success (and failure—you'll never get better if you don't make mistakes, and you learn a lot about what you do and don't want out of a job).

Top Revenue Streams
- Perl
- PHP
- Java programming

Pricing Structure
$45–$75/hour

Additional Cost Items

I obtained high-output Internet connectivity (DSL), which was a large regular expense. I avoided a lot of the upfront dumping of money because I leased computers as I found the need instead of buying. My largest expenditure has been on software (Macromedia Dreamweaver/UltraDev, SoftQuad XMetal, Microsoft Visual Studio) and technical books (most libraries don't have the latest books that I need to stay on top of the learning curve).

Recommended Resources
- www.hwg.org
- www.sba.org
- www.scguild.com
- www.prgjobs.com
- www.ework.com
- www.guru.com
- www.tjobs.com

WEB DEVELOPER/CYCLISTS

BENKA WEB DESIGN | www.benkaweb.com
Francoise Benka, 41 | Seattle, Washington | Age of Child: 10

Office Oasis
My office is in the living room, somewhat separated by the furniture arrangement but I can still see the TV from my desk.

Job Description
Design and develop web sites, maintain web sites I've created, find new customers, maintain contact with old ones, design and develop advertising for my own company, accounting.

Previous Career
Retail garden and nursery sales, landscape maintenance.

Transferable Skills
Retail sales experience really helps in dealing with customers. A good sense of design and what people want is essential. Expect to occasionally spend twelve hours a day at your job. It's not something you can "go home" from. When you have your own business, you develop a sense of dedication that makes a nine-to-five job seem like a cakewalk. You also learn all aspects of the business, not just the tiny part that is your "job," so you know all the ins and outs that make the business successful or not.

Knowledge, Skills, Experience, and/or Education Needed
A really good understanding of HTML is essential. The desire and the motivation to stay informed about the latest technology in your field is imperative. An artistic talent is extremely helpful. One can *learn* good design, but it's always easier if it comes naturally. No experience required, but the more you do and the more references you have, the more credible you will be. The ability to educate yourself is required.

Industry Insight
Right now I think the market for web developers is saturated beyond capacity. There are thousands of young twenty-somethings who are willing

to do the same work for half the price just to get their feet wet. It is helpful to work with another person or as a team because one person cannot specialize in all the different aspects of web development and make the whole company look good.

On Marketing
The majority of my advertising budget goes to print advertising, but I think the most effective form of advertising is word of mouth—and that takes time. Don't expect to be an IPO in two years. Write a business plan even if it's only for you; then do the things necessary to achieve your goals.

Top Revenue Streams
- Basic web site design
- Flash movies
- Banners

Pricing Structure
$50/hour routine web design work; flat rate of $100–$250 per page, for design, depending on complexity.

Additional Cost Items
None.

Recommended Resources
The most valuable resource I found was DigitalEve.com. The women on the mailing list were invaluable, not only for their knowledge but their support as well.

WEB DEVELOPER/GENERALIST

VIRTUAL IMPACT! | www.virtual-impact.net
Lori R. Stone, 42 | Germantown, Maryland | Ages of Children: 10, 14

Office Oasis
Family room.

Job Description
Web developer/consultant.

Previous Career
Paralegal for nine years.

Transferable Skills
The main skill I transferred from my previous career as a paralegal is my business savvy and my ability to draw up contracts for business. Other than that, since I went from a field that was not technical at all to a field that is very technical, I could not really transfer much. One of my business partners, however, was a technical writer prior to partnering with me, so he is still working those skills in my company as a documentation (help documentation and screens, etc.) specialist for Virtual Impact. My other business partner has been in the printing industry his entire career, so he has been able to transfer skills such as layout, color combinations, and general work flow.

Knowledge, Skills, Experience, and/or Education Needed
Computer industry knowledge, web development knowledge, www knowledge, various software and hardware knowledge depending on the task. Also, an eye for layout, design, color, and graphics is important.

Industry Insight
This is a very competitive field, and it's also a field that is gaining strength in an accelerated upward spiral. What you know today in industry knowledge is already outdated tomorrow, so it's a field that's hard to catch and keep up with. To break into it, you need to first learn as much as you can on your own, either through course work or independent study (there is a wealth of information right on the web, which you can exploit), and then attempt to come in as an entry-level person or an intern in a company that is willing to continue training you on the job.

On Marketing
I promote my web site to the search engines using effective meta-tags, join web-related member organizations that promote my business, and enter my business into skill-specific databases (like guru.com) so those

searching for my skills will find me. I also find that local clients have promoted my services via word of mouth. My most effective marketing effort has been to redesign my web site and resubmit it to search engines again. My least effective has been banner ad exchanges.

Top Revenue Streams
- Web designs, development, and redesigns
- Web site maintenance
- Writing help documentation for custom software

Pricing Structure
For most projects, we offer fixed-rate pricing based on specific package custom created for the client, but for other peripheral items we usually charge $60 to $80/hour, depending on the type of client and requested tasks.

Additional Cost Items
- A high-caliber computer (fast, a lot of storage space, etc.) with good graphics capability and a sound card is needed (approximately $2,100).
- Internet access is required via an ISP (DSL or cable is recommended, $25–$50/month).
- Various web development software is also needed such as graphics manipulation tools like Photoshop and Paintshop Pro ($100–$450).
- An HTML editor (Dreamweaver, Homesite) $99–$350
- An FTP program (~$20), plus any other types of programming software you might need (Java and associated compiler, etc.).
- A fast scanner (~$200), a laser color printer (~$300)
- A digital camera (~$200–$1,800)
- Domain name registration ($70 for 2 years)
- Renting space with a web host (costs vary from $10–$50 a month).

Recommended Resources
The SBA has a wealth of information for small business owners (my dad was a volunteer at SBA, so I consulted with him). Also the local Better Business Bureau is a great resource for meeting other small business owners for networking and other information.

WEB DEVELOPER/HOST

BLUE RIDGE WEB DESIGN | www.blueridgedesign.com
Jack J. White, 43 | Blue Ridge, Georgia | Ages of Children: 11, 16, 17

Office Oasis
In the loft of my cabin.

Job Description
Creating content, adapting existing content to a web-friendly format, creating and maintaining the logical structure of the content, running the web server software, running other web-related software, and performing system administration for the computer system(s) the web server runs on.

Previous Career
I am a former Air Force pilot. I flew helicopters with the Air Force Rescue and Recovery Service and then flew airplanes for the balance of the twenty years I was in the military.

Transferable Skills
Naturally the technical aspect is apparent (programming, graphic design), but it's the other qualities that are (in my opinion) more important. Traits like customer service, commitment, integrity, and a strong work ethic are what make an individual succeed whether in the marketplace or from a home-based business.

Knowledge, Skills, Experience, and/or Education Needed
Anyone with a love of computers who doesn't mind cracking a book to do a bit of studying can handle this line of work. As a pilot I was exposed to computers and cutting-edge technology on a daily basis so the transition came fairly quickly. While I think folks from a technical background may have an easier go of it, it's not a requirement by any means. Here in North Georgia we have a small college (North Georgia Technical Institute) that is now offering a certificate program in web design. Since the colleges are now meeting this demand with their curriculum, this might be an option for those interested in traditional forms of learning (vs. self-taught). I would also point out that the capabilities and

breadth of web design responsibilities are huge. Most of the designers doing what I do are small mom-and-pop operations that focus on web sites targeting the marketing aspect. There are firms that require a much greater breadth of experience and expertise because they develop high-end sites that are fully interactive and offer features such as shopping carts, credit card validation, and database integration.

Industry Insight

With the advent of WYSIWYG Editors that allow web site creation without a knowledge of HTML/JavaScript, there seems to be an explosion in small web site operations. Everyone is a web master it seems. To succeed, however, you need to go beyond this and really learn what you're doing. Hand-coding of HTML is a *must* because those fancy editors will not always give you what you are looking for, and they do have limitations that can only be solved via a hand-coded site. I would also advise against quitting your day job and moonlight to start. Once you have a dozen or so clients (and a working spouse!) then you might consider going it alone.

On Marketing

In this line of work, a web presence is certainly a requirement, but more important you should market in your local area of operations and not worry so much about getting jobs over the net from half a country (or world) away. If you market effectively in your local area, you'll probably have all the business you need. I live in one county but have joined the chambers of commerce of two additional counties in order to get listed on their web sites in the member sections. This assists in bringing business in. Rack cards and business cards should be placed in each chamber of course. I also ask each client if I may place a rack card holder in each place of business to increase exposure as well. Additionally, I have also been fortunate to secure a winning bid on a chamber site redesign, which will increase exposure because everyone who visits that site (and needs one themselves) will see my business logo at the bottom. They may think to themselves that if the chamber was willing to use me then perhaps they should also.

I have also been amazed by how many jobs have come in as a result of placing the business logo on our automobile windows. My wife works for the local newspaper and is always meeting clients around town. As a result the logo is taken all over town every day—it's a rolling billboard in effect.

Last, if a designer can come up with a business model to augment his income stream, that would be great. I recently launched a "For Sale by Owner" web site targeted to the tourist interest in housing here in the Blue Ridge area (www.fsbotoursonline.com). I've already set up the Yellow Pages and plan to order signs with the business URL. Homes are viewed by listing number on the sign which correlates to the listing number on the web site. I also plan to use VR technology to allow for 360-degree views of home interiors.

Top Revenue Streams
- Web design
- Hosting sites brings in some income but is certainly not a cash cow.

Pricing Structure
At the moment, I bill $295 for a home page and $95 for every page thereafter. I have been criticized by other designers for undercharging. My hourly rate is $30/hour.

Additional Cost Items
You bet. You need a digital camera, a digital film reader, and lots of specialized software if you're going to do the job correctly. Software titles include Adobe products such as Photoshop and Acrobat. The best deal is their $1,000 package that is targeted for web design and includes four different applications. The top of the line WYSIWYG editor is Dreamweaver by Macromedia for high-end sites. I also believe Microsoft Front-Page is a must because the Office Suite is so prevalent and many clients that want to do their own web site maintenance insist on this product. For a search engine, I purchased WebPosition Gold for $350 and for my VR application I spent another $350 on PixAround. I use AceHTML as my text-based editor ($79.95) and have also purchased several other web-related programs that I won't go into. As you can see, the bulk of your costs as a web designer are in software.

Recommended Resources
- My favorite resource is the Web Developer Virtual Library and the discussion list. Just join and watch the messages—you can learn so much from a list that it is amazing, and people are often very helpful if you have a problem.
- HTML Writers Guild

WEB DEVELOPER/MIDSIZE CORPS

SCARLET'S WEB | www.scarletsweb.com
Tara Lang, 32 | Pittsburgh, Pennsylvania | Ages of Children: 5, 8

"I think some of my clients appreciate what I am doing and hire me just because I am an EP."

Office Oasis

It used to be my fourth bedroom. Now it's my very cluttered, hard-to-walk-through office.

Job Description

Web master/programmer/designer.

Previous Career

Lots of them: international purchasing, library science, retail. My B.A. is in anthropology.

Transferable Skills

Computer skills! This can be self-taught, but resources like books and on-line tutorials are a must.

Knowledge, Skills, Experience, and/or Education Needed

In this day and age, a degree from a computer school in web development may help but is still not necessary.

Industry Insight

Well, there are hundreds upon hundreds of so called "web designers" out there, who bought a program like Microsoft FrontPage, and learned how to use it to slap some pictures and text on a page. In this business, you definitely get what you pay for. Designers who can program and do custom graphics, layouts, and hand-code are the ones who make it in the long term.

On Marketing

In the beginning, I sent out brochures and letters—but honestly? I don't have *time* to market. Most of my business is through word of mouth. Deliver a good product, and you'll get those referrals too.

Top Revenue Streams

- Programming!!!
- Start-up design (graphic layout of new sites)
- E-commerce

Pricing Structure

Every job is on a case-by-case basis. Programming work is $50 per hour, graphic design is $35. I also have standard web hosting, setup, and maintenance rates.

Additional Cost Items

I bought lots of books on different programming languages. Having up-to-date web software (browsers, etc.) is a must, as is a digital camera.

Recommended Resources

- Digital Women, www.digital-women.com
- Women's Business Network, www.wbninc.com
- Work at Home Moms, www.wahm.com
- Staying on top of my industry by reading the trade mags, entrepreneur mags, joining IEEE Computer Society and ACM to read their magazines
- Sarah and Paul Edwards' books *Working from Home, Secrets of Self-Employment, Getting Business to Come to You*
- Jessica Keyes' book *Internet Management*
- Joining regular email lists to get quick blurbs on my industry, such as www.itworld.com and www.computerworld.com

WEB DEVELOPER/REAL ESTATE

BELLA WEB DESIGN, INC. | www.bellawebdesign.com
Desiree C. Scales, 32 | Marietta, Georgia | Ages of Children: 6 months, 2½ years

"I really encourage EPs to build an office in their home especially designed for work. I started out working from my bedroom and that was quite difficult. I was interrupted all the time. Ever since we built our home office, I've had peace and quiet and a lot of privacy. Plus it is an environment conducive to my work—it helps me switch from 'Mommy' to 'CEO' quite easily."

Office Oasis
Basement, just built last year.

Job Description
CEO, web site designer, accountant, marketing guru, customer service, tech support, copywriter, graphic designer, sales manager, saleswoman, photographer, project manager. That about covers it!

Previous Career
I used to work in sales for an apartment complex, which helped me refine my sales skills. I was a flight attendant for United Airlines, which helped me learn how to handle customers. I was a reservations agent for Delta Airlines, which taught me good phone and sales skills. I was a web designer and communications specialist for Delta Airlines, which gave me the confidence and polish to write, design, and sell our web sites and services. I've been amazed at how my "careers" have really laid the path for my ultimate job of an entrepreneur. I didn't even know that being self-employed was what I wanted until Delta told me I couldn't work on the intranet I helped develop from home after I had my first child. I said, "I can do this from home and if Delta won't let me, I'll do it for myself and my family!" So here I am.

Transferable Skills
I think our success in growing our company and more than doubling our sales in the past year comes from having good alliances with other companies that bring business our way. (I learned that from the airline industry. It's called code sharing.) I also learned some important skills from the six months at Delta when I trained other reservations agents. I learned how to teach people very technical things in a simple way. Our clients now call me their Internet coach. They aren't very technically savvy, but they know they need a web site. They want someone to sit down with them and hold their hands through the process and give them a feeling of control. By treating our customers and business partners with respect, we've earned their trust and they've sent a lot of referrals our way.

As far as reentering the nine-to-five work life, I think you learn a great deal about multi-tasking and project management from working for yourself. You have to be everything to everybody, and you wear different hats every single minute of the day. You learn how to organize your workday to help you get things done in a more efficient manner. I think I am an even more valuable manager and team player now than I was before I started the business. I've learned how to fine-tune the important qualities of listening objectively and learning how to find a compromise in a difficult situation, both of which are very important skills when trying to sell or resolve a conflict.

Knowledge, Skills, Experience, and/or Education Needed

You have to be very tech-savvy as well as have the sales and customer care skills to pull off creating a successful web design company. You need to know HTML, plus a few editors like FrontPage and Dreamweaver, and have excellent graphics design skills. Most important, you need to know Photoshop and other image editors like the back of your hand. Those who keep their technical skills well honed do well in this business. Take classes and go to seminars. Also, read all of the trade magazines available. Arm yourself with knowledge and learn how to talk about new technology so that you're comfortable in a room full of people who are your peers as well as a room full of people who have never used a computer or seen the Internet.

Industry Insight

We have seen more people moving toward the web as a less expensive form of advertising. Our fourth quarter results this year (2001) were our strongest ever. The events in September have guided more people to leverage the Internet as an advertising and communications tool. We have seen a surge in database development, e-mail marketing campaign consulting, hosting, and web-site development. As far as breaking into the industry, do a few free sites for nonprofit organizations or for friends, family, or associates. Then get out and network! Join the chamber of commerce, your trade organizations, and on-line groups. Most important, make sure your own site is a real standout among your competitors and put your portfolio on-line immediately.

On Marketing

The best way to market ourselves is to partner with other companies that provide the same services on a larger scales or complementary services. We partner with a company called Storefront (www.storefront.net)

because they provide us with software we use to create our e-commerce sites. In turn, they send business our way as one of their preferred web development partners. We also partner with a larger web design firm that creates template sites for realtors. We have a division of our company, Realty By Design, www.realtybydesign.com, which creates custom web sites for realtors. This larger firm wants to keep its clients happy, and it uses our skills to do this. It has seen that once clients start out with a template site, after a few months they are so excited by their success on the Internet that they are ready to build a full-blown custom site with all the bells and whistles. This firm then sends the clients to us. We take over and create a client's custom site from the ground up. Again, our reputation with our clients helped bring us that business and the partnership.

Another thing we do is hold seminars for realtors and our local chamber of commerce on the topic of web design or other related topics. We have signed up a lot of our clients from these seminars. The only caveat is that the seminar has to leave your potential clients with a feeling that they've learned something from you. That is critical because they will trust you and you'll gain their respect and their business!

Top Revenue Streams
Referrals, seminars, and strategic alliances.

Pricing Structure
Our basic custom business package includes a five-page site priced at $1,500. We also host our sites starting at $35 per month, which includes thirty minutes of maintenance and basic search engine submission.

Additional Cost Items
A high-speed connection has made a big difference in the past couple weeks. We've had to pay $90 per month for IDSL because DSL and cable modem isn't available in our area yet. You also have to buy Photoshop, which is around $600, and FrontPage and Dreamweaver, which run about $200 to $400 each.

Recommended Resources
One of the things that has really helped us grow even more this year was hiring some freelancers to help us out on projects. Our goal is to use our

freelancers full-time and for me to take more of a project-management role. Our designers are the best around and work well as a team. And the most important piece of running this business are the people who help us care for our children while Rob and I are working. We couldn't do this without the collaborative help of my family, our baby-sitter, and our wonderful teachers at our preschool.

WEB HOST

Word.Net
David Holst, 30 | Springfield, Missouri | Ages of Children: newborn, 2

Office Oasis
We have a finished, walk-out basement looking out onto open farm fields nearby.

Job Description
I run my own web hosting business out of my home. My wife, Charla, runs her business, TheraPower.com, out of our home as well. I handle the special chores involved in storing all my client's sites on a server, including site security, data backup, power backup, and persistent connection from the server to the Internet, among many other technical tasks.

Previous Career
I was a computer programmer for Amdocs (www.Amdocs.com), in the Washington, D.C., metro area. We made the conscious decision to move and start our own businesses in order to have more time at home and start a family.

Transferable Skills
A background in computer science and/or web design is common, but several courses in any computer programming language can lay the foundation. With a knack for and understanding of programming languages, the rest of the skills needed can be self-taught over the Internet. Web hosts looking to reenter the job market can offer their technical skills to any larger, more established companies (dot-com or otherwise).

Knowledge, Skills, Experience, and/or Education Needed

- A good web host needs to have a handle on programming languages, especially Perl, and strong trouble-shooting skills.
- Ability to take technical concepts and explain them to lay people every day; 70 percent of a web host's daily tasks is e-mailing customers answers on how to fix their server problems, or talking them through it over the phone.
- The quantity of e-mail a web host receives increases astronomically as their customer base increases, so one has to enjoy and appreciate that form of communication.
- Ability to work well with people from many different disciplines and varying degrees of technical experience is important

Industry Insight

The millions of web sites and billions of web pages that make up the Internet are housed on specialized computers called "web servers," administered to by technicians like myself who are web hosts. Web hosting is critical to the existence and survival of the Internet, for without a place to store and secure all this electronic data, there'd be no "wild, wild web." To break into this field, read up on the industry and experi-

---

A Day in the Life

Early morning—Roll out of bed, eat some breakfast, walk downstairs, check e-mail, reply to urgent ones, prioritize to-do items, surf the web for daily tech news.

Late morning—Come upstairs for lunch; if it's a nice day play outside for an hour in the afternoon.

Early afternoon—Set up any new hosting accounts needed.

Late afternoon/early evening—Return calls around 3 P.M. Fix any urgent problems.

Early evening—Go upstairs for dinner. Enjoy family time.

Late evening—Back downstairs for a few more hours of e-mail/web surfing as necessary.

---

ment by designing and hosting your own site first. If your technical skills are strong, you can purchase a basic UNIX server, which has dropped down drastically in price in recent years. For a more "user-friendly" variety, try a Cobalt Raq that costs almost twice as much but has pre-installed software that allows you to use a web browser to set up new accounts and service them. Going forward, make sure to set up a merchant account and a toll-free line since the majority of your customers will be from out of state.

On Marketing

This business may be slow to grow, but once you have an established customer base, the focus shifts to customer service rather than acquisition. Expect to peak at 600 to 700 customers if you plan to remain working at home solo. Remember that once a customer sets up a web site, starts promoting their domain name, and sets up an account with you, they will depend on you for a core part of their business and are likely to stay on during the duration of their site's existence. Like a telephone company, your services are vital to their venture and would be the last thing they'd cut off. As for acquiring customers, consider a niche of site owners that typically generate low traffic so you have a larger customer-to-server ratio or a larger revenue-to-cost ratio. For instance, expect that each server (which is a fixed cost) can host from 50 to 200 sites, depending on how large the customer sites are and how much traffic they get. If you're an active participant in an Internet community, you can start spreading the word about your web hosting services there, so that your business and personal belief system are in sync. Count on heavy word-of-mouth advertising, and promote this method by offering customers a free month of service for referrals. Establish ongoing incentives like a generous discount if customers pre-pay annually for their monthly fees. And to ensure even cash flow, accept credit card payments only.

Top Revenue Streams and Pricing Structure

Our standard domain hosting accounts are priced to encourage pre-payment; for instance it's $15 a month if you pay by the month, but if you pre-pay a year in advance, it drops to $12.50 *and* you get more web space:

- $15/monthly, 75MB of web space (charged to a credit card)
- $150/year, 150MB of web space ($12.50/month)

- $240/two years, 240MB of web space ($10/month)
- $300/three years, 300MB of web space ($8.33/month)
- $360/four years, 360MB of web space ($7.50/month!)

Additional Cost Items
- UNIX Server / Cobalt Raq, $700 (basic) / $1500 (enhanced)
- Co-location fees, $200–$500 per month per server (depends on the traffic your customer's sites attract)
- Co-location installation fee, $200–$500
- High speed access to the Internet, $360–$600/year + $100–$300 installation fee

Recommended Resources
- The Web Host Industry Review, www.thewhir.com
- Web Hosting Survey, www.whsurvey.com
- Web Hosting Magazine, www.webhostingmagazine.com

WEB MASTER INSTRUCTOR

WEBFUT DESIGN | www.webfut.com
Laura Mercer, 33 | Henderson, Nevada | Ages of Children: 5, 7

"Financial freedom isn't everything, although some more furniture in our house would be nice. Patience will pay off for us down the road. We will most likely never be rich, but we'll at least be financially secure in a few years. I waited until my youngest was in kindergarten to start my business, and I plan to start out slow but gain momentum as the boys grow older."

Office Oasis
Converted small bedroom.

Job Description
I'm a certified web master and instructor for continuing education at UNLV. I work part-time because my youngest son is in school only half-days. Most of my work is via the Internet except for the web master classes in the evenings and/or weekends.

Previous Career
Stay-at-home mom.

Transferable Skills
The traditional work force prepared me in terms of handling paperwork, time management, personal skills, and marketing skills. Working out of my home has taught me to be highly productive in short periods of time; use of my time is highly optimized now. I feel that if I were to enter the traditional work force again, I would be a very efficient worker. I am now a "multi-tasking" type of person.

Knowledge, Skills, Experience, and/or Education Needed
You need to have a handle on what works and what doesn't for web site development in order to teach it, plus preferably some sort of certification and/or continuing ed courses on web development and business administration (as it relates to the on-line experience). A firm knowledge of HTML and other languages is important, and having an active web design portfolio will give you the confidence to handle questions that come up in the classes. One or more popular web site editors like FrontPage and Dreamweaver is a must if that's what your students will be using. In addition, since I concentrate on the business end of web development (marketing, e-commerce, customer service, etc.), I spend about one to two hours a day reading on-line articles so my teaching material stays fresh.

Industry Insight
There's more to becoming a valuable web master than churning out great-looking web sites—there's the marketing and business end of web development. Many universities offer some type of computer courses but would probably jump at the opportunity to offer web master, e-commerce, and/or on-line marketing courses to the local community. Of course establishing yourself in this local industry will have a great trickle-down effect on your own business. If you're a web master, find your niche in web development and create a course out of it—to the benefit of many local individuals and small businesses as well as your own home career.

On Marketing
My most effective marketing tool to date is word of mouth. I treat my clients like gold, and they seem to love referring people to me. I also do

A Day in the Life

7:00 A.M. The boys wake. Husband makes them breakfast, then leaves for work at 7:30. I focus on getting them dressed and doing their morning chores (make bed, clean up room).

8:40 A.M. We hop on our bikes and ride ¾ of a mile to their school.

9:00 A.M. I come home and get to work. Spend one hour checking on clients' needs, and the next hour reading and doing updates with other projects.

11:30 A.M. I get back on my bike to pick up my youngest son. We get home about 11:50 and eat lunch, review work he did that morning, talk and eat until about 12:30. At that time he and I work on some learning books and color until about 1:00. I will try to hit the computer at this time for another couple of hours and remind my son that it is now his time to play or color on his own. He plays with the neighbors' children and there is a steady parade of kids in and out until close to 3:00.

3:00 P.M. I finish work, get ready to bike back to school with my youngest in tow to get my oldest son (the biking is my free workout program).

3:30 P.M. Eat a snack and we all play outside or inside.

5:30 P.M. I'm back inside making dinner or burning dinner (I am not a great cook), and my husband arrives home on his bike (he also uses biking as his free exercise program) and takes over the parenting duties while I do the domestic stuff or at least try to do them. After dinner we do homework, play, and then read.

8:30 P.M. The boys are in bed and I go back to work. I am usually too tired to be productive at night so I mostly read or catch up on e-mail. For the evenings I teach the continuing ed classes, my husband is home with the kids.

11:00 P.M. Both parents are in bed. Phew what a day!

a lot of networking with local web masters as well, so when one needs help they can transfer their client to me and vice versa.

Top Revenue Streams and Pricing Structure

- Classes, $50/hour
- Web design projects, charged by number of pages and amount of graphic work, usually $50–$100 per page for basic design
- Web site marketing, a monthly fee of $50–$75

Additional Cost Items

The software for web site development can get costly, especially if you are into graphics programs and server side database development, but you can start out small with a couple of programs and develop slowly with about $1,000 to start. Grow with your abilities. Cable modem or DSL access is a must for Internet work, and can run about $50 per month. Reading all the material out there about web development and e-business is free, but if you're able to find a local certification program (which can cost from $1,000 to $3,000 depending on where you are and how many courses you take), I would highly recommend the educational investment. Digital cameras, which can cost between $200 and $1,000 depending on your needs, are also a good idea.

Recommended Resources

I received certification as a web designer, and all the courses I took helped me immensely. It cost about $2,000 for the certification but it gave me the knowledge I needed to move forward. I also really enjoyed each class. I definitely recommend getting some type of on-line or local certification.

WEB MASTER/SERVICE INDUSTRIES

SHADES OF WHITE | www.shadesdesign.com
Wendy Martin, 40 | Crystal City, Missouri | Age of Child: 7

Office Oasis

There is a room set aside the length of the left of our home; in it we have two computers, a drafting table, file cabinets, and bookshelves—and piles and piles of paperwork. It's a step down from the living room and is one of the two rooms in the house blessed with a door (the other one is the bathroom).

Job Description

I am a Jill-of-all-trades. I market, do collections, send billing, and do the design and bookkeeping. I also kiss boo-boos and answer the endless question "Honey, where is my (insert missing item here)?"

Previous Career

Before I was in web design, I was in graphic design (as an EP then). Before that I was a dog walker/sitter. That was what I did to get through college. I guess I've almost always been an independent. I did take full-time employee positions from time to time when business was slow, but they were short stints—never more than a year at a time.

Transferable Skills

I honestly believe the only difference in my line of work is the need to be self-motivated in bringing new clients. Other than billing these clients, all other aspects of my experience in the design business have been about the same skill set. I would say that as an EP, I get to flex my creative brain muscles a lot more often. There's no one else to hand over ideas for me to finish.

Knowledge, Skills, Experience, and/or Education Needed

I have a BFA in graphic design. It's not necessary, but the knowledge of good design is not something one can get from a computer program. I am *still*, even after studying art for more than three decades, learning something new about design every day.

It is a given that a web designer be computer savvy. There are so many things to know even before you get to the web site design and implementation. I think I probably use six or more high-end design and graphics programs in creating a web site. And then there are the programming languages like HTML, JavaScript, and CGI. I keep taking classes and trying to stay up-to-date, but with the fast pace of computer development right now, it's like I have a second job just staying current.

Industry Insight

It's such a new market, everyone and his brother is trying to get into the act. I think that the good and talented will survive, but only if they push the marketing envelope. Almost all the businesses I have approached are so turned off to yet another web site pitch. I've had business owners tell me that they've been approached at least twenty times already. I try to market my customer service aspect of my web hosting. Most places just throw together a site and put it on their server and then the client never hears from them again, except when it comes time to pay the bill. I have put together a program where the business owner can have as much or as little interaction with me as they want or need.

On Marketing

I try everything. If I read in a newsletter that this gimmick worked for XYZ company, I try and incorporate it into my own marketing efforts. Word of mouth has been my most reliable method of getting actual paying cliental. Least effective? Newspaper ads. I spend money and get bobkes. Oh, not true, I get a lot of people trying to *sell me* their services. I always turn it around on them and ask if they need my services or know of anyone who does. (So far, few leads or business that way!)

Pricing Structure

I price by the page. Also the complexity of the site design. If I am charging an hourly rate it's around $35, but that varies with the client and the skills needed.

Additional Cost Items

- I have a zip drive, a 21" monitor and a high-end Mac. I'd say close to $3,000 without programs; programs run another $5,000. Upgrades are usually a third of what the program is if you are starting fresh, and many manufactures offer what they call side grades. If you have a competitor's program, you can upgrade to their program for a fraction of the cost.
- I'm also in the process of deciding on a laptop purchase. Many clients don't have access to the web and this would be a good selling tool for my designs. Just plug in and play ("See what I can do for you, Mrs. Customer? And if you want one that does *this,* it's an additional $3,000.")

- Some basics classes like HTML writing and web site design specifics are an additional cost. I attend classes on-line, so I can do the class work when I have a few free hours and not be tied down to set class times. On-line courses start at $80 and go up from there.
- Art supplies can run around $15 per presentation, but that is a cost I add into the bill. I try and keep overhead to a bare minimum.

Recommended Resources

Would you believe your friendly Yellow Pages?

PART
II

ENJOYING
YOUR FAMILY,
YOUR WORK,
and
YOUR LIFE

Designing Your Own Solution

rying to track how the average EP family comes to be is like attending your child's graduation class and trying to define the average student. The composition of a "typical" student population is a veritable mix of talent, intellect, energy, and temperament, as is the "typical" household wherein an entrepreneurial parent (or two) resides.

While EPs are united in their desire to balance work and family on their own terms, each family unit is unique—with children of different ages, parents in different life stages, spouses with different attitudes and expectations, and households of different financial resources. That's why the challenge of "designing your own solution" to entrepreneurial parenthood is not about examining stats and pushing your life into the wedge of a pie chart. Rather, it's about giving yourself permission to break *out* of the chart and be that other one percent people wonder about!

Coming from speckled circumstances and points of view, we hope the following stories—including EPs who leapt out of the traditional work force for one reason or another, parents who were already home-based, single parents, couples who work at home, and parents who take their home career one step closer to their life goals—will help you as you write your own.

Permission Impossible? Breaking Away from the Traditional Work Force

Employee Scenario: You reach for the phone. A vaguely sick feeling begins to percolate in the pit of your stomach as you attempt to wrangle yet another extra sick day from your employer than your allocated annual days allow. Perhaps this time it's triggered by a child running a fever, a teen heartsick by a broken relationship or a failing grade, a sudden snow day, a child-care arrangement turned sour, or a critical parent-teacher conference. You dread making the call to work, feeling guilty as a professional if you do but even guiltier as a parent if you don't. And it's not that your boss is a cold-hearted ogre or anything of the sort—it's just that rules are rules and you naturally feel uncomfortable breaking them . . . especially over and over.

Perhaps the greatest benefit of striking out on your own is the freedom to be the parent you need to be without having to "ask permission" for the time and space to do it in. Again and again, we heard from parents who struggled to pull themselves out of the psychological grip of the employer-employee relationship, the steady-paycheck-for-steady-hours covenant that felt "safe" as a professional yet vulnerable as a parent. Even those who work in the most family-friendly companies feel inhibited in taking advantage of available policies that help them cope with their work-family responsibilities, fearing the backlash in performance reviews, co-worker attitude, and being labeled as a slacker.

Is giving yourself permission to parent—at your discretion, in privacy, and at a moment's notice—an impossibility in today's society? It may seem so at first, but given time you'll be able to put things in proper perspective. Bill Douglas, an instructor and video producer in Overland Park, Kansas, shares how becoming an EP first felt to him:

At first being at home feels a little guilty, as if you are skipping school or something. You don't know what to do with down time, and you feel like you're watching the world go by without you. (Of course, when the kids get home from school, you don't feel that way at all. You feel blessed to be with them, while everyone else is working or fighting traffic . . .) Over time, you begin to become more and more creative on how to promote or improve your business, and when you top that crest, you soon find that life is way too short to be able to complete all your ambitious plans. You must pick and choose, setting aside enough time for your family that makes being an EP worth it.

Sharon Hudak, a marketing consultant for software companies, found that giving herself permission to *change* her life was a lot easier than asking someone else's permission to *live* her life. "I was driven by two things: the desire to live my life by my own course, never having to say 'may I please, sir' to any middle-aged male boss; and to allow my son every opportunity to have a rich and rewarding childhood with a minimum of schedule-induced stress." Jo-Anne Penn-Kast of Designwweb, Inc., so succinctly puts it this way:

I have given myself permission to do what is important to the spirit and soul of my family—including myself.

Declaration of Parental Independence

I give myself permission to (your greatest desire)

_____

on (a specific date)

_____

because I have earned it by (your greatest sacrifices)

_____

_____

_____

Signed: _____

Second Baby as the Trigger

Sometimes giving yourself permission to break from traditional employment takes a period of many years, during which life and parenthood go by in a blur. After reading through the stories of what sparked an EP into becoming one, we found a popular pattern emerge that involved the birth of a second child activating a reevaluation of a parent's relationship to their firstborn. Erica Kuntz of BeHosting.com in Lakewood, Ohio, recounts:

> I had been working for about eight years in product management for a Fortune 500 company that produces greeting cards, at the rate of fifty or more hours per week right up to my maternity leave. Although I planned to return to work six weeks after Celia was born, during the leave I was afforded the opportunity to spend more time with my first daughter, who was then six years old. I had worked full-time since she was a year old, and after reconnecting with her, when the time came to return to work I just couldn't. It was sheer turmoil.
>
> It was the birth of my second daughter, more than anything else, that really helped me break free from the mindset that my "job" played such an integral role in my success as a person. I didn't believe at that time that we could financially afford having me at home, but when my husband and I did some number crunching, to our shock—at least on paper—it was looking like we could squeak by on one income. This opened the door to alternative possibilities, options I had never considered. The end result was a freedom where before there were limits.

The birth of a second child triggered the chain of EP events for A. Reneé Holmes of Lithonia, Georgia, as well. The major deciding factor in Holmes becoming an EP was her then four-year-old daughter who began to do and say things that she would *never* have taught her. Even with an eight-week-old son at the time, her elder child was the major reason for making the change. "And I must say, she's a beautiful person now," remarks Holmes. "She's almost eight and I can really see a change in her."

A second child also gave Annette M. Barron of Office Support Unlimited in Rochester, New York, the push she needed to pull her daughter out of a difficult day-care experience:

> I had my daughter in day care after she turned one. She was sick constantly and absolutely terrible when I brought her home

at night. It was killing me leaving her in someone else's hands every day, not knowing what was actually happening to her. I can't tell you how many times I got called at work saying that I had to pick her up because she was sick. When she kept getting bitten and scratched, I finally convinced my sister-in-law to watch her. Then my son came along and I went back to work for five months. My guilt was so extreme that I had no choice but to quit. I had to make this work. I feel like I missed two years of my daughter's life. It makes me ill to this day to think about it.

Living with a Layoff

While many EPs took a deliberate leap into self-employment with a running jump, others felt pushed more than pulled. These EPs didn't jump off the corporate bandwagon, but were rather thrown off by a company layoff. Shaken by the fall, they have become determined never to be pushed by someone else in an unwelcome direction again.

Linda Smith, a writer in Maplewood, Minnesota, used her severance and unemployment pay to give her a little grace period to get on her feet. Unfortunately, the immediate repercussions of the layoff are still being felt. "I'm still shaky," admits Smith, "and I have no cushion." Susan Heyboer O'Keefe, also a writer, has felt she traded financial security not only for more time with her son, but for the time and flexibility to do more creative writing.

> My home-based work certainly contributes a large part to our household income, but is it enough? Not when I look at the balance in my retirement account. I miss the economic stability, knowing there's a paycheck every other week. As a freelancer I know the check is **never** in the mail. I was able to survive the first year because I had the cushion of a profit-sharing account from my full-time job. I wish now I would have lived on a stricter budget that first year, put more money sooner into my retirement account, and tried to have at all times a bigger nest egg.

Despite the economic trade-off, Susan has never regretted her decision to freelance and only wished she'd had the nerve to do it sooner.

Making the Break

Although the resounding consensus from active EPs is that they miss "absolutely nothing!" about the traditional work force, there were a number of recurring laments. To assess your readiness to make the break, rate the following on a 1–10 scale of importance, then determine whether you feel each is primarily a "Benefit" to working outside the home or a "Trapping," with a checkmark in the selected column. Think carefully about what each means to you.

What You'll Give Up	Rate	Benefit	Trapping
Steady Paycheck	____	____	____
Company Benefits	____	____	____
Paid Vacations	____	____	____
Camaraderie/Sense of Community	____	____	____
Teamwork/Collaborating	____	____	____
Exposure to New Techniques	____	____	____
Administrative and Technical Support	____	____	____
New Clothes/Looking Sharp Daily	____	____	____
Regular Routine/Structure	____	____	____
Watching Your 401K Grow	____	____	____
Lunches Out	____	____	____

From VP to EP

Like Linda, Nancy Halpern used her severance package for "breathing space" while she transitioned into working at home. After many years in a number of high-level positions, Nancy decided to use this financial cushion to get her through her first year as an EP, admitting that the "real test" is whether she and her family can make it through the *second* year.

> My previous employment has ranged from being an executive director of a ballet company to a divisional vice president of a billion-dollar-plus importing company. Today I am an executive trainer and coach, working with both groups and individuals on two key areas: Internet-related job-search strategies, and improving oral and written communications for improved business

performance. My cash flow is now unpredictable—a few big chunks at a time, and I am always worrying about where the next gig is coming from. But I do have more time with my son, which is critical to both of us.

What has helped us is cutting way back on our expenses (no vacation this year, few major purchases), I took advantage of my husband's home office setup (paid for by his employer) to use the fax and supplies, and I created a good tracking system so that I could manage expenses and income. So far so good—not rich, but not losing. And we have saved a lot of money from my severance to carry us through this year. But next year will be the real test.

Moonlighting

Mustering up the courage to become an entrepreneurial parent was a recurring theme in the surveys we received. It was particularly poignant when we heard from respondents who were holding down full-time jobs "and a dream." A court processing specialist we heard from keeps her full-time job for the financial security it provides and moonlights on the side, hoping to situate herself soon so that she can become fully self-employed. "I would trade my whole salary now to be with my children full-time because there's no price tag that can replace time spent with a growing child," confesses Holly Jo West, the mother of three and an information systems analyst whose full-time job currently provides her family's health insurance. Moonlighting with a home business that creates children's photo ID cards, she and her husband are working on getting her back home. They are following the lead of EPs like a biological consultant in Hemet, California, who started to moonlight because he could only find a part-time job in his field. Over time, this dad began to make more money on the side than with his part-time salary, and that's when he felt prepared to become an EP full-time.

Home Economics: Breaking into Business
and Parenthood from the Home Front

> **Stay-at-Home Scenario:**   Remember when you first became a parent and the definition of who you "were" turned inside out immediately? It was like a line was drawn distinctly in your personal history, and there was a "you" before children and a "you" after. The decision to stay home with your child(ren) seemed clear and whole and right at the time, but as the weeks, months, even years passed, you knew there was something missing. This "piece" of you that was missing was either a part that had always been there but was behind you or a part that was always there up ahead of you. For a long time, you have hoped for some type of a reunion, a reconnection, or a renewal of sorts that would finally complete you.

Perhaps the greatest benefit for stay-at-home parents who have become work-at-home parents is the "happiness factor." Over and over, we heard from EPs who said, "If *I'm* happier, everyone's happier." Erin Stillman, who runs an office support service in Oakdale, California, refers to home-based entrepreneurship as being an "extended parent." Without a doubt, adding the pressures of work, clients, office decisions, and deadlines to your responsibilities as a caregiver becomes an extension of who you are—and sometimes a matter of extending yourself beyond recognition to those who love and live with you. Warns Stillman, "An at-home parent already has so many things to balance and take care of during each day, and adding more to it is interesting. It can either force you to be stronger, more independent, more organized . . . or it can break you."

Regardless of the exact motivation, the transformation of an at-home parent to an at-home *entrepreneurial* parent doesn't usually have the same financial impact on the family as those who have transformed from what our society coins a "working parent" to entrepreneurial parent. In households where a SAHP (stay-at-home-parent) turns into a WAHP (work-at-home parent), checkbooks are likely already being balanced off of one income and the family's lifestyle and spending/saving habits are in place. Of course, a shift in circumstance that triggers a fiscal crisis like the loss of a spouse's job, a divorce, an unexpected second (third or fourth) baby, an elderly parent turned ill, or an alarming medical diagnosis of a close family member can set the EP goal in motion. So can more low-key but important monetary goals like a desire to upgrade to a bigger home, encroaching college tuition costs, the yearning to travel more as a family, and more. But the financial "free fall" is not as common for SAHPs turned EPs, and the impact on the family more often than not is a gradual but exacting one.

Is giving yourself a professional goal while already filling the shoes of the primary caregiver in your family a selfish undertaking? It may seem so to others who have been quick to throw a label on your back, but nobody knows the dual-determinations of your heart and mind as well as you do. Parents who take a leave from their professional and/or educational aspirations to stay home with their children often experience a loss not felt in the pocketbook as much as in one's spirit and soul. "After two years at home I nearly lost my mind with boredom at times," confesses Suzanne Worsham, a freelance writer in Tecumseh, Michigan. "I really have enjoyed the benefits of staying at home with my child, but I also need the confidence and independence that comes from being self-sufficient." Bringing work back into their lives is a stepping stone to becoming "whole" again.

My Moments as an EP
By Melissa Bermea

Successful, fulfilling, delightful, educational, stressful, humorous, dexterous, multi-tasking, catching balls, disciplining, comforting, serious, inspiring, enlightening. I don't know what I would do without my business . . . I feel it somehow completes me!

Having Your Own Financial Leg to Stand On

Above and beyond the desire to feel "whole" again is the pressing concern of pulling one's financial weight in the family for any number of reasons. Even though Lisa Ivaldi of Bramton, Ontario, feels that her husband is supportive of her staying home, she sometimes feels that she's not pulling her weight financially. "I earned more than him when we first met and we always paid everything 50/50. Now I do not pay my

50 percent. I am sensitive to that fact. I just have to make sure that I re-mind myself that my self-worth is not connected to my 'paycheck.'" Karen Murray, a frugal-living consultant who bills herself as "The Coupon Lady," felt that her time at home with her kids was running out. She re-counts the private deal she struck with herself:

> They say that "Necessity Is the Mother of Invention," and that is how my business came to be. When our son entered kinder-garten, and our twin girls were two, I realized that they too would be going off to school before I knew it. I made a goal for myself that by the time my girls were in school full-time (first grade) I would be making enough money in my own business that my husband wouldn't say to me, "Okay, now that the kids aren't home during the day, you should go back to work outside the home." For me, it was *necessary* to be home and always available to our children. By January of that school year, I had started to teach classes to consumers on shopping wisely and finding good deals, and one thing led to another until I was hired by a local grocery store owner to be his "Consumer Advo-cate" as an independent contractor. On my fortieth birthday this past July, I was writing in my journal about how much I loved the work I am doing and how grateful I was to have it. And it suddenly occurred to me that in one month my girls would be starting first grade, and I had reached my goal for my busi-ness . . . I was making enough money, based out of my own home, that I would not need to go find a "job." What a heady feeling that was . . . to realize I had reached my goal by the time I had set for myself!

Defying Gender Roles

Working at home not only challenges the assumption that only an em-ployer ("a boss") can enable a person to grow professionally (by recogniz-ing talent and offering opportunities, promotions, raises, and "titles"), but also the assumption that only women can be the primary caregiver and nurturer to children. In fact, according to IDC, a research firm that tracks the Small Office Home Office (SOHO) trend, as well as Cyber Di-alogue, a research firm that tracks Internet usage, there are more men than women who work at home—offering ample opportunities for the dads among them to spin that assumption on its head and discover the joys, challenges, and splendor of caring for their own children.

This crossover of gender roles is not always easy, however. Robert Smith, a freelance writer in Elgin, Illinois, comments on what being the primary caregiver of his children is like for his family:

> My wife and I were strongly committed to one of us staying home with our kids, and after an unsuccessful job search, I was elected. We now have three children, with our youngest almost nine months old. At the onset of one of us staying at home, we both wanted to be that parent. By luck or fortune I was the one, and I always feel deep down that my wife resents me for not having had a secure enough job at the time. On the positive side, I think when the man stays home, the children benefit by having two committed parents. Sexist as it sounds, I feel mothers have a greater innate connection to their children and will maintain a stronger connection than fathers who work. By having the father stay home, he is by design "forced" to develop that level of connection and commitment.

Traditional Values

Other parents who have strong traditional values embrace entrepreneurial parenthood as a natural progression of family values in today's society. "The Bible tells of a virtuous woman who tends her home, weaves cloth, sews, spins, cooks and cleans, and tends the animals," says Laura Wheeler of Wheeler Computer Services. "We don't do that anymore—we buy those things—but I think my decision to work at a paying job from inside my home was really just a modern interpretation of that. I am, at heart, a stay-at-home mom. I have a traditional family, and I do not feel that this is really a departure from that, just a change in the tasks that an at-home mom does in our society today."

From Home-Based Entrepreneur to Parent

A handful of our survey respondents (5 percent) were already home-based entrepreneurs before they became parents. While they may have enjoyed an accelerated home career for years, pushing forth their professional goals in full throttle, the arrival of a newborn naturally slows them down. One mom we heard from waited until her forties to have a child and had already owned her own business for fifteen years. "I'm still struggling with the parenting part of working at home," she admits. "I'm used to working very efficiently and effectively from home. Now I get frustrated because I'm behind schedule and don't seem to be anywhere as efficient as before. And I don't like my son seeing my frustration, because the whole point of being an EP is to spend time with him. I'm still working on this one . . ."

To be the entrepreneur and parent she wants to be, Char James-Tanny, an on-line Help author and developer, has learned to segregate her time. "I am the financial support for my family and started my home-based business well before I got married or before I had my son. I have made adjustments since. For example, Jesse went into day care/private school at fifteen months, and the office is now 'closed' from 4:00 until 7:00 every day so that I can watch *Dragon Tales* and play in the dirt." For Char, giving herself permission to *not* be her son's round-the-clock caregiver (though she remains his primary one) keeps her entrepreneurial goals afloat.

Single-Parent EPs: Going Solo for Success

In our study we found single parent EPs among the most tenacious of all. Determined to offer their children financial and emotional stability after the relative instability of a parental divorce, many reach for the EP work option as a lifeline and source of emotional strength. Above all, they do not want to sacrifice any more time away from their children than any joint custody agreements permit.

"Becoming an EP was more of a forced decision than a choice because I got divorced and didn't want to give up the time with my son by working in an office all day," writes Liesl Johnson, an insurance transcriptionist in Phoenix, Arizona. "The first year after I made the decision to work at home was relatively easy because I was still married and my husband carried most of the monetary burden. However, the next year, *after* he and I were apart, was *wonderful*—I made more than he did that year!"

A teleworker in Tustin, California, used his EP status to gain joint custody during a divorce. "The high pay, combined with the ability to care for my one-year-old son, played an important role in retaining my joint physical and legal custody. Financial security as well as quality time with family and friends seems to be possible only through independent contracting from home. I refuse to live any other way."

Laurie Ayers, who runs an office support service in Grandville Michigan, remarks:

> It just grinds me when I hear people say they "can't" stay home with their children. Bunk. I'm the sole provider and head of the household and I manage to take care of my household just fine. Two-income families have no excuse at all. My kids and I don't live beyond our means and we're totally debt free (with the exception of a few years left on the mortgage). I'm thirty-something years old and it's possible. People may not *choose* to become an EP, but to say they *can't* is bunk!

Working at home affords the single parent EP more time with their children during their scheduled time together. An EP dad (wishing to remain anonymous) who is a consultant to nonprofits, values the flexibility inherent in his career choice. "Being an EP has given me more flexibility to see my daughter when she's available. Before working at home, I saw my daughter less and her mother provided the 'child care' or parenting." Unfortunately, being an EP has been a bone of contention in this dad's relationship with his ex-spouse. "It has not resulted in the court awarding more time for my daughter to be in our home. It's a constant court battle—my ex says I should be making more money like I was when doing international work overseas. She claims that I am not working to my full capacity because I am reserving the time for parenting." For this EP, more time to parent is the priority over a "full-capacity" income.

Bill Zimmerly, a systems engineer, became an EP at the onset of full custody of his teenage daughter. He recalls, "My previous employment was to work for a bank while my children lived with their mother. When their mother asked me to take physical custody of them, I accepted." Bill feels that becoming an EP has enabled him to be a better parent because he is there when his daughter needs him, which he feels would not be true if she needed him while he was working at an outside office.

Coupling Up: Taking the
Work-at-Home Oath Together

"We both do it all with our son—playing, reading, teaching, getting off to school, making lunches, volunteering in school, going to the park, on play dates, to the movies, doctor and dentist visits, learning on the computer, attending birthday parties, visiting great-grandma, doing chores, the laundry, cleaning the house, bath time, bedtime . . ."

—ANNE DULLAGHAN, MARKETING COMMUNICATIONS SPECIALIST

Out of the 10 percent of survey respondents who said they worked at home with their spouses, slightly more shared a joint business than worked side-by-side in separate EP activities. As part-time teleworking and remote staff opportunities take an increasing hold on the mainstream work force, we predict that the occurrence of husbands and wives sharing the same office space—or at least the same residential workplace—will grow more and more common, far surpassing the occurrence of husband-wife business partnerships.

While partnering successfully in life takes large doses of trust, respect, commitment, patience, and tolerance, successful partnering in business takes even more. On top of the delicate balance of shared goals and independent aspirations that form the basis of every marital relationship, couples who partner together in a home-based business also need just the right balance of a shared work ethic and business goals, *as well as* independent skills, talents, experience, and work habits that are complimentary. Scaling for the right combo can be easier for some couples than others.

Sarah and Paul Edwards began working at home because their individual careers, both of which involved a lot of travel, had been pushing them to spend too much time apart. Though at first they had separate businesses (Sarah as a psychotherapist; Paul as a public affairs consultant), they soon began to undertake as many joint projects as they could, including writing their first book, *Working From Home*. During this process, they spent several months of battling through how to write as a team, and that evolved into a working partnership they expect to continue for the rest of their lives.

"Working together," says Paul, "enables us to share our hopes, dreams, and our complementary creative talents. It enables us to be there for each other during the ups and downs of our days and assures that we'll never grow apart, only closer as the years pass."

Before having their first child, Morgen and Meghan Bahn started their joint home-based marketing design business in Santa Rosa, California. After nearly four years in business, they are able to keep up with their mortgage and other bills while taking turns watching their two-year-old daughter. Meghan is pleased that she and her husband are modeling non-gender roles, with both of them participating in the day-to-day raising of their daughter. "I think it's important for her to see that people can construct their lives to fit their dreams and personalities, regardless of whether or not it's what most people are doing," says Meghan.

Side by Side

The freedom to step out of traditional roles was a recurring theme among the EP couples we heard from. It wasn't until Pat McCann, a life and executive coach in Wilmette, Illinois, started working at home that his wife's business really began to take off. With Pat now lending his hand in household duties such as paying bills, scheduling doctor appointments, taxi-driving his daughter places, shopping, and cooking, his wife has been freed to grow her business "enormously." Pat says their combined home-based income generates more than enough to pay the bills, and in fact they are in the pleasant process of designing a new home and are ready to start construction. Without his launching his own home business, lending a ready hand in domestic duties as his wife needed, Pat feels this wouldn't have been possible for their family.

The decision for one spouse to become an EP can ignite the desire in the other. When David Holst and his wife packed up all their belongings to move from the Washington, D.C., area to Arkansas to follow his EP dream of launching a web hosting company, they engaged in a lively conversation during their cross-country travels in a U-Haul truck. His wife, who is an occupational therapist by trade, was triggered by the intellectual shakeout of a road trip and struck with the idea that "someone oughta write a book" about practical occupational therapy methods to which she was so accustomed in her own practice. David turned to her and cried out, *"You're that someone!"* A year later both the book *Empowering Occupational Therapy* and their first son Gabriel were born.

Living the EP Dream

Few EPs with unhappy spouses in the traditional work force will argue that their greatest hope in pursuing their home-based business is to become successful enough so that their spouses can quit their full-time jobs and join them. For a lucky few, this dream can and does become a reality.

After just one year of building her web design, hosting, and marketing business while her husband Rob held down his steady job, Desiree Scales of Bella Web Design felt confident enough to encourage Rob to join her full-time in their Marietta, Georgia, home. Desiree admits it's been a bit stressful on their marriage during the transition period, but they are helping and encouraging each other to live more balanced lives—he learning to help out with more child-care responsibilities and she learning how to "turn off" her work time in favor of more focused family time.

In Elmwood Park, New Jersey, Vickie Barnes' spouse covered all their household expenses while Vickie transitioned from a full-time early childhood teacher to owner of Earth's Magic, LLC, a company that designs and runs web sites. Now her husband has joined her in running their sites full-time, a move she feels has definitely strengthened their marriage. "Because he's home with me, it makes the web site more of an 'our' thing instead of a 'my' thing," says Vickie.

Getting Along

Whether or not couples share a home business, working and living 24/7 under one roof together can get challenging at times, to say the least. With each other's physical and emotional presence ever ready, communication can get redundant and stale patterns of miscommunication can take hold.

To avert verbal bickering, Kit Bennett of Amazingmoms.com communicates with her husband through e-mail. Even though they both work at home, she feels they spend little quality time together and have a tendency to take each other for granted. "He seems to take his business more seriously because it brings in more income right now," says Kit. "However, he tells me that he wants to work for me, which makes me feel pressure to succeed. There has been more bickering, but we *have* learned to communicate . . . even if it's through e-mail from one room to the next!"

For some couples, the only clear solution is separate home offices. Lisa Rudy, a freelance writer in Philadelphia, Pennsylvania, tried sharing the same office space with her husband, Peter Cook, former host of an NPR program called *CompuDudes* (www.compududes.com), for kids who love computers. Lisa counts the ways they didn't click as office mates:

> First, there's the basic "room of one's own" concept—you share every other aspect of your lives; you need some space to call your own, decorate with your own weird pictures, etc.
>
> Second, people have different working styles. I couldn't concentrate in that much chaos, nor could I think well listening to the radio, watching TV, hearing the sounds of gaming in the background. Peter needs a certain amount of "stimulation" to help him focus. I need quiet.
>
> Third, conducting phone interviews is central to my business, and I don't want to be interrupted in the middle—nor do I want the sounds of the latest game he's reviewing to intrude on my conversation.
>
> Fourth, STUFF. His office is always full of stuff. He collects antique computers, gets piles of hardware and software to review, and there are always new boxes and piles of stuff everywhere. It's fine if it's in his space . . . awful if it's in mine!
>
> Finally, I think the temptation to chat is just overwhelming. Every interesting conversation with a client, neat new web site, annoying software feature, technology glitch would become a half-hour conversation. It's a time drain we really couldn't afford.

After learning the hard way, Lisa and Peter chose their next house more wisely. They set out to hunt for a home with twin offices in mind, and they found a three-story, five-bedroom house in which they dedicated their entire third story to an office suite (two separate offices plus a bathroom).

Mary Ann DiGiaimo, who runs a secretarial service called "Beyond Words" in Pompton Plains, New Jersey, recently moved into a new office on the second floor of her home after sharing space with her husband on the first floor for two years, which she describes as being "interesting at times." Mary Ann jokingly says, "I tell people that we 'separated' this way instead of legally!"

Up, Up, and Away:
Taking the EP Life to New Heights

Once the doors of possibility fling open, some EPs come out of the gate flying. We were delighted to hear how truly liberating the decision to become an entrepreneurial parent was for many. Their decision to work at home became the catalyst or otherwise enabled them to fulfill other life goals and personal priorities. Here are just a few stories.

Traveling the World as an EP

How likely is it that a virtual assistant from Charleston, Virginia, would appear on vacation at the doorstep of a client who lives in *Russia*? If you're Barbie Dallmann of Happy Fingers Word Processing, it could happen. "Last summer I took my family to Moscow and we stayed with one of my clients for a week," she recalls. "It was an amazing adventure." Barbie finds that her business leads her to friendships all over the United States. She also has a client in her own hometown who is very active in the community and has given her and her husband tickets to many charity events that they'd never have been able to afford to attend. "It's fun rubbing elbows with the upper class on occasion!"

Phyllis Smith, who runs a business information and research consulting firm, picked up her business and went to Paris.

> My husband had an opportunity to take a short-term work assignment with his corporation that required a move to Paris, France. The decision was less difficult to make since I didn't have my own full-time employment to consider. Not all EPs

could just pick up their business and transport it to another country. I have had to curtail a lot of business development since I don't actually want to do business here. I'm fortunate that I don't maintain stock or require specialized equipment and materials. The bottom line is we have been able to take advantage of a great experience without my sacrificing my career interests. That wouldn't have happened as a full-time employee.

Some EPs take their families on the road with them during business travel. When Char James-Tanny's husband heard she had a speaking engagement in Seattle in July 2000, he turned the opportunity into a cross-country excursion for the whole family. "We were on the road the entire month of July," says Char, "and I worked over and back, plugging one and sometimes two laptops into converters."

On the Move

Nigel Hart, a Canadian technical illustrator, turned his last corporate layoff into a life-altering event. Instead of chasing jobs from city to city, he and his wife decided to finally move to where their family had always *wanted* to live rather than "another move to another job in another city." Even though he refers to his income as "spotty" now, he enjoys spending more time with his daughter and has "always enjoyed spending ridiculous amounts of time together" with his wife.

It was frustrating for Ginger Reid to find a job as an employee because her family moved so often, following her husband's career path. Rather than give up the possibility of a supplemental income, however, she decided to become an EP. Here's how:

My son fell very ill at the age of three months after contracting a respiratory virus while at day care. Shortly thereafter my husband's career took off and we began to move from state to state to follow his corporate ladder. I quit college to keep my family together, and I found out that employers didn't want to hire someone that put their family first and who had relocated as frequently as I did. So I put my skills to work and researched many fields before deciding that virtual assistance was the way of the future. Plus it's movable . . . just like us!

"Tag Team" Parenting

Mary E. Coe made a deal with her husband for both of them to work at home part-time (twenty-five hours each), equaling one full-time salary. They participate in "tag team" parenting—each taking on a different shift of the day or night—and homeschool as well. Says Mary, "We could both expand our businesses greatly and thus make more money, but we've chosen not to so that we can be with our kids." Mary is amused that her shared child-care arrangement with her husband was so equitable that when their first child was two, he'd simply call out the generic term "Mama-Dada" to summon whichever parent was home!

Foster Parenting

Susan Thesing and her husband are both self-employed, thereby enabling them to be the foster parents they had always wanted to be. Explains Susan, a graphic designer in Decatur, Georgia:

> My husband and I are foster parents, and so we have children who have unusually high needs. Behaviorally, these kids are often extremely needy, demanding, and prone to anger, violence, and throwing tantrums. They have many medical, educational, and psychological appointments as well as family/social worker visits that need to be arranged. We could not provide the care that these kids need without the flexibility of our schedules. We recently received a very angry six-year-old who consumes huge amounts of time and energy. Fortunately this coincided with a lull in work offers and I have not worked the phones at all to get more work. I could not deal with the stress of his anger if I had to also deal with an 8:00-to-5:30 job. I need the time during the day to deal with the little work I have and issues of running the house because afternoons/evenings are frequently consumed with tantrums.

Spiritual Awakenings

One mom we heard from has been able to reconnect with her strong religious beliefs now that she works at home, which allows her time to bake challah each week. Being able to fully celebrate the Sabbath is a priceless perk to her new employment status. And now that Bernadette Raferty is home-based, she is able to invite a previously homeless woman to live with her family. She and her husband are mentoring this woman in parenting skills.

Financial Affairs: Transitions and Trade-offs

Permitting yourself to live your own life is one thing. Paying the bills and taking financial responsibility of your life—and that of your family's—is quite another. Aspiring EPs may be in tune with the work-at-home lifestyle emotionally but terrified of the financial fallout. No doubt, many have reason, as nearly half of our survey respondents felt they had indeed traded financial security for more time with their children, and slightly more than half were making less money working inside the home than they had been while working outside the home.

For families that are used to full-time incomes, the financial transition to building a home-based career can be startling. In our study 74 percent transitioned into entrepreneurial parenthood from outside-the-home employment (53 percent were parents working outside the home and 21 percent were employees who came home to work at the onset of parenthood). When it comes to transitioning into this work option, these EPs seem to have had the biggest jolt. For some, it is truly an emotional free fall, from which they hang with conviction only by the strong thread of desire to be closer to their children. Laurie Ayers of Grandville, Michigan, sees it this way:

> I lost more than $45,000 annually by staying home. I lost my life and health insurance. I lost my retirement. *But* I gained time with my children. I don't have the discretionary income like I used to, but no amount of money could buy the satisfaction I have as an EP. We get by financially. That's all we need to do. We soar spiritually and emotionally.

Lizanne Fiorentino of The Administrative Edge, LLC, concurs. "We have made tremendous financial sacrifices in order to be more available to our children. My business does not currently make enough money to meet our needs because I choose to work a reduced number of hours per week in order to meet my children's academic, social, and spiritual needs." Part-time hours were indeed a trend we tracked from our survey respondents, contributing to the slight majority of parents in our study who were earning less than they had before. In addition, the symbolic "corporate ladder" is removed from one's sight, leaving one to feel "stranded" on the unfamiliar ground of self-employment. Remarks Sheri Wallace of Tuscan, Arizona, "I make enough money to pay our bills, but it is hard because I have to be constantly looking for the next month's work. I have no benefits, no ladder to move up, and no job security at all. So, yes, I do think that I have made a decision that has long-term consequences."

But EPs that make it through discover that the long-term consequences are more positive than they ever thought possible starting out. While letting go of the financial security blanket of a standard company paycheck can put the newly self-employed on edge, causing emotional stress for the entire family, working and living through it together can mend early wounds. Writes Bill Douglas who left a job as an administrator in human resources for a Fortune 500 company:

> The initial fear of financial insecurity caused stress in me that I am ashamed to say was externalized to my kids. I wish I could take my temper outbursts back now, because my life is so much more fulfilling and peaceful for having ridden out the storm, so to speak. But in the beginning I was scared of walking away from corporate security, and I didn't enjoy my kids to the fullest that I could have. But I think, all in all, the kids and I had opportunities to enjoy, understand, and deal with life issues that millions separated by nine-to-five jobs and endless traffic jams will never experience. Even though it wasn't always a bowl of cherries, I think the best thing about it was that my children saw me face my fears and move through them to realize my dreams. Them seeing me actually visualize, create, and market the value of my own dreams is a valuable life lesson that I hope will inspire them to walk off cliffs and scale insurmountable mountains in their future to fully realize their own life's limitless potential.

About Earning Less

Although more than half (55.5 percent) of our survey respondents indicated that they were earning less than they were before, the net income between employed workers and the self-employed does not accurately reflect the difference in *expenditures* between the two. What is not accounted for, for instance, are the wardrobe, commuting costs, and lunches out that often characterize the comings and goings of an out-of-the-home employed parent. While house bills such as electric, water, and gas can increase substantially, the decrease in auto gas, train tickets, clothing, dry cleaning, take-out or restaurant food, and especially day care can more than compensate. In addition, over-the-top expenditures that are deeply imbedded in the nine-to-five lifestyle, like impulse spending to and from work or overspending on errands in an effort to save time, rarely surface until one stops the cycle altogether.

As Phyllis Smith puts it, "One has to look carefully at the big picture. Although I am making less than I did while working outside the home, when we analyze the tax benefits that come from my working from home as well as the simple savings that are related to my being here, it clearly demonstrates that my current situation contributes to our family financial well-being just as surely as if I were bringing in a full-time employment income."

Alicia McColl, owner of McColl Communications, Inc., doesn't feel that she meets the financial needs of her household with her working from home, but she does feel that she has grown her business to the point where it wouldn't be worth placing her two children in full-time day care while she worked out of the house full-time. "We're talking maybe a benefit of $8,000 to $10,000 annually, which is not worth a year of missing those absolutely glorious days when you can pack a picnic lunch and head for the zoo, or make Play-Doh animals while waiting for the cookies to bake on a rainy morning." Similarly, a small press publisher we heard from in Olney, Maryland, feels the financial trade-off but can live with that feeling far better than she could live with an out-of-the-home job. "At times, I miss the guaranteed paycheck," she says, "but whenever I think about taking a job, I get a feeling of dread in the pit of my stomach."

Breathing Better with a Budget

To land on their feet, entrepreneurial parents who feel the loss of income the strongest are the first to create a strict household budget that accommodates their new economic reality. Tightening their belts does not center on simply cutting out discretionary purchases here and there, but a conscientious decision to change their spending habits. And like dieting, financial discipline can come easier to some than it comes to others. Sheri Goeser Stritof of Ocean Park, Washington, who is a partner with her husband in an e-commerce antique and novelty phone retail store, had to "downsize our lifestyle in order to keep our heads above water as EPs." When P. J. Rittiger of Pittsburgh, Pennsylvania, began freelancing, she went through charge card withdrawal, "a painful malady associated with a changing lifestyle." It was very difficult for her to stop buying some of the luxuries that they were used to, but her desire not to "trade back her child's welfare for a paycheck" kept her going.

On the other hand, Debbie Mancini, a technical recruiter in Alexandria, cut back wherever she could to make ends meet, but she found the experience a rewarding challenge. She was amazed at how little their family actually *needed*. Today she and her husband put at least 50 percent of what they both make in savings, just in case they need it in the future. "When you own your own business," points out Mancini, "you never want to be desperate for money. That's when business owners make the wrong decisions."

For EPs with strong negotiation skills, developing a new household budget can be likened to making a bargain with yourself. In Eagan, Minnesota, Gail Tanaka designed a "bare minimum budget" that includes no money for clothes or eating out but does provide for a $1,000 emergency account to which she adds $50.00 each month. As for health benefits, she currently relies on COBRA, making the monthly insurance payments with the gas money she used to spend commuting every day.

Tryna Bailey Fitspatrick, a web site manager in Winter Beach, Florida, describes how the tight budget plan she developed and adopted with her husband when they first started working at home led them to one day afford their "dream house":

> During the second year, after both my husband and I were working from home and operating our own respective busi-

nesses, we developed a decidedly achievable list of goals. We jokingly referred to it as "The Outline for Chapter Two." Here, we developed a time line for not only day-to-day tasks, but also long-term dreams. Since our aspiration was to become financially secure while working for ourselves from home, this meant making certain sacrifices in order to follow our "outline." Namely, we had to go without many effects. We had a ten-year-old Toyota that barely worked. We bought most of our clothes and house wares from the local Goodwill. We did not spend money on lavish vacations, gifts, or personal things. It may seem easier said than done; however, in retrospect, it was effortless and painless because we knew that our sacrifices were leading us to our common purpose.

Since then, we've been able to buy our dream house (out in the country on three acres) and live the kind of life that people were meant to live (in my opinion)—one that is filled with truly living, learning, sharing, growing, and caring. We spend more time with our daughter than most moms and dads are capable of spending with their children, yet we also have financial security and peace of mind. Some say it was luck, yet we know better. Luck is merely groundwork meeting opportunity.

Likewise, Angela Tesar, an Internet marketing consultant who was hit with a large income cut by working at home, now lives on a fixed budget, which is slowly relaxing a bit as she starts to earn more income from her on-line business. "My family has adjusted to the fact that we cannot just run out and buy whatever we want when we want," says Tesar. "We work for it, save for it, and only buy when the money is in the bank. Working on a budget has taught me more self-discipline which I am grateful for!" Strangely enough, Angela and her husband argue *less* about money now that they *have* less. "Before I was too tired, hurried, and stressed to sit down to talk to him. I complained all the time about not feeling well and problems at work. Now I talk more about my ideas and the kids . . . and with our new budget we seem to fight *less* about money!"

Sometimes the decision to become an EP has a much more dramatic affect on the household budget than simply adjusting expenditures. Sometimes EPs trade *their house* for the preferred *household* they long to live in. To better live within their means, Penny Craig and her husband "downsized" to a smaller home, relieving themselves of the stress of a huge mortgage on their backs. Now they live a much more comfortable and holistic life. Taking a house sale one step further, David Holst and his wife used the money they earned from the sale of their home in Laurel, Maryland, in 1997 to relocate to Little Rock, Arkansas, where the cost of living was nearly half the cost in the D.C. metro area. Then they used their stellar credit rating to get several 2.9% credit card transfer loans to help with the startup expenses for David's web hosting business.

Health Insurance

Perhaps those hit the hardest during the financial transition between employee to self-employed are EPs who have to fend for themselves when it comes to health insurance. The percentage of our survey respondents who were uninsured—17.2 percent—was above the national average of 15.5 percent. Of our survey respondents, 62.2 percent were covered under their spouse's employer, with an additional 3.3 percent covered by their own employer (either through part-time work or as a teleworker) for a total of 65.5 percent covered in the traditional labor force. (See Appendix, Figure 10.)

We found that 13.2 percent of our respondents paid their own way. For many of these EPs, the savings in employee-related expenses were a drop in the bucket compared to the added cost of health insurance. For instance, Pamela Stuart, an illustrator in San Diego, California, saw her health insurance costs shoot up from $40 per month as an employee to $400 a month, with a $1,000 annual deductible, when she became an EP. This is slightly above the average cost, according to our survey.

We found that health insurance companies run the gamut in terms of cost and coverage. In our survey, Blue Cross/Blue Shield was the most popular carrier, with family coverage averaging $293.50 a month. Other common health insurance carriers were Kaiser, Aetna U.S. Healthcare, and Cigna, with thirty-three others named. And while the range in monthly premiums for the varied other carriers were zero to $1,100 per month, when we lopped off these two extremes and averaged out the remaining costs, we found that the average EPs who are responsible for their own healthcare payments must set aside approximately $353.13 per month—or $4,237.50 annually—for their health care.

One way to lessen the sting of added health-care costs is to make a goal of earning more annual income to cover—for instance, aggressively pursuing that new account or client, earmarking those earnings for that annual payout. Other creative health-care solutions we heard of included:

Small Business Administration. Sarah of Garner, North Carolina, obtains health insurance for her family through the Small Business Administration. Through the Philadelphia American Life Insurance Company, she pays $105 per month that "covers everything," with no deductible and $10 co-payments for office visits.

Leasing Yourself. Mona of Rancho Santa Margarita, California, uses an employee leasing company to "lease" herself back to her company. Her company then provides health care ($90/month, HMO) and dental care and pays her taxes on her behalf.

Medical Savings Accounts. Peter of Herndon, Virginia, sings the praises of obtaining a medical savings account (MSA), which includes a high-deductible major medical health plan. His monthly cost is about $252 for full family coverage, with an annual deductible of approximately $4,500.

Life Partner Coverage. Gail of Atkinson, New Hampshire, "keeps things square with the IRS" by exchanging consulting services with her life partner. While both own their own businesses, Gail's business offers HMO coverage with Healthsource/Cigna for herself, her partner, and their son, and her partner's company reimburses her the $450/month since her company *would* cover domestic partner insurance if only the carrier would do so.

Insured by Parent's Company. Joanne of Hampden, Maine, offers administrative support to her father's company and is thereby covered through his insurance.

Insurance as a Student. Jackie of Montevallo, Alabama, is a student at the graduate program of the University of Montevallo, where she and her two children have limited health insurance coverage at the rate of $280 per month.

Climbing Out and Feeling Invincible

While becoming an EP pushes some parents to tinker indefinitely on the edge of a balanced checkbook, others find their financial salvation— but not "overnight" like some opportunists might want you to believe. Jo-Anne Penn-Kast of New Milford, Connecticut, recalls how becoming an EP helped her climb out of debt, but how hard she worked to do so:

> I began as a student in web design in February 1999, and the Job Training Partnership Act (JTPA) through the Connecticut Department of Labor paid my way. Prior to this, and practically overnight, my family was on food stamps, WIC, Medicaid, et cetera when my husband left. We lost and/or sold everything we owned of value except the house and computer. My skills were nil, I couldn't even turn on a computer before taking the classes. (My college degree was in anthropology/sociology and social science!) I did hateful, dull, boring office work before the "metamorphosis" of my life back in late 1998.
>
> I had no choice but to succeed. I worked so hard and so single-mindedly in the early days: making contacts, submitting résumés, following up, doing pro bono work, learning, teaching myself, investing in state-of-the-art programs when I didn't know how I was even going to pay the mortgage. My immediate need to succeed overtook everything. Unfortunately, the children were left to their own devices too often as I had no time for reading stories or playing games—not when I had to get résumés out, do on-line tutorials until 3:00 in the morning, pack in more than two years of schooling into six months, learn to adapt without my husband/kid's father. I can only hope I can "nip in the bud" any bad traits they learned from me from our difficult family experience.

A child of poverty determined to offer a better life for her own children, Tonya Parker Morrison, owner of an entertainment wire service based in Lake Charles, Louisiana, recalls the first year she and her husband became entrepreneurial parents:

> The first year was particularly hard because my husband and I were both laid off around the same time. Together we decided

that we never wanted to be that stressed out again and then have someone pull the rug out from under us. Call us control freaks, but we thought it would be much better if we could control our own destinies. Unfortunately, that meant we were broke while we were having babies (twelve months apart). Even now, when our children are five and six years old, the missing steady income puts a dent in the lifestyle we'd like to have. But at least I get to see my kids grow up and be here for them during this impressionable time. I've never heard a friend of mine complain about being broke when they were growing up, but I hear plenty of them griping about never seeing Mom or Dad. That always sticks in my mind. My husband and I are still both pouring ourselves into this business in the hopes of achieving our dreams on our own terms some day soon. I basically have to sell myself to every single client and hope they come back for more. You can't buy that kind of assurance and it certainly can't be measured in a job that could downsize at any moment. So most of the time, I feel invincible.

Feeling invincible is a shared emotion among EPs who can make that psychological break from the corporate tether and not look back. "My financial security is based on my ability to market my business and skills, and my family is part of this strength," remarks Mark Nathan, a multimedia, audio, and graphics consultant in Woodland Hills, California. "Whether I work on my own or for another company, I will *never* feel like I am substantially fulfilling my 'financial goals.' But being able to poke my head out of the office door and see my wife and children helps me get over that."

John Kirwan, owner of Carolina Financial Partners, LLC, who believes he has more financial security than ever before, also appreciates the psychological hold he has on his own life now.

Banks are notorious for going in different directions than earlier planned, and now the only person that can change minds is me. The first year was pretty tough, and I worked two part-time jobs to make it work (refereeing basketball and driving a delivery truck at night). But that was before kids, and my income now is more than when I worked for a bank, especially since my overhead is very low. We lowered our debt dramatically, cut back on non-essential items and lived lean as needed. My advice to others is that the "full-time" career can wait. The kids can't. I've had a lot of parents come up to me and say how envious they are. They shouldn't be envious; they should simply re-evaluate their priorities. We are not rich financially, but we're living our lives and raising our kids by our choice. It helps not to let "the day-care/career crowd" get to you. Success can be measured in many different ways. Ours is our kids are happy, healthy, and our home life is not crazy.

About Earning More

While most EPs who migrated from the traditional work force feel a loss of income at first, the flexibility to earn *more* than one's previous salary is also thrown into the mix. Gretchen Malik, a freelance writer, points out that breaking out of the nine-to-five time slot allows her to stretch her income alongside the hours she puts in. "When I worked outside the home, I made less because my hours were set. At home I can work as long as I want, thereby earning as much as I want."

Being a successful freelancer, however, has its drawbacks. When your income is directly tied to the time you put into your work, the decision to *stop* working can be difficult. Making a decision to go to bed early several nights in a row, or take a vacation, can cost money now. "I am the primary breadwinner and I definitely feel the pull of financial security over time with family," says Ann Dullagahn. "I'm lucky to have almost more work than I can handle—the freelancer's dream—but I'm working eight-to-ten-hour days, six to seven days a week. I miss the seemingly slower pace of the corporate world and the ability to tell your boss your plate is full and can't take on another project. I find it difficult to take time off as a freelancer."

In the end, one's choice of working at home becomes a public statement of one's value system *and* one's financial self-sufficiency. Mark DuRussel, a software engineer in Madison, Wisconsin, takes pride that his home-based income has afforded their family a larger home. Now, says DuRussel, "the rewards of our current arrangement (my working at home and my wife being a stay-at-home mom) are very visible not only to my wife, but to everyone who knows us!"

Defining "Financial Security"

Is "financial security" a matter of the mind, a "to each his own" viewpoint? Teresa Roebuck, a desktop publisher in Conway, Arkansas, reflects on the true meaning of the term:

> In my opinion, there is no such thing as "financial security" as most people understand it. It is a fallacy. You don't make your life better by throwing money at it; you make your life better by living it in a better way. As for leaving our loved ones with "security," unless the children are indeed young, then the best thing in the world that you can do for them is teach them how to make their own way in the world and to see opportunity in all things and not be limited by society's ideas about how "working" works!

Ida Rose Heckard, an educational specialist/school psychologist who provides educational and behavioral consultation and training for public and private schools, parents, and home educators in Kahului, Hawaii, recognizes the difference between "financial security" and "financial abundance":

> I haven't traded financial security for more time with the kids— but I've traded financial abundance. I used to enjoy going to the grocery store with a list and not worrying about the bottom line. I can no longer throw a couple thousand dollars at a vacation without months of careful planning. I made the transition to working at home by working part-time at first. A relocation almost sidetracked our progress, but the benefits of stay-at-home work far outweigh dashing out the door every morning.

Despite the financial crunch most EPs face when they first make the transition from a full-time income to entrepreneurial parenthood, they use their children as their guiding light. Bill Douglas points out, "Having time with my kids is the biggest dividend of all. To be at home each day when the school bus arrives and to see your kids come off safely is worth more than any Christmas bonus times ten." Adds Nigel Hart, an EP dad living in Gabriola, Canada, "Success is a balance of free time versus income." Often when your life is full of one, it is lacking the other. However, almost every entrepreneurial parent we've heard from has—from time to time—felt the harmony and the power of a work-life balance truly under control. "It doesn't always happen," adds Hart, "but when it does, life is just about perfect."

Is living in an EP household the perfect life? Hardly. Battles for computer time, family time, work time, vacation time, and simply *more time* plague even the smoothest-running EP household. Finding the right balance of income when your earning power is as flexible as the hours you put into your work is a tough juggernaut to crack, as are the engaging and disengaging of family members in your work-at-home goals. In the following chapters we'll explore these issues in greater depth. But first, if your home career plans involve a business, it's time to launch it officially and/or tie up any loose ends. Our next chapter gets straight to this critical step.

4

A Business Is Born

"After a few years of being a full-time mom who dabbled in web design, our financial situation demanded that I start to earn a steady income. My heart was breaking, but I knew we needed the money. So I told our six-year-old son, 'Mommy needs to get a job.' He cried out, 'But I'm your job!' Trying not to let him see how hard this was, I said, 'Yes, but I need a job that pays me money.' He then said 'I'll pay you,' ran to his room, got his piggy bank full of coins and gave it to me. That's when I decided I would find a way to make my 'web design hobby' a paying job. That's when I got serious about being an EP."

—SUZANNE SANZ, LIQUIDHTML.COM

For some, the idea of working at home while raising a family is a romantic one—full of hope and promise and good intentions. But like romantic love, taking all this to the next level (marriage) and beyond involves serious thought, legal commitment, and a public declaration. At some point on the way to becoming an entrepreneurial parent, it's time to get serious.

Whatever stage your business is in—whether you have a few clients on the side or a roster of repeat customers, whether you're still picking out your business name or you filed for an LLC years ago—this is a good time to take stock of where you are on the record and whether or not there are any loose ends you need to tie up to complete the entrepreneurial element of the EP equation.

In the next few pages, you'll find a "Show-and-Tell Showcase" of businesses that have been formed by EPs. On one side of the page the "face," or public image, of their business will be shown—in the form of business cards, brochures, stationery, web site home pages, and the like.

On the back of the page you'll see what's *behind* these businesses—what's supporting them and how they are being operated. Here EPs will tell you how they formed their companies—including selecting a legal entity, raising capital, setting up a bank account, registering for appropriate business licenses, and other universal start-up steps. You'll find out why one EP decided on a Limited Liability Company while another decided to incorporate, how one EP came up with capital through a formal business plan while another barely tested the market before diving right in, why one is a believer in using credit cards for start-up capital while another is not, how each is dependent on their professional support team that includes attorneys, web site designers, tech consultants, and more.

> "I think the best thing to do with regard to 'making the leap' is to make your business official! This means going to the city to get your business and/or zoning license and filing your DBA with the state. Once these tasks were completed, I felt that I had really created something and there was no turning back or chickening out!"
>
> —Tryna Bailey Fitzpatrick

We hope this "behind-the-scenes" approach to the formation of a business will de-mystify the process and help you assess where you are now and where you may need to go next.

"SHOW" PAGE

Federal Training Network

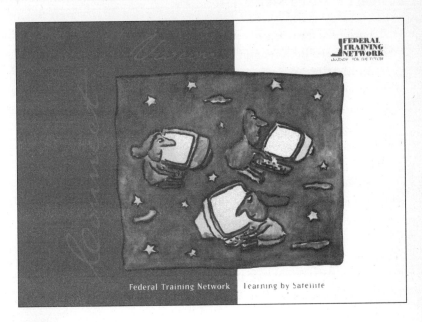

"TELL" PAGE

Chronological Order of Standard Business Start-up Steps:

1. Formed a legal entity
2. Registered for a federal ID number, business license, and other legal documents
3. Named business
4. Set up a business account
5. Wrote a business plan
6. Lined up a professional support team
7. Conducted market research
8. Raised capital
9. Planned a marketing campaign
10. Tested the market
11. Developed a "look" and marketing material for business

FEDERAL TRAINING NETWORK

Year of Formation: 1993

www.fedlearn.com
321 Bayview Street
Yarmouth, ME 04096
Ph: 207-846-5010
Fax: 207-846-0822
gshunter@fedlearn.com

EP: Shawn Hunter
Father of one (1), and another on the way

Business Plan: My father, Hal Hunter, developed a business plan in 1993 using experience, research, advice, and hope. At the time he developed the business model, we were not aware of any competition at all. Later we discovered a few companies doing the same thing.

Business Name: The parent company is Targeted Learning Corporation, a business founded around 1980 by my mother, Beverly Hunter. For the venture Hal developed in 1993, he used the same legal entity and changed the name to Federal Learning Channel. The Learning Channel contested our name and we eventually settled on Federal Training Network.

Bank Account and Capital: Our company has a savings, checking, and money market account—all owned and managed by the company. The initial capital came as a loan from my father, drawn from his retirement fund.

Business Structure: We are a for-profit corporation; we looked into establishing the company as a nonprofit foundation originally but was daunted by the strict requirements to do so.

Business Licenses and Registration: A federal, state, and/or local business license, a professional license, a federal ID number, incorporation papers, business name registration.

Record-keeping: We have a part-time accountant and bookkeeper who manages our files and accounting, as well as an independent accountant to prepare our annual taxes.

Professional Help: Accountant, bookkeeper, tax preparer, graphic artist, web site designer, baby-sitter.

Networking Organizations: Never, although I've often thought we should!

"SHOW" PAGE

BarbWired, LLC

BarbWired, LLC — The Public Image

Applications

Distance Learning is one of many applications of streaming media. In one recent example of how BarbWired offers value to customers, a corporate web development team approached us with a number of questions on how to deliver video over their intranet.

We researched the technology offerings of three major vendors and prepared a detailed technical description of the features, benefits, and drawbacks of each.

At the clients request, we prepared an executive summary for upper management and developed a glossary of terms that aided in their practical understanding of the technological jargon.

After the technology was chosen, testing of video compression parameters was conducted in order to establish a clear understanding of the quality of content delivered to their field service staff over various network connections.

Translating technology into business applications
A sampling of glossary terms:

.avi: movie file extension for audio and video content played back in Video for Windows or the newer DirectShow™ architecture

bandwidth: the amount of data that can be streamed over a network at any given time

codec: the mathematical algorithm that compresses and decompresses digital signals for delivery over limited bandwidths

JPEG: a standard compression format designed for still images

MPEG-2: a standard compression format for motion video and audio designed for delivery of standard definition DTV, HDTV and DVD

.mov: a cross-platform movie file extension for QuickTime™

VBR: variable bit rate encoding

.wav: a digital audio file extension used primarily on the Windows™ platform

▶▶ **BarbWired** LLC
4 Longmeadow Hill Road
Brookfield, CT 06804
Voice: 203.775.1796
Fax: 203.740.9428
barbwired@cyberzone.net

Give your video the competitive edge.

BarbWired
SPECIALIZING IN:

▶ Video Compression
▶ MPEG Processing
▶ Streaming Media
▶ DVD Technology

Technical Experience

Barbara Roeder holds B.S. and M.S. degrees in electrical engineering Her experience includes 10 years in the research and development of digital signal processing for advanced television and HDTV systems at prominent laboratories. She has written numerous technical reports and holds five patents relating to her

Professional affiliations include:

Institute of Electrical and Electronic Engineers (IEEE)

Society of Motion Picture and Television (SMPTE)

International Television Association (ITVA)

Danbury Area Computer Society

Barbara Roeder
Multimedia Technology Consultant
Voice: 203.775.1796
Fax: 203.740.9428
barbwired@cyberzone.net

Research

▶ Investigation and analysis of the technology that meets business investment strategy

▶ Executive summaries for planning

▶ Features and benefits analysis for purchasing decisions

▶ Independent source of information on available products and services

Engineering

▶ Testing methodologies that set expectations for digital media delivery

▶ Algorithm development for image format and digital processing of MPEG video

▶ Visualization software development for analysis of complex, multi-dimensional image processing applications including DTV and HDTV

Workshops

Focused, in-house training gives your staff the competitive edge without interrupting your demanding production schedule.

Workshops are customized to your application of CD-ROM, DVD, MPEG and streaming media delivery. Businesses that can benefit from our video capture and compression training sessions include:

▶ Corporate Intranet/Internet Development Teams
▶ Distance Learning Companies
▶ Video Duplication Facilities
▶ Video Production Departments

Call or write us for more details on current workshop offerings.

"TELL" PAGE

Chronological Order of Standard Business Start-up Steps:

1. Named the business
2. Raised capital
3. Tested the market
4. Developed a "look" and marketing material for business
5. Lined up a professional support team
6. Formed a legal entity
7. Registered for a federal ID number, business license, and other legal documents
8. Set up a business banking account
9. Wrote a business plan
10. Planned a marketing campaign
11. Conducted market research

> **BARBWIRED, LLC**
> *On the Cutting Edge of Digital Video Technology*
>
> Year of Formation: 1998
>
> www.barb-wired.net
> 4 Longmeadow Hill Road
> Brookfield, CT 06804
> Ph: 203-775-1796
> Fax: 203-740-9428
> Barbwired@cyberzone.net
>
> **EP:** Barb Roeder
> Mother of two:
> Theresa (10) and Stefan (8)

Business Plan: I buckled down and wrote the business plan after being in business for a year. I guess that was a year of market research and making some decisions about the direction I wanted my business to go.

Business Name: The name just came to me one day, not realizing it's the title of some B-rated movie starring Pamela Anderson! I have a tag line "BarbWired—On the cutting edge of digital video technology" but am continually trying to improve it.

Bank Account and Capital: I opened a separate checking account after the business was registered and I had an EIN. The bank I chose had the lowest monthly charges. In my area, they did not seem to give very good deals to businesses. Initial capital was about $3,500, but that included some money for part-time day care for my children.

Business Structure: I started out the gate as an LLC after consulting my lawyer. My decision was based on protecting my family from liability. The LLC was a simpler structure than getting incorporated, and I could still use Schedule C for my taxes. Plus I believe that an "LLC" (or an "Inc.") gives a much more professional impression.

Business Licenses and Registration: A federal ID number; forming an LLC; business name registration; trademarks/patents/copyrights.

Record-keeping: I put all receipts in an envelope and keep track of cash and mileage expenses on a running list on the envelope. Once a month I enter the data into QuickBooks Pro. I used Quicken for the first year as well.

Professional Help: Attorney, accountant, insurance agent (for business insurance), graphic artist, web site designer, baby-sitter.

Networking Organizations: I have found this to be the best network for clients. I go to International Television Association (ITVA) meeting four to five times a year, as well as some more engineering groups like Society of Motion Picture and Television Engineers (SMPTE) and a Consultant's Network (CT-CN). They are only useful if the current membership is very active. I couldn't find the time to start up a local group and a business at the same time.

Other Business Start-up Steps:
- An electronic Rolodex using HyperCard, which I can customize and on which I keep notes of what clients I have called and what we've talked about. Many are impressed with my memory!
- All the basic desktop software and hardware—printer, e-mail, word processing, modem, Internet service provider (ISP).
- Oh, yes, and a second phone line so my clients could call while I was on the Internet.

"SHOW" PAGE

Carolina Financial Partners, LLC

Carolina Financial Partners

2351 Fernridge Ln. • P.O. Box 1321 • Matthews, NC 28106
Website: www.carolinafinancialpartners.com

John R. Kirwan, President
Certified Investment Specialist
Financial Advisor

• Investments & Retirement Planning •

Planning For Your Financial Success One Step At A Time

704-845-1058 (business)
704-841-1487 (home/fax)
800-439-0188 (toll-Free)

Securities offered through Royal Alliance Associates Inc.   Member NASD / SIPC
Stocks • Bonds • Mutual Funds • Annuities • CD's

"TELL" PAGE

Chronological Order of Standard Business Start-up Steps:

1. Wrote business plan
2. Conducted market research
3. Named business
4. Formed legal entity
5. Developed a "look" and marketing material
6. Registered for a federal ID number, business license, etc.
7. Set up business account
8. Planned a marketing campaign
9. Lined up professional support team
10. Tested the market

CAROLINA FINANCIAL PARTNERS, LLC

Year of Formation: 1995

2351 Fernridge Lane
Matthews, NC 28105
Ph: 704-845-1058
Fax: 704-841-1487
jkirwan@carolina.rr.com

EP: John R. Kirwan
Father of two children:
Riley (3) and Casey
(20 months)

Business Plan: I wrote the business plan myself over a period of three to four months. I started the business before I had completed the business plan but have reviewed and rewritten parts of the plan over the past five to six years to keep current, assess my progress, and look for new niches. The main resource I used was a book called *How to Create a Successful Business Plan,* written by David E. Gumpert and presented by *Inc.* magazine. I also had some experience with developing a business plan since I set up a successful financial services sales department plan for my previous employer, Shelby Savings Bank, in 1991.

Business Name: When I first started my investment and retirement planning business, I just used my last name, Kirwan, and added "Financial Services" to it. But I didn't like how it looked or sounded. After two years of Kirwan Financial Services, I developed a name I thought really spoke of the mission statement of my business—"to be your trusted financial advisor throughout all your life stages."

That's how Carolina Financial Partners was named. I wanted to be my clients' trusted financial "personal consultant" or "partner" throughout their life stages. I have an interest and commitment in their financial life to help them plan for all their life stages. I am willing to be their "partner" for life.

Business Account and Capital: I have a separate business account that is titled like my business name. The bank I selected at first was because I was a friend of the branch manager. I am in the process of changing banks because the new one, BB&T, is much more small-business friendly. My initial capital expense was paid out of some of my severance package (former employer), savings, and cash flow. I bought a computer, two-line telephone, stationery, and business cards. It was definitely started on a shoestring budget and now has a pretty good monthly budget and cash flow. I'm not a proponent of credit cards or unnecessary debt, so I didn't use credit cards or loans to get started.

Business Structure: When I first started my business, I was a sole proprietor. This setup left open the door for excessive personal liability, so I formed an LLC, which owns all the assets of the business and is simple to keep up with, unlike being incorporated. As a one-person business, simplicity is a plus!

Business Licenses and Registrations: Federal ID number; local business license; professional license as a securities licensed representative; my LLC Articles of Organization; and business name registration.

Record-keeping: I use a file system on my desk, which covers everything from daily customer service requests, pending business, articles to be read, overnight shipping, to bill paying. I use a Dayrunner and Microsoft Outlook for scheduling, projects, and more.

Professional Help: Insurance agent, accountant, web site designer, assistant, baby-sitter and part-time day school (number one on list), and a computer tech consultant who helps me keep my business cost-effective and time-efficient by using the latest technology from hardware to software.

Networking Organizations: Local chamber of commerce, Kiwanis Club, active church member and youth adviser, youth sports program sponsor and referee, neighborhood homeowners association board member.

Other Business Start-up Steps:

Set up a retirement plan right from the start. I opened a SEP to start with and now a simple IRA. Since this is what I advise many of my clients to do, I do the same thing. A retirement plan, no matter how small at the start, helps you save for "after the business." You can't retire on your dream of owning your own business, but you can plan to "retire" comfortably *from* your business.

"SHOW" PAGE

e-conosystems

• Economics Research   • Information Brokerage   • Business Writing

---

Economic Outlook Reports

Forecast your sales, costs and future business conditions more accurately with insights gained from your customized economic outlook report. Econosystems will prepare an outlook report to help you with business planning, strategy and marketing. Your customized outlook report will:

- summarize trends in economic output, growth and employment levels of the local, national and international economy.

- track production or shipment levels of your company's key markets in order to estimate future demand for your goods or services.

- monitor income and buying patterns of your customers (consumers, companies, government agencies and overseas buyers).

- summarize changes in federal, state and local laws and regulations that will impact your business.

Your outlook report can be provided as a one-time project, or Econosystems can keep you informed of business conditions regularly with your own quarterly Economic Outlook Report.

THE Economic Consulting Firm for Small Business

- **Customized Economic Outlook Reports**

- **Market Research for Business Planning**

- **Information Brokerage for Your Consulting Contracts, Articles or Research Projects**

You *can* keep track of changes in your markets *without* having to hire a full-time economist. Call now for a free initial consultation.

Econosystems
2240 Camino a los Cerros
Menlo Park, CA 94025
USA

1-650-233-9613
1-650-503-7082 fax

www.econosystems.com

Economics Research •Market Research •Information Brokerage

Serving small businesses and independent consultants in the San Francisco Bay Area and Internet Communities.

http://www.econosystems.com

2240 Camino a los Cerros, Menlo Park, CA 94025
Telephone: 650-233-9613 Telefax: 650-503-7082
www.econosystems.com

"TELL" PAGE

Chronological Order of Standard Business Start-up Steps:

1. Named the business
2. Raised capital
3. Formed a legal entity
4. Registered for a federal ID number, business license, and other legal documents
5. Set up a business account
6. Wrote a business plan
7. Developed a "look" and marketing material for the business
8. Planned a marketing campaign
9. Conducted market research
10. Lined up a professional support team
11. Tested the market

E-CONOSYSTEMS
THE Economic Consulting Firm for Small Business

Year of Formation: 1999

www.econosystems.com
2240 Camino a los Cerros
Menlo Park, CA 94025
Ph: 650-233-9613
Fax: 650-503-7082
awenzel@econosystems.com

EP: Anne Ramstetter Wenzel
Mother of four:
Trent (20), Valerie (19),
Cort (16), and James (8)

Business Plan: I did minimal market research for my business because I already had clients asking me to do work for them. It was work I enjoyed and was well experienced in, and I could be paid well for it. I made sure to get two times my desired hourly rate (to cover overhead expenses) in my first big contract. Otherwise I did no financial planning.

As time went on I realized I could not even consider expanding my business without a business plan, so I worked with a personal business coach to help me finish my plan in order to submit it to a foundation for a grant competition. I did not win the grant, but it was an excellent source of inspiration to finish it by a deadline.

Business Name: My teenage daughter was disappointed when I told her I was going to use my maiden name "and Associates." Her belief that using my name was "boring" inspired me to search for a name. Many I thought of had the URL taken. I chose my business name and URL at the same time—the name I chose was dependent upon the URL being available. I looked in the dictionary and saw the word "ecosystem." I expanded that to "E-conosystems," because the world economy is interconnected—when something happens in one place in the world it can affect people in another part as the change works its way through the "economic system." My original thought for a logo was a drip making "ripple effects," but it was too hard to illustrate with a stationary (as opposed to animated) logo!

Econosystems.com was an available URL, so I went with it. A man I met at an SBA seminar suggested I wait to see what URLs were available before I named my company. My tag line is "THE Economic Consulting Firm for Small Business."

Bank Account and Capital: I have a separate banking account because I have credit card processing. ECHOtel set up a bank account for Econosystems at First Regional Bank in California.

My start-up capital came from a two-week vacation paycheck I received from the company I was laid off from. I also received severance that went directly into my family checking account for five months after I was laid off. Although the severance pay was never part of my business capital, it did act as my business paycheck during that five months. The sixth month after I was laid off was the first time I paid myself a salary out of the business funds.

My large contract with my former employer also served as start-up capital. I have signed my third annual contract with them and it serves as a steady stream of cash flow for my business.

I also use a personal for-business-use-only account for much of the money since it earns interest and my merchant account doesn't pay interest.

Business Structure: I am a sole proprietor (Anne Ramstetter Wenzel d.b.a. Econosystems) because it was the low-cost, simple alternative. I had originally wanted to incorporate, but three things changed my mind:

- The minimum tax. I didn't realize I'd be immediately profitable (I thought all new businesses took three years to stop operating in the red), and I didn't like the thought of paying the corporate minimum tax even if I was losing money.

- A lawyer I talked to said that working solo and being incorporated might not automatically protect my husband's and my personal assets in case of a law suit. The plaintiff could argue that since I was working solo as a professional it was actually ME who did the damages and not a corporation. We could argue that we had taken steps to prevent my being personally liable, but it made sense to me that if the corporation WAS in fact me, that I could in fact be held personally liable. That removed the major motive for me to take the expense of incorporating.
- After reading a home business book on selecting your company's legal entity, I realized that the only motivation to incorporate remained the name: I thought "Econosystems, Inc." sounded so cool. I decided it was too expensive an undertaking just to be able to place "Inc." after my company name.

Business Licenses and Registration: Business name registration, copyrights/patents/copyrights (I have applied for a service mark).

Record-keeping: I quickly write all expenses down in a book/journal, transfer them all to an Excel spreadsheet where I keep track of expenses by each quarter. I keep a running total of all expenses by date for the entire year, and now am on my third year of expenses in the spreadsheet. I am using the cash basis, so expenses put on my charge cards are recorded when I pay my Visa bill.

I also have a cash flow spreadsheet, where I keep track of all money spent. The entries have the date, source of funds/expense, the account the money goes to or is withdrawn from, and the balance of cash on hand.

I keep track of revenue in an Excel spreadsheet. When I invoice someone I enter the amount into the accounts receivable section, and when I receive payment it goes into the revenue received section. Each section has an add total, and I also keep track of a grand total to see how much I've made in sales throughout the year. At the bottom of this spreadsheet I subtract out taxes to estimate how much cash I've netted throughout the year. I keep one calendar year's record on this spreadsheet.

Professional Help: Insurance agent, graphic artist, web site designer, cleaning service, baby-sitter, research assistant. Although I have not yet hired an attorney, I will be doing so within the next month to help me negotiate licensing agreements and international contracts.

Networking Organizations: National Association of Entrepreneurial Parents; the Menlo Park (CA) Chamber of Commerce. Networking on-line, especially with the EP discussion group, has been an excellent way to pick up tips for business, balancing business and family, and emotional support. On-line networking *really* helps ease the feeling of isolation work-at-home entrepreneurs often experience.

"SHOW" PAGE

Goin' SOHO!

"TELL" PAGE

Chronological Order of Standard Business Start-up Steps:

1. Named the business
2. Developed a "look" and marketing material for business
3. Lined up a professional support team
4. Planned a marketing campaign
5. Formed a legal entity
6. Registered for a federal ID number, business license, and other legal documents
7. Set up a business account

GOIN' SOHO!
Work Efficiently. Live Deliberately.

Year of formation: 1996

www.goinsoho.com
P.O. Box 8263
Coral Springs, FL 33075–8263
Ph: (954)346-4393
Fax: (954)346-0251
jeff@goinsoho.com

EP: Jeffrey D. Zbar
Father to three:
Nicole (9), Zachary (7),
and Zoe (3)

Comments: These came in nontraditional order (as well as some otherwise important pieces didn't apply) because my business evolved over time. I had incorporated early on, only to let it lapse when I realized it was unnecessary at the time. By 1997, my business was generating enough annual revenues to follow my CPA's advice to incorporate, get the federal tax ID number, and set up the required business checking account (no co-mingling of personal and business funds!).

Business Plan: No formal business plan was written. Again, as the business evolved from journalism to subject matter, expert work, and authoring of books, it was very nontraditional in its evolution.

Business Name: I have several business names, all of which were created to boost my position as an expert in the field:
- Jeffery D. Zbar, Inc., is an umbrella corporation to make my relations with corporate clients cleaner (many would issue checks to

me personally and would therefore require me to return them for reissuance).

- Goin' SOHO! is a d.b.a. under JDZ, Inc., which helps brand my home office speaking and book-selling efforts. It was dot-commed, dot-netted (along with goingsoho.com and .net) and trademarked early on to protect the brand.
- Chief Home Officer.com is a further, more distinctive brand for my home office lecturing efforts. I own the .com and .net on that as well.
- I also own the .com domains for all my book properties—current and pending.

Bank Account and Capital: I opened a separate business account only after I incorporated (it was a requirement of incorporation). I did incorporate once before (around 1994), but soon let it lapse. No significant start-up capital was required to launch the business, except for my wife's steady income as a full-time contract registered nurse. With no kids at the time and very low overhead, it was not capital-intensive to launch a writing business. As sales have grown, we have "repaid" my wife, Robbie, by her now working less than twenty hours a week—if that.

I am a believer in maxing out credit cards to launch a business, but only on intro-loan rates of sub-prime and then only if you fully intend to pay back the balance within the typical twelve-month intro period.

Business Structure: I incorporated as an S-Corporation. This allows certain benefits regarding income, salary, and dividends.

Business Licenses and Registration: A federal, state, and/or local business license, a federal ID number, state sales tax certificate, county and city occupational and business licenses, articles of incorporation, business name registration, trademarks, no patents, and de facto copyrights (© 2001 Jeffery D. Zbar, Inc.) attached to all my written work.

Record-keeping: I use Quicken 6.0 as a simple cash account basis. It tracks accounts receivable, and I can easily track delinquent clients and dates. I also create "reports" to closely track weekly and month billings, so I can determine whether I am meeting projections.

Professional Help: Attorney, accountant, tax preparer, insurance agent, graphic artist, web site designer, cleaning service, mother's helper.

Networking Organizations: None. I instead rely on constant contact with my clients and allies out there to give me the juice to keep on going.

Business Start-up Commentary:

The two most important elements of launching a business is having the right mind-set and marketing yourself appropriately. Both have come easily to me. I enjoy working; I believe watching my billings grow in my accounting software is a true "passion" of mind. I also dig coming up with memorable marketing materials. It's fun, invigorating, energizing, and makes you memorable among your peers and clients—prospective and existing. That's way cool.

I could go on, but I do believe people need to conduct a pretty serious gut-check about the business they're starting, the climate they're starting it in, and whether they've fostered the support of family, friends, professional peers, and allies to make it a success. No person lives or works on an island, and while SOHO offers solitude, we often can use the help of others.

Ultimately, fun in the workplace—wherever you place that space—can help translate to satisfaction and enjoyment in your personal life, however you define it. I define my satisfaction in taking afternoon walks or shooting hoops with my three kids . . . during business hours. It's my way of saying, "This is my life, and this is how I live it."

"SHOW" PAGE

BeHosting.com, LLC

"TELL" PAGE

Chronological Order of Standard Business Start-up Steps:

1. Conducted market research
2. Tested the market
3. Lined up a professional support team
4. Named business
5. Set up a business account
6. Raised capital
7. Registered for a federal ID number, business license, and other legal documents
8. Formed a legal entity
9. Planned a marketing campaign
10. Wrote a business plan

BEHOSTING.COM LLC
Delivers the results you seek!

Year of Formation: 1999

www.beHosting.com
1480 Elmwood Avenue
Lakewood, OH 44107-3902
Ph: 216-225-5142
Fax: 216-221-4479
Youareimportant@
behosting.com

EP: Erica Anne Kuntz
Mother of three:
Nora (13), Celia (6),
and Oscar (4)

Business Plan: I still do not have a formal (GASP) business plan . . . it's in the works! I've always respected the importance of a business plan, and now that our business is coming into its own I know the plan I produce now will be so much more relevant and useful than one we initially would have devised. As for market research, since we were out among our peers and potential clients during the normal course of our on-line "existences," both personally and in relation to our web development business, we were able to feel the pulse of the client base we were interested in supporting—*and* of the competition!

Business Name: I first formed this company with a partner, whose name began with a "B" while mine began with an "E." We were looking for something halfway refined and whimsical—something that was non-threatening, easy to remember if not memorable. Our initials combined to form the word "be," a word with endless possibilities. "Hosting" was chosen to convey that we *are* a hosting company, not a firm that offers hosting on the side.

Bank Account and Capital: We had almost NO initial capital investment (a few hundred dollars), and even put off purchasing business cards until revenue from the business could cover the expense. (We are grateful and amazed at this still!) We started cautiously! In the beginning, we were actually resellers for another company. Once our client base was large enough (thirty customers), hosting fees covered the lease of our own server. Our first machine was solid, but basic. As we've grown, we invest in equipment that fits our growing needs. By taking baby steps early on and growing our infrastructure just a step ahead of our customer base, we've been able to avoid excessive debt.

We also use an American Express card for every payable possible. Our business checking account is housed at a local credit union. While American Express is huge and technologically advanced, and the credit union is small and more personal, both institutions make us feel that our success is important to them. That's the key.

Business Structure: The company is an LLC. We felt this was the ideal structure for us, offering the structure and room for the company's growth, while at the same time protecting our personal interests. The decision stemmed from research and casual conversations with business professionals (attorney) and those who'd been there, done that. Nolo.com also provided great resources.

Business Licenses and Registration: A federal, state, and/or local business license; a federal ID number; forming an LLC; business name registration; trademarks/patents/copyrights.

Record-keeping: Close your eyes, count to three, and imagine a wonderful blending of Eudora (e-mail program), QuickBooks, a filing cabinet, a CD burner for backups, scribbles on the backs of envelopes, a daily planner that notes payables and receivables as well as tallies new accounts and highlights of the day . . . and add to that some gray matter. That pretty much describes it.

Professional Help: Attorney, insurance agent, cleaning service, baby-sitter.

Networking Organizations: One of these days I'll send in that application to the chamber of commerce. Since we're an Internet company, the following organizations fit well with our business/networking mission. (I use mission instead of strategy because the whole basis that drives our company is to provide the means for others to success. Being out among our clients "networking" is what allows our mission to be realized.)

- Digital-Women.com
- en-parent.com
- HBWM.com
- Momsnetwork.com
- Apbiz.com
- WebGrrls International
- DigitalEve.com
- SFWoW.com
- ABWA.org

Other Business Start-up Steps:

I gotta quote Goethe: "Whatever you can do, or dream you can, begin it. Boldness has genius, power, and magic in it."

Just making the commitment and taking those first steps started the momentum that we're still running on. It sounds so simple. If you do it, it IS!

"SHOW" PAGE

PowerHour®, LLC

PowerHour®

Professional Business Coaching

"An hour a week delivers the results you seek!"®

PowerHour®

Professional Business Coaching

"An hour a week delivers the results you seek!"®

PowerHour®

Professional Business Coaching

"An hour a week delivers the results you seek!"®

E-Mail, ernest@powerhour.com
Visit our TeleForum website, http://www.coachingsuccess.com

CPBA

PowerHour®

Professional Business Coaching

"An hour a week delivers the results you seek!"®

1402 Cutter Lane, Park City-UT, 84098
435-615-8486

E-mail: ernest@powerhour.com
Website: http://www.coachingsuccess.com

"TELL" PAGE

Chronological Order of Standard Business Start-up Steps:

1. Conducted market research
2. Tested the market
3. Wrote a business plan
4. Named the business
5. Formed a legal entity
6. Set up a business account
7. Registered for a federal ID number, business license, and other legal documents
8. Planned a marketing campaign
9. Developed a "look" and marketing material for the business
10. Lined up a professional support team

POWERHOUR®, LLC

An hour a week delivers the results you seek! ©

Year of Formation: 1996

www.powerhour.com
402 Cutter Lane
Park City, UT 84098
Ph: 435-615-8486
Fax: 435-615-8670
ernest@powerhour.com

EP: Ernest F. Oriente
Father of three:
Thomas (6), Alexandra (8),
and Gabriel (10)

Business Plan: I read/learned about coaching from a *Business Week* article in 1995. My training as a coach began in January 1996, and my first paying client started in March 1996. My initial start-up costs required the purchase of a computer/printer, cordless telephone with headset, fax machine, and $5,000 of training to become a coach. Today, we coach/guide 300+ companies, clients, and executives in eleven countries around the world—all by telephone!

Business Name: My company name is PowerHour® and my copyrighted tag line is "An hour a week delivers the results you seek!" Most of my telephone coaching is done in groups by teleconference, and thus PowerHour® is a perfect fit for my clients. In addition, by using a more generic name for my company (rather than Ernest, Inc.), it will be easier to sell my company in future years, and it allows me to provide a broad array of coaching services (private coaching, group coaching, teleconference rentals, assessments for hiring, recruiting services, and more) under the *umbrella* of this business name.

Bank Account and Capital: We have a separate business account for our company, and we selected our bank because they *sweep* our checking account into an interest-bearing account each night. The start-up capital for our business was $10,000 in training/equipment, and another $35,000 over the course of the first year—primarily for telephone and marketing expenses.

Business Structure: Our company is an LLC. I followed the recommendation of my CPA on this decision, who said an LLC gives me the legal/liability protection of a corporation, but is taxed like a sole proprietorship. In addition, an LLC requires minimal paperwork/tax reporting each quarter and at the end of each year.

Business Licenses and Registration: A federal, state, and/or local business license; a federal ID number; articles in forming an LLC; business name registration; trademarks/patents/copyrights.

Record-keeping: We use Quicken to manage our finances. We invoice our clients by fax/e-mail in *advance* of each month's coaching services, and most of our clients pay by company credit card—thus we have no receivables.

Professional Help: Attorney, accountant, tax preparer, insurance agent, graphic artist, web site designer, telemarketer, secretary/assistant, cleaning service, baby-sitter.

Networking Organizations: We are very active in the business/professional associations for each of the niche/specialty areas we coach our clients. We speak at their annual conventions/meetings, we write monthly articles for their industry web sites/newsletters/magazines, and we coach/guide their board of directors.

Other Business Start-up Steps:

In 1996 we launched a free e-mail/fax newsletter as part of our attraction/marketing engine. Today, we have 9,000+ subscribers in 67 countries and write for 220+ web sites/newsletters/magazines each month. This newsletter has been the key for growing/expanding our business.

"SHOW" PAGE

E-Scent-ials

E-Scent-ials

All natural bath and aromatherapy products
inspired by Mother Nature.

WINTER/SPRING 2001 CATALOG

P.O. BOX 40
DES PLAINES, IL 60016
Toll Free 1-877-SCENT09 (877-723-6809)
847-298-3474
www.E-Scent-ials.com

"TELL" PAGE

Chronological Order of Standard Business Start-up Steps:

1. Formed a legal entity
2. Named the business
3. Registered for a federal ID number, business license, and other legal documents
4. Raised capital
5. Set up a business account
6. Developed a "look" and marketing material for business
7. Conducted market research
8. Planned a marketing campaign
9. Tested the market
10. Business plan (to be done!)

E-SCENT-IALS

Aromatherapy Products—
Because Nature Knows Best

Year of Formation: 1998

www.E-Scent-ials.com
P.O. Box 40
Des Plaines, IL 60016
Ph: 877-SCENT09
Info@E-Scent-ials.com

EP: Jeralynn Burke
mother of:
Girl (6) and boy (4)

Business Plan: While I haven't written a formal business plan yet, I have thought about the various aspects of the business plan in detail. I haven't been able to find the time to sit down and commit it to paper.

The business started as a partnership. The selection of our business actually resulted from a discussion that we were having regarding herbs and natural alternatives to treat my nephew's spina bifida. We were talking about all the synthetic ingredients we're exposed to and simpler times. Prior to that, we had gone through dozens of ideas but they just never clicked, or once we started doing the research, we decided that a particular business wasn't a good idea to pursue. It really was a situation where all of a sudden we looked at each other and said, "That's it!"

We investigated other sites carrying similar products, had read about the increasing trend in people looking for more natural products, and decided this was something that we could start on a shoestring budget. Of course, having a limited budget meant that we had to do a lot of legwork and learn how to do projects on our own, such as web design. Between our combined base of knowledge and a strong desire to start our own business we managed to figure it all out one step at a time.

Business Name: We started with the type of products we wanted to sell, which are normally scented, and coupled that with our belief that reducing our exposure to synthetic chemicals and getting back to a more basic, simpler way of life was essential to one's well-being. Scents can be powerful emotional triggers—think about how you feel when you smell the earth after a summer shower or when you smell the scent of a particular childhood favorite meal. We also wanted to convey the importance that the role of aroma plays in our lives.

Bank Account and Capital: Selecting our bank came after a frustrating day calling all the larger banks in our area. They all seemed to want an initial deposit larger than we could manage as well as had numerous fees for all transactions. Finally, we called the smaller local bank and they had a business checking account for small business that suited our needs.

Our initial investment was $375, which we raised from doing a craft show and getting an order from someone we knew who wanted to buy some of our items to put into gift baskets that they were sending out for their business for Christmas.

Business Structure: Sole proprietorship; former partnership. We spoke with the local SCORE representative. Our only other option was an LLC. Again, we didn't have the funds to become an LLC so we chose the partnership with the probability that one day we'll change it.

Business Licenses and Registration: A federal, state, and/or local business license; a federal ID number; business name registration.

Record-keeping: Currently working on a computer-generated system that will keep track of inventory as well as the sales and expenses. Previously we used the standard, manual method of bookkeeping: recording sales, purchases, expenses, etc., in a ledger and separate file for cost calculations of our products.

Professional Help: Insurance agent.

Networking Organizations: None.

Other Business Start-up Steps:

Meet with a SCORE representative. One of the first steps we took after researching as much as we could on the Internet and at the library was to meet with our local SCORE representative. Our goal in meeting with him was to get answers to the more specific questions we had at that time regarding business name registration, any licenses that were needed, handling sales tax, and other items along those lines. The rest, as they say, is history!

"SHOW" PAGE

Inner City Game Designs

INNER CITY GAMES DESIGNS

August 14, 2000

New Product Release Notice

Title: When Good Villagers Go Bad

Product Line: Micro-games
MSRP: $5.95

Release Date: 9/14/00

UPC: not coded ISBN: not coded

...-order Date: 9/12/00

...'x 5.5" Page Count: 16 + 7
...: hole-punched ziplock
...ris Clark
...: Jim Mitchell

...ting armies of irate villagers against
...100 stand-up pieces.

...t and happy residents is common to
...adventurers hit town with little or no
...dy. This tranquil scene can transform
...agers Go Bad. A simple logistics and
...ith separate miniatures or the stand-

...ages 10 and up. Impulse buy item.

INNER CITY GAMES DESIGNS

October 11, 2000

New Product Release Notice

Title: STARSHP War PIGs

Product Line: Micro-games
MSRP: $5.95

Release Date: 12/11/00

UPC: not coded ISBN: not coded

...re-order Date: 12/8/00

...5" x 5.5" Page Count: 36
...g: hole-punched ziplock
...ris Clark
...rk

...pitting armies of alien plastic insects

...re willing to invade Earth to get
...antry Guys army in this game of
...fast-paced miniatures game using
...players ages 10 and up.

...ages 10 and up. Impulse buy item.

INNER CITY GAMES DESIGNS

August 14, 2000

New Product Release Notice

Title: Abdul's Adventure

Product Line: Micro-games
MSRP: $6.95

Release Date: 10/3/00

UPC: not coded ISBN: not coded

...order Date: 10/2/00

...x 5.5" Page Count: 16 + 6
...: hole-punched ziplock
...iel Lewis
...: Angela Bennet

...planning and business techniques.
...200 stand-up pieces.

...e, and it is up to you to determine
...ruins will harass your caravans, but
...ls of the desert. If only the camels
...ement micro-boardgame for two to

...es 12 and up. Impulse buy item.

INNER CITY GAMES DESIGNS

September 20, 1999

New Product Release Notice

Title: CIVIL WAR PIGS

Product Line: Micro-games
MSRP: $5.95
Stock #: ICG 7305

Release Date: 11/15/99

UPC: not coded ISBN: not coded

Product Type: Miniatures micro-game	Format: 8.5"x 5.5"	Page Count: 32
Cover: 2-color uncoated 65# cardstock	Packaging: hole-punched ziplock	
Genre: Humor/tactical miniatures	Author: Chris Clark	
Cover Art: Chris Clark	Interior Art: Dale Ridder, Chris Clark	

Summary: A ready to play miniatures and logistics game pitting armies of plastic Civil War figures against one another.

Description: It was a time of great strife in the land of toys. A conflict that pitted friend against friend, brother against brother.... and PIG against PIG! Now you can re-create your favorite battles from the Civil War using Plastic Infantry Guys (PIGs) in this fast-paced set of rules. Morale, leadership, artillery, cavalry, and even the problems of loading a musket while someone is shooting at you are all covered within these rules.

Target Audience: Beginning and intermediate players ages 9 and up. Impulse buy item.

Sales Bullets:
- Humorous premise, art, and story line; as well as historic accuracy.
- Addictive game involving serious strategy and tactics.
- Inexpensive, easy to find miniatures.
- Impulse priced, easy to stock.
- An excellent introductory game to entice new customers.

Marketing Support:
- Events planned at Gen Con, Origins and other major conventions.
- Cross Marketing through Website advertising and the GPA.
- Plastic figures are also available.

Related Backlist and Comparable Product:
- War PIGs — ICG7300
- (_Your Name Here_) of the Jungle — ICG7302

"TELL" PAGE

Chronological Order of Standard Business Start-up Steps:

1. Conducted market research
2. Tested the market
3. Wrote a business plan
4. Planned a marketing campaign
5. Developed a "look" and marketing material for the business
6. Raised capital

> **INNER CITY GAMES DESIGNS**
>
> Year of Formation: 1982
>
> www.fuzzyheroes.com
> 36460 North Highway 45
> Lake Villa, IL 60046
> Ph/Fax: (847) 356-7484
> fuzhero@aol.com
>
> **EP:** Christopher Clark
> Father of two:
> Ages 4 and 9

Business Plan: Frankly, we started our business a *long* time ago, long before desktop computers were the norm—or even readily available. I was an amateur game designer first and had had several less than satisfactory work offers relating to my body of work at the time. I then, with the help of others, went out and researched the market to ascertain whether I was correct in assuming that the offers I was receiving were "underselling me." This research on the "cost of doing business" led to the "pipe dream" adaptation of a marketing and business plan (in my view, the two are inseparable) in hopes of attracting investors. We eventually did attract a single investor but wound up managing most of the funding ourselves. Inner City Games Designs was started in 1982 with a sum total of $4,200. Originally launched to sell designs, we soon discovered that the only means for paying running overhead was to actually publish the products ourselves. That is when I started looking for good folks with which to surround myself . . . a bit late, but you make a few mistakes when you're twenty!

Business Name: Our original slogan was "we make games out of life," because we were originally angling for a realistic approach to conflict simulation. We later discovered that humor products sold a lot better on our end of the business spectrum, and we abandoned the slogan. The company is actually named after our first product, the Inner City role-playing system, in a somewhat less than well-informed attempt to get some branding for both the product and the company. Funny thing is, it worked, at least to some extent.

Bank Account and Capital: We do have a separate business account, with checking, as we get a lot of checks that are made out to the business, and it makes things much simpler from an accounting standpoint if there is a "real" division of the funds. We chose our bank based on the service offered, the service fees, and the availability of the funds. Reasonably quick turnover can be (although isn't always) essential to good cash flow. We initially raised the money the old-fashioned way—I worked a few extra jobs and stockpiled the money. 'Course, I was a lot younger then . . .

Business Structure: A sole proprietorship. We chose this as it provided the best tax shelters for our type of business, and our product liability is low enough that I was and still am unconcerned about losing our personal funds to a liability suit. That protection, in my book, is the best reason to incorporate but is not necessary for our business.

Business Licenses and Registration: A federal, state, and/or local business license; a federal ID number; a sales license of permit; business name registration; trademarks/patents/copyrights; ISBN and UPC coding.

Record-keeping: I'm truly lucky in that I have someone do that—my wife. I know she uses Excel and a "first in-first out" inventory system. For my part, I keep client files that tell me at a glance the ordering pattern of the client, the last product ordered, pertinent specific information like contacts and adjunct marketing plans that they utilize, as well as their overall sales. You don't have to be completely prepared; you just have to be one iota more prepared than the client you call. I also keep running e-mail logs on any negotiations or client inquiries. The minute you delete them, in my experience, they'll come back to haunt you.

Professional Help: Attorney, accountant, tax preparer, graphic artist, web site designer, copywriter, sales rep, baby-sitter, workers on occasion to do pick-n-pack, assembly, and other manufacturing processes.

Networking Organizations: We are members of the Game Publishers Association and used to be associate members of the Game Manufacturers Association.

Business Start-up Commentary:

We started small, produced a prototype product, and got it placed in three local stores. This gave us the hard research to back up solicitations to distribution. Each industry has a different screening process of this nature, but it all amounts to "paying your dues." Know who you're trying to sell to, and then provide them the proof that they should buy, that's what it comes down to.

When we started our second company last year, Hekaforge Productions (a limited partnership with Gary Gygax—same industry, different products), we did *not* pre-market enough; the market has grown up a bit, and "paying your dues" is more involved than it once was. We're finally climbing the ladder with the new company, but we lost a full year by not "hyping ourselves" sufficiently before entering the market . . . and so we learn a new lesson.

"SHOW" PAGE

enScript

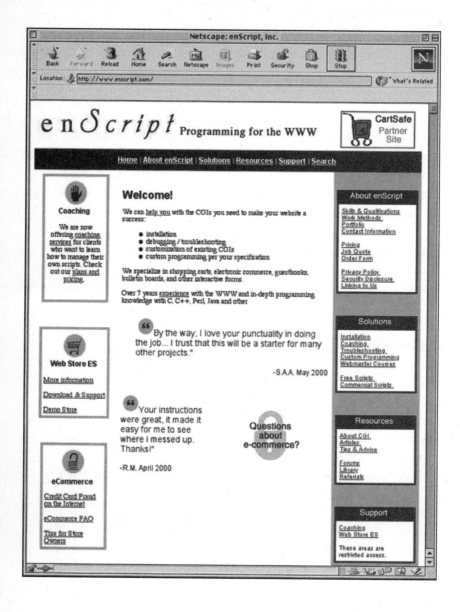

"TELL" PAGE

Chronological Order of Standard Business Start-up Steps:

1. Tested the market
2. Conducted market research
3. Named business
4. Formed a legal entity
5. Registered for a federal ID number, business license, and other legal documents
6. Set up a business account
7. Developed a "look" and marketing material for business

> ### ENSCRIPT
> *Programming for the WWW*
>
> Year of Formation: 1998
>
> www.enScript.com
> 8039 Callaghan Road, #418
> San Antonio, TX 78230
> Ph: 512-773-3077
> Fax/Toll Free: 877-682-1405
> info@enScript.com
>
> **EP:** Ashley Rosilier
> Mother of two:
> Zachary (4) and Aubrey
> (18 months)

Business Plan: I started out by running my own on-line retail business and setting up my own web site. I started having people contact me for help with their web sites and that led to doing the freelance work on the side. I really just fell into it; it was not that I intended to go into this business from the start. At the beginning I did mostly work for barter, to gain experience, and to test the waters. I then began to get many referrals from the initial clients within the business communities I participated in and started getting paid in real money. Since then I have never had to do much marketing since referrals keep coming in.

I did research enough to know that there weren't many businesses out there devoted to scripting only, most were full design firms. Also, I realized that many small design firms didn't know how *to do* the scripting. I also did research the going rates for design and programming, although none of this research was formalized (I wish it had been!). Eventually, I sold my retail business and devoted myself to the freelance work.

I think what kept me from formalizing my plan was the fact that I didn't need to convince anyone but myself and my husband, i.e. I didn't need any investors. I do wish now that I had done at least some formal planning up front, such as how to handle collections and draw up contracts. Eventually I do plan to implement something!

Business Name: I wanted something that indicated the business was focused on CGI scripting and not web design. Other requirements were that it was short and the domain (.com) was available. I liked enScript because the en prefix communicated that we can enable your site for scripting.

My tag line is simply "Programming for the WWW." I do have a banner ad that plays off the name, and I may start using that more in print:

> *enLiven your website*
> *enAble your customers*
> *enVision success*
> *enScript : Programming for the WWW*
>
> http://enscript.com/logos/banner1.gif

Bank Account and Capital: Yes, I have a separate business checking account and am planning to open a savings as well. I am very, very careful to keep my business income separate from my personal money. I will transfer money between accounts but deposits always go into my business account first so that I can track them.

I went through a lot of trouble finding a bank that I was happy with for the business. One bank in particular had a standard policy to hold all deposits over $100 that came from an out of state bank. This meant I couldn't access my money for seven to ten days after the deposit was made. This was totally unacceptable since 90 percent of my deposits were being held due to my national customer base. I did find another bank that didn't have this policy.

I had no initial capital investment since I just started freelancing on the side. Once I had gotten paid from a few customers, I launched my web site, and it took off from there. However I did already have a computer and the Internet connection.

Business Structure: Currently is a sole proprietorship. I went for simplicity since I didn't need to secure funding or hire any employees. This year I will be converting to an S-corporation primarily to protect my personal assets.

Business Licenses and Registration: A federal, state, and/or local business license; a sales license of permit; business name registration. NOTE: I have added all of these when I first started my business; however, currently I have none of them. My current county does not require a license or a name registration, and I've decided to not do any retail sales at this time.

Record-keeping: I use a program called Time Slice to record the time spent on individual clients. It runs on the computer and I can click start/stop when I begin and end any work. It also allows me to add comments for what I was working on.

When I bill clients, I enter the invoice into Quickbooks. I have categories for the different type of work I do (programming, design, script sales, etc.). When I get paid I also record that in Quickbooks, along with all expenses for the business.

I also use a program called Idea Keeper to keep track of project notes for each client. This is particularly useful for long-term clients who e-mail me with small requests from time to time.

Professional Help: Accountant, tax preparer, cleaning service, collections agency, occasionally I also contract work out to web designers or graphic artists. *Note:* Hiring a cleaning service for my house was a must. Hiring them to clean my whole house cost less than one hour of my billable time! I found it nearly impossible to focus on work when I was stressed about the house, yet I couldn't afford to spend my "free time" (i.e. kids asleep or with dad!) cleaning instead of working.

Networking Organizations: I did join several e-mail groups: Ap-biz, webgrrls. Networking via e-mail groups has been *essential* to my business. I also attended several meetings of the local women's chamber of commerce, which did produce some clients, although I didn't join as a member.

Business Start-up Commentary:

I am finding out now that I charged *way* too little for my services at the beginning. I wasn't confident enough in my marketability. Now I have a hard time (emotionally) telling my old customers to pay more, but I have to or else I can't justify working on old clients!

Also, I have always been too lax on billing and collections. I wish I had implemented a policy up front regarding finance charges and handling overdue accounts. It would have saved me *a lot* of trouble in the long run.

Follow the Three R's of Home-based Business Ownership: Read! Research! Review!
by Wendy Brown

Read everything you can find about your industry/field. Since you most likely don't have colleagues to help you with ideas or problems, you need to stay current on the issues that effect your particular job—especially trends and legal issues. And further, read everything you can find about running a business, home-based or otherwise.

Research your customer base, your competition, and your product. Know as much as you can, because an expert is always in demand, and as an extra income, you can always be a consultant or an expert contributor for print periodicals and e-zines.

Review your business goals every few months. Businesses are dynamic and growing, like people, and they need to be closely monitored or they will get out of hand. Make sure you know where you're going with your business and be prepared to change directions if the need arises.

Business Formation Checklist
(in no particular order)

To Do:

____ Develop a "look" and marketing material
____ Line up a professional support team
____ Name your business
____ Plan a marketing campaign
____ Raise capital
____ Register legal documents
____ Research the market
____ Select and register a legal entity
____ Set up a business account
____ Test the market
____ Write a business plan

To Obtain:

____ Business name registration
____ Federal ID number
____ Federal, state, and/or local business license
____ Incorporating or forming an LLC
____ Professional license
____ Sales license or permit
____ Trademarks/patents/copyrights

To Hire:

____ Accountant
____ Attorney
____ Baby-sitter (or other paid child care)
____ Bookkeeper
____ Business insurance agent
____ Copywriter
____ Graphic artist
____ House cleaning service
____ Publicist
____ Sales Rep
____ Secretary/virtual assistant
____ Tax preparer
____ Telemarketer
____ Web site designer

Time Management

"Sometimes it's hard to keep things in perspective because we want to do everything all at once and we want to get from point A (idea) to point B (success) at lightning speed. I admit that I sometimes get frustrated because I can't get more accomplished in a day, but when I think about how much I actually do get done it's no wonder that I don't get to everything."

—Jeralynn Burke, E-Scent-ials.com

Time is at such a high premium for EPs that we challenge any one of our readers to pick up this book and read it from cover to cover. Can't do it? We're not surprised. You've either been interrupted twelve zillion times during the course of your reading *or* you have a to-do list the size of this entire book yourself. Most likely, both are true.

There's no question that finding enough time in the day is a quest that every working family is on, whether parents are working inside or outside the home. But for some reason, an EP's time is so often thrown under scrutiny and into question. Perhaps it's because EPs work and live under one roof, where the walls of society-sanctioned work time are knocked down indefinitely and the physical separation that characterizes traditional work outside the home is completely eradicated. Without a "rule book" of expectations, how an EP spends their time can be a magnet of controversy and judgment.

It may not be until after you've been working at home a few years that you wake up one morning and realize that time is not the matter it used to be. Instead, how you spend your work time is on display and constantly monitored by family members. One can't simply declare, "I'm going to work now," and take off, then walk through the door eleven hours later and announce, "I'm home." You are at home *all* the time, you are working *all* the time, and you are parenting *all* the time. Yes, even those of you with set office hours, even those of you who get out of the house regularly to network, volunteer at the school, or exercise at the gym, even those of you with firm childcare arrangements in place, are still *on call*—as both an entrepreneur and as a parent—*all* the time, ready to pull back into the E or P role at a moment's notice.

Like it or not, these expectations are imposed on you from within and without, and they can lead some EPs to ongoing feelings of restlessness and exhaustion. Without the sanctity of an employer's hours, all your time is deemed discretionary—whether by spouses and children; parents and relatives; friends, neighbors, and school teachers; and, most relevant, by *yourself*. If how you spend your time is always at your discretion, then are you spending it wisely? Are you spending it productively? Are you having fun with it, teaching and learning with it, growing with it? Are you wasting it, abusing it, throwing it to the wind? If you are not asking yourself these questions, then chances are there's someone else in your life asking them of you.

This chapter will attempt to offer a fresh perspective on *time* from the entrepreneurial parent point of view, inching towards a new blueprint for living, working, and being. While we can't promise that after reading through these pages you'll be totally "understood" by the non-EPs in your life, we do hope you'll walk away understanding *why* time management can be such a struggle for you and *how* you can take measures to ease your chosen path. Don't have any issues about managing your time? You'll sail through this chapter and perhaps reconnect with us on the next one. For the rest of you, draw a deep breath and release. You'll get there. Time, after all, *is* on your side!

Work Schedules: Finding
"A Day in the Life" You Can Live With

"I would say the biggest challenge for me has been shifting be-tween mommy mode and entrepreneur mode. I spend two hours with my daughter in the morning before school . . . that's mommy mode. Then I work for three and a half hours while she's in school . . . that's entrepreneur mode. Then I pick her up and hang out with the other preschoolers and their mommies for about an hour . . . mommy mode again. Because I have these switches several times a day and because each requires such a dif-ferent attitude and intensity (one is slow and patient; the other is fast and sharp), it can be tough."

—SMALL PRESS PUBLISHER, MARYLAND

Stop. Go. Stop. Go. The jerky work-life rhythm so many entrepreneurial parents are familiar with is like no other. Because family life is the natural anchor of an EP's routine—from nap and feeding times when children first enter your life, to nursery, elementary, middle, and high school hours as they grow—work life tends to bend and flex around that anchor like an unwieldy vine. If working at home is billed as the holy grail of perfect work-life balance, EPs know it just ain't so.

In Part I we included several "A Day in the Life" diaries so you can get a feel for how your fellow EPs have carved out their flexible work schedules. Now it's your turn to assess your daily agenda and evaluate what is and what isn't working for you or think about how you'll orchestrate your days if you're just starting out. This section will cover work styles, child-care options, night owl schedules, and part-time hours—all tried and true coping tools EPs have used to develop work schedules they, and their families, can live with.

Integrator/Segregator—What's Your Personality Type?

Personality indicators can be useful tools in solving all kinds of life problems—career path dilemmas, marital difficulties, academic approaches, and more. The premise is that if you can identify your true personality type and follow its innate path, you'll live, work, learn, and love more successfully and with less stress.

When it comes to working at home, the personality indicator that surfaces to the top from the onset is whether you're primarily an "integrator" or a "segregator." Work-at-home integrators thrive on weaving business, child care, and household tasks in, around, and through each other, and they are natural multi-taskers. Work-at-home segregators thrive when the various facets of their lives are separated physically, intellectually, and by the clock.

How do you spot an EP integrator at the local playground? More often than not, they're the ones who have a business magazine in their lap, a pen in their hand, or are swinging their toddlers with that far off "strategizing" look in their eye. Walk into the home of an EP integrator and you just may find a computer in the living room, business papers spread all over the dining room, and toys in the office. Much like a natural cook may throw in a handful of this ingredient and a pinch of that and whip up something wonderful—without paying much attention to a specific, strict recipe—an integrator's approach to their day is fluid, open-ended, and flexible.

On the other hand, if anything sets a segregator apart at the local playground it's their unbridled enthusiasm playing with their children, fueled by their fresh "all work" and "all play" take to their daily schedules. Walk into a segregator's home and you'll likely find nary a trace of work until you step into their office, which is surely set off from the main traffic of the house and has a sign on the door saying "Dad at Work: Keep Out!" A segregator prefers to compartmentalize—much like a diner who prefers a meal where the meat doesn't touch the vegetable, which doesn't touch the potato—turning their *full* attention to the child, or the business, but rarely both at the same time.

When developing and/or revising your work schedule, it would

Profile of a Segregator:

- Thrives in a well-organized, structured environment
- Plans ahead
- Takes control over situations
- Decisive
- Needs closure

Profile of an Integrator:

- Thrives in a fluid environment
- Shifts priorities easily (will shuffle a to-do list around as needed)
- Invites and accepts input from others

help you (and everyone who lives with you) to first identify your preferred work style before even thinking about setting your "office hours." In our extended survey, 55.4 percent identified themselves as primarily integrators, 32.6 percent said they were segregators, and 7.75 percent said they were both. Likewise, when we asked specifically whether they ever involved their children in their work (a strong indicator of being an integrator), 54.6 percent said they did, while 45.4 percent did not.

Don't worry about which style you gravitate towards—both integrators and segregators can be successful in their work and live harmoniously with their families. What's troublesome is if you have workaholic tendencies that push your personality type beyond its limits. For instance, it's hard to tell whether this EP is a natural segregator or integrator, but clearly she's simply working far too much:

> They (a two-year-old and a four-year-old) tear up the house, unmake made beds, pull clothes off hangers, fight with each other, climb on the counters . . . and right this minute, for instance, my four-year-old is kicking on my leg to get off the computer and do something with her.

Another snag is when you work *against* your type. Here the following two EPs believe they have found the "secret" to working at home, but really they have just discovered the personality type that "centers" them after perhaps suffering first in the wrong type. (Can you tell which one is the natural integrator and which is the segregator?)

| It all comes down to planning, flexibility, and mental attitude. If you're a linear kind of person, you'll never make it as an EP; true multitasking is the central key. You have to be able to switch gears in an instant, juggle many ongoing tasks at once with many interruptions, especially when the kids are small. | Work and kids DO NOT MIX. You must work one around the other. Trying to work while they are at your feet will make you a very grumpy and frustrated parent! Know how to separate your work and your home life, NEVER mix them together. My kids rarely see me work, I am there 100 percent when I'm with them. |

To help clarify, here are the voices of two strong segregators. Can you relate?

I recently banned my children from my office. As they got older, they became too noisy . . . I want my office to be the place that is set aside to do WORK.	I made a conscious decision **not** to "childproof" my home office to help me resist the temptation to work with my daughter around. She's still quite young, and I feel that both realms of my life deserve and demand my full and undivided attention.

Now here are the voices of two natural integrators. Can you relate better to these two?

We are a fully-integrated family! Despite building a dedicated office adjacent to our home, the kids have always used my 24' × 28' office as if it were their own, and I encourage this. From when they were little—when three playpens were staggered strategically around my workstation—to their present ages (twelve, twelve, and ten), they've always been very welcome in my office. These days they spread their homework on my conference table, work at one of the computers here, and all three sons work in my business stuffing envelopes, processing postage on the Pitney-Bowes machine, making copies, doing faxes, etc., for pay.	I moved my office into the living room. I used to have it in a spare bedroom and felt like I was away . . . now I can work more, enjoy my kids, and take family breaks when I need to! My children actually help me with increasing my business. At first I wanted them to be quiet but I realized that is why I am home . . . to hear them! And when someone else hears my kids they wish they were home too!

Of course opportunities to integrate your work with your family or segregate these spheres from each other can also depend heavily on the ages of your children, *their* personalities, and/or the nature of your business (for instance writers may need the house quiet while businesses involving children's products are sure to initiate and promote interaction with the kids). However, your innate personality type is bound to surface to the top as the weeks, months, and years go by. Letting expectations and images of other EP households go so you can feel free to find the right mix for you may help you bypass one of the greatest stress factors of working at home as a parent.

Child Care

"I have had to put my son in his crib and let him cry while I finished something. I hate doing that, but when I need to submit something by noon, or if I need to have a phone meeting at a certain time, I can't play with him or have 'baby noises' in the background. I try to schedule things around his naps, but as soon as I think we're down to a pattern, he changes it on me, so he spends some time (albeit infrequently) alone in his crib not really wanting to be there. I really don't like that, but compared to the alternative . . ."

Whether primarily an integrator or segregator, there are inevitably times when an EP needs blocks of uninterrupted time to focus and produce. Beyond a preferred work style is the basic premise that sometimes you gotta work hard to play hard—and hard work usually demands total concentration. Securing steady and reliant supplemental child care is highly recommended for those EPs who are consistently missing deadlines, running late, and experiencing guilt feelings that they're neglecting their children.

Yet one of the most surprising survey results we came across is that the majority of our respondents, 63 percent, did *not* use outside child care, even though they are working parents with professional commitments that need to be met. Not surprisingly, then, was a related survey result that meeting deadlines was by far the most difficult challenge facing EPs and finding backup child care the next most difficult. With 79 percent of EPs surveyed being the primary caregivers to their children, and 34 percent stating that their desire to spend more time with their children was the catalyst to entrepreneurial parenthood (the largest percentage reported), child care is perhaps the most thorny issue of all. Eager to "be there" for their kids but distracted so often by work, are the children *or* the parent really better off with a work-at-home arrangement?

Although I'm much happier now that I'm self-employed, I find it difficult to cut my hours back and so I feel that my son is just as neglected as if I worked outside the home. Since my business is just over a year old, I'm often distracted when I'm with my son and don't plan as many fun activities as I used to when I worked outside the home.

Chances are the answer is yes, both the parent and child in each of the above circumstances are better off primarily at home, where they can bond and grow together on a daily basis . . . "bumpy" moments and all. But a little supplemental child care to help the parent catch up with work and the child to enjoy an adult playmate other than a perpetually distracted mom or dad can be a very healthy habit for all.

As you develop your work schedule, consider your child-care needs thoughtfully. Worried about the cost? Remember that, along with a house cleaner, a baby-sitter is perhaps the most inexpensive form of hiring a helping hand *for your business*. Hourly rates are far below that of an accountant, web designer, public relations specialist, attorney, and other high-end professionals, yet the impact on your bottom line in

Child Care Options

Here's how the EPs in our study secure supplemental child care:

After-school camp
After-school care
Baby-sitter
Church-sponsored
College student
Co-op pre-school
Day care center
Day care provider
Friend's home
Grandparents
In-home family day care
Learning center
Licensed home child care
Montessori school
Mother's helper
Parent's day out
Play school
Preschool
Sister-in-law
Summer camp
Summer-only baby-sitter
YMCA

terms of freeing up your time to earn increased income can be significant. In fact, it could make all the difference in your turning a profit as well as meeting or exceeding your financial goals.

Sleep Deprivation

"I find it's very hard to get a full eight hours of work completed without working late at night."

—DENNIS HESTER, PEOPLE POWER TRAINING

Squeezing a full-time workweek out of an extremely flexible schedule is the bittersweet by-product of work-at-home parenthood. Burning the midnight oil may get a rare mention in a proposed business plan when an EP first starts out, but it's a widespread habit many slip into as they try to make up for time lost during the day. And some EPs feel so strongly about spending their children's waking hours with them "100 percent" that they do indeed prefer sleep deprivation over paid child-care options.

EPs who push their bedtime past the stroke of twelve find the extra yawns the next day par for the course. "I find time at night to accomplish my work," says Melissa Bermea of Gilroy, California. "This cuts back on my sleep time, but it's well worth it for financial reasons and my own self-gratification!" If it's not a regular habit, working late can be used as a backup plan. Explains Bobbi Dempsey, "I will often be found typing up a short press release at 3:00 A.M.—a technique I use when I've been thrown off track during the day by a family emergency."

Other EPs are more in tune to their pre-industrial revolution forbearers who lived by the early to bed, early to rise mantra. Ann Hinderholtz of Caledonia, Wisconsin, misses the ability to have eight hours (or more) in a day to get something accomplished, without interruption. To compensate, she regularly rises at 4:00 A.M. to work before her kids awaken. Kimberly Lainson, the mother of four boys and co-owner of The Party Works with her mom, pushes that early bird envelope a bit further. She lives with her family in rural Chewelah, Washington, and her mornings begin like this:

> I get up at 2:30 to 3:00 A.M. with my husband and head straight for the computer, eyes still shut. Turn it on and my husband showers and brings me coffee. I work until around 6:00 A.M. on

web site/e-mail and then wake the kids up. Make breakfast, get them ready, pick up the house, do dishes, and start laundry. Feed the dogs, cat, and chickens. Then at 7:30 they leave for the bus. I then shower/dress and leave for the office/warehouse—four miles away on my parents' rural property.

For EPs suffering from sleep deprivation, Melissa Morris, who gets up at 5:45 A.M. and goes to bed by 1:00 A.M., has some sage advice. "Listen to your body! When you need more sleep, catch up on it. Every week I have one day for crashing early and when it hits, I go with it!!"

Setting Realistic Professional Goals

Finally, one more solution to creating a reasonable work schedule is to simply tone down one's professional goals and expectations while being a parent of young children. EPs learn soon enough that what's far more important than the *quantity* of their workload is the *quality*. Since time is always of the essence, it's a practical matter to pick and choose one's projects and clients carefully—keeping the goal of having an impressive and updated résumé on hand to use if ever a financial crisis puts you in a pinch and you need to head back into the traditional work force for a full-time steady paycheck.

"As soon as money and business growth become your primary focus, then your focus on family responsibilities starts to slide into the background," reminds Phyllis Smith, a knowledge worker who describes her definition of success as having nothing to do with how much money she is making or how many clients she gains each year. To her, making smart choices like having a smaller clientele and "building a good foundation for the time when my family responsibilities require less of my constant presence and I can give more energy to the business," is the higher road to follow.

Dennis J. Hester, a Southern Baptist minister, is careful how much work he takes on so he can be available to his children first. "I choose assignments that will not interfere with my children's schedule, which is my first priority," he says.

Got 10 Minutes? Get Busy!

Members of the EP discussion group (EP@yahoogroups.com) compiled a to-do list for when you have only ten minutes "to do" something. Says Paula Polman, "With a twenty-month-old toddler running about, my whole life is organized around ten- to fifteen-minute cycles . . . ten minutes here, five minutes there. The only extended periods of time that I do get I use for business, which is either early in the morning, during nap time, and late at night. Other than that, the day is filled with abbreviated time slots, according to the demands of my young son!"

So the next time you have ten minutes, see if you can:

- Send out an invoice/late payment notice.
- Sort pile of receipts.
- Find one new e-zine/magazine/newspaper to submit article/promo.
- Draft twenty-five-word ad for newsletters.
- Write up a new marketing ad for one product.
- Return one or two e-mails that need answering.
- Start up second computer to get ready for the next project.
- Make one or two phone calls where you're sure the answering machine will pick up.
- Check voice-mail.
- Check e-mail and mentally "sort" the next steps.
- Start a sales letter or brochure.
- Add recent expenses to accounting program.
- Make a to-do list.
- Practice two-minute "elevator speech," telling people about your business.
- Edit the sales letter you started.
- Add one or two names to your mailing list.
- Delete unused/outdated files from hard disk.
- Delete outdated e-mails from e-mail box.
- Start outline for promotional article.
- *Refine* outline for article.
- Begin writing one section of article.

Finally, if you have ten minutes on your hands, write to: EP-subscribe@yahoogroups.com and join the discussion!!

Learning to Work and Live with Loved Ones

"When my oldest son, Bryan, was four and I had been home work-ing all day, he said to me while I was fixing dinner, 'Can we just spend a little time together tonight?' I thought to myself that I'd been with him all day, but then realized I was only with him phys-ically, not emotionally. It was a wake-up call and still is today, six years later."

—PATTI HATHAWAY, THE CHANGE AGENT

Worried that staying home with your kids may lead them to mistak-enly believe they're the center of the universe? Don't be. "I think I'm passing a strong work ethic on to my son but also unfortunately showing him that *the computer* is the center of the universe," comments Jodie Gastel, a virtual assistant in British Columbia. Jodie is wrangling with an issue far too common in the EP household, according to our sur-vey respondents. With PCs becom-ing the primary business tool for more and more EPs, it can look from a distance that their fingertips are permanently attached to the key-board and that the computer screens have taken a strange hold on their loved one. *"Why are you always in the office?" "Why are you always at the computer?"* These questions haunt EPs and are frequently the source of guilt, anger, and frustration.

"My daughter complained to me one day that I'm always on the com-puter," comments Tara Lang, a web designer in Raleigh, North Carolina. "I said, 'Yeah, and Dad goes to the office every day!' I think she got my point. Sometimes they don't look at this as a job." Justifying one's work time/computer time can be a never-

"On the Lighter Side"

"I remember when I was still working as an art director when my daughter was about two, three months old. I was in the kitchen, working on backgrounds for a jewelry shoot, and there was my daughter—lying in her car seat—my one foot keeping it rocking. I talked to her while I worked, and then asked her if she wanted to eat. I swear the biggest smile came over her face, and she actually began rocking the seat all by herself. That was when I knew that she'd always come first in my life. Work would always take a second seat."

—Joi M. Lasnick

> ### Beat-the-Clock Tip
>
> *"As a work-at-home parent, I learned something truly liberating: that I can live my life with just one calendar (complete with client meetings, family activities, project deadlines, playgroup dates, and doctor's appointments). When I blended my personal and professional lives, I realized I needn't be two people with two schedules. I can be one beautifully balanced person. And I'm so proud of the message we're sending to our child: that work is but one steady beat in the rhythm of life, and that people can excel at both career and family without sacrificing either."*
>
> —Alisa Ikeda

ending chore. Like most EPs, Ida Rose Heckard of Kahului, Hawaii, can get absorbed in a project, but she has learned that this sometimes projects the wrong message to her children that her work is more important than they are. "It has taken my kids truckloads of explanations for them to understand that when I'm working I really *need* to be working and it's not that I'm rejecting them!"

Compounding the situation is that most kids and even spouses may be accustomed to using the home computer for recreational activities—games, socializing with friends, and other assorted activities. While you may be plugging away at a deadline, it may look to others like you're just "fooling around" on the computer instead of spending time with the family or keeping up the house. "My wife comments to friends and family that she thinks all I do is 'play' on the computer all day," sighs David Vallieres, an electronic publisher in Utica, New York.

In fact, as EPs we may even be inadvertently teaching our kids the perception that "working" at the computer is the same thing as playing. Eager to invite our children into our home offices while we chip away at some business tasks, we may ask our three-year-old if he wants to "work" with us, setting him up on a second computer with a few educational software games. Our child then learns that playing games is called "work"—a difficult misconception to shake as he grows up watching Mom or Dad put so many hours into *their* computer "work."

It's no wonder that EP kids seem prone to frequently interrupt your work sessions, especially when you're hard at work *at the computer*. To them, it seems like a recreational activity like watching TV, only they can't even pass the time with you by sitting down to watch the same program. The "parallel play" they might have enjoyed sharing with you at two or three years of age, where you both "played" in the same room together, has long since lost its appeal. Now, both you and your children may feel misunderstood and short-changed.

Dealing with Frequent Interruptions

To deal with frequent interruptions, festering resentments, and ongoing power struggles, entrepreneurial parents use the following tools to cope:

Hold Family Meetings. Frequent and consistent communication is key to clarifying expectations and dispelling resentments. Family "business" meetings is a popular and effective method of staying on track as a family. Says Nicki Conroy of Endicott, New York, "The family needs to know that they have to let you work. No money comes in if you are not allowed to work. A family meeting at the beginning of the week to go over all details is the best method to managing all our schedules."

Set Consistent Office Hours. Because EPs generally select work they love to do, and because work is always there, so is the pull to spend time in the home office. Comments Wendy Hogan of Kirkland Lake, Ontario, "It's easy to get caught up in work, work, and more work when you work from home. Since you are always there, at work so to speak, every free moment can be a 'get one more thing done' moment." Setting office hours that your family members can count on can make all the difference in living harmoniously at home. Jeff Zbar of Coral Springs, Florida, finds that "time shifting" (working early or late), working during naps, and getting family or a mother's helper to help out regularly helps, as is "realizing when to say when and just have fun." Points out Jeff, "That's what this gig is all about. My kids will be grown and out of the house sooner than I care to think. I don't want them to remember me as being tethered to my PC."

Foster Team Spirit. Read up on how to be a successful sports coach and you'll be surprised at how appli-

> ### "On the Lighter Side"
>
> *"Whenever I become short tempered, I pick up my daughter and start kissing that beautiful little face. Immediately, the stress and pressure melt away!"*
> —Jackie Eastwick

"On the Lighter Side"

"As I plan my week I decide what I want to do for fun and then schedule my work hours around that."

—Darla

cable these skills are to you as an entrepreneurial parent. Remember that a successful season is not all about "winning" (i.e., earning income) but how you come together as a team and play the game (i.e., meeting a project deadline). Success to each team player comes from offering specific direction as well as the time and space to make mistakes and practice until they get it right—so be abundantly clear with your kids on what you expect in terms of cooperation, and be patient if they are slow to learn. (Also, always remember that ice cream sandwiches at the end of a "game" makes everything just a little more fun.)

Have Heart-to-Heart Talks as Needed. Maybe years ago when you first became an EP you explained to your family why you were doing so. But as children grow, so do their needs, perspectives, and assumptions. Sometimes another heart-to-heart talk is needed. When Janet Drez's daughter found her work interfering with her social plans, Janet sat her down:

> About four years ago, my daughter was upset with me because she couldn't go to a friend's to swim because I had work to finish. She was mad and said very firmly, "WHY did you start this dumb business in the first place??" I was hurt because, after all, I had done it for her! So I said, "Well, sweetie, do you really want to know?" Still pouting she said, "Yes," so I sat her down and explained. "Here were my choices. You were three months old when my maternity leave was up. So I could either go back to my job and drop you off at day care at 7:00 A.M. and pick you up at 6:00 P.M. OR I could try to start a business at home. So that's what I did." Then I prayed a quick prayer, "Oh please let that be the right answer!" My daughter thought for a moment and then smiled and hugged me and said, "I'm glad you started a business at home." Whew!! I was so relieved! She understood.

Check Up on the Kids Frequently. When child care and work hours do need to overlap, plan on taking frequent computer breaks to check in with the kids and see if any issues have popped up that need resolving . . . *before* any fighting breaks out! While "kids will be kids," let them know you're monitoring them and can check in on any moment. Says one EP, "I can't discipline my kids as much as I'd like because I can't watch over them constantly. By disciplining I mean that when my daughter throws potato chips all over the floor, I am not always near her to see what she is doing to stop this behavior immediately." You may not be able to follow through with immediate time-outs as needed, but you can have children reenact situations where a lesson needs to be learned.

Pull Away to Play. Taking fifteen- to thirty-minute breaks from your work to play with your child can go a long way in building a trusting bond between you *and* helping you get your work completed. Sometimes all it takes to settle the restlessness of a young child is to stop everything and read a book or go for a short walk or put a jigsaw puzzle together side by side. Debbie Williams, a professional organizer with an only child, takes her cues from her son. "I sometimes feel guilty about working when my son's friends are playing outside, or when he wants me to read a book or play a game with him," says Debbie. "That's usually when I 'bookmark' my work, take a short break, and enjoy him. He'll only be little for a short while, and I want to show him that working from home is a wonderful thing, not something that is to be competed with or resented."

Schedule Weekly Fun Activities. Schedule "play dates" with your kids just like you would schedule a client meeting. Don't let their young years pass you by without building those endearing memories. Shares Tryna Bailey Fitzpatrick of Winter Beach, Florida:

> We take our sixteen-month-old to functions at the local library and community center. These type of activities take up approximately three to four hours per week—a small sacrifice for such fun times with my child!! In my golden years, I think I'll enjoy the wonderful memories of me, my husband, and my daughter sitting Indian-style on the floor of the library singing 'Five little monkeys jumping on the bed . . .' I doubt I'll even think twice about all the deadlines that I was able to meet.

Marital Accord

Perhaps family members who are hardest hit by the-computer-hijacked-my-loved-one problem are the spouses, as so many EPs we heard from

---

"On a Bad Day . . ."

"When Jesse was about eighteen months old, he was walking around naked in the house . . . and stopped to pee in my shoe in the kitchen. I could see him from my chair (my office is off the dining room), but I was on the phone with a client. I couldn't do a darned thing about it (except throw out the shoe!)."

—Char James-Tanny

"My son hid the keys for the company van in his sand box the day before we had to leave for a show. He brought them back about a year later (yes, after we had punched out the ignition)."

—Chris Clark

"One day when my day-care provider was sick, I was on a big conference call and my son decided to take his diaper off and poop/pee on my desk to get my attention. Yuck!!"

—Rebecca Hart

"Dog vomits on the floor, client on the phone, my son is screaming, the other dog grabs The Silly Putty from the counter and trys to eat it. I have to pry the Silly Putty out of the dog's mouth and then he's trying to bite me."

—Sheryl Joy Christenson

"It's hard to keep your composure, trying to sound like a professional on the phone, while your undiapered child is peeing in your lap (yes, this happened to me)."

—Lisa Ivaldi

"My son was sick a couple weeks ago, and right in the middle of a conversation with a potential employee on the phone, my son started to throw up. I explained to the client and after apologizing, told him I'd call him back. (He was a Dad himself so totally understood.)"

—Marie Stroughter

---

try to catch up on work or even have their set office hours at night, after the kids are in bed. This eats into previously sanctioned husband-wife "down time" and can lead to what we call "spousal neglect."

Sheri Wallace, a freelance writer in Tuscan, Arizona, laments, "We don't have much quiet time alone. In fact, we have none. I am always working if I have a minute." Adds Barb Roeder, a multimedia consultant

in Brookfield, Connecticut, "Marriage has been yet another thing to balance, and often the one that slips through the cracks because time alone
is when we're exhausted at night." Holly Urie seconds that notion, "When
you have to take time from somewhere, it necessarily has to come from
your spouse because there isn't anywhere else to take it from—other than
sleep, and I've already whittled that down to the bare minimum." Jennifer
Dugan, a travel agent in Los Alamos, New Mexico, put it clearly, "My husband sometimes complains I love my computer most of all!"

In addition to night-time office hours, work can easily pour into the
weekends, creating even more of an upheaval in family life. Melissa
Bermea, a transcriptionist in Gilroy, California, admits, "There's definitely more added stress on everyone when Mom has to work on weekends. For hours lost during the week, it must be made up when Dad's
home." For a spouse who has already put in traditional full-time work
hours during the week, this expectation may cause hidden resentments.

So how do you get your computer to hold its proper position in the
home—as a money-generating business tool rather than "the competition"
that causes your loved ones hurt feelings? Here's how some EPs cope:

Stay Focused. Melissa Bearmea advises to stay focused on the reason
you're an EP (to spend more time with your family), because if you lose
sight of that you'll lose your family's support. That means walking away
from the computer and focusing on the *family* as much as possible.
Laura Wheeler comments, "How my business affects our marriage has
been entirely a choice that I make by how much attention and time I am
willing to give my husband when he needs it. If I let myself be con-
sumed with business, then surely our marriage suffers."

Go to Bed Together. A recurring theme we heard from both EPs and
their spouses is to *not* work after the family has gone to bed for the
night. Working into the wee small hours of the morning should be re-
served as a backup plan under severe deadlines, not a regular daily
habit. Sensitive to this issue, Kim Lainson, a party supply site producer
in Chewelah, Washington, tries to go to bed at the same time as her
husband every night, "just to be near him."

Remember the "Good Old Days." Are your work hours really much
longer than they were when you worked outside the home? Or is it just
that they're now under the family microscope? Mark DuRussel, a tele-

Beat-the-Clock Tip

"I imagine that I am losing money every time I dawdle. I imagine that I won't be able to afford skating lessons for my daughter if I don't complete a project. I have clocks everywhere and lists in several places. I also use Outlook reminders, and I bill using an Excel spreadsheet. When I am done with a part of the day, I log on and record my hours. This is an important way to keep track of how much time I am spending and how much I've devoted to each project."

—Leah Magid

worker, finds that his wife sometimes complains that he's working too much, even though he's just trying to put in his forty hours per week. When his hours do stretch to accommodate a project deadline, he tries to remind her that at least it's nicer with him working late at home rather than working late at the office.

Get a Hot Tub. "One of the best investments we made is in an outdoor hot tub/spa which forces us to just talk and listen to each other without other distractions in the evening hours," says Patti Hathaway, a certified speaking professional.

Have a Date Night. If hot tubs aren't your style, a weekly "date" with your spouse can work the same wonders. Go out to dinner, take a walk on the beach, take in a baseball game, play racquetball—whatever you enjoy as a couple, make it a regular thing. This can be recreational in nature *or* business-related. Kathleen Menard has regularly scheduled "meetings" with her spouse for the sole purpose of discussing business issues. "My husband and I have meetings on a regular basis—every two weeks for financial purposes and other meetings to discuss purchase of computer systems, problem clients, and more."

Phone Foibles—Maintaining a Quiet Zone for Business Calls

"I was on the telephone in my second-floor office with a rather snotty representative of a well-known international corporation. Downstairs on the first floor, my children were mopping the kitchen floor to earn the opportunity to go to the movies. I know it sounds unlikely, but mopping was one of their favorite chores, especially when they could play golden rock-and-roll oldies and

sing along. On this particular day, 'Itsy Bitsy Teenie Weenie Yellow Polka Dot Bikini' was blaring from the tape player when a wildly swinging mop knocked the telephone receiver off the hook in the kitchen. My telephone conversation with the corporate representative was disrupted by the inane lyrics, then giggles, and finally loud clunks as my sons attempted to replace the receiver. When silence resumed, the corporate representative asked, 'What WAS that?' and I replied, 'I'm very sorry—that was my cleaning service. I'll have to speak to them when we're done. It's so hard to get good help these days!' I got off the phone, laughed, and went downstairs to hug my boys and share the story."

—DARLA DERNOVSEK, CU VILLAGE

If you're an EP, you've had one. A "phone foible." A time when you were on an important call—with a client, a reporter or producer, co-workers back at the office, someone important—and your kids made their presence all too clear. Perhaps it's a daily event that you've gotten used to or an early lesson learned that you have made certain will never repeat itself. Either way, how you handle the kids and the phone is a lifestyle issue you'll need to address early on, and keeping a sense of humor, like Darla, is a really good idea. Tonya Parker Morrison of The Star Wire shows how to stay on the sunny side of a sticky situation here too:

One time, I had a client in California, a big newspaper outside Los Angeles that I had never worked with before, asking a million questions about an arti-

---

Beat-the-Clock Tip

"Probably the biggest time and sanity saver for me was the development of a 'suspense file' system. I took a stack of thirty-three file folders, labeled one of them 'To Read,' another 'Next Month,' and the rest with a day of the month (1–31). I keep the hanging files on my desk, and each day I check that day's corresponding folder for what needs to be done, paid, or otherwise handled. If something comes in on the fifth that I don't need to worry about for a few days, I'll put it in the folder for the eighth. It organizes information and action items, saves time, and wards off the frustration of sifting through papers to find what you need!"

—Tonya Poole

cle submission. My daughter, then two years old, came into the room with blue hands. She was pointing to herself and saying "potty is full," which was great since we were potty training and she'd yet to go on the potty for me. I tried to hurry my client off the phone while taking the cordless with me into the bathroom. When I entered the bathroom, I realized she was saying "potty is full" because she had taken twelve rolls of toilet paper and crammed them down the toilet . . . then flushed. There was blue water and wet, sticky toilet paper everywhere—even on the ceiling! It was such a completely ridiculous sight that I cracked up instantly, which put me at ease, but confused the editor I was talking to. Even if I wanted to be mad, I couldn't, because my daughter had this look of pride that made her just glow, blue hands and all. Suddenly, the cantankerous editor on the other end wasn't nearly as intimidating as this little, tiny creature of mine capable of stopping up an entire neighborhood's sewage system!

Besides a healthy sense of humor, here are a few more ideas on coping with phone foibles:

Beat-the-Clock Tip

"I keep a journal of everything: mileage, phone calls, billable hours, ideas, schedule, notes, everything. I staple receipts to that day of my journal and only keep two months of daily sheets with up to a year in advance of month-at-a-glance. That way, I don't lose anything and I have a clear record of the operations of the business. I don't ever have to worry about being audited and not having records!"

—Lori Ruff

Schedule Calls. Return calls at one specific time each day. For David Holst of Springfield, Missouri, 3:00 P.M. works well because he can catch clients on the East Coast before they leave for the day, and West Coast clients right after they are getting back from lunch. By isolating phone work to a solid block of time, you can eliminate the distractions of periodic phone calls throughout the day *and* hold down the domestic fort with a special video or child-care arrangement for that hour and a half or so.

Pick a Conference Room. Find one room in the house that's relatively quiet (up in the attic, down by the boiler room, out in the greenhouse?) and call it your conference room. You'll want to avoid Annette Baron's situation—where there have been "dozens of times when the kids start fighting while I'm on the phone and I run upstairs or down the cellar to try and get away from them, and they follow me!" No need to let your family in on your "little secret" conference room; just pick up the cordless phone and discreetly close the door behind you. Teri Hirko uses her bathroom as her conference room.

Dance a Jig. To counter her three-year-old daughter's "super power" to detect deadlines and important phone calls, Anna Baron entertains her daughter with a special dance while on the phone. "It never fails when on a call, she will scream—loudly," says Baron. "I think it's just to see the way I bounce up and down and the gestures I make trying to keep her quiet. She always starts laughing in between screams. She just kills me sometimes . . ."

> ### Beat-the-Clock Tip
>
> *"An answering system is a godsend because many of my friends will call to 'chat' during the day. I also try to avoid checking my personal (non-work-related) e-mail during the day so I don't get distracted. I try to get my least favorite tasks out of the way first thing in the morning, so I don't spend the whole day worrying about them. I also take advantage of any time-saving devices, such as voice-recognition software and portable computers that allow me to get some writing done while waiting in the doctor's office."*
>
> —Bobbi Dempsey

Train Them Well. Teach your kids to behave when you're on the phone by either offering them incentives or disciplining them with consequences afterward. Incentives might include a basket full of special toys that only make an appearance during a phone call (this is also an effective technique when changing a diaper on a wirey baby!). Consequences might be fifteen minutes of weeding the garden or cleaning the bathroom after a bad call. When phone issues involve older children, let them know what it feels like by disrupting their next phone call. Bobbi Dempsey, a PR specialist in Drifton, Pennsylvania, confesses, "I have resorted to tossing Oreo cookies, toys, and even cash at children who refused to behave while I was on the phone with a celebrity or other VIP."

<table>
<tr><td>

Beat-the-Clock Tip

"Rely on voice-mail, which can be checked via cell phone while sitting for pickups at a soccer game or religious education class. Love my Franklin Planner and couldn't live without it; it has client appointments, doctor appointments, basketball and soccer games, golf dates, dates with my husband, you name it. I never leave home without it. I use one credit card for all business purchases; makes input to Quicken infinitely easier. Multitasking: I never do one thing at a time. I buy dozens and dozens of the exact same kids' socks so I never have worries about matching. I cook double batches of sauce, freezing half, and I bake a turkey or chicken every Sunday and have great leftover meals throughout the following week (chicken pot pie, grilled chicken salad, etc.)."

—Jan Melnik

</td></tr>
</table>

She adds, "The plumber, meter reader, and UPS man have all become accustomed to my answering the door with a phone at my ear, while whispering, 'deadline.' And if my son's teachers call during the day, they've taken to inquiring if I'm on deadline before they address whatever it is they called about." (Training, as we see, is not only kid-related!)

Play Mess-Making Mania. Next time you're on the phone while on child-care duty, play the game "Mess-making Mania." Talk in the kitchen and watch how big the mess can get—butter spread in a line down the refrigerator door, puddles of juice under the kitchen table, chairs pulled up to the kitchen sink, and water sprayed all over the walls. No, we're not saying to *encourage* this behavior—just expect it, watch it happen, and laugh when it's all over. Darlene Walker can try this the next time she's caught off-guard. "There's nothing like trying to answer the phone professionally with the faint whine of 'Mama, Mama, more juice' in the background," says Darlene. "My son tends to believe that NO one but Mommy can make juice!" If Darlene hands over the juice box and a plastic cup to her son, her son may have fun playing "Mess-Making Mania" and eventually, some day, learn how to pour *himself* a glass of juice!

Model Proper Phone Etiquette. The flip side of phone foibles is the impressive ability children have to model proper phone etiquette and knock the socks off of clients and friends of the family alike. Patrick

Dexter's children, ages eight and ten, regularly answer his business phone in a very professional matter. Although Dad "did have to resort to showing them the hold button for screening purposes," he is proud of how well they've picked up on this vital form of business communication at such early ages. Linda Novelli sees the phone as an entrepreneurial opportunity she wished she had as a youngster herself. "The best is when people hear my five-year-old answer the phone, 'Novelli Residence, Renee speaking, may I help you?' and it blows their mind that such a young girl can answer the phone and remember who called when I come home!" Adds Linda, "I wish they taught entrepreneurial skills in school because I always knew I wanted to be one, but just didn't know what it was or how to spell it." Teri Hirko relays this tale:

> When I first started working at home, my youngest daughter was very young. I found that setting up a small office for her in a corner greatly reduced my stress as she was naturally curious about all my 'toys' such as telephones with many push buttons, fax machines, and more. I purchased inexpensive toy models of a telephone, cash register, and fax and gave her some broken items like a stapler and answering machine. She also had her own "business supplies" like paper, pens, stickers, envelopes, and a briefcase. So she would emulate me during the day by working in her office when I worked in mine and sometimes would begin her nap at her desk by just nodding off to sleep while "at work." It made my day the first time my mom babysat after I had been in business only a few weeks, and I heard that while away my daughter answered her telephone by saying hello, announcing my business name, and then asking, "How may I help you?"

School Days: Making the Most of Them

Once your children start boarding the school bus in the early A.M., not to return until six or seven hours later, a world of work opportunity truly opens up for entrepreneurial parents. Finally there are long blocks of time that can be devoted to the singular pursuit of earning an income, and all the awkward tiptoeing around the behaviors and physical needs of very young ones becomes a thing of the past. However, school days bring a new set of issues that EPs must face and take on. Here are some of the more common ones.

Responsible Volunteering at School

Ever in pursuit of a reasonable work-life balance, entrepreneurial parents of school-aged children have strong views about how involved they are in their children's schools. For some, a big draw of entrepreneurial parenthood is the opportunity to have a strong presence in the PTA and other school-generated activities, and earning a maximum income at home isn't as important as living a balanced life. For others, the pull to volunteer is an unwelcome pressure that distracts the EP from staying on task with their business goals. Most EPs find a rhythm of involvement that works for them, but if you're having trouble, here are some options open to you.

Just Say No. If there's one thing that stay-at-home parents can agree on, it's that the call to volunteer will come as often as it is encouraged. With so many parents working outside the home, many school systems are short of parental involvement and every mom or dad who "can be reached during the day" finds out that they surely will be. For Neeley Spotts, a graphic designer in Oxford, Pennsylvania, the view that a work-at-home mom is someone who doesn't really "work" hits a raw nerve. "I feel that I'm expected to volunteer more than parents who work outside the home, and find myself sometimes taking on too much because of this," says Neeley. "As a result, the negative traits I'm passing on to my children include stress, poor planning, and habitual lateness. I meet my work deadlines above all else, but those countdown minutes tend to bring out the worst in me." To tame expectations, sometimes it's best to just say no every once in a while. If this is hard for you, going cold turkey from all volunteer activities for a period of one school year may help you regain your entrepreneurial footing.

Volunteer Responsibly. Perhaps volunteering at the school is an important priority but your availability is not consistent due to the ebb and flow of your work. Staying flexible but firm is the right move. When Kathleen Menard was asked to fill in at her children's school because their regular helper was out sick, she rearranged a client meeting so she could do so just that once. But when the teacher asked her to then help out every other week on a regular basis, she had to very reluctantly turn it down because she couldn't *promise* every other week. As much as she enjoyed visiting her sons in their classrooms, she needed her home-based income to support her family, so her first alliance was to clients rather than the teacher. She agreed to continue to help in an emergency or if she had a day off, and the teacher, of course, understood.

Keep It Simple. If you're eager to get involved in your children's school but have limited time, resist the temptation to lead up any activities and instead volunteer as a "helper." That means let someone else be the Girl Scout leader or the Little League coach, but don't hesitate to assist at special events or an afternoon game as your free time allows. Tammy Sadler tries to limit school-related volunteer work by selecting one to two activities that she can control, something that requires a set date and time to do it "and be done." She doesn't want to let the school think they can call her any time and she'd pop in. This could mean volunteering to coordinate one class party per child and/or attending one or two field trips per child, but not raising your hand to be the room mom, which requires ongoing involvement all year long.

Use Your Business Skills. One way to reconcile the time volunteering takes away from time for your business is to make sure you choose volunteer activities that highlight your skills and talents. This can help you polish your skills or showcase them to the community or both. A publicist by profession, Janet Drez uses her business experience and knowledge to take the good news happening at her daughter's junior high school to the media as a publicity parent volunteer. She also enjoys being in charge of the fund-raising sock hop at her son's elementary school for the past two years. Both skills of fund-raising and writing news releases are vital services she offers paying clients.

Go to Town. Some EPs are a whirlwind of productivity and find their children's school system and community a natural platform for their multiple interests. Angela Roberts of San Jose, California, finds her volunteer activities help her lead a "full and busy life, filled with lots of family and friends." In addition to serving on the board of directors for a local chapter of Association of Business Support Services (ABSSI), she is the vice president of the school board, a room mom for her son, a Girl Scout leader for the past nine years, a Boy Scout leader for the past five years, and a volunteer at her church. Right alongside Angela's high level of energy is Jan Melnik, who is a room mom too for her ten-year-old son's classroom, where she also teaches a writing class and art class regularly. Jan serves on the parent-teacher council of two schools (elementary and middle), publishes the school newsletter for each, and is the elected planning and zoning commissioner for her community for the past twelve years. "I really feel it's important to give back to the community that, in part, supports my business," explains Melnik. If you've got this high energy in your blood and you're meeting your financial goals, go for it!

Homeschooling

There is certainly no parent who volunteers more in their child's school than the homeschooling parent. Homeschoolers are avid advocates of their children's education so much so that they have elected to educate their children themselves, outside of a public or private school system. With roots in both liberal and conservative segments of our society, the homeschooling movement has ballooned in recent years, with more than one million children involved nationwide, estimates the U.S. Education Department. Without question, the homeschooling movement has indeed strengthened as a unified voice in recent years due in large part to the powerful community magnet known as the Internet—a tool home educators know and use well.

What motivates parents to homeschool their children? While homeschoolers are often portrayed in the media as motivated by strong religious beliefs, our survey respondents pointed to various reasons. First we heard from Dave Ratz, a computer programmer in Gunnison, Colorado, who did seem primarily motivated by his Christian faith. He has found a new set of wings from his dual role of work-at-home and homeschooling parent—wings that will allow him to sell all his belongings and buy a mobile home for him and his family to travel around the country, as a kind of missionary spreading his faith. In Dave's story we see the convergence of modern technology and traditional family values take a new hold:

> When we first moved to Colorado, we bought forty acres in the mountains that was "off the grid." We installed a solar system for electricity, melted snow for water in the winter, heated the

house with wood and coal, and used an outhouse in the middle of winter. Each year we improved the place with the entire family helping to build a barn and new cabin, including carpentry work, painting, finish work, etc.

The city is a place where your kids can get hurt "morally" by hanging out with the other kids on the street. In our woods, the only thing they can do is get hurt "physically." When they get restless in the house, we send them out to "play in the woods." During the winter, we have to snowmobile twelve miles to where we park the truck. The kids missed the city at first, but after seeing the activities they can do here, they like it better here because there are just some things you can do here that you couldn't in the city!

We are now getting ready to enter a new phase of our lives. We are selling our property in the mountains and are looking to buy a large motor home. We want to travel around the country giving "health and healing" lectures and cooking schools. With a nationwide ISP, I can stay connected wherever we stop. Since I work through the Internet, and the kids are homeschooled, why not?! We are wanting to work on the "front lines" with God and to be involved with work that "really counts." If L.A. had the "big one," would all the reports we produce really be important anymore? But if I am reaching people with the happiness that Christ offers, then when the "big one" hits, the work I have done is even more important.

Unlike Dave, Lu Anne Colmery, a paralegal in Fort Myers, Florida, homeschools for academic reasons. In fact, just her ninth grade daughter who had fallen behind in private schools is taught at home, but not her son. Ida Rose Heckard, "The Homeschool Coach" in Kahului, Hawaii, also sounded motivated primarily by academic as well as social goals and has found that her role as an EP enabled her to meet these goals. "We decided to home educate our children and the results are incredible. I couldn't meet this goal if I had even a part-time school psych job. It's taken about two and a half years to get adjusted to this lifestyle, but we're starting to reap the rewards. By having regular extended periods of time with my elementary age children, I am able to strongly influence their values, social skills, and academic achievement."

Couples who homeschool together enjoy the shared responsibility. Writes Mary E. Coe, an indexer in Rockville, Maryland, "We are homeschooling, a task that requires a lot of time and energy, and one that we probably wouldn't attempt if it was one parent all day long. Having two parents with different skills adds to the homeschooling experience, plus we are both relatively fresh for our 'half' of the day. The combination of work and 'child care/teaching' each day (we each work half a day) is very satisfying and, I think, really helps limit burnout on either end. I also think it's a good example for our kids of a satisfying lifestyle. We both enjoy our careers but are not totally absorbed in them."

But how can a parent who is a full-time teacher *and* a full-time caregiver possibly find the time to run a home business as well? Homeschooling EPs use a holistic approach to life that is as philosophical as it is instructional. Laura Wheeler is the mother of seven, with children ages four to fourteen, and a self-taught computer technician whose business, Wheeler Computer Services, offers everything from technical support to web design to computer sales. Recently Laura began to rent an office outside the home in an attempt to separate some arenas of her life, but she brings her "home" to her office in terms of all her children and their schoolwork heading down there with her every day. Laura states her case clearly, "I am my children's school. So sometimes we take time off and have a field trip. We often walk home at night and have lessons from the sky, or we talk about whatever questions are on my kids' minds." As we take "a walk" with Laura through a typical day we get a sense of the rhythm of what her life is all about:

> We have a six-day workweek, but the kids do school the traditional five. We get up in the morning, have breakfast, and do chores. Our day starts late because my husband works swing shift, and we like to spend as much time with him as we can. The house is cleaned up before we leave for the office, which is only a half mile away.
>
> After we get to the office, we start school and often start something in the crock pot for dinner at the same time (our office has a small functional kitchen). The kids are given their assignments, and I check and answer e-mail while they are doing their assignments. I can stop e-mail simply to answer their

questions or offer help. I do some assignments with the younger kids after e-mail has been dealt with.

Usually school takes until lunchtime, and after lunch we clean up. The kids work on fun projects, go outside to play on the lawn, and play games indoors while I get down to serious work, either repairing computers, researching prices for custom orders, or doing web site design or administration. I occasionally have a walk-in customer, but this is such a small town that it is rare. My husband leaves for work at noon, so sometimes he is with us for school, sometimes he is working at home, and sometimes he is sleeping late after a double shift.

In the late afternoons, we sometimes baby-sit for a friend, and my older kids do much of the tending there too, so I can continue to get a little done in between providing snacks and supervising frequent cleanups. Often this is when I put away units I have been using for testing, pull out the next one and set it up, or do other small organizational tasks that do not take much concentration and can be broken down into actions that only take a few minutes.

Sometimes the younger kids will go over to play at a friend's house, which gives me a couple of hours of uninterrupted time. Funny though, I get restless after about an hour of silence and can't seem to work as well! If we need anything to supplement dinner, I send two of the older children on an errand to get it from the store (this is such a small town it is safe to do so), and we also have dinner, at the office.

After dinner the older kids clean up, and I will check up on them and work with them for a few minutes at a time, but since my business is largely web-based, I get the most e-mail after dinner and have to break up that time between cleanup and on-line technical support.

After cleanup, the kids settle down to read, play with Legos, and use the computers. I put in another one or two hours of intensive work, and then we get ready to go home.

Once we are home, the kids bathe, read, talk, play games, or watch a movie, while I read, and check the e-mail one last time. Then it's bedtime and we start it all over again the next day.

Homeschooling EPs are a growing phenomenon, as both the work-at-home and homeschooling movements are enjoying parallel growth spurts. While homeschoolers by number remain a small minority of the work-at-home community, their voice stands out as a particularly strong one.

School Holidays and Summer Vacations

Perhaps the most telling comment by a survey respondent that describes just how all-consumng it is to juggle child care, home education, and a home career came from Cheryl R. Carter, a professional organizer in Uniondale, New York. When asked about her workday, she wrote, "Of course, I get more done in the summer and on school breaks when I'm not homeschooling . . ."

Being a full-time, home-based teacher notwithstanding, for most EPs the thought of school breaks and summer vacations generate a long, loud sigh. While infinitely easier to handle as an at-home parent than a working parent outside the home, the days the kids are off from school—either because of snow days, sick days, scheduled school holidays, winter and spring breaks, and especially the long summer vacation—bring an entire new set of rules and expectations than any other. "Summer is tougher," says Darla Dernovsek of CU Village.com. "My older son needs a ride to his job. My younger son needs rides to camps and other activities. When he's home, he needs companionship. Summer vacation makes me CRAZY, but I wouldn't miss it for the world!"

Here's some summer stock to take stock in:

Take Your Work to the Beach. Yes, sometimes the commercials get it right. Sometimes it's best to just pack up the kids, a picnic basket, and a bucket full of sand toys and head to the beach. When the heat is on—both in terms of the weather and deadlines—just don't forget your laptop or cell phone. "In the summer it is more of a challenge," says Deborah Braun. "I enroll them in lots of fun and educational classes and take my laptop and cell phone along. I have developed web sites, drawn illustrations, and talked to many a client in lots of parks over the summer!"

Schedule Your Work Around the Beach! Remember that the "crazy, hazy, lazy days of summer" are sweet childhood memories. Don't spoil them for your kids—take as much time off as you can. "All of my children are happy to have me around more," writes Nickie Conroy. "The summer has been so much more enjoyable since I have been able to work pool and lake time around my businesses so that the children can get to these activities."

Become a Night Owl. A recurring theme we heard from survey respondents is that they tend to work late into the night during summertime to catch up after days filled with fun and activities.

Quit Work Altogether. Bill Douglas, a video producer in Overland Park, Kansas, takes off from work the entire month of August. "Our son always played in summer tournaments for baseball, including the Little League World Series. Therefore, we scheduled zero commitments in August so that we could travel, and we brought some work to do while driving to Florida or wherever the tournaments were held. My wife's school volunteerism simply fits within the framework of her filling orders and doing the bookwork of our business. She weaves them together."

On Your Own

Because working at home goes a bit against the mainstream workforce tide (at this point in time), EPs tend to be individualistic by nature. However, being an independent doesn't necessarily mean being an introvert, and being a parent *or* an entrepreneur doesn't necessarily mean those are your only sources of identity. In the rush of developing the professional you and the parental you, don't forget to take care of the *natural* you!

In addition, just like you may enjoy seeing the "person" behind the "child," children enjoy getting to know the "person" behind their "parent." That can only happen when you stay true to your inner self. Taking time for yourself and taking care of yourself should be the foundation of your day, not what's thrown haphazardly on the top of everything else.

Staying Healthy

"Take time in the morning to get healthy before starting work. If you do, you'll be more coherent, more efficient, more pleasant, and more creative."

—BILL DOUGLAS, SMARTAICHI

Who has time to exercise? We can almost hear EPs all over the country with very young children yell a resounding, "Not me!" In between running up and down the stairs, processing stacks of paper, changing diapers, collecting bills, and picking up crayons, who needs exercise anyway?

Well, Ann Betz, for one. She finds that regular exercise makes her calmer and more patient. Adds Susie Michelle Cortright of Alma, Colorado, "It's really important to avoid neglecting your own needs so you have the energy to meet the day's demands. That means eat right, exercise, and indulge in a little 'me time' every day."

On top of the common conflict of working just a few feet away from a stocked refrigerator that all work-at-homers wrestle with is the popular kid food that many parents tend to buy. The urge to splurge on a Yodel here and a chocolate milk there can really add up. In fact, the word "snack" was mentioned thirty-eight times in the survey responses we received! Snack time for, with, and *in between* the kids can add unwanted pounds and increased lethargy.

How can you snap out of it? Start substituting those processed snack foods for healthier ones. Then find a baby-sitter for your kids and a buddy for you who will pull you out of the house and take a walk with you, play racquetball, or work out at the gym. Put your small kids in a stroller and walk briskly through the neighborhood, or in a bike seat and ride down to the park. Try in-line skating with your teen or hiking with your ten-year-old, swimming with your baby or playing basketball with your teen. Teach your three-year-old how to play hopscotch and jump rope. Do whatever it takes to get some fresh air and move your muscles and bones about!

As for the athletes among you, becoming an EP can give an old dream a new lease. Kelly Dobben-Annis always wanted to run a marathon but wasn't able to train when locked in her nine-to-five job. Now that she works for herself she's run one marathon and will complete another soon. "It's a dream I couldn't have achieved working for someone else," says Kelly.

Combating Isolation

"Sometimes I worry about stagnating, working all by myself. I miss the creative interchange. It can also get lonely, so you have to

*make sure that you make time for yourself as well as your child.
Jazzercise is really important for that reason, as well as finding
some sort of support group or professional organization. Otherwise, it's really tempting to work all day long . . ."*

—CHRISTINE PRADO, GRAPHIC ARTIST

Becoming an EP can polarize your personality—from high-energy extro-
verts who are constantly on the go to low-energy introverts who cocoon
into homebodies. If your home career does not involve clients coming in
and out of your home, it may take a real push to get yourself out the
front door and back in the circle of civilization. Whether that push is
needed to exercise with a buddy, chat with a neighbor, or network with a
colleague, it's a shared goal among nearly every work-at-homer we've
ever heard from. Says Pat McCann of Wilmette, Illinois, "Being an EP
can be lonely. It is imperative to have an active network of humans to
communicate with in order to keep from being isolated."

This is why joining professional organizations is such a popular
move among the self-employed—not only to network and make vital
business contacts, but to *be* with other people. Pamela Waterman, a
technical writer, has networked from "day one" through the Society of
Women Engineers and has found the association an invaluable resource
in terms of generating work, comparing notes, and socializing. She also
recently joined the local chapter of the Entrepreneurial Mothers Association and wish she'd known about it sooner.

As a parent, you also have ample opportunities to socialize with
other stay-at-home parents—at the park, on play dates, volunteering at
the school. To cater to both her entrepreneurial and parental need to
mingle, Leslie Corcoran of Stuart, Florida, formed an informal networking group for parents who work at home or want to. "With this
group we hope to share information such as how to avoid scams, how to
handle health insurance needs, how to work with kids underfoot, and
how to reach our business goals," says Leslie. "Also, I hope we can do
some bartering too!"

Stress Management/Burnout

*"I do have my meltdowns. I get exasperated when the washing ma-
chine is running, my kid is crying, and my business phone rings. I*

> *sometimes feel about as far from professional as my bunny slippers*
> *take me . . ."*

—ALISA IKEDA, WRITER/EDITOR

Like "time management," "stress management" is a popularized term that is a by-product of the modern-day pressure to seek all, do all, and be all. Entrepreneurial parents certainly have their share of stress management issues—so much so that a "stress management center" was among the first resource channels created at en-parent.com. Desiree Scales, Owner of Bella Web Design (www.bellawebdesign.com), was the EP contributor who developed the center by locating top-notch stress management web resources and writing a monthly column for six months. Her first column started as such:

> When you plug in the words "stress management" into any search engine on the Internet, you'll find thousands upon thousands of sites totally dedicated to the subject. Lots of remedies pop up—anything from Kava Kava, meditation, and a technique called "drumming" which involves rockin' and rollin' your way through stress on a drum set. There's even an American Institute of Stress! It's no surprise the world has gone on stress overload. I'm getting stressed looking through the list of stress management sites!
>
> For those of us trying to balance working at home and raising a family delicately on our tension-filled shoulders, it's a real balancing act. The number of members in our ranks grows quickly each year. How should we handle all this stress so we can enjoy the benefits that working at home brings us? That's what this monthly column is all about.

In her first and ensuing columns Desiree goes on to suggest the following coping tools for EPs to manage their stress:

Get Organized. "I know I would feel less stressed if I could actually find a pen in five seconds instead of five minutes."

Exercise. "My favorite thing about exercising is that you can still engage your mind and use your exercise time as a productive business tool. The best time for me to work through a problem with a client or think

Time-Management Shorts

- Take advantage of every peaceful moment the kids give you.
- Keep your shades down where you work, and wait until your children are home from school before you even *think* about housework.
- Remember that "planning" is only an educated *guess*!
- Keep the school and outside activities organized and limited, in terms of one place for all the papers, a master calendar, and choices (one sport, one religion class, one group like Scouts, etc.).
- Use a small digital timer in your office every day, to remind you it's time to stop working and do the school pickup.
- Make a list of occasional household tasks (cleaning out closets, putting pictures in a photo album, etc.), so that if a project gets canceled or postponed you can effectively make use of your free time.
- Try to use a family calendar on the refrigerator with a different color for each school's activities OR for each child.
- Put pictures up of your goals on your desk.
- Put pictures of your kids nearby to help center you.
- Do financial work just one day/month.
- Answer e-mail periodically, not as they come in.
- Use the EP "power nap"—when your child naps, work fast and furious!
- Touch every piece of paper only once.
- Carpool with other moms when possible.
- Set up "telephone appointments" rather than play "phone tag."
- Keep an in-office postal setup. Always have the U.S. Postal Priority Mail envelopes ready to go, with a $3.20 stamp for as much as you can stuff in an envelope.
- Make lists of what to do for the week or the day, and then chunk them up by two-hour slots.
- Set a stove timer to go off ten minutes before you need to get off the computer, as a reminder.
- Plan, schedule, adjust plan, insert all emergencies. Anticipate moderate daily accomplishments.

about a new business strategy is while I'm taking my walk through the neighborhood, pushing my daughter's stroller."

Simplify Your Life. "Meditation is a wonderful way to focus on your ultimate business goals and to reduce the stress involved in meeting them."

Help Your Children Manage Stress. "As I sat here thinking about this month's column and watching my one-year-old daughter deal with getting off the bottle (complete with tantrums and tears), it hit me that teaching our children to manage stress was a very important part of managing our own stress."

Remember How to Play. "One of the best things I've found to help me reduce stress is to play like a big kid. Remember how we used to get so absorbed in the moment while playing that we forgot everything around us?"

Change Your Perspective. "Think about the positive in every stressful situation and weed out negative thoughts. Break the problem down into bite-sized pieces and ask yourself how to handle each part in a positive way."

One of our survey respondents, Bill Douglas, was so distressed by the busy life of being a parent that he carved his entire home career out of managing his stress. Bill is the author of *T'ai Chi & Qigong, The Complete Idiot's Guide to T'ai Chi & Qigong* (Macmillan Reference, 1999) and retells his story here:

> Actually, the stress and strain of juggling kids, jobs, and home economics pushed us to find personal stress management tools. They worked so good, we found that other parents and co-workers wanted to learn them. So we mass-marketed them. My wife and I now teach stress management, tai chi, and qigong, and create video and audio instruction for adults and children, and write columns for magazines and e-zines on the subject. Beyond that, we found that our kids really enjoyed the exercises too. So I began to create fun kids' relaxation therapy techniques, and now we sell the audios to schools, individuals, etc.

Other "Me" Time

"Once a week, I take an entire afternoon for reading a book, taking a bath or a nap."

—Leah Magid, Remote Office Consultants

Take a *proactive* stance on nurturing your personal needs instead of *reacting* to work-life burnout. That can mean winding down or winding up—whichever way your personality naturally swings. For Darla Dernovsek, winding up is the way to go. Serving on the local school board has been very fulfilling for her but not enough. So she has taken the opportunity that being an EP gives her to explore her other interests, including becoming the accompanist for the choir, learning to play the organ for her church, directing a 4-H play, learning to braid rugs, and walking four hours a week. Explains Darla, "Because I work at home, I have time for my family, but I also have time for *me!*"

Other EPs tone things down a bit and find more soothing activities in which they can "just be me." For Pat McCann, that means getting a chance to "indulge in my ability as a cook." Bill Douglas likes to "take time to make a nice cup of cinnamon spice tea in the afternoon, take a few moments to stretch, pet the dog, and watch the squirrels play outside." Finally, Sharon-Kaye Hector just bookmarks the time without any stated expectations or commitments:

I make sure that I have dates with myself where I am just being . . .

It's a Family Affair

"We have a 'Wall of Dreams and Goals' in our home office and the kids know that the work we do will pay off for them as well. Their biggest dream right now is to go to Disney World. There are a couple of pictures of Disney World on the 'Wall' and we have set a goal to take a family vacation when we generate enough income from our business."

—TAYLOR SPARKS, SPARKS AND ASSOCIATES

Other than a traditional family business, perhaps no other work option involves family members to such depth as entrepreneurial parenthood. While the traditional work force continues to grapple with creating and implementing family-friendly *policies*, EP households are the quintessential family-friendly *workplaces*. Kids and work don't mix? Try convincing an EP of that one (especially an integrator!). They have a very different story to tell, to be sure.

The entire EP work option is built on the premise that kids, spouses, and work can live and breathe and grow together in harmony, much like the rhythm of American life before the Industrial Revolution. While in the previous chapter we've seen the pitfalls of mismanaged expectations and perceptions through the lens of time management, in this chapter we'll explore the potential EP families have to get it right and the magnitude of possibility when that happens.

Feeling overloaded as an EP? Remember that on the most basic level, this is truly a family affair. So go ahead and share your work with your family and maybe your load will lighten a bit. And if your family members do not happen to have the personality or skills to chip in directly with your work, remember that sometimes the biggest help of all is just stepping out of your way and/or being the beacon of light to comfort and guide you. Whatever they can give, on whatever level, appreciate them. They are what makes this work option work optimally.

Kid Power: Involving Your Children in Your Work

"In business, often we put the bar too high, always looking, reaching for the stars, and we lose sight of the things at eye level and below . . . like our children."

—Yvonne Koulikov, Access Capital Services Corp.

Here's looking at you, kid. As EPs move into a high-gear work cycle, it helps to remember that looking at, listening to, and involving their children can elevate their work experience to heights unheard of in the traditional labor market. Stuck on an administrative, client, marketing, or technical problem? Tap into the talents, fresh perspectives, and surprising competencies of your co-inhabitants . . . who may be far more eager to help you out than any co-worker ever did back in the competitive environment of the conventional office. Well, yes, perhaps the pool of human resources under your own roof is somewhat limited in ability, experience, education, and aptitude, but if you know how to harness what you've got they'll make up for it in attitude, insight, and adaptability. Just start small and simple and see how it works out. In this section, we'll take a look at how some EPs handle their personnel issues with inspired ingenuity, nurturing the entrepreneurial spirit within us all.

The Funny Things EP Kids Say

"My six-year-old son is quite a character. While working on a current assignment, my oldest daughter and her girlfriend were sitting in my living room talking. As my daughter's friend prepared to leave, my son approached her. Smiling and winking his eye at her, he handed her a phone card and said, 'Call me.'"

—Gretchen Mailk

Who's Hiring EPs . . . and Why?

We questioned the "other side of the coin"—the clients themselves—to hear what made that first sale from *their* point of view. What motivates a client to hire? Most EPs will be happy to hear the following reasons:

The Soft Sell. Cleanse your mind of the Willy Loman image. It's not necessarily the fast-talking, I'm-your-best-friend persona that seals the deal between EPs and their clients. "I don't like to be approached by someone who tells me I need to do this or that right off the bat," reveals Dan Birk, a jewelry and art retailer who hired Janet Drez of A Perfect Solution as his PR specialist. "Janet was referred to us by a neighboring store owner, and when we first met she asked questions about our business and did a little research before offering any suggestions." Because Janet listened first and dispensed advice later, she got the account. Likewise, it was Roseanne Kupiec's natural instinct *not* to push the sale at the first contact that encouraged her now satisfied client, Dr. Judith Logue, a psychoanalyst who has been self-employed for over thirty years, to give Roseanne a try. "Roseanne left me alone," explains Dr. Logue, who was first approached by Roseanne after filling out an application at the virtual assistant registry. "I told her I wasn't ready yet and she believed me." Roseanne's patience paid off—when Dr. Logue was ready she gave Roseanne a call as promised and has been working with her ever since.

A Catchy Name. Both Jeff McCroskey, executive director of Community Access, Inc., which offers job training and placement for persons with disabilities, and Rich Robb, mayor of South Charleston, West Virginia, and an attorney, used the word "catchy" to describe the name of Barbie Dallman's "Happy Fingers WP and Résumé Service" business. Barbie, who offers a wide array of office support services from typing and desktop publishing to editing and writing to accounting and bookkeeping, has built up a strong clientele over seventeen years in the business. Her regular clients include a minor league baseball team, a magazine, an author, a small retail business, an artist, a cleaning service, and four overseas clients. Both McCroskey and Robb first spotted "Happy Fingers WP" in the Yellow Pages, and the image of a pleasant personality behind the ad prompted them to pick up the phone, after which they found Janet to be "super competent" and "very dependable."

(continues)

A Local Address. While some clients who regularly outsource are comfortable with a virtual working relationship, others are not. Pat Roed of Jackson and Associates, a philanthropic fund-raising consultancy who helps health-care organizations raise money, tried recruiting grant writers from all over the United States, thinking the phone and Internet were sufficient communication tools. But again and again the grant writers she hired did not pan out over the long haul. "Sometimes the grant writer wasn't devoted to the project as much as we would like," explains Roed, "sometimes the working relationship among us, our client, and the grant writer simply did not *or could not* evolve, and sometimes the writer needed more help than I realized and I didn't give it because we were not face-to-face." Because Linda Regensburger of Westminster, Colorado, could meet with Roed on occasion in person, she has been able to build a strong working relationship with her as well as with Roed's clients with whom she interviews for feasibility studies. Adds Roed, "And Linda has been very good about the little steps that lead up to the big project. Several writers in the past would skip that plotting work, and it showed in the end."

For more on breaking through the sales and marketing barrier that keep so many aspiring EPs at bay, turn to the EP Profiles and read through their marketing tips and top sources of revenue. Also, *Getting Business to Come to You: A Complete Do-It-Yourself Guide to Attracting All the Business You Can Enjoy*, by Paul and Sarah Edwards and Laura Clampitt Douglas has nearly 700 pages of marketing strategies for the fledgling to highly successful home business.

Administration

How young is too young to put a child to work? We heard from one EP whose two-year-old models her inventory (a line of children's clothing) and "sure tries hard to unpack/re-pack packages and decorate them with crayons." Monika Ortiz of Office Etc. and Picture Patchwork has her little one dumping small office trash into the big kitchen trash, organizing office supplies in their proper containers, and filing papers with her. We also heard about three-year-olds stapling small stacks, punching three holes in paper, and sticking stamps on envelopes, and from an editor's daughter who separates the red pens from the blue and black ones so her mom can get to work.

The Funny Things
EP Kids Say

"My son James, age four, often walks up to me and says, 'After you go to your work.com, then can you [fill in play activity]?' Or 'Why do you always have to go to your work.com?' Keep in mind that I never told him about any 'work.com,' just that I am working. He added that cute little 'dot-com' in there, and it gives me a whole lot of extra guilt. . . ."

—Mario Costanz

Relax—there's no need to alert the child labor authorities. Yes, these kids are "working" but in a very supportive environment and for very short spurts of time. Plus the value of involving small children in an EP's work is often reflected in the sparkle in their eyes. Little ones hardly care whether you are working on a jigsaw puzzle with them or a mass mailing, as long as you're doing something *together*. Labeling the time (kid time) instead of the task (mailing) can help curb your patience. In British Columbia, Christine Nicholls runs a mail order crafts business called Creative Kids at Home. She points out, "Today my five-year-old daughter helped me put together the craft kits and she loved the time we spent together. Yesterday I was doing lots of e-mail (alone) and she hated it!"

While there's no question that teaching little children to do simple administrative office tasks can soak up an exorbitant amount of time, by the time they are seven or eight years old, they often have learned how to be a tremendous help. Lisa Roberts sends out an annual press release about The Entrepreneurial Parent (en-parent.com) every summer to more than 400 media contacts—and her children, ages five to fourteen, know the score. They clear the dining room table, line up the press packet pieces (usually a release, a flyer, a response postcard, and a business card or Rolodex card), envelopes, stamps, labels, and paper clips. The fun part for them is when each large envelope is sealed and they get to stick a small fluorescent-colored label that boldly declares, "Assembled by EP Kids!" somewhere on the outside . . . and the more crooked, the better!

EPs who run office support services seem to have particularly competent children. Lori Ruff of Document Solutions of North Carolina remarks that her daughter is involved in "brainstorming and brain-dump sessions," marketing ideas, answering phones, data entry and typing, checking her e-mail to clean up junk mail, and even searching the paper for potential clients. Holly Urie has been in this business for more than twenty years, and her kids have a long history of helping out. Through middle school and high school, her children ran errands, made copies, filed, stuffed envelopes, and entered data. Recalls Holly:

> We once had a 10,000-piece mailing project that had to be zip sorted. We had the kids spread out on the garage floor with 9 × 11 cake pans assigned to their zip number for sorting purposes. This was when my sister was my partner, so her two and my two were kept very, very busy.

By the time your children are "tweens," however, the serious entrepreneur in them can kick in and your "co-inhabitants" may turn into "co-workers," asking for reasonable compensation for their work. Says Anna Baron, a virtual assistant in Allen, Texas:

> My thirteen-year-old charges me $5.00 per hour. She can type, file, research, invoice, and more, and our agreement is that half of the money she earns weekly will come to her in cash and the other half goes into the bank to save for the car she wants when she turns sixteen. It teaches her to work for what she wants and to save money as well. The best part is she can put it on a résumé when she goes job seeking!

Bookkeeping

Older children with strong math skills can be a strong ally when it comes to record-keeping. If a budding accountant is in your midst, this is a perfect opportunity to hone some real-life skills and experience. The risk here is that you must be willing to share your bottom line income with your child, which may be awkward for some. James Saddler of Heaven Scents doesn't mind. "Our oldest runs the register, handles sales, and is currently learning the books."

The Funny Things EP Kids Say

"When we first started our business in 1991, our youngest daughter was almost three. One night she said to me in all seriousness, 'When are those people Daddy works for going to pay him so he can come out of the basement?'"

—Mary Ann DiGiaimo

Building a Client Base with Children

"When I first started out, my office was in a bedroom that faced the front of the house. Prior to it being my office, however, it had been my son's room, and he had the habit of locking himself in that room. We turned the lock to the outside so he couldn't do that any longer, but when I took the room over and moved him to another room, we never turned the handle around. Yep . . . he locked me in one day just when my client—the president of a large electronics firm in the area—was pulling into my driveway to pick up a project I had been rushing to finish. He pulled in as I was climbing out the front window, back end first. His comment? 'Interesting way to come out of your house, Holly!' We laughed about that for many years to follow!"

—HOLLY URIE, COMPLETE
OFFICE SUPPORT

The Funny Things EP Kids Say

"We have a very talkative two-year-old daughter named Abby. Given her age, we're constantly amazed at the things she says, and how keenly she's aware of everything. Abby knows that I sometimes work late into the evening after she goes to bed (in order to make up time spent with her during the day!). But perhaps I'm making too much of a habit out of this, because the other night, as I tucked her in and gave her a kiss good night, she said, 'Good night, Daddy—hope you have a 'ductive work.' After a giggle and a sigh, all I could say was, 'Thanks, sweetie—hope you have a good sleep.'"

—Mark DuRussel

Client-children clashes are all the rage among work-at-home parents, and for good reason. There are so many sitcom-like situations that arise when EPs are trying to build client relationships under the curious eye, active behaviors, and honest renderings of small children. Here's another "scene" out of the widespread situation comedies that occur in EP households all over the country:

"I remember, when I first started out, giving a preliminary lecture to my kids on how important it was for them to stay upstairs when a new client was expected to come over and drop off/discuss an assignment. I took care of all

the drinking, snacking, and anything else I could think of that would make it necessary for them to come downstairs. I was a little nervous about my own presentation but felt confident that if nothing else we can at least count on no interruptions. My client arrives, I show him to my 'conference room' (kitchen table), and we start discussing his job. Two minutes later my then four-year-old arrives at the bottom of the stairs. 'Yes, Emma?' I say, horrified. 'Mommy, I forgot to tell you something.' 'Yes, Emma?' 'Mommy, I'm gonna stay upstairs when that man comes like you said. But Mommy, you forgot to tell me what's that man's name!'"
—NEELEY SPOTTS,
INKSPOTS CREATIVE SERVICES

The clients of Neeley and Holly were amused by the children and took the escapades in stride. Unfortunately, not all EPs are that lucky. In Mt. Laurel, New Jersey, Suzanne McCoach-Casey adopted the stand early on that clients "Take me as I am (a mother with kids) or not at all!" When her oldest was an infant, she had a new client tell her she should put her daughter in day care because it wasn't very professional to have her in the room while she was meeting with him (she was babbling softly in a bouncy seat). "He may have been right," says Suzanne, "but it was then that I realized I didn't want to work with people who had that type of attitude."

The Funny Things EP Kids Say

"My business partner (Terri White) and I own WhiteSmith Marketing Group, Inc. We operate the business out of our homes. We do market planning, research, and advertising for a diverse customer base. One day, after overhearing me on a business call, my son Zach came in and said, 'Mom I know who "WhiteSmith" is.' I asked, 'Who?' He said 'Terri is White and you are Smith and that makes WhiteSmith.' I said, 'You are so right.' He then continued, 'And I know who the "Group" is.' Curious, I asked, 'Who?' He said 'Us, the kids . . . me, Mollie, Ross, and Liam.' (Mollie is my daughter, and Ross and Liam are Terri's boys.) I never thought of it that way before but I assured him that yes, the kids WERE the 'Group' in WhiteSmith Marketing Group. After all, the reason we work from our homes is to be available for our children . . . so why not!"
—Jeanie Garcia

What can surprise many EPs is that for the most part, in cases where clients and children do come into contact—especially on a regular basis—the relationships that develop are endearing and long-lasting. Kids can be real charmers, dissolving awkward circumstances more than causing them. They can become an invaluable magnet for new business as well, immediately touching the nurturing nature inside most adults.

"Some of my best memories are when I took my son with me to business meetings," says Julie McMann, owner of Effective Results in West Jordon, Utah. "He's even traveled out of town with me. Having a child in the room seems to brighten everyone's day and gets them to relax a bit and see things from a less stressful point of view. Though it may take longer to accomplish your goals, mixing business with a bit of child play reminds you of what's really important in life—having fun with it!" Adds Bobbi Dempsey, a PR specialist in Drifton, Pennsylvania, "The child's presence seems to put the interviewee at ease, especially if it is someone who doesn't regularly deal with writers or the media. And a child sometimes shocks you by asking a very interesting question, which can really help the story."

Breaking the ice is a special knack EP kids have, taking everybody by surprise again and again. After a while, though, an EP can catch on and become accustomed to positioning themselves as a parent in the eyes of their contacts to make current work easier or bring new work in. Tonya Parker Morrison, who runs the entertainment wire service and web site The Star Wire (www.thestarwire.com), has learned that parenting tales work like a charm, even with VIPs in the business.

> When I am interviewing a celebrity who is also a parent, I relay personal stories about my own experiences to them and it really ilumminates a whole new side of them. As long as it is a sincere effort on my part to connect, I think they pick up on that. I always get a second interview and everyone comments on how comfortable they were talking to me, which means a lot in scoring more people from the same PR firm or agency. More interviews in return mean more income for me, since I get paid only when I keep churning out new stories for everyone.
>
> For example, when I recently interviewed Cindy Williams

and Eddie Mekka from *Laverne & Shirley*, I related a story about how my daughter Alexa has been watching the show with me for years, but used to call it "Early & Shaverne." Cindy thought that was so cute, she called Penny Marshall (who played Laverne on the show), and I got a referral to interview her as well. Plus, Alexa and the rest of the family got to meet Cindy when she came on tour with *Grease*.

Eddie Mekka, on the other hand, has a five-year-old daughter as well, and was more than happy to swap stories with me. Plus, my six-year-old daughter is a good movie critic, so she gives me insight into kids' movies that I have to review or kid TV characters, like Steve from *Blue's Clues* whom I have to interview, to help me get inside the characters better.

Regular clients can develop special relationships with EP kids that seem to stretch beyond the exchange of time, services, products, and money. Over the years, clients may watch a baby blossom into a preschooler and then into a school-aged child and enjoy the friendship and warmth that grows over time. "My clients have come to enjoy my children at their various stages and ages and even look forward to visiting with them while I get their projects ready," says Suzanne. "I have had clients stop by with coloring books or some other item to present to my kids regardless of the work I am doing." Suzanne remembers one time when a client stopped by unexpectedly, announcing she was there to see the kids and not her. "She had come with some crafts and told me to go to work while she played with them." Talk about support of a home career!

In turn, EP kids often look forward to welcoming their parent's clientele, responding kindly to pats on the head, friendly smiles, pleasant remarks, and even gentle hugs. During holiday seasons, Laura Tobita's children in San Francisco, California, paint their large front window with holiday pictures and greetings which, says Laura, her customers love and look forward to seeing every holiday.

Creative Process

For artists, graphic designers, writers, and web developers, involving children in the creative process of their work is a distinct joy. As

Suzanne Sanz, owner of LiquidHTML.com puts it, "My son is only six, but I frequently ask for his input. A 'pre-literate' viewpoint can be invaluable when trying to create 'a picture worth a thousand words.'"

Preschool perspectives can surprise and delight EPs. Jo-Ann Penn-Kast is a multimedia designer in New Milford, Connecticut. She writes:

> In fact, my children "test" much of my work for function, aesthetics, and on more than one occasion, my four-year-old has offered me real, viable ideas and inspirations that I have used successfully. They often sit nearby and color, ask questions, and analyze my work from a truly fresh perspective!

Like other personality traits, creative talent seems to pass on from parent to child. Sandra Linville-Thomas is a freelance writer in Shawnee, Kansas, and says of her daughter, "She is an excellent writer and has helped me brainstorm advertising headlines, copy ideas, and more." Teresa Roebuck, a desktop publisher in Bloomington, Indiana, occasionally consults her sixteen-year-old who is "a very talented artist and has a good eye for detail" on page layouts. Adds Neeley Spotts of Inkspotts Creative Services, "When I'm painting, my older daughter (nearly ten) loves to sit and watch for hours. She is a budding artist herself, and I often find myself taking her frequent observations and developing new techniques from them."

For administrative EPs who need to churn out creative work in their promotional material, consulting their children can help stimulate ideas as well. Wendy Brown, a virtual assistant, finds that "just reading my marketing materials out loud to my teenage son helps me generate ideas and check my wording." In addition to being a horseback riding instructor and running an office support service, Suzette Fleming tutors on the side. She finds that asking her young children questions that are related to the subject she is teaching an older student helps her put the material in terms her student can easily understand.

Many EPs of all industries also mentioned that their children played a vital role in developing and/or selecting their logo, business name, and tag lines.

Marketing, Advertising, and Promotion

"My daughter and her friends wanted to have a big end-of-school party last summer. I told them that I would pay for it if they distributed flyers around the neighborhood for me."
—GINGER REID, 4VIRTUALASSISTANCE, INC.

Once EP kids grasp the concept of what you do, they can become your favorite sales reps, marketing experts, and PR specialists. Seeing opportunity that you may miss in the rush to get from here to there, children can become mighty effective promotional allies. "During my oldest's first fund-raiser for school," recalls Ena Regnier of Aloha, Oregon, "my son mentioned my gift business and I received orders from neighbors whom we didn't even know." Relates Kendra Bland who sells gourmet sauces in Mequon, Wisconsin, "Once I was doing a sampling of my product at a grocery store. [My son] said to an eager taste-tester, 'My mom's sauce is the best.' He is now my public relations specialist!"

Sometimes kids don't take the initiative but are happy to tout a parent's services or products if asked. Holly Jo West equips her children with bag tags on their school backpacks in an effort to make her products visible so people inquire about them. When Andrea M. Pixley was moving into a new home and neighborhood, she made "business cards" for her son before they moved so his friends would have their new address. Not to miss a golden opportunity to keep her business name in the forefront of her old stomping ground, she put her business information on the back of the card for their parents.

Operations

Keeping a business running smoothly employs a lot of people in the traditional work force, but it all falls on the shoulders of an EP who's working solo at home. Spreading certain tasks among family members can help a great deal. J. R. Allen, a business plan writer in Saddle River, New Jersey, has found that paying his son to take phone calls instills greater responsibility and respect for the task. He writes, "My son answers the phone when I'm away, which has given him a sense of responsibility and he knows how important clear messages are. He charges me $.50 per call."

Errands being run by older children with their driver's licenses was mentioned several times in our survey. In addition to providing errand services, the children of Mary Ann DiGiaimo of Beyond Words also conduct research for her at the library. And when Judith K. Diamond, who rents stork lawn signs in Redondo Beach, California, goes to work, her young children will often accompany her on deliveries and "help carry my tools." A horseback riding instructor, Suzette Fleming often has her children carry her supplies as they go to riding lessons.

One type of support system that is gravely missed by many EPs when they leave the corporate office behind is tech support. Luckily, just as some have a strong aptitude for math, many parents find one or more of their children have a strong aptitude for computer science—which is nurtured over the years by computer system hand-me-downs. While the conventional life span for a personal computer is two to three years (before it's cheaper to buy a whole new system than upgrade an old one), those PCs often find new life and new use in a child's bedroom, encouraging the learning of new and advanced skills. Bonnie Rozean of Topaz Office Pros, declares, "My son is my live-in tech support!"

Product Development with Children

"When it comes to dreaming up product names, the whole family has a great time brainstorming together. One product line had names drawn from the kitchen metaphor—BreadBoards, Toast Timers, Sync Strainers, and Sync Traps. And after the products are produced, my daughters take them to school for show-and-tell—it's like having my own personal team of PR agents and sales reps!"

—BRUCE ROBERTSON, INDEPENDENT
ELECTRONICS DESIGN ENGINEER

Involving children in developing a product for sale can be a fun family event. Rosey Dow is an author who produces one to two books every year. Her books are truly a family affair as she involves her children directly in the creative process:

When I'm plotting a new story, we have family brainstorming sessions. We sit at the dining room table with a stack of blank notecards in front of each person. We set up a topic such as the personality of the story's hero and then each person writes an idea on a card, speaks the idea, and throws the card in the center of the table. At the end of the session, a moderator gathers up the cards and we discuss the ideas, discarding some and keeping others. The results are fun and often hilarious. The children enjoy this as much as game night!

For EPs involved in parenting-related businesses, children have natural roles as "advisers." Kawai S. Brown is a consultant for Mommy and Company and asks her children to be her toy testers. "When I receive a new toy product, I give it to them to try out and they will tell me how interested they were and the level of difficulty." Adds Jenny Wanderscheid of ChildFun, Inc., "With a parenting site, my kids are my inspiration, my testers, and everything in between!"

A baker opening up a pastry shop, Tanya M. Jackson already has a title for her daughter's role in the family business—manager of children's services. "When we open the doors for Heavenly Pastries she'll be coming up with the menu for children," explains Tanya, "and she'll also assist me with a monthly Saturday activity for children of our customers."

Sometimes the "product" is actually a service that needs "development." Penny Craig spends a good deal of her workday transcribing tapes for her clients. "When I can't understand a word or phrase on a tape, I ask my kids to listen to it. Sometimes with really poor quality tapes we all hear silly things—it's like that game 'telephone'—so that's fun. I also frequently share the funny or interesting things I've learned on my tapes . . ."

Web Site Development

From assisting a parent who's a web site designer to becoming the parent's web designer themselves, EP kids enjoy the language known as "HTML." Laura Mercer of Webfut Design sometimes consults her young children on the color schemes of a site she may be working on, or shares a cool new tool she's implemented on a site. By volunteering to manage and develop their elementary school's web site, Laura hopes to involve her children in web development that way as well.

As for Penny Craig, the transcriptionist mentioned above, her son learned HTML over summer vacation one year and developed his own web site. Now that he's got one site under his belt, he's offered to create a business site for his mom.

A Little Bit of This, A Little Bit of That

The versatility of EP kids often mirror that of their parents. Over the years they pick up "a little bit of this" and "a little bit of that" to grow into highly competent young adults. In Chapter 7 we'll see how deep that entrepreneurial seed is planted as we track the "next generation" of EPs. For now, here are three examples:

From Marsha Simms, a professional organizer in Miami, Florida, mother of three sons aged fifteen to twenty-two:

> My children are completely involved with my business. One of my sons goes with me on location with clients. Another son helps with mailings and bookkeeping. My oldest son does artwork for my booklets and presentations. My sons have become my peers for brainstorming. Every idea I have has to pass by at least one of them. I couldn't do it without them!

From Bill Douglas, a stress management author and instructor in Overland Park, Kansas, father of two:

> My daughter helped my wife teach her Tai Chi classes and was a model demonstrating Tai Chi movements in my book. My son was also a model for the book and helped as an assistant instructor with a Tai Chi class for kids that I ran. Both children help with organizing big public marketing events, and asking people to sign mailing lists, handing out clip boards. And both kids read my brochure and flyer drafts before they go out, critiquing all the articles I write for magazines. My son also served as my cameraman and videotaped the graduation ceremony of a class I taught for developmentally disabled students, which I used to market to other schools. Nowadays, my son hooks up all the new hardware and software I get for my business computers, because he knows how and I don't!

From Laura Wheeler, an all-around computer systems guru, mother of seven children, and a homeschooler:

My children often will seek out newcomers in our small town to tell them about my services. My older ones help me with making legal software duplicates, with some hardware testing, computer system assembly, and other tasks I can delegate. Since my children are in the office with me and we have numerous computers here, my youngest are highly computer literate and that has served as a powerful advertising tool also. My kids also help me select usable designs from proof as well as just the right word to use in ad copy. In return, my work has provided ideas for school assignments for them and has made some science lessons quite easy.

On Educating EP Kids

You don't have to be a homeschooling teacher to educate your children as an EP—informal lessons come with the territory. From teaching kids their ABCs as they help you file papers in a well-organized file drawer, to challenging them to count to fifty *silently* while you make a quick return business call, to asking them to read the instructions out loud as you build the mail-order desk that arrived by UPS that morning, there's ample opportunity to extend one's schooling in an EP home.

"My file cabinets are covered with letter magnets," says Debbie Mancini, a technical recruiter in Alexandria, Virginia, and the mom of a one-year old. She also has a spare, unattached keyboard that she lets her little one use to develop dexterous fingers. Clarissa Chestnut, a candlemaker in Holt, Florida found that delegating the task of alphabetizing her scents helped her daughter stay in step with the class when she started kindergarten.

Most entrepreneurs would agree that combining educational and entrepreneurial opportunities is a natural. A monetary incentive to learn something new is the carrot on the stick at every turn. A business referral consultant and owner of the Wisconsin chapter of BNI, Craig Campana has been teaching his son how to make a living out of learning from early on:

> I can remember that my son Corey learned his numbers when we were riding in the car together. If he saw a vehicle with a sign on the car and a phone number, he would call out the numbers and I would write them down (or record them on audiotape). His

incentive: if I called that business and I was able to get them to visit a chapter and consider becoming a member, I paid Corey a quarter. Later as he learned to write, he jotted down the numbers we saw on the road himself. He also is a keeper of business cards. Frequently we'll go to trade shows together and we'll have a contest to see who obtains the most business cards. His incentive here: I pay him five cents per card he collects.

Marriage Wows:
Lending a Helping Hand as a Spouse

"My husband says it's only a matter of time before I sell that blockbuster novel or screenplay. Better still, he says what I do makes me interesting and fun and a delight to be with. Pretty cool, huh?"
—CARMEN LEAL, LIVING HOPE, INC.

How are EPs loved and supported by their spouses? Let us help you count the ways. Beyond (but not above!) the unpolished skills of eager children can lie the constructive assistance of a fellow adult who by virtue of age has mastered certain skills and talents that can be of great use to a home-working solo EP. Granted, not every work-at-home parent is blessed with the unwavering encouragement of their significant other, and even the great majority of married survey respondents who happily reported that their spouses were *primarily* a support know all too well how the pendulum can swing. But such is the nature of a long-term relationship, and there's no question that whatever the nature of your marriage, it is sure to be tested and confirmed with an EP in the house. That's why you can dog-ear the following pages and either give them to your spouse with a massage and a thank-you—or a pinch in the arm and a date to talk! In this section, we'll learn of some innovative ways spouses are lending a helping hand to re-energize the entrepreneurial battery of their life partner. But before we get started, we have to call attention to our favorite expression of support, which has to go to Heidi Piccoli's husband who asked her "just the other day":

Teach me what you are doing so I can help when you need me!

Domestic Duty

Perhaps mentioned more than any other description of support was the simple but monumental relief from domestic duties such as child care and housework. Holding down the home front so an EP can catch up with work (see Chapter 5) can be offered on a daily, weekly, or emergency basis. For Holly Urie, it's weekly: "On the weekends my husband and my daughter will do a 'daddy thing'—go to the zoo, the ocean, some kind of an outing so I can get some quality work hours in." For Laura Mercer, it's as needed: "He always tries to work with his schedule to accommodate me. Today he is coming home at 2:30 P.M., allowing me to take a web course for the afternoon." And Janette Fennell recalls an emergency: when she received a call from an associate in Washington, D.C., on a Saturday morning "desperately" requesting her help for the following week, causing a drastic change in her schedule, her husband was happy to take over the family's entire week's activities.

Home Office Help

Like every other room in the house, a lot goes into the "moving into" of a home office—from painting the walls and putting up window treatments to moving furniture around and hanging pictures (or certificates) on the wall. Add to that the assembly of office furniture, installing of computer equipment and extra phone lines, and making sure there's enough electrical power behind the walls to handle all the office apparatus, and it's easy to see how many opportunities there are for spouses to demonstrate their support.

"My spouse completely set up my office, from the electric to the office partitions," says Jackie Eastwick. Jackie points out that her husband has always been actively engaged in the peripherals of home employment, but "doesn't actually perform any of the work." His active engagement in the "peripherals," however, is a job that most big business owners hire full-time workers for, so clearly that type of help can impact your bottom-line profit.

It's also common for a parent to start working out of a bedroom, dining room, or even hallway when first starting out. If a spouse later suggests clearing space in the garage for the computer, turning a guest room into an office, or even remodeling the home to accommodate dedicated

office space, that's a sure and strong sign of cooperation and encouragement. Even more modest enhancements, like the encouragment from
Darla Dernovsek's husband to buy a new desk to improve her office, can
feel like a firm and welcome pat on the back.

Financial Support

Another subtle but certain way spouses offer support is financially—especially when two-income couples downsize to one-income so a parent
can be home with the children. Everyone's budget tightens and all the
pressure to pay the bills falls on the shoulders of the full-time working
spouse until the EP starts turning a profit. This could take months to
years, depending a great deal on the amount of time an EP decides to
put into their business.

Aside from the steady flow of income coming into the household, a
spouse can informally "buy stock" in their favorite EP's business instead
of a stranger's on Wall Street. Investing in a spouse's new business venture can be formal as well—owning a certain percentage of the company in exchange. "My husband continually offers to transfer money
into my personal and business accounts," says Judith K. Diamond. "To
date, I haven't had to take him up on his offer, but it's nice to know he
would rather help me than see me worry about 'my' financial situation."

Smaller gestures work to build confidence in each other as well.
"For years my husband supported me in making purchases of books
to learn from, even when money was so tight we often had to choose
between paying the bills and buying food," recalls Laura Wheeler. "He
still juggles the use of our single car so I can accomplish my business
demands."

Moral Support

An extension of the kind of vote of confidence mentioned above is a
generic understanding between couples that the EP is on the right personal and professional track. Says Ena Jenee Regnier, "I once looked for
a regular job and he suggested I not look unless I am paid three times
the amount we would lose in child care."

Playing a "cheerleader" role can have long-reaching effects. "Although my business has yet to turn a profit, my husband has never wa-

vered from his conviction that this business will succeed—and do so grandly. That is the most important level of support," remarks a small press publisher from Maryland.

Operations

Many EP spouses we heard about really rolled up their sleeves and pitched in when deadlines had to be met and the clock was running out. Susan Segars' husband has been at Kinko's at 2 A.M. printing reports for her, and Penny Craig's husband regularly acts as a courier, picking up and delivering transcription tapes for her.

Bernadette L. Raftery recalls this incident:

> Once my husband traveled four hours roundtrip to pick up specialty stock for me from a warehouse vendor so that I could produce a project that the client wanted the next day. What had happened was I originally had the stock and for some reason my computer had the wrong date on the clock and all the Rolodex cards were printed ($200 in stock) with the wrong production date. My husband wanted to help me save the name and reputation of my business.

Promotion

Spreading the word about what your husband or wife does for an entrepreneurial living is a popular way to express support for your spouse. We heard from lots of EPs who say their spouses "brag" about them at work—to colleagues, bosses, assistants, and anyone/everyone who'll listen. Jack Jerome White's wife takes the promotion of her husband's business seriously. She drives around town in her Landcruiser with his business logo prominently drawn on the side of her car!

Tech Support

"Techie" spouses are a stroke of luck for any EP. "When I need to upgrade software and/or hardware and my budget doesn't allow for it, my husband chips in," says Toni Johnson, a word processor. Suzette Flemming's husband provides all the computer hardware/software technical support, loading all her new gadgets and programs as needed. Adds A. Renee Holmes, "He makes sure my computer is up-to-date and capable of all the demands that I put on it."

A Little Bit of This, A Little Bit of That

Like EP kids, EP spouses can offer help on many fronts. From Jo Shea, owner of Kanggah.com and Danjo Creations:

> When my husband arrives home, he'll take my packages to the post office and pick up some groceries while I fix dinner. After dinner, he'll play with the kids, give baths, and get them off to bed so I can work alone in my office. On weekends I tend to sleep in while my husband takes care of the kids, then I work all day. He does the evening and weekend child care to free me up to work and even hands out my catalogs and business cards at work. He also does programming and network maintenance for Danjo and some customer relations.

In summary, interaction among family members of an EP household can lead to exceptional opportunities to grow and strengthen as a family unit. In our next and final chapter, we'll take an in-depth look at how one family set out on the winding backroad of entrepreneurial parenthood nearly thirty years ago, and where that road has led each of them today. While the name of their homestead has been dubbed by the family as "The End of the Road," those of us who visit and the many who will now read their tale know otherwise. In truly dedicated EP homes there *are* no ends . . . just a series of new beginnings!

CHAPTER 7

The End of the Road: Growing Up in an EP Home

As many veteran EPs are well aware, electronic cottages are nothing new. From electric typewriters to wireless communications, pioneering parents have lassoed advancing technologies, tamed their inherent potential and put them to work supporting their families. In the process, they develop an affinity for technology and its integration into everyday life much like farmers who work the land day in and day out cultivate a kinship to the earth beneath their feet. And, like any lifestyle that combines work and family, it becomes a way of life that is passed on from one generation to the next.

How do children who grow up in an EP household see themselves and their place in the work world? In this last chapter we'll take a close look into the lives of one family, the Hunters of Amissville, Virginia, who began their home-based career odyssey back in 1972. Bev and Hal Hunter are a husband-wife team who have switched back and forth as EPs and outside-the-home employees for nearly thirty years now, spotting each other with the financial security of a steady paycheck when one wanted to take a more risky career move at home. While over the years the two worked together only once, and briefly at that, their professional partnership was measured more in terms of serving as each other's career consultants. "We brought two different backgrounds to working at home which was synergistic in creating an entrepreneurial environment," explains Bev. "Hal brought his background as a training expert and I brought my background as an engineer. I brought the technology and he brought methodology."

As pioneers of home-based computer technology, the Hunters' adult children, Cynthia (age thirty-four) and Shawn (thirty-two) were early users of electronic communication, developing "virtual" relationships in the early dawn of the Internet age. Both have home careers of their own today, and Shawn became a parent just about a year ago—furthering family tradition along one day at a time.

The story of the Hunters is one filled with ingenuity and cautions, triumphs and setbacks, and ever-evolving professional and personal growth. With a full half (52 percent) of our survey respondents less than three years into this work option, the Hunters have much to teach about the long-term ebb and flow of belonging to the independent work force. Rather than closing the full loop of entrepreneurial parenthood, this final chapter serves as a pause in the lifetime education of one particular EP family. The Hunters—every one of them, as every one of us—continue to learn.

Working at Home Works for Me

In 1972, Bev and Hal Hunter, parents of Cynthia, then five years old, and Shawn, then three years old, moved from their home in Alexandria, Virginia, to Gainesville, Florida, when Hal was offered a position as associate professor at the University of Florida. At that time, Bev was a senior staff scientist at the Human Resources Research Organization (HumRRO), specializing in educational technology. Not wanting to lose her to a long-distance move, HumRRO invited Bev to stay on staff as a remote employee, thereby introducing the concept of working at home—effectively and professionally—to the Hunter family.

About one and a half years later, the oil crisis and oil embargo hit, with gas jumping up from 35 cents per gallon to 65 cents. "I bought a book by Harry Brown about what to do in an economic crisis, and he suggested to his readers to find yourself an ecological bomb shelter," recalls Hal, who was still based in Florida with his family at the time. This was just the catalyst the couple needed to build their dream home on

The Hunters: Early Pioneers of Technology

The mid to late 1960s was an era of explosive growth in the computer industry, and Beverly Hunter was in the center of it all. Early on in her career Bev was a technical manager in IBM's mainframe business. Years later, Bev received one of the first Macintoshes as one of ten who served on the Educational Advisory Board at Apple. "During board meetings, Steve Jobs would wander around and one day he handed each one of us this new machine," recalls Bev. "I *loved* the Mac—it was a dramatic breakthrough in my field. In those days we used Apples for education work and IBMs for business work and Radio Shack for recreation."

Constantly trying, tweaking, and taming the latest technology as it broke through the field, the Hunters were often on the "cutting cutting edge," as their son Shawn describes, of the information age. One of the Hunters' most indelible memories was New Year's Eve, 1977. As the clock struck twelve, Bev was communicating at 300 baud to a close friend in Anchorage, Alaska. "The rate was so slow you can see the letters crawl across the screen," remembers Hal. But that's when the moment of awareness hit, and the seed of instantaneous global communication that is today the Internet was planted in Bev's consciousness.

Consulting to IBM, Bev was asked to write a resource directory for the educational market. Hal still chuckles at the recollection:

"A lot of ad people based in New York City who didn't know anything about the technology were involved in the production of the manual. The title was *Guide to Learning Resources for the IBM PC*, but since it was too long they had to put it on two lines." The end result was a printed version entitled:

**Guide to Learning
Resources for the IBM PC**

Recalls Shawn, "I remember when I was maybe eight, nine, my mom sitting me down one day, describing a vision that she had of children collaborating with each other around the world, sharing ideas, research. I thought

(continues)

it was a nutty idea and didn't see how it would work." Meanwhile, in 1979 about that very age, Shawn, while visiting his mother at work at HumRRO, struck up a dialogue on-line with a student at the University of Illinois, using a nationwide educational network called Plato. Equivalent today to an "instant message" but at a very slow speed, they exchanged information and ideas. Shawn was awestruck that the student believed he was conversing with a fellow undergrad . . . not a child!

This visualization that so inspired Bev was finally realized during the years of 1993 to 1997, when she worked at BBN in Massachusetts, an advanced technology center that was one of the inventors of the Internet and where an engineer developed the first e-mail. There her projects and teams involved partners, contractors, and clients all over the world, and operating largely in cyberspace finally became "just a normal way of life." That seed planted years ago in her consciousness has finally come to full bloom.

the thirty-five acres of land they owned back in Amissville, Virginia. "We figured if the sky fell down it would be a good place to be and if it did *not* fall down it would be a good place to be." So one mile away from the closest state-maintained road, with a mile-long driveway between the front door and its mailbox, the home the family has dubbed "The End of the Road" was built, using specialized wood from abandoned barns in the surrounding rural area. The convergence of modern technology with yesteryear (such as a wood cook stove) has been the foundation of this EP home ever since.

Before moving into their newly constructed home, Hal landed a

two-year contract with the National Institute for Dental Research to work with expanded function dental assistants. He formed his first company, Rappahannock Associates, to take the contract. Not yet ready for a home office, Hal rented a small office space in Little Washington while Bev went back to her full-time position at HumRRO, commuting to Washington, D.C. Shawn remembers, "In the morning my sister and I would catch the school bus from the end of my driveway while my parents commuted to their jobs, then on the return bus we'd get off in Little Washington and hang out at my father's office."

About one year into Hal's first contract as an EP, the federal government announced that another two-year contract was available, but only for a nonprofit organization. To woo the decision-makers, Hal established a new company called the Piedmont Research Center as a 501C3 and won the second contract. The one-year overlap between the two contracts kept him busy for a period of three years. "My only problem," cautions Hal, "was that I was so busy I didn't pay attention to the fact that all contracts end." Without having lined up another one, he was back to work in the city with a suit, a tie, and a commute.

With Hal back at a nine-to-five job and Bev still a full-time employee of HumRRO, Bev wrote a proposal to the National Science Foundation to research, write, and produce a pioneering work that created a curriculum in all subject areas using educational software, and she was awarded the grant. Unfortunately, the grant ran out before the project was completed. Believing the work "too important to stash away in a file drawer," Bev left her paid employment and self-funded the completion of the book at home.

It was in the basement of "The End of the Road" that *My Students Use Computers*—which is still being used and distributed worldwide—was realized, followed by ten more books and fifteen educational databases. With the successful publication of *My Students Use Computers* in 1984, Bev was offered several contracts by Scholastic Publishers to produce educational curriculum databases in all subject areas. Breathing new life into the Targeted Learning Corporation (TLC), a company her husband had incorporated in the late 1970s but then "abandoned when he went off to do consulting," Bev reactivated the company, which the family still uses as an umbrella organization for various ventures.

"For seven years my mom worked in the basement," recalls Shawn. "It was her personality to just go in the basement for hours and hours and hours." Often Shawn was enticed by his mother with some new software application, and was asked by her to test, play, and review her work since he was in the age group it was being developed for. Shawn remembers his mom actively trying to get his attention. "She'd have me go through a database and learn about a tiger, and I'd click the button and hear the tiger roar. Today this is nothing, but twenty years ago this was absolutely the edge of the edge of the edge." He remembers his mom spending weeks trying to assemble a single audio clip and get it on the database—something he believes would take about two hours to do today. While he'd get a "kick out of" the software, in the back of his mind he knew she was developing the equivalent of textbooks and couldn't shake the feeling that he was being asked to do more school-work. So it would hold his interest—"but not for long."

Shawn's extroverted personality helped him set limits in how involved he became in his mother's work, while Cynthia's introverted personality did not, she now believes. A natural integrator, Bev could think of all kinds of ways to share her work with her kids—if they seemed ready and willing to cooperate. So while Shawn didn't hesitate to say "No thanks," Cynthia felt compelled to say, "Sure, what do you need?" For the most part, Cynthia enjoyed helping her Mom out. She recalls:

> I was probably ten to fifteen years old when my mom was work-ing for Scholastic. She'd develop a database and the user man-ual that went with it and also conducted training workshops with teachers. I was very hands-on helping her with beta test-ing, designing, data entry, but I loved the training workshops the most. For those I'd help her pack up all the computers and material (manuals, disks) she needed; then we'd go into the classroom and set everything up. I'd make sure the computers were turned on and ready to go, make sure there were enough disks and made copies when there weren't. Then the teachers would all come in, each sitting down to their own computer. My mother would do the introductions and explain the purpose of the workshop. As she walked them through the program, I'd walk around the room as an assistant, showing teachers where the menu was or anything else they were confused about. When

it was all over, I'd help my mom pack everything up, using a checklist to make sure all the materials we came in with we were also leaving with.

While Cynthia recalls the workshops fondly, she also talks of her mom's "workaholic" tendencies and how that made her feel growing up. Just as in Chapter 5's "Learning to Work and Live with Loved Ones" section, the ever-present pull of work—especially compelling work—against the pull of family time was at issue here too. Looking back, Bev feels that she spent more time on work than she should have "because it's there all the time." If she were to do it again, she'd set up more predictability for the kids, like "I'm working now until noon and then we'll do something fun." Cynthia adds this advice for today's EPs, "Set the time aside, like you'd go to an aerobic class a few times a week, you have family fun time on a scheduled basis. This is great not just for the kids but for the parent, who may have a hard time breaking from their work but could use the break anyway."

By 1989 Bev "climbed out of the basement," realizing she had gone as far as she could without having the resources of a large organization behind her. She joined the National Science Foundation as a program manager, and she then left there in 1993 to become a manager for Educational Technology Systems for BBN, commuting from a rented apartment in Boston until 1997.

A Father-Son Team

Meanwhile, in the early 1990s Hal was catapulted into a work situation that turned his own career on its head. A business contact who was moving from one company to another was put in charge of forming the nucleus of a new research and development division that offered training for federal government employees. He enticed Hal with a large salary to be one of the key senior staff. Because the mission of the division seemed right up Hal's alley, he took the job, but without fully realizing that his role would be one of a "rainmaker"—someone who'd bring in lots of money. After a year and a half in this role, he was told at Christmastime that he needed to produce a quarter of a million dollars by January or they'd let him go.

"Getting fired turned out to be a very good thing," Hal comments.

"It was nuts dealing with all the bureaucracy and office politics, and I realized I wanted more from my work than a paycheck." Hal assessed his situation. He was in his late fifties. His children were grown and on their own. He had a wife earning a large, steady income. He had a couple of hundred thousand dollars accumulated in a retirement fund. And he had an idea whose time had come . . . he hoped.

Hal's idea was to create a company that would offer management training by distance learning to federal government employees via telecommunications—incorporating his expertise as a trainer, his experience working with the federal government, and advanced technologies he was so comfortable working with. Today we would call it web-based training, but this was before there was a web. Back then it was called computer conferencing. He called the company the "Federal Training Network" and started digging into his retirement fund to get it up and running.

By this time his son, Shawn, was out of college, having spent his first four post-graduate years bicycling across the United States and then from Virginia to the Gulf of Mexico, working as a ski instructor and on a ranch in Montana, and finally trying his hand at teaching English in Korea. When he came back to the United States he didn't know what he wanted to do, only that he didn't want to go back to his "freestyle, free-wheeling" way of life. He wanted more direction.

Shawn heard "only that my dad was starting a new company and spending his retirement money." Shawn asked him what he was doing, found it "pretty interesting," and asked if he needed any help. With $6,000 saved from his year of teaching overseas, he put his money on the table and a father-son partnership was born.

It's All About Sales

With two heads together and a generation of experience and attitude between them, the company took shape. "But the trouble," Hal recalls, "was that while computer conferencing had a long tradition, I couldn't explain it to anyone who had enough money to buy it." What prospective customers did seem to understand was "satellite conferencing"—students and instructors connected by television sets that communicated by satellite and telephone—and while Hal began to produce the satellite events at a cost of $10–20,000 a pop, Shawn took on a marketing and sales role that was conducive to his gregarious personality. After a couple of years of "hemorrhaging cash" by producing the events but not selling them fast enough, Hal was about ready to give up. Recalls Shawn:

> I'll never forget this. I had been working for maybe a year and my dad said, "OK, I'm going to take another $20,000 from my retirement account, put it into our business account, and if that runs out, then that's it. Then we'll just say we did the best we could and it didn't work out." And it was at that moment that it all became very real. That I realized the money wasn't endless. That I realized *it was all about sales.*
>
> And so we started to get creative. We started cutting back on our expenditures. We realized all our money was going to these TV studios to develop our content, but we weren't selling enough. So we said forget it; we'll halt production all together; we'll start on the other side of the house and just learn how to sell. That's when we turned to our competitors and started identifying them as partners. We said we're also in this business and we have an audience for you—how's about we help you distribute your programming for a commission, no retainer fees whatsoever. I thought this was a beautiful idea because on someone else's nickel *we could figure out how to sell!*

By the spring of 1997 the Federal Training Network had regained some financial footing and was ready to produce some more satellite events. Shawn continues:

> This time we were very tentative. We surveyed our customers very carefully. We chose topics they specifically said they wanted. We only did two events in a season instead of eight or nine, and that was a moderate success, so based on that in the fall we did three events. Simultaneously, we continued to develop more partnerships. We already had a group of content providers; distributing other people's content added a little bit of revenue, our own content we developed added some more revenue, and partnering with other distributors who sold our content added a bit more revenue. With some gentle, slow steps we started to gain more customers, gain their trust and loyalty,

offering more content tailored to their responses and requests, and started getting our heads above water.

Now we produce a lot more, we distribute a lot more, and the depth of the accounts—the dollars invested by our clients— have grown enormously. As our clients' success increases using our training seminars, so does our success increase. The only marketing we do now is our web site and a 30–40,000 piece mailing every year. The rest is word of mouth and repeat customers, and I'm thinking we'll be dropping the direct mail soon too.

Today the Federal Training Network grosses well over a million dollars annually. Shawn, who is the father of a one-year-old son and married to Amy Hunter, a high school biology teacher, works from his basement office in Maine while his business partner is based in a second-floor loft at "The End of the Road" in Virginia. "The international headquarters of FTN is located on a teeny laundry table in a home in a little village in Maine," muses Shawn. "I'm now a parent working out of the basement and I have to admit, it's sort of nostalgic . . ."

Lessons Learned

Aside from setting up time boundaries so both kids and their parents can get a break from home office work, Bev had some career advice for entrepreneurial parents. In contrast to the dot-com companies that have recently gone bust, the Hunters never borrowed money for any of their ventures. Instead they financed them by leveraging one contract at a time, getting that first contract and building on it. "We didn't go out and get venture capital because it gives us so much more freedom financially. You can just follow your interests and opportunities and take more risks when the investment in the company is just your own."

What were the biggest risks each took professionally? Hal didn't hesitate to say it was dipping so deeply into his retirement funds to finance FTN. Bev shares this:

My biggest risk professionally was to go off in the corner and do my own thing without the power of an organization behind me. It's hard to leverage yourself without the resources, the diversity of talents you can draw upon in a large organization—the accountants, engineers, managers, lawyers, all the infrastructure you get there that you just don't have as an individual. You can hire a consultant but it's just not the same.

Bev adds that when you're working independently it's important to be really agile. "You have to think quickly and when you see a project isn't working because you're missing some critical talent, you have to move quickly to find that talent."

Over the years Bev has worked as a freelancer, remote staffer, or full-time employee for the federal government, state governments, nonprofits, academia, and large corporations. When asked which work force sector seemed most friendly toward outsourcing, she responded, "I'd say the private industry is far more open to flexibility in terms of work arrangements, pace of change—light-years, really—and the reason is that they're worried about the bottom line. Productivity *matters* to them. In the other sectors there are other factors at work like tradition, loyalty, procedures, and checks and balances that are more important than productivity. These are important values but not as conducive to alternative work arrangements."

Finally, when asked what project she worked on in her long and varied career that she was most proud of, and whether that happened as an EP or as an employee, ironically enough she immediately brought to mind her book *My Students Use Computers*—which took a marriage of both to be born! This is the project that was launched when she was an employee and initially funded through a grant by a large nonprofit, but finished only through her determination to follow the project through— at home, on her own, and with her own finances. Because of her dedication to the project itself—both as a salaried employee and as an entrepreneurial parent—the impact of this work is still being felt today.

The Next Generation

Checking back in with Cynthia and Shawn today, we see what an indelible mark growing up in an EP household can make. Swimming in a current that's not mainstream but getting closer and closer to it as the currents begin to merge, these two are navigating the waters with finesse. Cynthia works at home, technically proficient. Her web site, www.contingent.com, is an information portal for anyone who works in the temp work force—educating human resource management on the preparation, training, orientation, and selection of a temp worker, while also educating the temps on how to select an agency to work for and what to expect going in.

In the meantime, Shawn is getting used to being an entrepreneurial *parent*. When his son was first born, his office was located smack in the middle of the house they recently purchased because he and his wife initially planned to build him a separate office above their garage. When those plans fell through, he tried conducting business where he was but found it very disruptive. "My son was then two to three months old, and if I was caring for him and my business phone would ring, I'd have to make a decision as to whether he was settled and comfortable and quiet so I could talk . . . or not. So many times I thought I made the right call, and then as soon as I started talking, he'd start to cry. Everybody of course was always understanding, thinking it was so cute, but then they'd say 'Oh, your son's crying, you better go and we'll talk later.' The trouble was that 'later' wasn't necessarily any better time to talk!"

So after three months, he got the basement painted and carpeted and moved on down, his wife Amy went back to work, and they hired a nanny. The couple's maternity/paternity leave was over. These days his schedule is getting up with his son at 7:00 A.M. when his wife is leaving for her classroom, getting him dressed, feeding him breakfast and playing until the nanny comes at 8:30, then going downstairs to work. At 2:00 or 2:30 Amy comes home and takes over their baby's care until family time at 5:00, when Shawn usually quits for the day.

Isn't working in the basement like his mom all day hard to handle? "Well I couldn't be in production because my personality wouldn't sustain it. I'm too extroverted. But I'm really not lacking colleagueship because I spend most of my time in a marketing/sales role so I'm constantly exchanging phone calls, e-mails with customers, providers, partners. I've developed strong collegial relationships with people all over the United States—they're just not within my own company." In addition Shawn breaks up his day by running, bicycling, playing with his son, walking his dog, and playing in a racquetball league.

Shawn is certain that his success today is a reflection of his parents' role modeling that working at home was a viable option, that it was an "OK thing to do." The only time he ever considered getting a "real job" was when he was getting married and developing a life together with his wife, who he describes as coming from "a conservative, New England family." Amy expressed her concerns when FTN was not turning a profit after three years, and she suggested he perhaps find a steady job. "I considered it briefly but dismissed it very quickly. I have always felt that I would have greater job security being responsible for my own business than my peers do, who can lose their job for lots of different reasons that they have absolutely no control over."

Now an entrepreneurial parent in his own right, what are Shawn's long-term plans? "My life goal," Shawn explains firmly, "is never having to submit a résumé. Ever."

National Survey of Entrepreneurial Parents

The **National Survey of Entrepreneurial Parents** was a two-part on-line survey that ran from early September 2000 to early January 2001, for the sole purpose of conducting research for this book. The first part was a short survey that was a quantitative questionnaire to which 606 people responded; the second part was an extended survey that invited verbatim responses to which 258 people responded, generating more than 700 pages of information and insight into the lives of EPs. This National Survey was distributed via site links and e-mail primarily though The Entrepreneurial Parent web site, en-parent.com, as well as by the following survey sponsors:

- **Aquent (www.aquent.com),** the world's largest specialized talent agency for creative, web, and tech contract workers

- **Monster Talent Market (www.talentmarket.monster.com),** the world's first on-line, auction-style marketplace connecting free agents with hiring organizations in need of contract work

- **Ants (www.ants.com),** the fastest-growing marketplace for freelance work

- **MBA Free Agents (www.mbafreeagents.com),** a leading executive recruiting and venture talent agency for the New Economy

- **Oxygen Media's ka-Ching.com (www.ka-ching.com),** a business and finance site for women

Throughout this book, you heard the voices of the EPs who responded to our extended survey as well as those from the on-line community of entrepreneurial parents at en-parent.com (who have contributed to the site but not necessarily the survey over the years), and other EPs we have interviewed by phone. We hope their tips, stories, advice, and musings have given you inspiration and guidance as you explore the world of entrepreneurial parenthood for yourself and your family.

EP Survey Data Summary

Compiled and Reported by Janet Gardella,
Janet_Gardella@prodigy.net

Out of the 606 people who responded to the survey, the great majority were American, with 8 percent international (Figure 1).

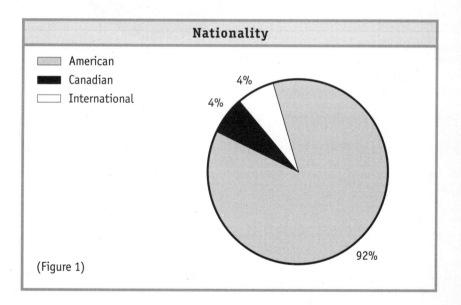

(Figure 1)

This database is primarily comprised of females (82 percent), as shown in Figure 2. However, it is misleading to ascertain that most EPs are moms, but rather that the moms are more likely to hear about and respond to an entrepreneurial parenting survey distributed via on-line communities.

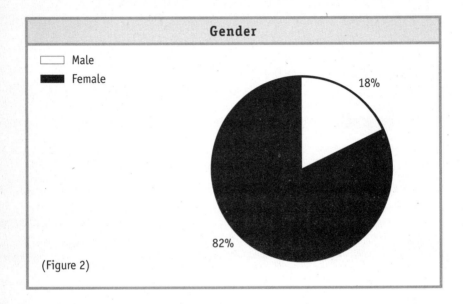

(Figure 2)

A full 59 percent of the respondents stated that they had a college degree or higher, while 16 percent had a Ph.D. (Figure 3).

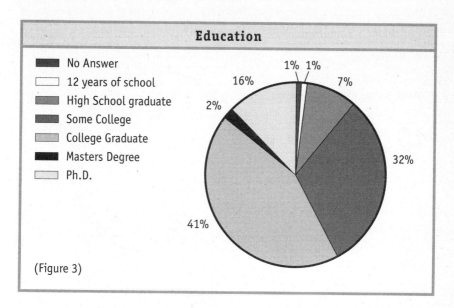

Education

- No Answer
- 12 years of school
- High School graduate
- Some College
- College Graduate
- Masters Degree
- Ph.D.

1% 1%
16%
7%
2%
32%
41%

(Figure 3)

Fully half of the base of 606 respondents were "thirty-something." Those in their forties made up almost one-third of the database (Figure 4).

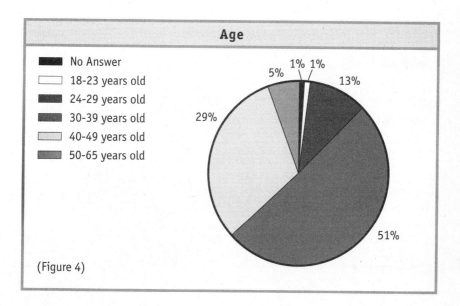

Age

- No Answer
- 18-23 years old
- 24-29 years old
- 30-39 years old
- 40-49 years old
- 50-65 years old

1% 1%
5%
13%
29%
51%

(Figure 4)

Figure 5 illustrates the marital status among the respondents. The great majority are married (81 percent).

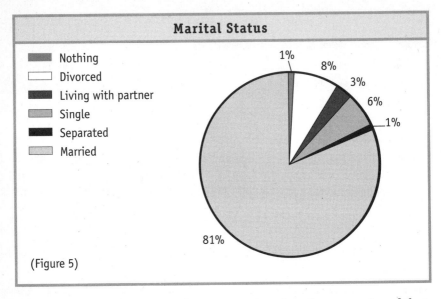

(Figure 5)

When asked whether or not their spouse is primarily supportive of their working at home, most (69 percent) responded yes, they do receive support—be it physical, emotional, or psychological—from their spouse (Figure 6). Of married EPs, a full 80 percent were supportive.

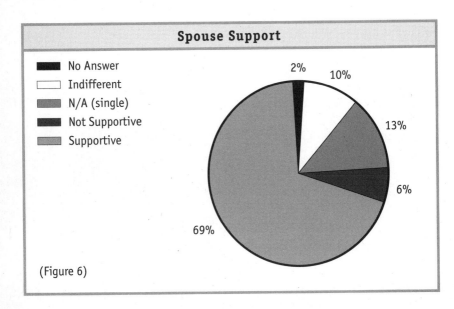

(Figure 6)

Of the entrepreneurial parents in our study, 43 percent had two children, while almost one-third had 1 child (Figure 7). (One parent reported having 9 children.)

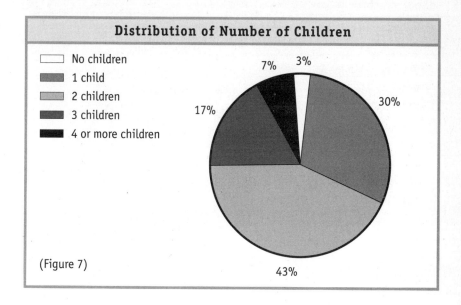

Distribution of Number of Children

- ☐ No children
- ▨ 1 child
- ▨ 2 children
- ▨ 3 children
- ▨ 4 or more children

3%

7%

30%

17%

43%

(Figure 7)

Figure 8 illustrates the breakdown in ages of all the children of our database. Young teens, from eleven to fifteen, took up the largest piece of the pie (25 percent), followed by elementary (six to ten) and preschoolers (three to five).

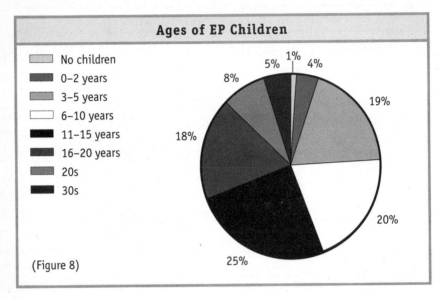

(Figure 8)

Figure 9 illustrates how the spouses of our EPs are employed. The vast majority are full-time workers outside of the home.

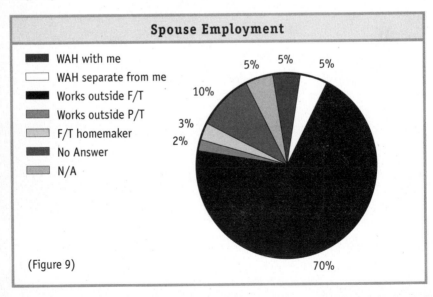

(Figure 9)

Of those surveyed, 62 percent are covered under their spouse's employer, 13 percent cover the payments on their own, and a full 17 percent are uninsured (Figure 10).

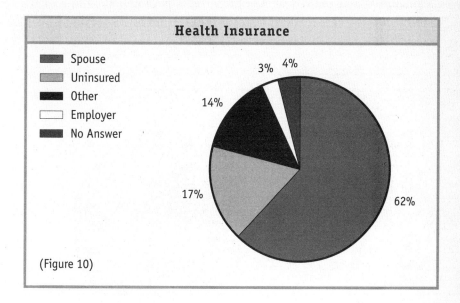

(Figure 10)

Prior to becoming an EP, 74 percent of respondents worked in the traditional work force, with 53 percent already a parent working outside the home and 21 percent making the jump from outside of the home employment to home employment at the onset of parenthood. Only 15 percent of current EPs made the transition into home employment as a stay-at-home parent (Figure 11).

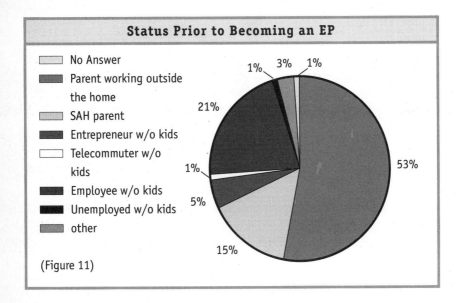

(Figure 11)

Not surprisingly, over one-third of EPs cite the reason they became EPs was to spend more time with their children, while only 5 percent were concerned about day-care issues. Doing the work that they love, supplementing household income, and working on their own schedule rounded out the top four catalysts to becoming EPs. Incidentally, the percentage (13 percent) of "supplementing income" as a catalyst nearly matched the percentage of stay-at-home parents who became EPs (Figure 12).

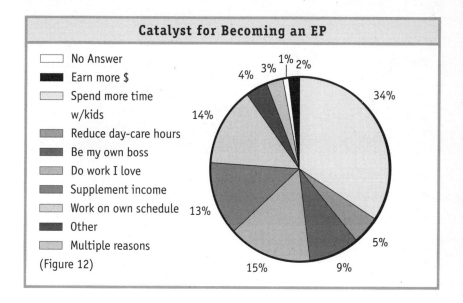

Catalyst for Becoming an EP

☐ No Answer
■ Earn more $
☐ Spend more time w/kids
▨ Reduce day-care hours
▨ Be my own boss
▨ Do work I love
▨ Supplement income
▨ Work on own schedule
■ Other
▨ Multiple reasons

(Figure 12)

1% 2% 3% 4% 14% 13% 15% 9% 5% 34%

Freelancers (39 percent) and small business owners (34 percent) constituted the majority of survey respondents, with only 2 percent identifying themselves as network marketers/MLM consultants and 5 percent as teleworkers. More prevalent were EPs who worked in more than one capacity (10 percent) and those who worked both at home (self-employed) and outside the home (employee), at 7 percent (Figure 13).

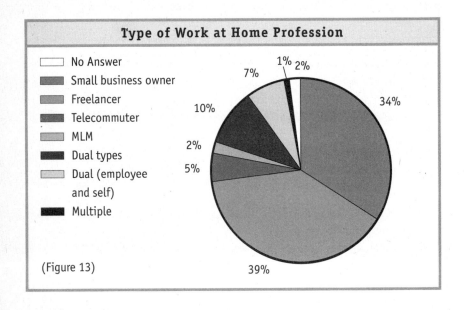

Type of Work at Home Profession

Legend:
- No Answer
- Small business owner
- Freelancer
- Telecommuter
- MLM
- Dual types
- Dual (employee and self)
- Multiple

1% 2% 7% 10% 2% 5% 34% 39%

(Figure 13)

A little more than half (52 percent) of the EPs surveyed began working from home within the last three years. 7 percent have been at it for more than ten years (Figure 14).

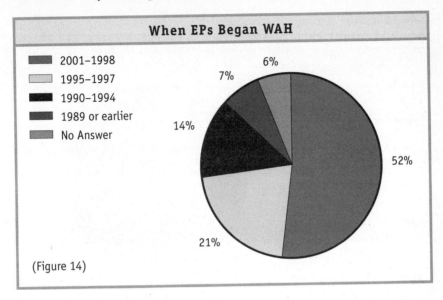

When EPs Began WAH

- 2001–1998
- 1995–1997
- 1990–1994
- 1989 or earlier
- No Answer

6%
7%
14%
52%
21%

(Figure 14)

Whether due to time constraints or lifestyle preferences, 58 percent of the EPs who responded to the questionnaire stated that they were part-time workers, putting in less than forty hours per week (Figure 15).

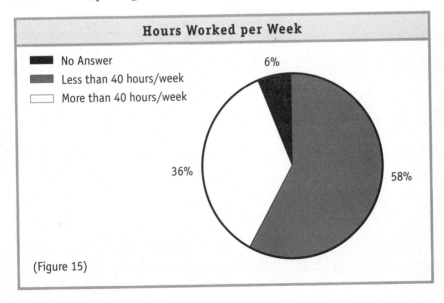

Hours Worked per Week

- No Answer
- Less than 40 hours/week
- More than 40 hours/week

6%
36%
58%

(Figure 15)

Consequently, the majority (52 percent) of those surveyed said that they make less than they did before working from home, while 41 percent said they made as much or more (Figure 16).

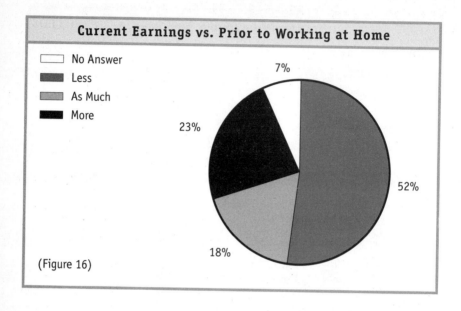

Current Earnings vs. Prior to Working at Home

- No Answer
- Less
- As Much
- More

7%

23%

52%

18%

(Figure 16)

To highlight the relationship of hours worked to income earned, Figure 17 illustrates the breakdown in income versus the hours worked per week of our respondents. Those working twenty hours/week overwhelmingly earned $20,000 or less per year, while the rate of income for 49% of those EPs who put in over 40 hours per week shot up to $30,000–$100,000.

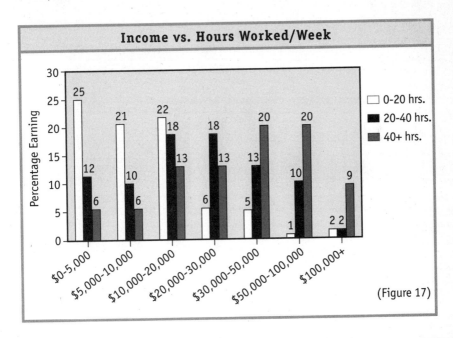

(Figure 17)

We also found that of those who worked full-time at home (40 or more hours/week), 69.5 percent of the men earned $30,000 or more per year, while only 38.9 percent of the women did. (The ratio of full-time EPs were 31.7 percent dads to 68.4 percent moms.)

Part-time hours seems to be the greater cause of income limitations than number of years working at home. In Figure 18, we see the correlation between the years as an EP vs. income earned, with a full third of those working two to five years at home earning $20,000 or less per year and 50.29 percent earning more, and nearly half (49.7 percent) who have been an EP for five years or more earning $30,000 or less.

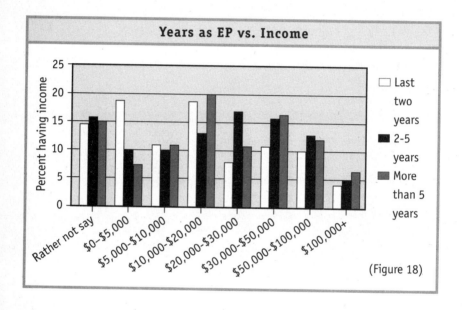

(Figure 18)

Figure 19 shows the distribution of income earned by the EPs surveyed, while Figure 20 shows the overall household income of the families. Unfortunately, 12–13 percent gave no answer to each of these questions so it's difficult to determine true income potential. In short, a very close 43 percent reported earning $30,000 or more annually to 42 percent reporting earning less than $30,000 from their home employment. For 54 percent, combined household income was $50,000 or more.

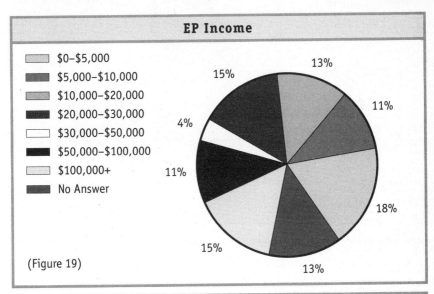

EP Income

- $0–$5,000
- $5,000–$10,000
- $10,000–$20,000
- $20,000–$30,000
- $30,000–$50,000
- $50,000–$100,000
- $100,000+
- No Answer

(Figure 19)

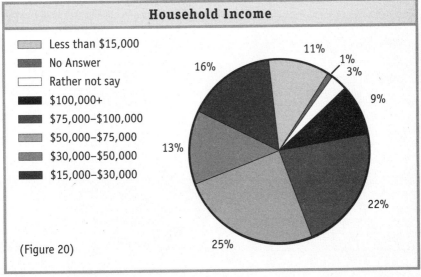

Household Income

- Less than $15,000
- No Answer
- Rather not say
- $100,000+
- $75,000–$100,000
- $50,000–$75,000
- $30,000–$50,000
- $15,000–$30,000

(Figure 20)

Also curtailing income potential is the fact that most of the EPs surveyed (63 percent) do not use outside child care (Figure 21).

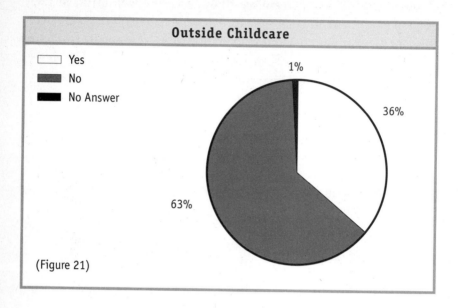

(Figure 21)

Not surprisingly, the vast majority of EPs surveyed (79 percent) are the primary caregivers to their children (Figure 22).

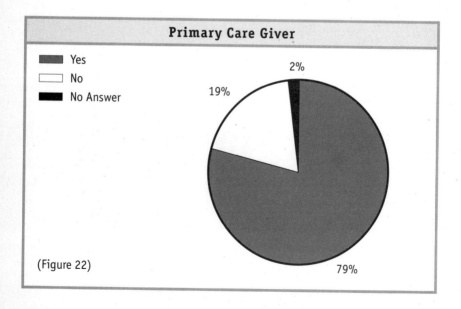

(Figure 22)

When asked what kind of difficult challenges EPs find themselves dealing with, meeting deadlines was the challenge mentioned most often. Getting backup child care was the second most frequent response (Figure 23).

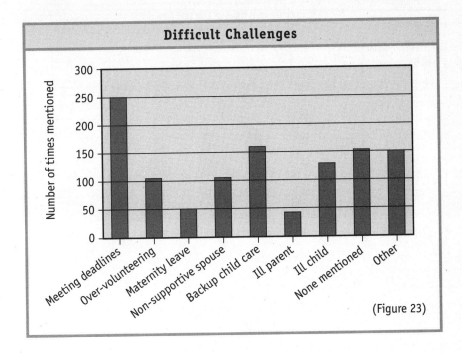

Difficult Challenges

(Figure 23)

Happiness and well-being is the area that parents surveyed cited most often as improving in their children. Behavior was mentioned second most often, with social skills being third (Figure 24).

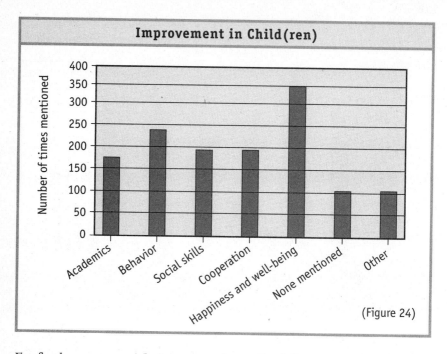

(Figure 24)

For further survey analysis, contact Janet Gardella at Janet_Gardella@prodigy.net.

Index